PROSPERITY

DEFINING DOCUMENTS
IN AMERICAN HISTORY

Political Campaigns, Candidates & Debates

(1787-2017)

AT HOME, PRESTIGE ABROAD.

COMMERCE.

CIVILIZATION.

DEFINING DOCUMENTS
IN AMERICAN HISTORY

Political Campaigns, Candidates & Debates

(1787-2017)

Volume 1

Editor

Michael Shally-Jensen, PhD

SALEM PRESS
A Division of EBSCO Information Services, Inc.
Ipswich, Massachusetts

GREY HOUSE PUBLISHING

Publisher's Cataloging-In-Publication Data
(Prepared by The Donohue Group, Inc.)

Names: Shally-Jensen, Michael, editor.
Title: Political campaigns, candidates & debates (1787-2017) / editor, Michael Shally-Jensen, PhD.
Other Titles: Political campaigns, candidates and debates (1787-2017) | Defining documents in American history (Salem Press)
Description: [First edition]. | Ipswich, Massachusetts : Salem Press, a division of EBSCO Information Services ; [Amenia, New York] : Grey House Publishing, [2018] | Includes bibliographical references and index.
Identifiers: ISBN 9781682177006 (set) | ISBN 9781682172995 (v.1) | ISBN 9781682173008 (v.2)
Subjects: LCSH: Political campaigns--United States--Sources. | Campaign debates--United States--Sources. | Speeches, addresses, etc., American--Sources. | United States--Politics and government--Sources. | Political oratory--United States--Sources.
Classification: LCC JK2281 .P65 2018 | DDC 324.70973--dc23

FIRST PRINTING
PRINTED IN THE UNITED STATES OF AMERICA

Contents

THE FIRST AND SECOND PARTY SYSTEMS, 1787–1854

THE THIRD PARTY SYSTEM, 1854-96

THE FOURTH PARTY SYSTEM, 1896-1932

Complete List of Contents

Volume 1

THE FIRST AND SECOND PARTY SYSTEMS, 1787–1854

THE THIRD PARTY SYSTEM, 1854-96

THE FOURTH PARTY SYSTEM, 1896-1932

Volume 2

THE FIFTH PARTY SYSTEM, 1932-60

THE SIXTH PARTY SYSTEM, PART I, 1960-1974

THE SIXTH PARTY SYSTEM, PART II, 1974-2016

THE SEVENTH PARTY SYSTEM? 2016-

APPENDIXES

Publisher's Note

Defining Documents in American History series, produced by Salem Press, offers a closer look at important historical documents by pairing primary source documents on a broad range of subjects with essays written especially for the series by a diverse range of writers. This established series includes twenty-seven titles that present documents selected to illuminate specific eras in American history—*Exploration & Colonial America (1492 -1755)* through the *1910s*, for example—or to explore significant themes and developments in American society—*Civil Rights (1954-2015); The Cold War (1945-1991); Environment & Conservation (1791 -2015); Native Americans (1451-2017)* and *LGBTQ+ (1923-2017)*.

This set, *Defining Documents in American History: Political Campaigns, Candidates & Debates (1787 -2017)*, offers in-depth analysis of sixty-four speeches, letters, inaugural addresses, pamphlets, and debates.

The material is organized under seven historical groupings:

- **The First and Second Party Systems, 1787-1854**, beginning with James Madison's *Federalist Papers* and George Washington's inaugural address and concluding with the Kansas-Nebraska Act, a hotly debated piece of legislation that led to the Civil War;
- **The Third Party System, 1854-96** features Lincoln's "House Divided speech, hotly contested presidential campaigns such as Greeley versus Grant, Tilden versus Hayes), and William Jennings Bryan's fiery "Cross of Gold" speech
- **The Fourth Party System, 1896-1932** includes Teddy Roosevelt's Progressive Party platform, Woodrow Wilson's second inaugural speech, and the establishment of the country's national anthem
- **The Fifth Party System, 1932-60** begins with a fireside chat from Franklin Delano Roosevelt and includes the ratification of the twenty-second amendment, and the famous Truman versus Dewey presidential campaign.
- **The Sixth Party System, Part I, 1960-74** delves into the Kennedy-era and LBJ's Great Society, as well as the Vietnam War and the election of Richard Nixon.
- **The Sixth Party System, Part II, 1974-2016** begins with Gerald Ford's remarks on assuming the presidency and on the U.S. bicentennial celebration, the decision to determine the outcome of the Bush/Gore presidential campaign, and the landmark case regarding campaign contributions in *Citizen's United v. Federal Election Commission*.
- **The Seventh Party System? 2016-** considers the current political climate, from Hillary Clinton's acceptance speech at the 2016 Democratic convention, "fake news" stories such as the erroneous report that Pope Francis supported Donald Trump's bid to become president, and another crucial court case, this time related to voting districts, in *Cooper v. Harris.*

These documents provide a compelling view of what makes America's political system so engaging and enduring: discussion, debate, and free, open elections leading to the order transfer of power. The documents prove that the system is not always polite, but it is always vibrant, as well as vital to a strong democratic government.

Designed for high school and college students, the aim of the series is to advance the study of primary source historical document as an important activity in learning about history.

Essay Format

Political Campaigns, Candidates & Debates features sixty-four documents that span the country's history. The set begins just as a new nation has been declared, in 1787, and continues through the 2017 election of the nation's first openly transgender official.

Each document is supported by a critical essay, written by historians and teachers, that includes a Summary Overview, Defining Moment, Author Biography, Document Analysis, and Essential Themes. An important feature of each essay is a close reading and analysis of the primary source that develops broader themes, such as the author's rhetorical purpose, social or class position, point of view, and other relevant issues. In addition, essays are organized by sections, listed above, highlighting major issues of the apolitical process: slavery, global wars, civil rights, voting rights, transgender equality and nationalism.

Each section begins with a brief introduction that defines questions and problems underlying the subjects addressed in the historical documents. Each essay also includes a Bibliography and Additional Reading section for further research.

Appendixes

- **Chronological List** arranges all documents by year.
- **Web Resources** is an annotated list of websites that offer valuable supplemental resources.
- **Bibliography** lists helpful articles and books for further study.

Contributors

Salem Press would like to extend its appreciation to all involved in the development and production of this work. The essays have been written and signed by scholars of history, humanities, and other disciplines related to the essays' topics. Without these expert contributions, a project of this nature would not be possible. A full list of contributor's names and affiliations appears in the front matter of this volume.

Editor's Introduction

The U.S Constitution's requirements relating to the electoral process are relatively few; the nation's founding document leaves to the states, by and large, the control that process. In the modern era, of course, the right to vote cannot be denied on the basis of race (15th Amendment), gender (19th Amendment), or age (18 years or older; 26th Amendment). But beyond those requirements, the states are relatively free to specify voting requirements and methods of electing representatives and casting votes.

The Constitution limits the terms of president and vice president to four years and requires that elections be held at the end of those terms. The Framers, however, did not prescribe popular election by the masses but rather devised a unique institution, the electoral college, to nominate and elect persons for these high offices. Each state would appoint electors, and on a specified day the electors would meet in their respective states and cast their ballots (or otherwise vote) for two individuals as presidential candidates. The candidate with the most votes was declared winner of the presidency for that state, while the second highest vote winner was deemed vice president. The results were reported to the U.S. Congress. The individual receiving the most votes among all the states was named president, the runner-up, vice president. If no individual won a majority, the election was thrown to the House of Representatives. Such elections occurred in 1801 and 1825, not without controversy.

The Framers had thought that under the electoral college system, elections would be free and fair but not politicized events. And, indeed, for many years presidential candidates took little part in election campaigns, seeing any solicitation of public favor as beneath the dignity of a national leader. They met delegations of electors and occasionally wrote letters but generally let others speak on their behalf. As political parties began to emerge, from the 1790s, however, the nomination and election process became increasingly politicized. The electors began voting by party affiliation rather than acting independently. For reasons related to this, and to lessen the likelihood of a tie, the 12th Amendment was adopted in 1804, requiring electors to vote for a president and a vice president instead of just two top candidates.

Initially, electors were chosen either by state legislatures or by popular vote within districts. By the 1830s, though, the most prominent method was the nomination of slates of electors by parties, which slates were then voted on by citizens. Also developing in the 1830s was the party-based national nominating convention for presidential elections. This meant that electors, as party members, met and pledged to vote for their party's choices. Thus, a candidate who won a majority (or in some cases a plurality) of votes among electors "carried" the state by virtue of gaining the remaining pledged votes from that state. This practice is called the "winner-take-all" rule, and it produced a good deal of behind-the-scenes politicking on the part of party bosses and special interest groups who favored one candidate or another. For much of the nineteenth century, and the first part of the twentieth century, candidates were chosen in these kinds of electoral bargains made in "smoke-filled rooms" inside the convention halls.

During the Progressive Era, some reforms were instituted, including the primary election, or the preliminary election of candidates. Under the primary system, voters express their preference for their party's candidates directly, thus eliminating the need for back-room deals. Today, most states have some form of primary election; others have a party caucus, or meeting of supporters. With primaries and caucuses, victories racked up state-by-state by successful candidates can act to winnow the field, allowing a leader to emerge by the time of the national convention. One effect of primaries, then, is to render the nominating convention a largely ceremonial event, as the choice has already largely been made by then.

Another major effect of the rise of state party primaries was the development of political campaigning, or efforts designed to raise a candidate's chances. Even during the nineteenth century, party activists had worked vigorously to advance their favorite candidates, printing promotional biographies, generating enthusiasm among crowds, speaking poorly of the candidates' opponents, and generally playing up the wondrous future that lay ahead under their candidates as opposed to the disasters that await all under the opposition. Still, it was not until the twentieth century that presidential candidates themselves routinely went out to "stump" on the campaign trail, making "whistle stop" tours in key parts of the country, or traveling, in later years, by airplane or bus caravan. Mass media such as radio and television also became more important, although for decades these were considered secondary tools aimed simply at making candidates more familiar to voters. They were not employed directly to celebrate candidates, to pound on the issues, or to blacken the reputations of opponents until later in the century. (Print continued to be used in those capacities.)

By the late 1950s, as television became more widespread, this began to change. A watershed moment came during the first televised debate between John F. Kennedy and Richard M. Nixon (1960), which revealed the power of the medium. Since then, presidential campaigns have regularly hired marketing and media experts, often concerned with image and "likeability" over substance and experience. Social media has multiplied this effect, even while it also allows the building of connections and pertinent exchanges among voters on topics of interest. The proliferation of "fake news" reports on social media during the 2016 election, however, caused some rethinking of this process. Citizens and politicians alike became concerned that the campaign process could be disrupted, or even hacked into by foreign powers (Russia, in this case).

It is at the general election that voters cast their ballots for the presidential candidate—the party nominee—of their choice. Technically, citizens today still vote for electors rather than presidential candidates, although rarely do the names of electors appear on the ballot. (A ballot might instead present a choice between "The Electors of" JOHN DOE and "The Electors of" JANE SMITH.) The number of representatives that a state has in the electoral college matches the number of senators and representatives it has in Congress. And, the electoral college "winner take all" rule continues to apply, with the candidate who garners the largest number of votes in a state receiving the full support of that state's delegation in the electoral college. (The are some variations of this among the states, though.) The successful presidential candidate must receive a majority of the votes in the electoral college. On five occasions, however, the winning candidate lost the national popular vote yet won the presidency based on the electoral college results. These are: John Quincy Adams, 1824; Rutherford B. Hayes, 1876; Benjamin Harrison, 1888; George W. Bush, 2000; and Donald J. Trump, 2016. Over the years, there has been discussion of scrapping the electoral college as an outmoded institution, but whether the political will is there to make such a significant change remains to be seen.

As noted, the presidential term is fixed at four years. The first three presidents, George Washington, Thomas Jefferson, and James Madison, retired after two terms, thus establishing a precedent. Ulysses S. Grant in 1880 and Theodore Roosevelt in 1912 sought (unsuccessfully) to win third terms; and Grover Cleveland served in two nonconsecutive terms (from 1885 and from 1893). It was not until the presidency of Franklin Delano Roosevelt that a candidate sought, and won, a third and even a fourth term (1940, 1944). As a result, the Constitution was amended in 1947 (22nd Amendment; ratified, 1951) to limit presidents to two terms.

* * *

Historians and political scientists have described the political culture of the post-1960s United States as the "sixth party system," a reference to different stages of evolution in the politics and party rivalries of the nation.

The first party system, or first period of American political history, involved a contest between Federalists and the Jeffersonian Republicans in the 1790s and early 1800s. It was an unsettled period in which a number of the Constitution's tenets and the political process that stemmed from it were put to the test

The second system, operating between 1828 and 1854, was made up of rivalries between Jacksonian Democrats, Whigs under Henry Clay, and what remained of John Quincy Adams' National Republican Party; the period produced campaign rallies, additional partisan newspapers, and the expectation of loyalty to party.

The third party system, ranging between 1854 and the mid-1890s, was rooted in growing nationalism, modernization, and the issues of slavery/race and, later, Gilded Age wealth; from it came the then-new Republican Party, in opposition to the Democratic Party.

The fourth party system extended from about 1896 to 1932, roughly paralleling the Progressive Era; it was marked by an increasingly successful Republican Party, except for a split in 1912 when Theodore Roosevelt broke from his party, and Democrats, under Woodrow Wilson, took the presidency.

The fifth party system was characterized by the dominance of the New Deal Democratic coalition from the 1930s through the 1950s; this coalition was made up of Southerners, labor unions, urban political "machines," progressive intellectuals, and populist farm groups.

Scholars have debated whether the fifth party system ends at the start of the 1960s, the start of the 1980s, or at some other time; in the present volume, we assume the earlier date (1960) as the starting point.

Thus, the most recent, or sixth party system, from 1960 on, is characterized by increasing Democratic-Republican rivalry, popular disenchantment with politics, the critical role of media, a decline in the importance (for voters) of parties *per se* relative to candidates, and the skyrocketing cost of election campaigns. Some observers would further divide this sixth system into 1) an early phase, concluding with the disruptive 1968 election and the denouement of the Nixon-Watergate scandal; and 2) a later phase, involving the rise of Ronald Reagan's political philosophy, Evangelical voters as a bloc, and the use of targeted, negative campaign ads as a key driver in electoral politics.

A shift among Democrats under Bill Clinton in the 1990s, whereby Democratic voters moved to the center of the political spectrum (and even to the right of center), is another notable event during this period. So too is the election of the first African American president, Barack Obama, on the Democratic ticket, in 2008.

Additionally, some commentators have speculated about the possibility of a *seventh* party system having emerged with the 2016 election, when Donald Trump, a nonpolitician, broke precedents in both primary races and the general election and essentially took over the Republican Party, demanding loyalty to him (above party) and overturning decades of Republican thinking on matters such as free trade, deficit reduction, international alliances, faith in the justice system, and even personal morality. Electoral disruptions caused by fake news on social media, some of it foreign (Russian) produced, as well as the hacking and leaking of private emails and other data, contribute to the idea of an ostensive seventh system. Only the future will tell.

The plethora of information now available on media/social media has not to date translated into major increases in voter participation, but the expectation is that such increases could occur in the near future as American electoral politics continue to evolve.

—*Michael Shally-Jensen, PhD*

Bibliography and Additional Reading

Baylor, Christopher. *First to the Party: The Group Origins of Party Transformation.* Philadelphia: University of Pennsylvania Press, 2018.

Critchlow, Donald. *American Political History: A Very Short Introduction.* New York: Oxford University Press, 2015.

LeMay, Michael C. *The American Political Party System: A Reference Handbook.* Santa Barbara, CA: ABC-CLIO, 2017.

Wilentz, Sean. *The Politicians & The Egalitarians: The Hidden History of American Politics.* New York: W.W. Norton & Co., 2016.

Contributors

Anna Accettola, MA
University of California, Los Angeles

Michael P Auerbach, MA
Marblehead, Massachusetts

William E. Burns, PhD
George Washington University

Steven L. Danver, PhD
Walden University

K. P. Dawes, MA
Chicago, Illinois

Jonathan Den Hartog, PhD
University of Northwestern – St. Paul

Amber R. Dickinson, PhD
Oklahoma State University

Tracey DiLascio, JD
Framingham, Massachusetts

Bethany Groff Dorau, MA
Historic New England

Ashleigh Fata, MA
University of California, Los Angeles

Gerald F. Goodwin, PhD
Syracuse, New York

Kevin Grimm, PhD
Regent University

Aaron Gulyas, MA
Mott Community College

Mark S. Joy, PhD
Jamestown University

Tom Lansford, PhD
University of Southern Mississippi

Karen Linkletter, PhD
California State University—Fullerton

Laurence W. Mazzeno, PhD
Norfolk, Virginia

Scott C. Monje, PhD
Tarrytown, New York

Michael J. O'Neal, PhD
Bloomington, Indiana

Jonathan Rees, PhD
Colorado State University—Pueblo

Michael Shally-Jensen, PhD
Amherst, Massachusetts

Michele McBride Simonelli, JD
Poland, Ohio

Robert Surbrug, PhD
Bay Path University

Vanessa E. Vaughan, MA
Chicago, Illinois

Anthony Vivian, MA
University of California, Los Angeles

Donald A. Watt, PhD
Middleton, Idaho

DEFINING DOCUMENTS
IN AMERICAN HISTORY

Political Campaigns, Candidates & Debates (1787-2017)

THE FIRST AND SECOND PARTY SYSTEMS, 1787–1854

The founding era in American politics is also what some scholars consider the "first party system," in reference to a model used in history and political science to periodize the entire 230 years of U.S. political history, breaking it down into segments that reflect the nature of parties, campaigns, and elections during each period. This first party system existed in the new nation roughly between 1790 and 1828. (We start in 1787, here, to set the context.) It featured competition between two national parties—the Federalists, associated with Alexander Hamilton, John Jay, John Adams, and others; and the Democratic-Republicans, under Thomas Jefferson, James Madison, and others. The first elected president, George Washington, though a Federalist in sentiment, was nominally an independent. He served two four-year terms (1789–97). During Washington's time, the Federalists were the dominant party in government. After 1800, control switched to the Democratic–Republicans.

Political parties at this time, however, were not at all the rigorously organized, activist machines that we know today. They were grounded in philosophical (or ideological) differences, yes, but they operated more like loose assemblies or societies than as distinct professional organizations. Nevertheless, newspapers served as party organs, campaign techniques were devised to make candidates known and to get out the vote, and issues were debated among proponents—rarely directly or publicly by candidates themselves. By the time of the so-called Era of Good Feelings (1812–25), which corresponds roughly with James Monroe's presidency (1817–25), partisan disputes had lessened somewhat and the Federalist Party had faded away as a growing sense of national unity took hold. The Democratic–Republican party broke up as well, but a faction representing the old anti-federalists formed, in 1828, the Democratic Party.

The second phase of U.S. political history, or the "second party system," runs between about 1828 and 1854.

Much of the period is associated with Andrew Jackson (served 1829–37), who largely founded the Democratic Party and shaped it in its early years. Jacksonian democracy is defined by greater participation by "the common man" in the political process—and indeed voter participation rose sharply during this period, as did population growth generally. Jackson also distrusted central banks and believed in a strong executive and the "spoils system," whereby the winning majority in an election may largely disregard the losing minority and can hand out patronage assignments to its supporters. The other parties competing in this era were the waning National Republican Party, under John Quincy Adams, and the Whigs, under Henry Clay. Jackson and Clay, in particular, had become sharp rivals. The Whigs, for their part, supported central banks, mercantile-friendly tariffs, the rule of law, and the protection of minority interests against the "tyranny of the majority." In the election of 1824, Jackson won the most votes, but since no candidate won a majority the election went to the House of Representatives to decide. In what Jackson later called a "corrupt bargain," he was denied the presidency in the House vote; he accused Adams of having bought Clay's support.

Slavery was not yet the massive issue it soon would become, simply because organized opposition to it was still in development. The abolitionist movement was heating up and gaining notice. Yet, during this second period of U.S. political history, the South emerged as a political power, challenging the traditional dominance of the mid-Atlantic and Northeastern states. Where slavery did cause intensified debate was in considering the status of western and/or frontier areas such as Texas, Kansas, and Nebraska. Although the Compromise of 1850 was supposed to settle the issue, little came of it in the long run. The resolution would come, in blood, during the Civil War, in the next phase of political realignment.

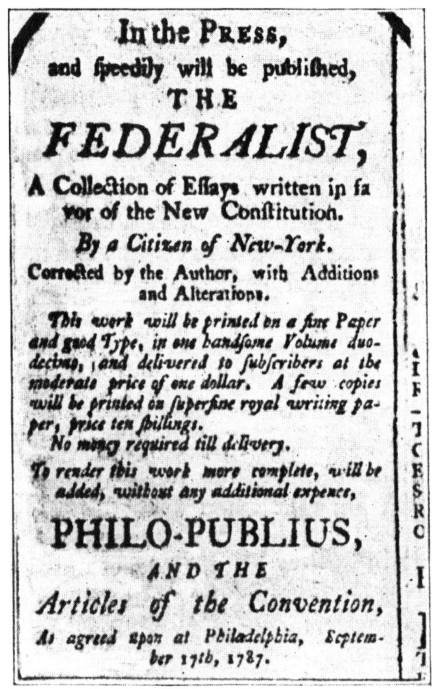

An Advertisement of *The Federalist* (Project Gutenberg eText).

Federalist No. 10

Date: 1787
Author: James Madison
Genre: Essay

Summary Overview

As the newly independent United States began to build its system of government, it became clear that the new nation could easily be fractured from within. Writing in favor of the Constitution and a federal government, James Madison, under the pseudonym Publius, suggested ways in which the new union could mitigate the negative effects of factionalism. He believed that the primary cause of factions was the unequal distribution of property, which in turn fostered a system of political inequality. In "Federalist No. 10," Madison suggests that a representative democracy, rather than a direct democracy, could prevent the political disenfranchisement that occurred in society as a result of this inequality.

Defining Moment

In 1787, the newly independent United States of America began the difficult task of establishing a new national government. This effort was marked by considerable controversy between two main camps. The first group, led by such figures as George Washington, Alexander Hamilton, and Madison, advocated for a strong central government that would oversee matters of nationwide concern, such as foreign relations and defense. Supporters of this position came to be known as the Federalists. On the other side of the constitutional debate were the Anti-Federalists, who advocated for a more decentralized form of government that would empower each state to manage its own affairs. The group, led by such figures as Patrick Henry and George Clinton, expressed great concern that a strong federal government would inevitably abuse its power and infringe upon the basic rights of the people.

As the Constitution was completed, it needed to be ratified by each state. During this period, however, a series of Anti-Federalist pamphlets and letters were published and distributed in large volume. These writings argued that American liberties were at stake and encouraged citizens not to ratify the document. In order to counter this movement, Madison, Hamilton, and John Jay wrote another series of essays, letters, and pamphlets that advocated for the federal approach and particularly sought to convince the residents of New York to support ratification. These papers later became known as the *Federalist Papers*.

Each author wrote under the pen name Publius, taking inspiration from the famous Roman statesman Publius Valerius Publicola, who helped establish the stable Roman Republic after the fall of King Tarquin the Proud in the sixth century BCE. They are believed to have written a total of eighty-five papers, though the authorship of a number of the essays continues to be debated among historians. "Federalist No. 10" is one of the best known of the *Federalist Papers*. The previous paper in the series, written by Hamilton as a letter to the people of New York, warned that the nation was in danger of domestic insurrection and the development of factions that could undermine the new government. Madison examines this issue further in his essay, suggesting that factions are caused by inequities in the political economy and proposing the adoption of a republican form of government in order to address this issue.

Author Biography

James Madison was born on March 16, 1751, in Port Conway, Virginia, to James Madison Sr. and Nellie Conway Madison. He was raised and educated on his family's plantation, Montpelier, before enrolling in the College of New Jersey (now Princeton University) at the age of eighteen. There, he became strongly influenced by the writings of such iconic seventeenth- and eighteenth-century thinkers as John Locke and Isaac Newton and helped found the American Whig Society, a debate club. Madison graduated from the college after two years.

During the American Revolution, Madison joined the cause by gaining election to the Virginia Convention in 1776, where he helped draft the state's new constitution.

He also served in the Virginia House of Delegates. In 1780, Madison was elected to the Continental Congress in Philadelphia, where he honed his belief that Britain's rule should be replaced with a centralized, federal government. He attended the Constitutional Convention in 1787 and contributed heavily to the writing of the new Constitution. Seeking to encourage the states to ratify the document, Madison collaborated with Hamilton and Jay on the *Federalist Papers*. Their efforts were successful, and the Constitution was ratified by the required number of states in 1788 and by all thirteen states in 1790.

Madison served as secretary of state during Thomas Jefferson's presidency, during which time he helped to negotiate the purchase of the extensive French territory known as Louisiana; this purchase dramatically increased the geographical size of the country, a possibility Madison had predicted in "Federalist No. 10." He won the presidency in 1808, serving two terms. Following his presidency, Madison returned to Montpelier, although he would later advise his successor, James Monroe, on foreign policy matters. He also remained true to the cause of federal government, speaking out on issues that arose under the auspices of states' rights. He died at Montpelier on June 28, 1836.

HISTORICAL DOCUMENT

The Utility of the Union as a Safeguard Against Domestic Faction and Insurrection

Daily Advertiser
Thursday, November 22, 1787

No man is allowed to be a judge in his own cause, because his interest would certainly bias his judgment, and, not improbably, corrupt his integrity. With equal, nay with greater reason, a body of men are unfit to be both judges and parties at the same time; yet what are many of the most important acts of legislation, but so many judicial determinations, not indeed concerning the rights of single persons, but concerning the rights of large bodies of citizens? And what are the different classes of legislators but advocates and parties to the causes which they determine? Is a law proposed concerning private debts? It is a question to which the creditors are parties on one side and the debtors on the other. Justice ought to hold the balance between them. Yet the parties are, and must be, themselves the judges; and the most numerous party, or, in other words, the most powerful faction must be expected to prevail. Shall domestic manufactures be encouraged, and in what degree, by restrictions on foreign manufactures? are questions which would be differently decided by the landed and the manufacturing classes, and probably by neither with a sole regard to justice and the public good. The apportionment of taxes on the various descriptions of property is an act which

seems to require the most exact impartiality; yet there is, perhaps, no legislative act in which greater opportunity and temptation are given to a predominant party to trample on the rules of justice. Every shilling with which they overburden the inferior number, is a shilling saved to their own pockets.

It is in vain to say that enlightened statesmen will be able to adjust these clashing interests, and render them all subservient to the public good. Enlightened statesmen will not always be at the helm. Nor, in many cases, can such an adjustment be made at all without taking into view indirect and remote considerations, which will rarely prevail over the immediate interest which one party may find in disregarding the rights of another or the good of the whole.

The inference to which we are brought is, that the *causes* of faction cannot be removed, and that relief is only to be sought in the means of controlling its *effects*.

If a faction consists of less than a majority, relief is supplied by the republican principle, which enables the majority to defeat its sinister views by regular vote. It may clog the administration, it may convulse the society; but it will be unable to execute and mask its violence under the forms of the Constitution. When a majority is included in a faction, the form of popular government, on the other hand, enables it to sacrifice to its ruling passion or interest both the public good and the rights of other citizens. To secure the public good and private rights against the danger of such a faction, and at the same time to preserve the spirit and the form of popular government, is then the great object to which our inquiries are directed. Let me add that it is the great desideratum by which this form of government can be rescued from the opprobrium under which it has so long labored, and be recommended to the esteem and adoption of mankind.

By what means is this object attainable? Evidently by one of two only. Either the existence of the same passion or interest in a majority at the same time must be prevented, or the majority, having such coexistent passion or interest, must be rendered, by their number and local situation, unable to concert and carry into effect schemes of oppression. If the impulse and the opportunity be suffered to coincide, we well know that neither moral nor religious motives can be relied on as an adequate control. They are not found to be such on the injustice and violence of individuals, and lose their efficacy in proportion to the number combined together, that is, in proportion as their efficacy becomes needful.

From this view of the subject it may be concluded that a pure democracy, by which I mean a society consisting of a small number of citizens, who assemble and administer the government in person, can admit of no cure for the mischiefs of faction. A common passion or interest will, in almost every case, be felt by a majority of the whole; a communication and concert result from the form of government itself; and there is nothing to check the inducements to sacrifice the weaker party or an obnoxious individual. Hence it is that such democracies have ever been spectacles of turbulence and contention; have ever been found incompatible with personal security or the rights of property; and have in general been as short in their lives as they have been violent in their deaths. Theoretic politicians, who have patronized this species of government, have erroneously supposed that by reducing mankind to a perfect equality in their political rights, they would, at the same time, be perfectly equalized and assimilated in their possessions, their opinions, and their passions.

A republic, by which I mean a government in which the scheme of representation takes place, opens a different prospect, and promises the cure for which we are seeking. Let us examine the points in which it varies from pure democracy, and we shall comprehend both the nature of the cure and the efficacy which it must derive from the Union.

The two great points of difference between a democracy and a republic are: first, the delegation of the government, in the latter, to a small number of citizens elected by the rest; secondly, the greater number of citizens, and greater sphere of country, over which the latter may be extended.

The effect of the first difference is, on the one hand, to refine and enlarge the public views, by passing them through the medium of a chosen body of citizens, whose wisdom may best discern the true interest of their country, and whose patriotism and love of justice will be least likely to sacrifice it to temporary or partial considerations. Under such a regulation, it may well happen that the public voice, pronounced by the representatives of the people, will be more consonant to the public good than if pronounced by the people themselves, convened for the purpose. On the other hand, the effect may be inverted. Men of factious tempers, of local prejudices, or of sinister designs, may, by intrigue, by corruption, or by other means, first obtain the suffrages, and then betray the interests, of the people. The question resulting is, whether small or extensive republics are more favorable to the election of proper guardians of the public weal; and it is clearly decided in favor of the latter by two obvious considerations:

In the first place, it is to be remarked that, however small the republic may be, the representatives must be raised to a certain number, in order to guard against the cabals of a few; and that, however large it may be, they must be limited to a certain number, in order to guard against the confusion of a multitude. Hence, the number of representatives in the two cases not being in proportion to that of the two constituents, and being proportionally greater in the small republic, it follows that, if the proportion of fit characters be not less in the large than in the small republic, the former will present a greater option, and consequently a greater probability of a fit choice.

In the next place, as each representative will be chosen by a greater number of citizens in the large than in the small republic, it will be more difficult for unworthy candidates to practice with success the vicious arts by which elections are too often carried; and the suffrages of the people being more free, will be more likely to centre in men who possess the most attractive merit and the most diffusive and established characters.

It must be confessed that in this, as in most other cases, there is a mean, on both sides of which inconveniences will be found to lie. By enlarging too much the number of electors, you render the representatives too little acquainted with all their local circumstances and lesser interests; as by reducing it too much, you render him unduly attached to these, and too little fit to comprehend and pursue great and national objects. The federal Constitution forms a happy combination in this respect; the great and aggregate interests being referred to the national, the local and particular to the State legislatures.

The other point of difference is, the greater number of citizens and extent of territory which may be brought within the compass of republican than of democratic government; and it is this circumstance principally which renders factious combinations less to be dreaded in the former than in the latter. The smaller the society, the fewer probably will be the distinct parties and interests composing it; the fewer the distinct parties and interests, the more frequently will a majority be found of the same party; and the smaller the number of individuals composing a majority, and the smaller the compass within which they are placed, the more easily will they concert and execute their plans of oppression. Extend the sphere, and you take in a greater variety of parties and interests; you make it less probable that a majority of the whole will have a common motive to invade the rights of other citizens; or if such a common motive exists, it will be more difficult for all who feel it to discover their own strength, and to act in unison with each other. Besides other impediments, it may be remarked that, where there is a consciousness of unjust or dishonorable purposes, communication is always checked by distrust in proportion to the number whose concurrence is necessary.

Hence, it clearly appears, that the same advantage which a republic has over a democracy, in controlling the effects of faction, is enjoyed by a large over a small republic,—is enjoyed by the Union over the States composing it. Does the advantage consist in the substitution of representatives whose enlightened views and virtuous sentiments render them superior to local prejudices and schemes of injustice? It will not be denied that the representation of the Union will be most likely to possess these requisite endowments. Does it consist in the greater security afforded by a greater variety of parties, against the event of any one party being able to outnumber and oppress the rest? In an equal degree does the increased variety of parties comprised within the Union, increase this security. Does it, in fine, consist in the greater obstacles opposed to the concert and accomplishment of the secret wishes of an unjust and interested majority? Here, again, the extent of the Union gives it the most palpable advantage.

The influence of factious leaders may kindle a flame within their particular States, but will be unable to spread a general conflagration through the other States. A religious sect may degenerate into a political faction in a part of the Confederacy; but the variety of sects dispersed over the entire face of it must secure the national councils against any danger from that source. A rage for paper money, for an abolition of debts, for an equal division of property, or for any other improper or wicked project, will be less apt to pervade the whole body of the Union than a particular member of it; in the same proportion as such a malady is more likely to taint a particular county or district, than an entire State.

In the extent and proper structure of the Union, therefore, we behold a republican remedy for the diseases most incident to republican government. And according to the degree of pleasure and pride we feel in being republicans, ought to be our zeal in cherishing the spirit and supporting the character of Federalists.

PUBLIUS

GLOSSARY

cabal: plot, or a group involved in a plot

desideratum: something highly desired or needed

opprobrium: disgrace

republic: government in which elected representatives and officials rule based on the laws of the country and the interests of the electorate

theoretic: concerned primarily with theoretical rather than practical considerations

Document Analysis

The *Federalist Papers* were written as a counterpoint to another series of pamphlets and position papers introduced to New York readers, calling upon the people to reject the proposed Constitution and embrace a small, decentralized government that deferred power to the states. In "Federalist No. 10," Madison, writing under the pen name Publius, does not take to task the notion of states' rights (or, for that matter, the basic rights due all American citizens under the new government) stressed by Anti-Federalists. Rather, he focuses on the negative effects of political factions on the political system as a whole and argues that a large, republican form of government, as defined by the Constitution, would make public policy and public administration more efficient and focused on the public good.

Madison begins his letter to the people of New York by commenting on the nature of people living within a political system. He states that within this context, all people are inherently biased toward their own interests. Therefore, he writes, no individual can be relied upon to judge his or her own cause impartially. However, a body politic requires political leaders and infrastructure to facilitate the public policy and public administrative process. In a society, bodies of citizens have to develop and introduce legislation and laws to the rest of the society, despite this bias toward personal interest. In fact, legislatures, he writes, are composed of individuals who are expected to serve the interests of their various constituents. This diversity inevitably leads to different perspectives on certain types of legislation and laws. For example, Madison offers, a legislator whose constituency serves entrepreneurs with foreign interests would be more inclined to support legislation that bolsters foreign-based manufacturers, while other legislators may support legislation that is supportive of domestic businesses.

The only area in which all involved parties do not seem to have a diversity of interest but instead a degree of impartiality, Madison suggests, is taxation. This is due to the fact that property values are set based on existing statutes and not easily changed to satisfy the whims of a few. Then again, he warns, not all aspects of taxation are set in such a manner. New taxes on income levels, products, and services could be levied, much in the same manner by which taxes were levied on colonial goods during the years leading up to the Revolution. Madison cautions that certain socioeconomic classes, once placed into positions of political power, could use that influence to "trample on the rules of justice" by imposing taxes on other classes, keeping them at bay while benefiting financially from the revenues generated.

Madison's point is that factions—groups with a common interest—form within a political system because of the diversity of groups in a society. These factions could be regional in nature, composed of members devoted to local interests such as rural areas, or economic in nature, composed of wealthy merchants as opposed to impoverished farmers. Furthermore, factions could be focused on a singular issue, such as the establishment of a paper currency or the lowering of taxes. The leaders sent forth by factions, Madison argues, are thus dedicated to their factions rather than the entire population.

Under ideal circumstances, legislators who represent different factions would find commonality in passing laws. Put simply, these legislators would ideally form a singular, powerful faction dedicated to the governance of the new nation. However, Madison writes, such a scenario would only be possible if the most "enlightened" legislators assumed the top levels of political power in the country. Such ideal leaders would be able to write laws that would place all competing interests at a lower priority level than that of the common good. Based on the notion that it would be far too difficult to place enlightened leaders in a majority position in government and therefore ensure that the development of political factions would be stymied, Madison concludes that factions are inevitable, and so the task is to control their effects.

Madison states that the very nature of a faction is the key to success in this endeavor. A faction, he reminds his readers, is often a group that is in a political minority. To be sure, a minority faction has the power to clog the political process and disrupt society. However, in a republican form of government, the majority would be capable of defeating a faction's "sinister" endeavors through a simple vote. But, Madison states, when a faction is part of a governing majority, that majority loses its incentive to act in the public interest rather than the narrower factional interest, and this is the problem that the new government of the United States will need to address.

Next, Madison explores the means by which the absorption of factions into a popular government could take place. He notes that the majority could either be prevented from acting upon the interests and passions that defined the faction or be rendered unable to create laws that would be oppressive. In either case, should factions pursue disruption of the government, Madison writes, neither religious nor other "moral" arguments could be expected to control that impulse. After all, he writes, such arguments often have little effect on the actions of individuals.

Madison next states that a pure democracy, a government system in which all eligible members of a society play an equal role in its governance, offers no solution to the "mischiefs of faction." He writes that a democracy by its very nature does not feature any safeguards against the tyranny of an oppressive majority. For this reason, pure democracies have historically fallen victim to turbulence, infighting, and controversy, becoming detached from the ideals of protecting personal and property rights. He criticizes "theoretic" politicians who have advocated for such systems, arguing that their support for such a form of government has been erroneously based on a notion that all citizens therein would enjoy equal standing, equal property, and unfettered ability to voice their political passions. On the other hand, Madison writes, the republic offered to Americans by the proposed Constitution includes systems that could "cure" the political system of the problems created by factions.

Having described the dangers of factionalism inherent in a democratic system of government, Madison next seeks to convince his readers that the republican system would prove more effective in mitigating factions than a pure democracy. He begins by describing the differences between the two types of systems. Madison identifies two major differences, the first of which has to do with the delegation of government: In a republic, a small group of representatives is elected by the people to write laws and carry out the other functions of government. The other major difference of concern to Madison is that unlike a pure democracy, a republic is designed to grow with both the population and the geographical size of a country. This latter point proved to be important as the citizenry and boundaries of the United States expanded over time, particularly following the Louisiana Purchase during Madison's term as secretary of state.

The effect of the first of these differences, in Madison's estimation, is a broadening of the public's perspectives on government. The elected representatives, of which there would be a limited number, would use their wisdom, patriotism, and respect for justice to serve the best interests of the people. Madison notes that while these interests may not be consistent with public opinion, they would be consonant with the public good. Seemingly anticipating the objections of some of his readers, he admits that elected leaders who demonstrate "factious tempers" or biases toward local interests could potentially use their positions, through the political process or in a corrupt manner, to betray the public good. However, Madison argues that a republic, through its size and composition, would keep such corruption to a minimum.

No matter how small the republic might be, he writes, its leadership would need to be large enough in number to guard against the pursuits of dangerous factions. On the other hand, should the republic grow to a considerable size, the number of leaders to govern it must not exceed a certain number, as placing into power a multitude of officials would cause confusion. The key, he argues, is in creating the right proportion between citizens and their elected officials. Additionally, Madison notes that a larger republic would feature a greater number of voters who elect only a relatively small number of officials. In this dynamic, it would be more difficult for leaders who remain committed to their factional interests to gain success by taking advantage of the electoral system. Furthermore, because the people themselves would be free to vote for any candidate, it would be more likely that a majority of the people would elect an upright candidate who would best represent them.

Madison acknowledges that there is a flaw in creating a large republic to govern the country. Because the limited number of elected officials would be put into office by sizable voting blocs, these officials might not be knowledgeable on every local matter. In fact, he writes, there is a risk that the people might, out of a perceived connection, link candidates to local issues with which they are not fully familiar. Furthermore, because of this connection to local interests, the person being elected might not be able to pursue national matters with great skill. Fortunately, Madison notes, the Constitution provides a solution to this flaw. By creating the jurisdictions of the national, state, and local governments, the document ensures that local matters are addressed by local officials and national matters are handled by those who focus solely on such large-scale issues.

Madison next returns to the advantage a republic holds over a pure democracy within the context of growth of population or expansion of geographical boundaries. In a smaller society, there are likely to be fewer differences among a small number of parties. Indeed, majorities will be more easily attained and retained by smaller groups of people. The direction of the country will also be easily established by these majorities, as leaders will share a singular focus on their preferred goals. Then again, the ease by which these majorities would be gained, according to Madison, also means that oppressive measures could be applied at greater rates of speed and efficacy.

As the society grows, however, so too would the number of factions and interest groups. Madison argues that this trend would make obtaining a majority extremely challenging. If a majority is obtained, the leadership, beholden to the interests they serve, would have great difficulty in unifying the rest of the society to its cause. In a republic, however, distrust of a large, strong government would be mitigated by interparty communication and the proportionally smaller government's pursuit of common goals.

Madison reiterates that based on these benefits, a large republic such as the one he and his fellow Federalists advocated was more advantageous than a smaller republic or a purely democratic system. In a republic, it would be more likely that "enlightened" leaders would take office, even if there is the chance that those dedicated to more provincial interests could be among them. Additionally, because the new Union would allow for many different parties, the republic would feature safeguards preventing the establishment of a single, dominating party. Furthermore, the republic would consist of a series of "obstacles" that would hinder the success of any "unjust" party seeking majority powers.

Madison indicates that the republic would not, however, be able to prevent the effects of factions on the state level. Because of the common perspectives among residents at these levels, factions could gain prominence in state governments, and "factious leaders" could influence a push for power in their respective states of residence. However, Madison notes that such influences would not be able to spread into other states. He cites, as an example, the presence of certain religious sects in some states. These sects might prove successful in generating a following among a state's populace. However, because there are so many other sects, a single sect's ability to cement support from other state religious groups would be stymied.

Furthermore, Madison writes, there is a multitude of political issues that might garner passionate support in the states. He cites the examples of interest in the abolition of debt, the equal division of property, and the pursuit of paper currency. In such cases, interest among the like-minded voters in a state might fan passions on such issues, but these likely would not carry into other states in which voters have other priorities. He adds that similar conditions might occur within states, as factions and voters in certain counties or regions are likely to be more passionate about certain issues than their state government personnel are.

Madison completes his essay by offering an appeal to the reader to endorse the republican style of government advocated by the Federalists in the Constitution. He refers to the republican system as a "remedy for the diseases" that afflict the new Union, a comment directed specifically toward interest groups that were more concerned with addressing their own provincial issues than the national public good. Madison saw such factions as dangers to the integrity of the new United States. He cites the great swell of pride he and other founding fathers feel with regard to this particular form of government. In light of this passion for republicanism as well as the fact that many prominent Federalists were highly respected by most Americans, Madison encourages his New York readers to eschew the rhetoric of the Anti-Federalists and embrace the many public policy and public administration advantages of the republican system of government.

Essential Themes

"Federalist No. 10" is particularly known for its discussion of the dangers of factionalism. Madison believed that factions had the power to undermine a government's ability to serve the people effectively, though he acknowledges that in light of the wide array of different factions in the new United States, dismantling or preventing the development of factions would be an exercise in futility. Such factions continued to be of concern following the adoption of the Constitution, and although Madison believed that the influence of many factions would be confined within individual states, he did not anticipate the rise of the mass media and its effects on politics and society. In later centuries, regional factions became able to disseminate information about various causes nationwide, and their influence was able to spread beyond state boundaries.

Madison's work is also significant for its support of the federal government proposed in the Constitution and advocated by the Federalists. He believed that a strong, large republic, as opposed to a pure democracy or other popular forms of representative government, was designed to prevent factions from gaining power by fostering the election of more enlightened leaders who would focus on national matters and the common good. Popular governments akin to the pure democratic model, he argues in his essay, only lead to confusion and a larger number of disruptive factions. The Federalists were eventually successful in convincing the states to ratify the Constitution. However, the debate regarding the size and scope of government has continued, with some politicians arguing that more power should be given to the states.

—*Michael Auerbach, MA*

Bibliography and Additional Reading

Beschloss, Michael, and Hugh Sidey. "James Madison." *The Presidents of the United States of America*. Washington: White House Hist. Assn., 2009. 12–13. Print.

Brookhiser, Richard. *James Madison*. New York: Basic, 2011. Print.

Gutzman, Kevin R. C. *James Madison and the Making of America*. New York: St. Martin's, 2012. Print.

Kesler, Charles R., ed. *Saving the Revolution: The Federalist Papers and the American Founding*. New York: Free, 1987. Print.

Ketcham, Ralph, ed. *The Anti-Federalist Papers and the Constitutional Convention Debates*. New York: Signet, 2003. Print.

Madison, James, et al. *The Federalist Papers*. Lib. of Cong., n.d. Web. 25 May 2012.

———. "The James Madison Papers." *American Memory*. Lib. of Cong., n.d. Web. 23 May 2012.

Meyerson, Michael. *Liberty's Blueprint: How Madison and Hamilton Wrote the Federalist Papers, Defined the Constitution, and Made Democracy Safe for the World*. New York: Basic, 2008. Print.

■ George Washington's First Inaugural Address

Date: April 30, 1789
Author: George Washington
Genre: Address; speech

Summary Overview

George Washington's inaugural address of 1789 was the first by an American president. Although the setting has changed through the years—Washington's was given on Wall Street in New York City—every inauguration has featured a speech by the incoming president. Many of them have followed the same general pattern as Washington's: a mixture of modesty, reflection on what has come before, and thoughts on what lies ahead. Knowing that there was great uncertainty about the new system, Washington tried to assure everyone that he did not want any more power than the Constitution gave him. Understanding the struggles through which the country had come, Washington had confidence that the various factions within the government would come together to find the "enlarged views" that would make the government and the nation successful.

Defining Moment

Almost thirteen years after the Declaration of Independence was signed, and eight years after the Battle of Yorktown, in which the colonists defeated the British and ended the War of Independence, the United States was still struggling. Although foreign relations with Great Britain were not ideal, that external threat had subsided for the moment. The real threat to the existence of the United States was internal. The Articles of Confederation, the predecessor to the Constitution, had not resulted in a viable national government. A new Constitution had been written and was in the process of ratification by the thirteen states. Members of Congress had been chosen and electors from the states had selected George Washington to be the first president. Arriving in New York, the nation's temporary capital, almost two months after his term should have begun, Washington was sworn into office. After a brief public ceremony, he went into the congressional chambers to deliver his inaugural address. He understood the importance of the situation, not just for his presidency or his legacy, but for the entire

future of the nation.

Although Congress had been in session for almost a month, the appointive positions in the executive branch and members of the judiciary were yet to be nominated and confirmed by the Senate. All of this awaited the president's taking office, truly marking the beginning of government under the Constitution. The United States Constitution is considered brief and spare in that many of the powers, at all levels, were laid out in only general terms. Thus, Washington had some flexibility in defining the office of president. Even the members of the Electoral College, all of whom had voted for Washington, did not fully know what he would do as president. The text of his first speech would be essential to making his intentions clear to the entire nation. The eight pages of his handwritten speech contain a call for those in the government to put the interests of the nation first. It contained a pledge that he would do his utmost to serve the people of the United States. He called for mutual respect of all citizens and harmony within the very diverse nation. Through this speech, Washington set the tone for all future presidents to follow as they entered the highest office in the land.

Author Biography

The son of Augustine and Mary Ball Washington, George Washington was born on February 22, 1732. His father died when Washington was eleven, so his older half-brother, Laurence, raised him on one of the family plantations, Mount Vernon, Virginia, which Washington later inherited.

Joining the Virginia militia as an officer, Washington's first major assignment was to deliver a message from the British general to the French commander in what is now northwestern Pennsylvania. Washington took detailed notes of the trip and of the French forces and defenses. When this was published after his return, Washington was rapidly promoted. He participated in the French and

Indian War, although he temporarily resigned from the militia to protest the difference in pay between British and American troops. From participating as an officer in the war Washington learned much regarding civilian-military relations, in addition to military tactics. Once the war moved beyond the Virginia colony, Washington resigned from the militia and entered politics. Elected to Virginia's House of Burgesses in 1759, he served for fifteen years while operating his plantation. His objection to the double standard of giving the British advantages over the colonists was a major reason for his political activism.

Beginning in 1774, Washington represented Virginia at the Second Continental Congress, which declared the colonies' independence from Great Britain. In 1775, he was appointed commander-in-chief of the American forces. From the successful battle to expel the British troops from Boston in 1776 to the campaign at Yorktown in 1781, Washington continually led the main forces in the northern part of the colonies. Although not successful in every battle, he ultimately prevailed, with a peace treaty recognizing the independence of the United States signed in 1783.

After the war, he resigned his commission, stayed out of politics, and enjoyed life on his plantation. However, the new nation was in need of Washington's political leadership. In 1784, he hosted a meeting between leaders of Maryland and Virginia to develop a compact regarding navigation on the Potomac River, part of their mutual boundary. When it became clear that the Articles of Confederation were too weak to govern the United States, he was asked to lead Virginia's delegation to the Constitutional Convention. Once there he was unanimously elected president of the convention.

When Congress convened in 1789 following the first presidential election, they received the results of the votes by the electors of the various states, showing that Washington was unanimously elected as the first president of the United States. During his two successful terms in office, he worked hard to establish a system of government that would endure. Refusing to be considered for a third term, Washington retired to Mount Vernon in March 1797. After a brief illness, he died on December 14, 1799.

HISTORICAL DOCUMENT

Fellow Citizens of the Senate and the House of Representatives.

Among the vicissitudes incident to life, no event could have filled me with greater anxieties than that of which the notification was transmitted by your order, and received on the fourteenth day of the present month. On the one hand, I was summoned by my Country, whose voice I can never hear but with veneration and love, from a retreat which I had chosen with the fondest predilection, and, in my flattering hopes, with an immutable decision, as the asylum of my declining years: a retreat which was rendered every day more necessary as well as more dear to me, by the addition of habit to inclination, and of frequent interruptions in my health to the gradual waste committed on it by time. On the other hand, the magnitude and difficulty of the trust to which the voice of my Country called me, being sufficient to awaken in the wisest and most experienced of her citizens, a distrustful scrutiny into his qualifications, could not but overwhelm with despondence, one, who, inheriting inferior endowments from nature and unpractised in the duties of civil administration, ought to be peculiarly conscious of his own deficiencies. In this conflict of emotions, all I dare aver, is, that it has been my faithful study to collect my duty from a just appreciation of every circumstance, by which it might be affected. All I dare hope, is, that, if in executing this task I have been too much swayed by a grateful remembrance of former instances, or by an affectionate sensibility to this transcendent proof, of the confidence of my fellow-citizens; and have thence too little consulted my incapacity as well as disinclination for the weighty and untried cares before me; my error will be palliated by the motives which misled me, and its consequences be judged by my Country, with some share of the partiality in which they originated.

Such being the impressions under which I have, in obedience to the public summons, repaired to the present station; it would be peculiarly improper to omit in this first official Act, my fervent supplications to that Almighty Being who rules over the Universe, who presides in the Councils of Nations, and whose providential aids can supply every human defect, that his benediction may consecrate to the liberties and happiness of the People of the United States, a Government instituted by themselves for these essential purposes: and may enable every instrument employed in its administration to execute with success, the functions allotted to his charge. In tendering this homage to the Great Author of every public and private good I assure myself that it expresses your sentiments not less than my own; nor those of my fellow-citizens at large, less than either. No People can be bound to acknowledge and adore the invisible hand, which conducts the Affairs of men more than the People of the United States. Every step, by which they have advanced to the character of an independent nation, seems to have been distinguished by some token of providential agency. And in the important revolution just accomplished in the system of their United Government, the tranquil deliberations and voluntary consent of so many distinct communities, from which the event has resulted, cannot be compared with the means by which most Governments have been established, without some return of pious gratitude along with an humble anticipation of the future blessings which the past seem to presage. These reflections, arising out of the present crisis, have forced themselves too strongly on my mind to be suppressed. You will join with me I trust in thinking, that there are none under the influence of which, the proceedings of a new and free Government can more auspiciously commence.

By the article establishing the Executive Department, it is made the duty of the President "to recommend to your consideration, such measures as he shall judge necessary and expedient." The circumstances under which I now meet you, will acquit me from entering into that subject, farther than to refer to the Great Constitutional Charter under which you are assembled; and which, in defining your powers, designates the objects to which your attention is to be given. It will be more consistent with those circumstances, and far more congenial with the feelings which actuate me, to substitute, in place of a recommendation of particular measures, the tribute that is due to the talents, the rectitude, and the patriotism which adorn the characters selected to devise and adopt them. In these honorable qualifications, I behold the surest pledges, that as on one side, no local prejudices, or attachments; no separate views, nor party animosities, will misdirect the comprehensive and equal eye which ought to watch over this great assemblage of communities and interests: so, on another, that the foundations of our National policy will be laid in the pure and immutable principles of private morality; and the pre-eminence of a free Government, be exemplified by all the attributes which can win the affections of its Citizens, and command the respect of the world.

I dwell on this prospect with every satisfaction which an ardent love for my Country can inspire: since there is no truth more thoroughly established, than that there exists in the economy and course of nature, an indissoluble union between virtue and happiness, between duty and advantage, between the genuine maxims of an honest and magnanimous policy, and the solid rewards of public prosperity and felicity: Since we ought to be no less persuaded that the propitious smiles of Heaven, can never be expected on a nation that disregards the eternal rules of order and right, which Heaven itself has ordained: And since the preservation of the sacred fire of liberty, and the destiny of the Republican model of Government, are justly considered as deeply, perhaps as finally staked, on the experiment entrusted to the hands of the American people. Besides the ordinary objects submitted to your care, it will remain with your judgment to decide, how far an exercise of the occasional power delegated by the Fifth article of the Constitution is rendered expedient at the present juncture by the nature of objections which have been urged against the System, or by the degree of inquietude which has given birth to them. Instead of undertaking particular recommendations on this subject, in which I could be guided by no lights derived from official opportunities, I shall again give way to my entire confidence in your discernment and pursuit of the public good: For I assure myself that whilst you carefully avoid every alteration which might endanger the benefits of an United and effective Government, or which ought to await the future lessons of experience; a reverence for the characteristic rights of freemen, and a regard for the public harmony, will sufficiently influence your deliberations on the question how far the former can be more impregnably fortified, or the latter be safely and advantageously promoted.

To the preceding observations I have one to add, which will be most properly addressed to the House of Representatives. It concerns myself, and will therefore be as brief as possible. When I was first honoured with a call into the Service of my Country, then on the eve of an arduous struggle for its liberties, the light in which I contemplated my duty required that I should renounce every pecuniary compensation. From this resolution I have in no instance departed. And being still under the impressions which produced it, I must decline as inapplicable to myself, any share in the personal emoluments, which may be indispensably included in a permanent provision for the Executive Department; and must accordingly pray that the pecuniary estimates for the Station in which I am placed, may, during my continuance in it, be limited to such actual expenditures as the public good may be thought to require.

Having thus imported to you my sentiments, as they have been awakened by the occasion which brings us together, I shall take my present leave; but not without resorting once more to the benign parent of the human race, in humble supplication that since he has been pleased to favour the American people, with opportunities for deliberating in perfect tranquility, and dispositions for deciding with unparellelled unanimity on a form of Government, for the security of their Union, and the advancement of their happiness; so his divine blessing may be equally conspicuous in the enlarged views, the temperate consultations, and the wise measures on which the success of this Government must depend.

GLOSSARY

aver: to affirm

felicity: happiness or bliss

pecuniary compensation: monetary payment, in this case a salary

Republican: of a republic, a country governed by the representative form of democracy

vicissitudes: changes

Document Analysis

George Washington opened his first term as president of the United States with an inaugural address that lay out his approach to this new task given him by his country. While his introduction and conclusion should not be ignored, the heart of his address dealt with the issues facing the new Congress and the new president. In the nearly six-year period since the Treaty of Paris was signed, recognizing the independence of the United States, the new country had struggled to remain united. Two years prior to Washington's inauguration, the Constitutional Convention had been called to create a more effective system of government. Seven months prior, enough states had ratified the Constitution to begin its implementation. Washington was standing before the members of Congress who were waiting with great anticipation to hear what he had to say. The Constitutional Convention had tried to seek a way to truly unify the thirteen states by writing a Constitution that put more power in the hands of the federal government and only a few powers in the hands of the states, the opposite approach of the failed Articles of Confederation. The challenge that faced Washington was how to execute the statutes put forth by the Constitution and gain the support of the fiercely independent states. How could the new government overcome "local prejudices" and be unified? This was the task before Washington and Congress, and this was the tone that Washington needed to set as he started his first term.

First page of George Washington's First Inaugural Address. (National Archives)

Washington began his speech with an affirmation that he understood the magnitude of the current situation. For one so familiar with the battlefield, who had commanded a desperate army searching for a way to defeat a major European power, he affirmed the tremendous challenge facing him by stating, "No event could have filled me with greater anxieties than that of which the notification was transmitted by your order." Although as the result of his earlier leadership, he knew to expect the call to be president, Washington still had to prepare himself for the challenges that lay ahead. In the time between the end of large-scale fighting in 1781 and the signing of the peace treaty in 1783, some within the army offered to support any move he might want to make to become king of the United States. He had refused that offer, but now had been made president— not the king, but the leader nonetheless—of the nation. This speech had to establish the precedent of a republican leader of a strong central government, while at the same time not claiming for himself or Congress more power than was appropriate under the Constitution. This was the challenge of the situation in which he found himself.

Having served Virginia and the united colonies for most of his adult life, Washington declared that in this new phase of the history of the United States he could not refuse another call to service. Since Washington was the only U.S. president who did not campaign for office, his humility was sincere. The country had sought him out; he was "summoned" by his country, who, he states, he could never hear "but with veneration and love." Yet, his hesitation to accept the presidency is evident. He spoke of his "fondest predilection," the desire to continue his retirement at Mount Vernon. Fifty-seven was not an exceptionally old age, but his health was failing him. Although he did not explicitly refer to the hardships he had experienced, he said that his health had a "gradual waste committed on it by time." He went on to comment that any person, even the person with the greatest skills for governing, would question their ability to meet such a call, and that he was far from the most qualified person for the position. Although he admitted to having some experience that would assist him as leader of the new nation, throughout the opening paragraph he is continually modest, and hopes for success even as he wondered if the electors did not take into consideration his limitations and inexperience at this level of government. But even with these uncertainties, Washington proclaimed that he would accept the call. And if he failed, he hoped that Congress would remember that he took the position

to serve his country, and not to serve his own interests.

Washington opened the second paragraph of his speech with a statement of thanks to God for the blessings that had brought the nation to this point in history. The religious beliefs of many of the Founding Fathers, including Washington, have been the subject of great debate, especially in recent years. Some have tried to prove that many of the Founders were not Christians at all, while others have asserted that the Founders' beliefs were devoutly Christian.

In this paragraph and the closing one, Washington made it clear that he was not on either extreme. Those who would call him a deist (one who believed that God's only action was the creation of the universe, which he then left alone) should be able to clearly see in this passage, as well as in other speeches and writings, that Washington saw God as "the invisible hand, which conducts the Affairs of men." Thus, as with other members of the Anglican/Episcopalian church, Washington believed that God was active in the world and had blessed the people of the United States by the creation of the new nation. Washington said it would have been wrong not to give thanks to God, "that Almighty Being who rules over the Universe."

On the other hand, Washington does not refer to Jesus in this speech, and rarely did in any public speech or writing. Thus, when he gave his "pious gratitude" to God, Washington did not use the type of personal language for God that many Christians would use in similar circumstances. As a believer in God, Washington gave thanks, and as a political leader he did not think it inappropriate to do so in the context of an official speech. However, his neutral tone reflected not only his personal faith, but his desire for religious tolerance in the new nation as well.

Within Washington's thanksgiving to God, he outlined some of the unusual steps that had occurred in the creation of the new nation and this new system of government. He reminded the members of Congress that it was the people as a whole who created "a Government instituted by themselves for these essential purposes." He stated that while the "providential agency" (God) had been with them throughout the process, it had been a united effort of the people that had allowed the new nation to reach its goal of a "free Government." For Washington, unity was key. The advancement was only possible because of the "voluntary consent of so many distinct communities." Unity allowed the constitutional system of government to develop peacefully, unlike the "means by which most Governments have been established." By this, he meant the hereditary monarchies that were more common in the eighteenth century.

He was optimistic about the future and believed that the past predicted the possibilities of the future. Washington told the members of Congress, and indirectly the population of the United States, that the blessings of this new form of government were the best possible foundation upon which to build the future.

Moving on to specifics, Washington discussed the duties of the executive branch. He clearly understood his responsibilities in making proposals to Congress regarding various issues before the national government. However, he had decided that since this was a ceremonial occasion, he would not make a series of specific requests regarding legislation for what might be considered day-to-day issues. This he would do later. In place of outlining specifics, Washington focused on some of the general issues that would confront him and Congress. He once again called for unity within the nation and the government. In the process of ratifying the Constitution, the Federalist and Anti-Federalist factions had crystallized throughout the country. While most members of Congress represented those in favor of the strong federal system that was being implemented, a minority were elected because of their Anti-Federalist views that emphasized states' rights. Rather than focusing on the political debates that had preceded the election of the members of Congress, Washington lifted up the qualities that he believed were in all members of Congress. Thus, he stated that he wanted to pay homage to the "talents, the rectitude, and the patriotism" that were found in all the members of Congress. While he was probably sincere in making this statement, it was also an attempt to unify the Congress, since the political process required Congress to pass the laws that Washington proposed.

The second general point Washington made was that Congress was to serve the United States of America. No secondary attributes should come before the desire to create and sustain a truly democratic government. After his previous appeal to lawmakers' individual characteristics, Washington made a pledge that he would work for the nation, and asked members of Congress to act in a similar fashion. He listed the two most common barriers to cooperation at that time: rivalries among the states and differences of opinion between the emerging political factions. Rather than create legislation based on what Washington saw as negative qualities, he asked Congress to build the new system of government based on "the pure and immutable principles of private morality; and

the pre-eminence of a free Government." In doing so, Washington asserted that the citizens living under this new system of government would proclaim its goodness and other nations would see its integrity and accept the new system of government. Washington's belief that personal morality and a good and successful government were closely related was in line with many political thinkers of his day.

Washington then proceeded to list what he considered dualities of truth and the challenge that confronted the American people and their system of government. He stated that he was certain and fully satisfied that the new nation could live out these truths and meet the challenges before it. He said, "There is no truth more thoroughly established, than . . . an indissoluble union between virtue and happiness, between duty and advantage, between the genuine maxims of an honest and magnanimous policy, and the solid rewards of public prosperity and felicity." In other words, living a moral life brings forth happiness; doing one's duty creates opportunities; open and honest government allows for generosity; all of which combine to create wellbeing and happiness in all parts of the society. These are maxims in which Washington truly believed, ones that he sought to have members of Congress follow. He also believed that if all citizens of the United States followed these guidelines, then God's blessings would assist the nation in doing great things.

Washington understood that the entire world was watching this new nation and its experimental government. If the nation's republican form of government succeeded, others might follow its example, whereas if the United States failed in its experiment, democracy in that form might not survive. The challenge before the nation, and especially before Congress, was the "preservation of the sacred fire of liberty." This belief in America's special role in the world has long been a part of its heritage and often its foreign policy.

In the next paragraph Washington took on one the major issue dividing the Federalists and the Anti-Federalists. Although promises had been made to secure the ratification of the Constitution, it was now time for action. Washington referred to the Fifth Article of the Constitution, the article that deals with amendments. The major complaint that Anti-Federalists had concerning the Constitution was that it did not place sufficient limits on the power of the central government—the same issue that led to the American Revolution. In addition, the Constitution did not explicitly guarantee the basic rights of the states or their citizens. Washington indicated his support for changes to the Constitution, but did not try to direct the members of Congress in the specific changes that were to be made, probably because the U.S. president does not have a role to play in amending the Constitution; constitutional amendments are a matter between Congress and the state governments. However, by mentioning the need for additional civil rights, Washington was urging the Congress to add such amendments as quickly as was practical. These must include "reverence for the characteristic rights of freemen, and a regard for public harmony." Washington asserted that a balance between those two ideals must be reached. Often reminding them of this charge, left over from the campaign for ratification, he stated that he was confident they would deal with this matter in an "expedient" manner.

In the next to last paragraph, Washington addressed the House of Representatives regarding something unique to him. This was financial compensation. Throughout his previous service to the colonies, Washington had refused to draw a salary. He had land in Virginia and a plantation, which had been run by his family during his time of service. Even so, the donation of his time and talents meant that he was less financially secure than would have been the case if he had worked full-time on his plantation. Nonetheless, he desired to do the same while he served as president. He did not want people thinking he was using service to the country as a way of getting rich. He addressed this concern to the House, because under the Constitution, all bills appropriating money for expenditure had to originate in the House. He understood that in developing a budget for the United States, Congress had to establish "a permanent provision for the Executive Department." However, while he served as President, he requested the House only appropriate money to cover "actual expenditures," expenses having to do specifically with the office of the president.

As in the earlier passage of his speech, Washington closed with a statement of thanksgiving to God, as well as a remembrance of the steps that had been taken by the American people to reach their present situation. Washington believed that a part of this blessing had been the ability of the people's representatives to peacefully and rationally develop the constitutional system. The previous system of government, the Articles of Confederation, had been put together in the midst of the Revolutionary War, a war fought because the British withheld from the colonies powers of self-

government or representation in Parliament. Fearing a strong central government that might usurp power as the British did, the Articles created a very weak central government. Washington spoke positively of the fact that the Constitution was only possible because of the "opportunities for deliberating in perfect tranquility." Through this unique opportunity, Washington was certain that the nation had created a system giving "security of their Union and the advancement of their happiness." He closed with the admonition that everyone in the new government must work for the country as a whole, through "temperate consultations" that will ensure "success." Washington was certain that this new system being inaugurated with him would truly fulfill the Preamble to the Constitution, with implementation leading to "a more perfect union."

Essential Themes

Washington set a precedent, which all presidents have followed, of giving an inaugural address. Although his was shorter than most, it was arguably the most significant because it laid out the most important issues that his administration and the nation as a whole would face for decades to come. Again, this is the norm for inaugural speeches. In Washington's first term, even more important than legislation establishing the operations of the government, was the need for assurances to the citizens of the new nation regarding their civil rights. Washington strongly urged Congress to take up this issue, and the result was what is known as the Bill of Rights. These first ten amendments to the Constitution have served the nation well and their adoption ended most of the disagreements over whether to have a federal system of government. Political disputes then became focused on policies and implementation. Washington's strong desire was for the Congress to complete what the Constitutional Convention had started. The stress he laid on this point made it perhaps more important than any other set out in his inaugural speech.

In addition to his belief in the need for a Bill of Rights, Washington was also successful in demonstrating his personal beliefs the nation's future, based on its successes in the past decade or so. He thought it was almost miraculous that the colonies had come together as states in the new democratic federal system of government. His assertion was that "every step" on the way could be seen as guided by a force greater than human intellect. The idea of "one out of many" rang true to Washington. Because of this, he indicated that he believed the future was assured. During his presidency, his certainty inspired many who had more mixed feelings about the path from thirteen colonies to the new, restructured United States. Even though there were divisions within his administration, and Congress did not automatically give him everything he requested, Washington's certainty about the near and long-term future gave stability to the new system, which it otherwise would have lacked. Although he did not use the twentieth-century term "American exceptionalism," Washington did believe that the United States had a special role to play in the world. His belief that the United States carried "the sacred fire of liberty" rang true for many. The democratic example of the United States helped inspire many others in Europe and the Americas to follow suit.

—*Donald A. Watt, PhD*

Bibliography and Additional Reading

Beschloss, Michael, and Hugh Sidey. "George Washington." *The Presidents of the United States of America.* White House Hist. Soc. 2009. Web. 23 Apr. 2012.

Brookhiser, Richard. *Founding Father: Rediscovering George Washington.* New York: Free Press, 1996. Print.

Chernow, Ron. *Washington: A Life.* New York: Penguin, 2010. Print.

Ellis, Joseph J. *His Excellency: George Washington.* New York: Vintage, 2005. Print.

Flexner, James Thomas. *Washington: The Indispensable Man.* Boston: Little, 1974. Print.

Washington, George, and Howard F. Bremer. *George Washington, 1732–1799; Chronology, Documents, Bibliographical Aids.* Dobbs Ferry, NY: Oceana, 1967. Print.

———, and John H. Rhodehamel. *Writings.* New York: Lib. of America/Penguin, 1997. Print.

■ Thomas Jefferson to Elbridge Gerry

Date: January 26, 1799
Author: Thomas Jefferson
Genre: Letter

Summary Overview

President John Adams and his vice president Thomas Jefferson had long been working together towards common goals, such as fighting for independence and creating the constitution that would guide the country for decades upon decades. However, in 1800 the two men found themselves pitted against one another in a heated battle for the presidency, divided by party politics. Adams, a Federalist, and Jefferson a Democratic–Republican, had found themselves in this same campaign competition just four short years earlier, with Adams ultimately achieving victory. While the two men had seemingly worked together in harmony as president and vice-president regardless of their previous electoral competition, they engaged in a bitter rematch during the 1800 elections. While presidential candidates during this time were not known to actively campaign as it seemed undignified, this particular campaign eventually boiled down to name-calling and insults. Regardless of the campaign tactics employed, the result of the election of 1800 occurred due to a flaw in the Electoral College. The language regarding the Electoral College mechanism did not differentiate between presidential and vice-presidential candidates. Because Jefferson and Aaron Burr (who was campaigning as Jefferson's running mate) both received an equal number of electoral votes, the tie had to be settled in the House of Representatives as outlined in Article II, Section 1 of the Constitution. After days of deliberation, the House declared Jefferson the winner, thereby naming him the next president of the United States.

No one historical document brings together all the different threads of this important election. A 1799 letter by Jefferson to the Massachusetts statesman Elbridge Gerry, however, serves to introduce the subject by laying out Jefferson's thoughts on running for president.

Defining Moment

Although the letter reprinted here precedes any actual maneuvering for the presidency, in the 1800 contest for that office, Adams and Jefferson found themselves in the middle of an election that was not unlike the modern elections we know today. The candidates, Adams, Jefferson, and their running mates Charles Pinckney and Aaron Burr, were jockeying for Electoral College votes, divided by region, and encountered intense mudslinging campaigns. Adams was the sitting president and had enjoyed some popularity as a president due in large part to the Alien and Sedition Acts that gave the president the power to deport disloyal citizens and provided for the prosecution of people with dissenting political opinions. Adams was a Harvard graduate, a lawyer, and served as George Washington's vice president for two terms. Jefferson had previously served as the Governor of Virginia, George Washington's Secretary of State, and Adams' vice president. Pinckney, running as Adams choice for vice president, had no modest resume himself, as he was present for the signing of the U.S. Constitution, and served as the Governor of South Carolina. Burr, who was slated to fill the role of vice president if Jefferson secured the win, had also achieved greatness as the New York State Attorney General and as a U.S. Senator. All were seemingly viable candidates in the race for the presidency, but it would come down to just two who might not have been the obvious final contenders: Jefferson and Burr.

At this point in history, active campaigning on the part of presidential candidates was not commonplace—as illustrated in Jefferson's letter to Gerry. In fact, Adams and Jefferson spent most of the campaign season at their respective homes. However, this did not mean campaigning did not take happen. In fact, some of the most negative campaigning of the time occurred during the election of 1800. Some historians believe Jefferson hired a man named James Callendar to drag Adams' name through the mud during the election. Adams was portrayed as a fool, hypocrite, criminal, and a tyrant, while those fighting against Jefferson claimed he was a weak coward who was also an atheist. In addition to the name-calling, newspapers at the time were extremely partisan and did not shy away from taking sides in campaigns. Once a newspaper decided to back, or perhaps more importantly, oppose a candidate, there was nothing that could be done to stop the paper from writing stories that reflected their presidential preference. With the Federalist Party attacking Jefferson as un-Christian, and the Democratic Republicans voicing objections to Adams' expansion of military forces and tax increases, the battle for the office of the president was intense even though the two main candidates themselves were not visibly involved in the fray. When the campaign was over and electoral votes were counted, a shocking revelation was made: Jefferson and his running mate were tied for president. Each man had received 73 Electoral College votes each, meaning the race was to be decided in the House of Representatives. John Adams was out of the race officially, and would not be serving another term as the president.

Author Biography

Thomas Jefferson was born in 1743 to a prominent Virginia family. As a young man, Jefferson received a rigorous private school education and went on to study at the College of William and Mary. Jefferson was a successful lawyer, land-owner, and farmer. He worked diligently for American independence as a Founding Father and was the draftsman of the Declaration of Independence. Jefferson served as the nation's first Secretary of State, the second vice president, and the third president.

HISTORICAL DOCUMENT

Jefferson to Elbridge Gerry, January 26, 1799

MY DEAR SIR,
—Your favor of Nov. 12 was safely delivered to me by Mr. Binney, but not till Dec. 28, as I arrived here only three days before that date. It was received with great satisfaction. Our very long intimacy as fellow-laborers in the same cause, the recent expressions of mutual confidence which had preceded your mission, the interesting course which that had taken, & particularly & personally as it regarded yourself, made me anxious to hear from you on your return. I was the more so too, as I had myself during the whole of your absence, as well as since your return, been a constant butt for every shaft of calumny which malice & falsehood could form, & the presses, public speakers, or private letters disseminate. One of these, too, was of a nature to touch yourself; as if, wanting confidence in your efforts, I had been capable of usurping powers committed to you, & authorizing negociations private & collateral to yours. The real truth is, that though Dr Logan, the pretended missionary, about 4, or 5, days before he sailed for Hamburgh, told me he was going there, & thence to Paris, & asked & received from me a certificate of his citizenship, character, & circumstances of life, merely as a protection, should he be molested on his journey, in the present turbulent & suspicious state of Europe, yet I had been led to consider his object as relative to his private affairs; and tho', from an intimacy of some standing, he knew well my wishes for peace and my political sentiments in general, he nevertheless received then no particular declaration of them, no authority to communicate them to any mortal, nor to speak to any one in my name, or in anybody's name, on that, or on any other subject whatever; nor did I write by him a scrip of a pen to any person whatever. This he has himself honestly & publicly declared since his return; & from his well-known character & every other circumstance, every candid man must perceive that his enterprise was dictated by his own enthusiasm, without consultation or communication with any one; that he acted in Paris on his own ground, & made his own way. Yet to give some color to his proceedings, which might implicate the republicans in general, & myself particularly, they have not been ashamed to bring forward a supposititious paper, drawn by one of their own party in the name of Logan, and falsely pretended to have been presented by him to the government of France; counting that the bare mention of my name therein, would connect that in the eye of the public with this transaction. In confutation of these and all future calumnies, by way of anticipation,

I shall make to you a profession of my political faith; in confidence that you will consider every future imputation on me of a contrary complexion, as bearing on its front the mark of falsehood & calumny.

I do then, with sincere zeal, wish an inviolable preservation of our present federal constitution, according to the true sense in which it was adopted by the States, that in which it was advocated by its friends, & not that which its enemies apprehended, who therefore became its enemies; and I am opposed to the monarchising its features by the forms of its administration, with a view to conciliate a first transition to a President & Senate for life, & from that to a hereditary tenure of these offices, & thus to worm out the elective principle. I am for preserving to the States the powers not yielded by them to the Union, & to the legislature of the Union its constitutional share in the division of powers; and I am not for transferring all the powers of the States to the general government, & all those of that government to the Executive branch. I am for a government rigorously frugal & simple, applying all the possible savings of the public revenue to the discharge of the national debt; and not for a multiplication of officers & salaries merely to make partisans, & for increasing, by every device, the public debt, on the principle of its being a public blessing. I am for relying, for internal defence, on our militia solely, till actual invasion, and for such a naval force only as may protect our coasts and harbors from such depredations as we have experienced; and not for a standing army in time of peace, which may overawe the public sentiment; nor for a navy, which, by its own expenses and the eternal wars in which it will implicate us, will grind us with public burthens, & sink us under them. I am for free commerce with all nations; political connection with none; & little or no diplomatic establishment. And I am not for linking ourselves by new treaties with the quarrels of Europe; entering that field of slaughter to preserve their balance, or joining in the confederacy of kings to war against the principles of liberty. I am for freedom of religion, & against all maneuvres to bring about a legal ascendancy of one sect over another: for freedom of the press, & against all violations of the constitution to silence by force & not by reason the complaints or criticisms, just or unjust, of our citizens against the conduct of their agents. And I am for encouraging the progress of science in all its branches;

and not for raising a hue and cry against the sacred name of philosophy; for awing the human mind by stories of raw-head & bloody bones to a distrust of its own vision, & to repose implicitly on that of others; to go backwards instead of forwards to look for improvement; to believe that government, religion, morality, & every other science were in the highest perfection in ages of the darkest ignorance, and that nothing can ever be devised more perfect than what was established by our forefathers. To these I will add, that I was a sincere well-wisher to the success of the French revolution, and still wish it may end in the establishment of a free & well-ordered republic; but I have not been insensible under the atrocious depredations they have committed on our commerce. The first object of my heart is my own country. In that is embarked my family, my fortune, & my own existence. I have not one farthing of interest, nor one fibre of attachment out of it, nor a single motive of preference of any one nation to another, but in proportion as they are more or less friendly to us. But though deeply feeling the injuries of France, I did not think war the surest means of redressing them. I did believe, that a mission sincerely disposed to preserve peace, would obtain for us a peaceable & honorable settlement & retribution; and I appeal to you to say, whether this might not have been obtained, if either of your colleagues had been of the same sentiment with yourself.

These, my friend, are my principles; they are unquestionably the principles of the great body of our fellow citizens, and I know there is not one of them which is not yours also. In truth, we never differed but on one ground, the funding system; and as, from the moment of its being adopted by the constituted authorities, I became religiously principled in the sacred discharge of it to the uttermost farthing, we are united now even on that single ground of difference.

I turn now to your inquiries. The enclosed paper will answer one of them. But you also ask for such political information as may be possessed by me, & interesting to yourself in regard to your embassy. As a proof of my entire confidence in you, I shall give it fully & candidly. When Pinckney, Marshall, and Dana, were nominated to settle our differences with France, it was suspected by many, from what was understood of their dispositions, that their mission would not result in a settlement of differences, but would produce circumstances tending to widen the breach, and to provoke our citizens to consent to a war with that nation, & union with England. Dana's resignation & your appointment gave the first gleam of hope of a peaceable issue to the mission. For it was believed that you were sincerely disposed to accommodation; & it was not long after your arrival there, before symptoms were observed of that difference of views which had been suspected to exist. In the meantime, however, the aspect of our government towards the French republic had become so ardent, that the people of America generally took the alarm. To the southward, their apprehensions were early excited. In the Eastern States also, they at length began to break out. Meetings were held in many of your towns, & addresses to the government agreed on in opposition to war. The example was spreading like a wildfire. Other meetings were called in other places, & a general concurrence of sentiment against the apparent inclinations of the government was imminent; when, most critically for the government, the despatches of Octr 22, prepared by your colleague Marshall, with a view to their being made public, dropped into their laps. It was truly a God-send to them, & they made the most of it. Many thousands of copies were printed & dispersed gratis, at the public expence; & the zealots for war co-operated so heartily, that there were instances of single individuals who printed & dispersed 10, or 12,000 copies at their own expence. The odiousness of the corruption supposed in those papers excited a general & high indignation among the people. Unexperienced in such maneuvres, they did not permit themselves even to suspect that the turpitude of private swindlers might mingle itself unobserved, & give its own hue to the communications of the French government, of whose participation there was neither proof nor probability. It served, however, for a time, the purpose intended. The people, in many places, gave a loose to the expressions of their warm indignation, & of their honest preference of war to dishonor. The fever was long & successfully kept up, and in the meantime, war measures as ardently crowded. Still, however, as it was known that your colleagues were coming away, and yourself to stay, though disclaiming a separate power to conclude a treaty, it was hoped by the lovers of peace, that a project of treaty would have been prepared, ad referendum, on principles which would have satisfied our

citizens, & overawed any bias of the government towards a different policy. But the expedition of the Sophia, and, as was supposed, the suggestions of the person charged with your despatches, & his probable misrepresentations of the real wishes of the American people, prevented these hopes. They had then only to look forward to your return for such information, either through the Executive, or from yourself, as might present to our view the other side of the medal. The despatches of Oct 22, 97, had presented one face. That information, to a certain degree, is now received, & the public will see from your correspondence with Talleyrand, that France, as you testify, "was sincere and anxious to obtain a reconciliation, not wishing us to break the British treaty, but only to give her equivalent stipulations; and in general was disposed to a liberal treaty." And they will judge whether Mr. Pickering's report shews an inflexible determination to believe no declarations the French government can make, nor any opinion which you, judging on the spot & from actual view, can give of their sincerity, and to meet their designs of peace with operations of war. The alien & sedition acts have already operated in the South as powerful sedatives of the X. Y. Z. inflammation. In your quarter, where violations of principle are either less regarded or more concealed, the direct tax is likely to have the same effect, & to excite inquiries into the object of the enormous expences & taxes we are bringing on. And your information supervening, that we might have a liberal accommodation if we would, there can be little doubt of the reproduction of that general movement, by the despatches of Oct. 22. And tho' small checks & stops, like Logan's pretended embassy, may be thrown in the way from time to time, & may a little retard its motion, yet the tide is already turned, and will sweep before it all the feeble obstacles of art. The unquestionable republicanism of the American mind will break through the mist under which it has been clouded, and will oblige its agents to reform the principles & practices of their administration.

You suppose that you have been abused by both parties. As far as has come to my knowledge, you are misinformed. I have never seen or heard a sentence of blame uttered against you by the republicans; unless we were so to construe their wishes that you had more boldly co-operated in a project of a treaty, and would more explicitly state, whether there was in your colleagues that flexibility, which persons earnest after peace would have practised? Whether, on the contrary, their demeanor was not cold, reserved, and distant, at least, if not backward? And whether, if they had yielded to those informal conferences which Talleyrand seems to have courted, the liberal accommodation you suppose might not have been effected, even with their agency? Your fellow-citizens think they have a right to full information, in a case of such great concern to them. It is their sweat which is to earn all the expences of the war, and their blood which is to flow in expiation of the causes of it. It may be in your power to save them from these miseries by full communications and unrestrained details, postponing motives of delicacy to those of duty. It rests for you to come forward independently; to take your stand on the high ground of your own character; to disregard calumny, and to be borne above it on the shoulders of your grateful fellow citizens; or to sink into the humble oblivion, to which the Federalists (self-called) have secretly condemned you; and even to be happy if they will indulge you with oblivion, while they have beamed on your colleagues meridian splendor. Pardon me, my dear Sir, if my expressions are strong. My feelings are so much more so, that it is with difficulty I reduce them even to the tone I use. If you doubt the dispositions towards you, look into the papers, on both sides, for the toasts which were given throughout the States on the 4th of July. You will there see whose hearts were with you, and whose were ulcerated against you. Indeed, as soon as it was known that you had consented to stay in Paris, there was no measure observed in the execrations of the war party. They openly wished you might be guillotined, or sent to Cayenne, or anything else. And these expressions were finally stifled from a principle of policy only, & to prevent you from being urged to a justification of yourself. From this principle alone proceed the silence and cold respect they observe towards you. Still, they cannot prevent at times the flames bursting from under the embers, as Mr. Pickering's letters, report, & conversations testify, as well as the indecent expressions respecting you, indulged by some of them in the debate on these despatches. These sufficiently show that you are never more to be honored or trusted by them, and that they await to crush you for ever, only till they can do it without danger to themselves.

When I sat down to answer your letter, but two courses presented themselves, either to say nothing or everything; for half confidences are not in my character. I could not hesitate which was due to you. I have unbosomed myself fully; & it will certainly be highly gratifying if I receive like confidence from you. For even if we differ in principle more than I believe we do, you & I know too well the texture of the human mind, & the slipperiness of human reason, to consider differences of opinion otherwise than differences of form or feature. Integrity of views more than their soundness, is the basis of esteem. I shall follow your direction in conveying this by a private hand; tho' I know not as yet when one worthy of confidence will occur. And my trust in you leaves me without a fear that this letter, meant as a confidential communication of my impressions, will ever go out of your hand, or be suffered in anywise to commit my name. Indeed, besides the accidents which might happen to it even under your care, considering the accident of death to which you are liable, I think it safest to pray you, after reading it as often as you please, to destroy at least the 2d & 3d leaves. The 1st contains principles only, which I fear not to avow; but the 2d & 3d contain facts stated for your information, and which, though sacredly conformable to my firm belief, yet would be galling to some, & expose me to illiberal attacks. I therefore repeat my prayer to burn the 2d & 3d leaves. And did we ever expect to see the day, when, breathing nothing but sentiments of love to our country & its freedom & happiness, our correspondence must be as secret as if we were hatching its destruction!

Adieu, my friend, and accept my sincere & affectionate salutations.

I need not add my signature.

GLOSSARY

Federalist Party: an early political party that wanted to see the Constitution adopted by the states, and favored a strong central government.

Document Analysis

Although this letter is revealing of Jefferson's intentions before the 1800 election, it is the wider picture of the election that is historically notable. Both Adams and Jefferson genuinely wanted to win the race for the presidency in 1800, and both men honestly believed the other's party would lead the burgeoning nation to ruin. Therefore, the stakes were phenomenally high during America's fourth presidential election. Tensions had been rising among the parties since the French Revolution, and Adams' passage of the Alien and Sedition Acts had driven tensions even higher. Jefferson expressed his sincere desire to uphold a country with a strong central government, and stood by the Constitution. Jefferson wanted a "frugal & simple" government, and this sentiment seemed in direct contradiction to Adams' stance as evidenced by his creation of the Alien and Sedition Acts.

In addition to party disagreements over major issues and policies, the campaigns had resorted to hurling slurs directed at the opposing candidates. Adams was cited for having an "ungovernable temper," while Jefferson was called a "howling atheist." In fact, Jefferson was greatly troubled by the mudslinging and felt he was personally being demolished, in terms of reputation, by the press and the people. Other, more unsavory labels were attached to the candidates, proving the negative campaigning familiar to us in modern campaigns has actually been occurring for hundreds of years. Even though the focus of the campaign was primarily on the two candidates vying for the presidency, Adams and Jefferson, the final contest would actually be between Jefferson and his own running mate, Aaron Burr.

Jefferson and Burr, each having received seventy-three Electoral College votes were tied for the office of the president. How could it have been that Adams was no longer in the running? Part of the explanation for Adams' loss has to do with the ⅗ Clause created at the Constitutional Convention. The ⅗ Clause states that all slaves were to be counted as ⅗ of a person in terms of the population count. Had this clause not existed, slaves would not have been counted for the purposes of Congressional apportionment, and the vote could have easily tipped in Adams' favor. Another major challenge Adams faced in the race was not a law or Constitutional provision, it was another man: Alexander Hamilton. Throughout the course of the campaign, Hamilton tried to convince people to put their support behind Pinckney which may have cost Adams votes in the election. With Adams out of the race, and the decision being left to the House of Repre-

sentatives, the final battle for the presidential win began.

For six full days Jefferson and Burr ran against one another in the House to determine who the victor would be. Hamilton once again inserted himself into the election and argued on behalf of Thomas Jefferson. This was not an indication that Hamilton by any means truly favored Jefferson, it was more likely that Hamilton believed Jefferson to be the lesser of two evils. The debate in the House was impassioned, so much so that Virginia even threatened succession if Jefferson was not named the winner of the election. Finally, a member of the House, under pressure from Hamilton, agreed to abstain from the vote. This abstention put an end to the debate and officially declared a winner. On February 17, 1801, after months and months of campaigning, Jefferson was officially the president of the United States, with Aaron Burr agreeing to serve as the vice president.

Essential Themes

Although the Jefferson–Gerry letter may not hint at this, historical evidence suggests the 1800 campaign was just one of the first in a long line of nasty, negative, contentious races for the office of the president in America. Jefferson's choice to employ Callendar to smear Adams' name would eventually come back to haunt him. Although some historians bill this as propaganda, others genuinely believe Callendar, feeling as if Jefferson did not properly compensate him for his work in the 1800 election, was responsible for leaking the story about Jefferson's relationship with Sally Hemmings, a woman who served as a slave for Jefferson. DNA evidence was presented in 1998 linking Jefferson to members of the Hemmings' family, suggesting not only was there an affair but children resulted from that union. Rumors of this affair would ultimately tarnish Jefferson's reputation. In addition to political scandal stemming from the fallout of the 1800 election, there were legal ramifications as well.

The founding fathers did not anticipate a tie occurring between a presidential and vice-presidential candidate, which accounts for the original flaw in the Electoral College plan. As a result of the Jefferson/Burr situation, the Twelfth Amendment to the U.S. Constitution was passed in 1804, which officially separated the Electoral College votes for the president and vice-presidential candidates. The unique situation of the election of 1800 would never happen again due to the ratification of this amendment.

Overall, the election of 1800, also referred to as the "Revolution of 1800," would go on to be known as a realigning election that brought about a generation of Republican Party rule in the United States. This would lead to the eventual downfall and dissolution of the Federalist Party in America. This election marked the first time in history when power transitioned from one political party to another, that along with the unique nature of the final battle between the presidential and vice-presidential candidate makes this campaign truly distinct.

—*Amber R. Dickinson, PhD*

Bibliography and Additional Reading

Ferling, John. 2004. *Adams vs. Jefferson: The Tumultuous Election of 1800.* Oxford University Press.

Hitchens, Christopher. *Thomas Jefferson: Author of America.* Atlas & Co./Harper Perennial, 2009.

Lepore, Jill. "Party Time for a Young America." *The New Yorker,* The New Yorker, 18 June 2017, www.newyorker.com/magazine/2007/0d9/17/party-time.

Swint, Kerwin. "Founding Fathers' Dirty." *CNN,* Cable News Network, www.cnn.com/2008/LIVING/wayoflife/08/22/mf.campaign.slurs.slogans/.

"Thomas Jefferson." *Biography.com,* A&E Networks Television, 7 Feb. 2018, www.biography.com/people/thomas-jefferson-9353715.

Wills, Garry. *Negro President: Jefferson and the Slave Power.* Houghton Mifflin, 2005.

■ Thomas Jefferson's First Inaugural Address

Date: 1801
Author: Thomas Jefferson
Genre: Political speech

Summary Overview

As Thomas Jefferson assumed office as the nation's third president, his first task was to seek reconciliation between the Federalist and Democratic–Republican parties, the latter of which Jefferson was a founding member. After a contentious and controversial election, Jefferson's inaugural address struck a conciliatory tone. He called upon both major parties to put aside partisan differences for the good of the nation. In the new United States Capitol in the capital District of Columbia, he encouraged Americans to take advantage of the peace and stability the country was experiencing to continue building and strengthening the young republic.

Defining Moment

At the end of the eighteenth century, the United States closed the book on nearly half a century of tumult and dramatic change, marked by the increased oppression from Great Britain, the Revolutionary War, and the adoption of the United States Constitution. As figures such as George Washington, John Adams, and Thomas Jefferson (all of whom were once dubbed radicals and revolutionaries) evolved into the country's political leaders, they were charged with continuing the construction of the new nation's government. While many of these Founding Fathers stood side by side during the Revolution, their ideas about shaping the new government eventually pulled them in different directions, forming distinct and disparate political parties.

On one side of the American political landscape were John Adams, the country's second president, and his Federalist Party. The Federalists had long seen the need for a strong central government to oversee matters of national interest, including foreign policy, and to maintain cohesion among the states. On the other side were Anti-Federalists, like Thomas Jefferson, who believed the country should defer greater power to the individual states and stress the basic rights of the people. In 1792, Jefferson transformed this group into a political party known as the Democratic–Republicans.

In 1798, President Adams signed into law a series of measures collectively known as the Alien and Sedition Acts, which were introduced as the country stood on the brink of war with France. The acts made it more difficult for foreigners to become American citizens and made it possible for the president to imprison or deport aliens who were perceived dangerous. The acts also included provisions that significantly restricted any speech that was critical of the government. This latter set of provisions sparked a major backlash—particularly in political circles, where it was seen less as a security measure and more as an attempt to hamper the Democratic–Republicans. Consequently, Adams's reelection chances in 1800 were low. Jefferson, the most prominent of the Democratic–Republicans and an outspoken critic of the Federalists, became the most viable challenger.

During the election, the candidates were Jefferson and Aaron Burr on the Democratic–Republican ticket and Adams and Charles Pinckney on the Federalist ticket. Jefferson and Burr tied with seventy-three electoral votes, while Adams received sixty-five and Pinckney received sixty-four. With Adams and the Federalists defeated, the House of Representatives took up the task of selecting one of the two Democratic–Republicans.

The House then faced a period of lobbying and campaigning. Alexander Hamilton pushed hard for the representatives, including the Federalists, to vote for Jefferson, owing to his dislike of Burr. Meanwhile, the Federalist Party threw its support behind Burr in an attempt to defeat their biggest critic in Jefferson. In the end, Jefferson won largely thanks to Hamilton's efforts. Nevertheless, great animosity remained between the two parties, tearing at the fabric of the government of which Jefferson was now the leader.

Author Biography

Thomas Jefferson was born in Shadwell, Virginia, on April 13, 1743. His mother came from a prominent Virginia family and his father was a successful planter and surveyor. Jefferson was educated at a prestigious private school near Shadwell before he enrolled at the College of William and Mary in 1760 and went on to study law under the mentorship of an established attorney, George Wythe. Jefferson worked as a successful attorney from 1764 to 1774. During this period, he met his wife, Martha Skelton, with whom he had six children.

In addition to his tenures as a magistrate and county lieutenant, Jefferson was elected to the Virginia House of Burgesses. There, he connected with a group of radicals, including Patrick Henry and George Washington. In 1774, he wrote his first major political document, "A Summary View of the Rights of British America," which cemented his reputation as an individual who could eloquently present colonial issues.

In 1775, Jefferson attended the Second Continental Congress, which appointed Jefferson's colleague, Washington, as commander in chief of the newly established Continental Army. A year later, in light of the reception of "A Summary View of the Rights of British America,"

Jefferson was asked by the Continental Congress to work with John Adams, Roger Sherman, Benjamin Franklin, and Robert Livingston to draft the Declaration of Independence, although most of that document would be credited to Jefferson alone.

Jefferson returned to Virginia as a member of its House of Delegates from 1776 until1779 and then served as Virginia's governor from 1779 until 1781. Although he desired to return to his Monticello home after leaving office, his wife's death drew Jefferson back into public service in 1782. He returned to Congress in 1783 and was named the American minister to France in 1785. Upon returning to America in 1789, he was appointed as President Washington's secretary of state, a post he held until 1794.

In the 1796 presidential election, Jefferson ran against Federalist John Adams as the candidate to succeed President George Washington. He narrowly lost the election to Adams, but according to the rules of the time, had enough votes to become vice president—an office he held from 1797 until 1801. Jefferson defeated the incumbent Adams in 1800 and became the third American president. In 1809, Jefferson returned to Monticello and founded the University of Virginia. He died in 1826.

HISTORICAL DOCUMENT

FRIENDS AND FELLOW-CITIZENS,
Called upon to undertake the duties of the first executive office of our country, I avail myself of the presence of that portion of my fellow-citizens which is here assembled to express my grateful thanks for the favor with which they have been pleased to look toward me, to declare a sincere consciousness that the task is above my talents, and that I approach it with those anxious and awful presentiments which the greatness of the charge and the weakness of my powers so justly inspire. A rising nation, spread over a wide and fruitful land, traversing all the seas with the rich productions of their industry, engaged in commerce with nations who feel power and forget right, advancing rapidly to destinies beyond the reach of mortal eye — when I contemplate these transcendent objects, and see the honor, the happiness, and the hopes of this beloved country committed to the issue and the auspices of this day, I shrink from the contemplation, and humble myself

before the magnitude of the undertaking. Utterly, indeed, should I despair did not the presence of many whom I here see remind me that in the other high authorities provided by our Constitution I shall find resources of wisdom, of virtue, and of zeal on which to rely under all difficulties. To you, then, gentlemen, who are charged with the sovereign functions of legislation, and to those associated with you, I look with encouragement for that guidance and support which may enable us to steer with safety the vessel in which we are all embarked amidst the conflicting elements of a troubled world.

During the contest of opinion through which we have passed the animation of discussions and of exertions has sometimes worn an aspect which might impose on strangers unused to think freely and to speak and to write what they think; but this being now decided by the voice of the nation, announced according to the rules of the Constitution, all will, of course, arrange themselves under the will of the law, and unite in common efforts for the common good. All, too, will bear in mind this sacred principle, that though the will of the majority is in all cases to prevail, that will to be rightful must be reasonable; that the minority possess their equal rights, which equal law must protect, and to violate would be oppression. Let us, then, fellow-citizens, unite with one heart and one mind. Let us restore to social intercourse that harmony and affection without which liberty and even life itself are but dreary things. And let us reflect that, having banished from our land that religious intolerance under which mankind so long bled and suffered, we have yet gained little if we countenance a political intolerance as despotic, as wicked, and capable of as bitter and bloody persecutions. During the throes and convulsions of the ancient world, during the agonizing spasms of infuriated man, seeking through blood and slaughter his long-lost liberty, it was not wonderful that the agitation of the billows should reach even this distant and peaceful shore; that this should be more felt and feared by some and less by others, and should divide opinions as to measures of safety. But every difference of opinion is not a difference of principle. We have called by different names brethren of the same principle. We are all Republicans, we are all Federalists. If there be any among us who would wish to dissolve this Union or to change its republican form, let them stand undisturbed as monuments of the safety with which error of opinion may be tolerated where reason is left free to combat it. I know, indeed, that some honest men fear that a republican government can not be strong, that this Government is not strong enough; but would the honest patriot, in the full tide of successful experiment, abandon a government which has so far kept us free and firm on the theoretic and visionary fear that this Government, the world's best hope, may by possibility want energy to preserve itself? I trust not. I believe this, on the contrary, the strongest Government on earth. I believe it the only one where every man, at the call of the law, would fly to the standard of the law, and would meet invasions of the public order as his own personal concern. Sometimes it is said that man can not be trusted with the government of himself. Can he, then, be trusted with the government of others? Or have we found angels in the forms of kings to govern him? Let history answer this question.

Let us, then, with courage and confidence pursue our own Federal and Republican principles, our attachment to union and representative government. Kindly separated by nature and a wide ocean from the exterminating havoc of one quarter of the globe; too high-minded to endure the degradations of the others; possessing a chosen country, with room enough for our descendants to the thousandth and thousandth generation; entertaining a due sense of our equal right to the use of our own faculties, to the acquisitions of our own industry, to honor and confidence from our fellow-citizens, resulting not from birth, but from our actions and their sense of them; enlightened by a benign religion, professed, indeed, and practiced in various forms, yet all of them inculcating honesty, truth, temperance, gratitude, and the love of man; acknowledging and adoring an overruling Providence, which by all its dispensations proves that it delights in the happiness of man here and his greater happiness hereafter — with all these blessings, what more is necessary to make us a happy and a prosperous people? Still one thing more, fellow-citizens—a wise and frugal Government, which shall restrain men from injuring one another, shall leave them otherwise free to regulate their own pursuits of industry and improvement, and shall not take from the mouth of labor the bread it has earned. This is the sum of good government, and this is necessary to close the circle of our felicities.

About to enter, fellow-citizens, on the exercise of duties which comprehend everything dear and valuable to you, it is proper you should understand what I deem the essential principles of our Government, and consequently those which ought to shape its Administration. I will compress them within the narrowest compass they will bear, stating the general principle, but not all its limitations. Equal and exact justice to all men, of whatever state or persuasion, religious or political; peace, commerce, and honest friendship with all nations, entangling alliances with none; the support of the State governments in all their rights, as the most competent administrations for our domestic concerns and the surest bulwarks against antirepublican tendencies; the preservation of the General Government in its whole constitutional vigor, as the sheet anchor of our peace at home and safety abroad; a jealous care of the right of election by the people — a mild and safe corrective of abuses which are lopped by the sword of revolution where peaceable remedies are unprovided; absolute acquiescence in the decisions of the majority, the vital principle of republics, from which is no appeal but to force, the vital principle and immediate parent of despotism; a well-disciplined militia, our best reliance in peace and for the first moments of war till regulars may relieve them; the supremacy of the civil over the military authority; economy in the public expense, that labor may be lightly burthened; the honest payment of our debts and sacred preservation of the public faith; encouragement of agriculture, and of commerce as its handmaid; the diffusion of information and arraignment of all abuses at the bar of the public reason; freedom of religion; freedom of the press, and freedom of person under the protection of the habeas corpus, and trial by juries impartially selected. These principles form the bright constellation which has gone before us and guided our steps through an age of revolution and reformation. The wisdom of our sages and blood of our heroes have been devoted to their attainment. They should be the creed of our political faith, the text of civic instruction, the touchstone by which to try the services of those we trust; and should we wander from them in moments of error or of alarm, let us hasten to retrace our steps and to regain the road which alone leads to peace, liberty, and safety.

I repair, then, fellow-citizens, to the post you have assigned me. With experience enough in subordinate offices to have seen the difficulties of this the greatest of all, I have learnt to expect that it will rarely fall to the lot of imperfect man to retire from this station with the reputation and the favor which bring him into it. Without pretensions to that high confidence you reposed in our first and greatest revolutionary character, whose pre-eminent services had entitled him to the first place in his country's love and destined for him the fairest page in the volume of faithful history, I ask so much confidence only as may give firmness and effect to the legal administration of your affairs. I shall often go wrong through defect of judgment. When right, I shall often be thought wrong by those whose positions will not command a view of the whole ground. I ask your indulgence for my own errors, which will never be intentional, and your support against the errors of others, who may condemn what they would not if seen in all its parts. The approbation implied by your suffrage is a great consolation to me for the past, and my future solicitude will be to retain the good opinion of those who have bestowed it in advance, to conciliate that of others by doing them all the good in my power, and to be instrumental to the happiness and freedom of all.

Relying, then, on the patronage of your good will, I advance with obedience to the work, ready to retire from it whenever you become sensible how much better choice it is in your power to make. And may that Infinite Power which rules the destinies of the universe lead our councils to what is best, and give them a favorable issue for your peace and prosperity.

GLOSSARY

benign: kindly

bulwark: line of defense

felicities: good feelings

habeas corpus: due process of the law

presentiments: premonitions

temperance: self-restraint

March 4, 1801, Draft of First Inaugural. (The Thomas Jefferson Papers at the Library of Congress)

Document Analysis

Thomas Jefferson's first inaugural address was, in style and substance, designed to give Jefferson a sense of connection with all Americans. The Capitol Building and White House were not yet completed, but Jefferson still chose to give his address in a simple setting without ornate trappings. His language would be equally humble, as his task was to reach out to the deep political divisions that had formed during the election. The speech was to serve as an olive branch to these opposing factions and as a call for all Americans to join together to set the republic on a forward path.

Jefferson begins his speech by showing his appreciation to the people who had called upon him to take the office of president. He acknowledges that the tasks he has been given are daunting, particularly given that he entered office with under a cloud of doubt, as citizens had "awful presentiments" about his effectiveness as president. Although humble about his position, he expresses his awe and feelings of inspiration with regard to the country's direction. The nation, he says, is growing across wide expanses, and its commercial interests are expanding along with it.

Although America's economic and political influence was expanding beyond its borders, the young nation's growing cosmopolitanism also presented risk. Indeed, Jefferson contends that many of the other nations with which the United States would have contact were hungry for power and consequently willing to disregard that which is right. Nevertheless, he adds, when he compares the ideals of those nations with those of the newly formed United States, he appreciates the hope, honor, and "happiness" the latter nation demonstrated even in pursuit of the same interests as the former. These "transcendent objects" elate Jefferson, who says he is further humbled by such outstanding characteristics.

However challenging he sees his new position to be, however, Jefferson is buoyed by the presence of so many wise, zealous, and virtuous people holding constitutional offices. He addresses them during his presentation, saying that, when the enormous challenges of the presidency come to bear, he can call upon these constitutional officers to assist him. He also addresses the members of the legislature, stating that they too have an important role to play in steering the new nation through the difficult issues it would face in the "troubled world." In this regard, he is stating a desire to work in partnership, rather than in competition, with members of the judiciary, legislative, and executive branches.

Jefferson next moves into a reflection on the events of the 1800 election. According to Jefferson, the campaign was supposed to be a "contest of opinion." However, it ultimately became rife with animated and charged debates that, Jefferson says, might have seemed alien to people unfamiliar with the extents to which the notion of free speech could be carried. He notes that, with the end of the election, the voice of the nation had spoken. Under the rules of the Constitution, he affirms, the question of who would lead the nation had been answered and it was time for the United States to move forward.

Although Jefferson expects that some division will remain, he maintains that these groups could unite "in common efforts for the common good." Still, he acknowledges that in all cases, the will of the majority (which his party, the Democratic–Republicans, held) will prevail. Jefferson also states that the majority has a responsibility to ensure that the minority's voice in government would be heard and given consideration. Furthermore, the minority party was to have equal rights under the government, and the law would protect those rights in the same manner that it would protect the majority.

Jefferson asserts that violating those rights would amount to oppression.

Jefferson then states it is time to "unite with one heart and one mind" to restore America's harmony and social order. Without such harmony, even the liberty that was at the core of the nation's heritage would be of little value. Jefferson also maintains the need for tolerance in the new government. After all, he argues, Americans had long before banished from their shores the notion of religious intolerance, which had caused so much hardship throughout history. If a similar form of intolerance—political intolerance—is allowed to fester in the country, Jefferson warns, the nation will become as despotic and persecutory as the nations that advocated religious intolerance.

Jefferson notes that throughout history, humanity had fought with great zeal and bloodshed for freedom and that such violence continued to rage around the world even at the time of his speech. This violence approached America, threatening to affect and to divide Americans. Jefferson argues that the differences such conflicts generate are mere differences in opinion, not differences in principle.

Despite the gulfs between Federalists, Democratic–Republicans, and other political parties, Jefferson claims that the groups share the same principles even if they differed in opinion. Despite ideological disparities, he declares, "We are all Republicans, we are all Federalists." If any individuals looked to dissolve or dramatically change the republic, they should be allowed to speak as a testament to the tolerance on which the country was based.

Jefferson next turns his attention to those who doubt the viability of the republic and the government that was formed to oversee it. He challenges the "honest patriot" to allow what he describes as the "successful experiment" to follow its course. After all, he says, this new government keeps Americans free and without the fear of a political system that will seek more energy from the people than it should. This government, he asserts, is the world's best hope, with a system of law that is responsive to each person. Furthermore, the American government makes the security of the nation's borders a matter of interest for every citizen, ensuring that the people, regardless of their locations, are safe from foreign invasion.

Jefferson emphasizes that the republican form of government framed by the Founding Fathers is the optimal system. He reminds his listeners that there are those who believe that individuals cannot be trusted with their own governance. Then again, could they be trusted with a government managed by those whom they did not elect? In other words, Jefferson is asking if monarchies and other such authoritarian governments are more beneficial to the people than democracies. History, he says, provides a clear answer to this question. The American people were stymied by an oppressive monarchy before they opted for dramatic change. Similar events had occurred throughout Europe as well.

In light of this fact, Jefferson encourages all Americans to continue to support the federalist and republican principles that permeate the representative government. This support was critical, especially since nearly one-quarter of the world beyond the United States was in a state of war and political turmoil. He adds that Americans are indeed fortunate to live in such a nation, geographically separated from this turmoil, with "high-minded" leaders who can withstand the degrading rhetoric of those who would undo the nation's government. Furthermore, Jefferson adds, the country has such a wealth of resources and geography that it is able to support not just the present population, but its descendants as well, spanning the "thousandth generation." The people themselves, he says, are able to understand and use the rights and abilities given to them under the government for the purposes of building the society and honoring and serving one another.

Even the many religions that developed in America had, despite their different traditions, many concurrent themes that Jefferson cites as "benign": honesty, truth, temperance, and love for others. He adds that each of these religious faiths worship a god who approves of their happiness and peaceful ways (as opposed to injuring or oppressing others), which further fosters goodwill within the society.

Furthermore, Jefferson cites the "wise and frugal" government as one of the many blessings given to the United States. The government would enact laws that protect the people from the attacks of others but would not otherwise interfere in the citizens' affairs. The people were free to pursue their own interests and goals, with minimal taxation and regulation on their entrepreneurship. These qualities comprised what Jefferson called "the sum of good government."

Good government, diverse religious faiths, the people's intellectualism and respect for one another, and relative safety from the tumult in which European and other nations were mired were among the most significant of the "felicities" that were evident in the United States. Americans should, Jefferson says, be appreciative of these blessings and stand united against any force that would undo this positive way of life.

Jefferson next moves into a summary presentation of his vision of the principles of the government and his plans for administering those principles. The first of these principles is the equal and exact application of America's laws. Regardless of geographic location, religion, or political ideology, justice must be applied equally to all citizens who commit acts against their fellow Americans, Jefferson asserts.

The second principle Jefferson outlines is that the United States should seek honest and peaceful commercial and political relationships with other countries, eschewing what he calls "entangling alliances" with only a few nations. Adopting such an ideal would afford America many trade options and help the country avoid being drawn into conflicts between competing groups of nations. The Adams administration had shown favor toward Britain, both politically and commercially, and the Federalists had opposed the French Revolution; the Democratic–Republicans, Jefferson's own party, favored the rival French, in part due to France's support during the American Revolution. Jefferson's foreign policy recommendation here seeks to bridge this division between the parties.

The third principle Jefferson identifies is support for state governments. The states, in the views of Jefferson and the Democratic–Republicans, were critical institutions within the republic, representing the "surest bulwarks" against those who would tear down the country's government. The nation's entire system of government itself was the fourth principle—the framework established in the Constitution was, as Jefferson suggests, the anchor for the nation's domestic peace and safety from foreign attacks.

The fifth principle Jefferson discusses is the nation's electoral system. He believes that the nation should be zealous in its protection of the people's rights to elect their leaders. After all, elections represented what he calls a "mild and safe corrective" for people to use when their leaders abuse their power, affirming that it is only possible to engage in revolutionary activities when an election or other similar peaceable events cannot remove an oppressive leader.

Sixth, Jefferson identifies the need for the people to fall behind the political majority as it maintains leadership. Although he calls for a majority to make an effort to receive input from the minority parties (as failure to do so stood dangerously close to an act of despotism), he makes this statement to remind the defeated Federalists that the election had determined the country's leadership for Jefferson's term as president.

Next, Jefferson describes the need for the nation to have a strong network of militias. Militias—forces of civilians organized to supplement a nation's regular army—played an essential role in protecting the nation during peacetime and the earliest stages of war until the regular army could replace them in combat. Jefferson also expresses his preference that civilian leadership maintains management of the military at all times.

Turning his attention to the nation's economy and the government's role therein, Jefferson argues that the nation's businesses and labor should be "lightly burthened." This principle meant that government should be careful to maintain the public faith by demonstrating sound fiscal policies and paying the nation's debts in open, honest fashion. In keeping with Democratic–Republican values, he adds that the government should support the country's most prominent business sector—agriculture—with commerce serving as that industry's "handmaid."

Another principle of high priority to Jefferson was the education of the people; he believed that an enlightened citizenry was paramount to the success of self-government. He therefore used this speech to advocate strongly for the dissemination of information to the people so that they could be educated on issues of importance to them and their country as a whole.

Jefferson further cites several concepts introduced in the Bill of Rights—the freedoms of religion and the press, as well as the right to due process of the law and the right to a trial by an impartial jury of peers. Jefferson states that, under these principles and the many others cited above, American society is guided, like ships following the stars, out of the conflict of revolution and reformation, and into an era of enlightenment and wisdom.

Jefferson says that those who fought and died in the Revolutionary War did so to protect these principles. To honor them, Jefferson insists, these principles should be part of the American political system as well as the civic education offered to all Americans. In the event that the United States ever drifts away from these ideals (which Jefferson warns could happen in times of crisis), the people should retrace America's steps and recapture these principles in order to return to liberty, peace, and safety.

Jefferson concludes his address by reiterating his experience, from the days of the Revolution through his political rise, describing the path that led him to the presidency. He acknowledges that, although he enters office with strong public backing and appreciation for his experience and knowledge, it is likely that he will leave office (as had so many leaders before him) with that reputation in such high standing. Therefore, he asserts that he will not act with pretentiousness with regard to his position but rather with gratitude to and respect for the position and the people it serves. Thereafter, history would judge his accomplishments, and he expresses the hope that it would be fair.

He next looks to both peers and rivals together, admitting that it is likely that he will make mistakes, although those errors will not be intentional. He asks for the people's support when he errs and when his detractors seek to undermine him. Jefferson further states that he takes solace from his voters' past confidence, adding that he will continue to take comfort in their support of his presidency.

Jefferson ends his first inaugural speech by saying that he will carry with him the support of the people as he takes office. He adds that when the people decide that he is no longer the best man for the position, he will retire out of respect for their will. He concludes with an appeal for divine guidance, asking the "Infinite Power" that rules over destiny look with favor upon his government, providing its officials with the wisdom to make the right choices and to do what was best for the United States.

Essential Themes

Thomas Jefferson took the office of president after an election filled with controversy and divisiveness. To be sure, the gulf between Federalists and Democratic–Republicans had been growing for years—a fact underscored by the former's efforts to stymie the latter's criticisms via the Alien and Sedition Acts. However, during the 1800 election, the two disparate parties injected a number of personal attacks into their competitive pursuit of the majority, particularly when the House of Representatives was tasked with reconciling the tie between Jefferson and Aaron Burr. Although the United States had reached a state of relative stability after the Revolutionary War, considerable disharmony remained over how the relatively new nation would move forward in the nineteenth century.

Jefferson understood that if his presidency were to prove successful, he would need to strike a conciliatory tone with the Federalists. His speech was therefore marked by numerous calls for political unity and mutual respect between parties, especially in light of the continued development of American government and ongoing conflicts overseas. Jefferson also used the speech to call for political tolerance akin to the religious tolerance on which America was founded. Although he admitted there would be unfounded criticisms from those whose goals only involved undoing Jefferson's administration, he called upon Americans to allow constructive input and commentary from the minority Federalists.

Jefferson's speech also outlined the principles of American government and society that he held dear. These ideals included many of the points outlined in the Bill of Rights, such as the freedom of the press and the rights of accused criminals to a fair legal process and trial. Some of the principles he described focused on the positive qualities of Americans themselves, including their honesty and intellectualism. Jefferson also outlined many of what he deemed the attributes of a strong government,

including the nation's electoral system and the development of strong defense infrastructures and diplomatic institutions. Finally, he emphasized the need for government to be minimally invasive with regard to commerce and individual citizens and maintain sound fiscal policy.

Jefferson expressed both confidence and humility in his presidency, acknowledging that his term would likely be filled with great challenges. Some of these challenges would be natural for any president—ensuring the safety, security, and prosperity of the nation and its citizens. He also understood that some rivals would seek to tear down both president and republic through harsh rhetoric and unfounded accusations. Jefferson said that although he knew such challenges would test his leadership, the vote of confidence he received from the electorate would bolster and carry him through his term.

—Michael Auerbach, MA

Bibliography and Additional Reading

"Alien and Sedition Acts." *Library of Congress.* Library of Congress, 2010. Web. 6 June 2012.

"Brief Biography of Thomas Jefferson". *The Jefferson Monticello.* Thomas Jefferson Foundation, 2012. Web. 1 June 2012.

Ellis, Joseph J. *American Sphinx: The Character of Thomas Jefferson.* New York: Vintage, 1998. Print.

Ferling, John. *Adams vs. Jefferson: The Tumultuous Election of 1800.* Oxford: Oxford UP, 2005. Print.

Larson, Edward J. *A Magnificent Catastrophe: The Tumultuous Election of 1800, America's First Presidential Campaign.* New York: Simon, 2007. Print.

Sharp, James Robert. *The Deadlocked Election of 1800: Jefferson, Burr, and the Union in the Balance.* Lawrence: UP of Kansas, 2010. Print.

"Thomas Jefferson Biography." *Biography.com.* A&E Television Networks, 2012. Web. 21 Apr. 2012.

"Thomas Jefferson: The Revolution of 1800" *PBS.* Public Broadcasting Service, 2012. Web. 10 June 2012.

Bernstein, R. B. *Thomas Jefferson.* Oxford: Oxford UP, 2005. Print.

■ Andrew Jackson to Henry Lee

Date: October 7, 1825
Author: Andrew Jackson
Genre: Letter

Summary Overview

The presidential election of 1824 was significant for the contentious nature of the contest, culminating in the race being thrown into the House of Representatives. The subsequent selection and inauguration of John Quincy Adams triggered the nearly immediate nationwide organization of efforts to ensure Jackson's victory in the next presidential election. The controversial election also, as this letter from Jackson to Henry Lee illustrates, ushered in questions over political appointments and patronage and how these might influence the electoral process. Most of all, what one sees in this letter is Jackson's frustration over clearly being the choice of the people but being kept out of the White House by what he can only see as the corrupt actions of his enemies. This discussion of a "corrupt bargain" between John Quincy Adams and Henry Clay would be one of the factors that would propel Jackson to the presidency in 1828 and forever taint Henry Clay's political career, with many historians believing that it was an insurmountable obstacle in Clay's attempts to become president in the future.

Defining Moment

The presidential election of 1824 was one of the most divisive of the nineteenth century, and perhaps all of American history. The first political party system, which pitted Federalists against Republicans, had passed away with the collapse of the Federalists after the War of 1812. With no national parties, American politics became increasingly sectional, with northern, southern, and western regions of the country supporting candidates that promised to pursue policies that supported those regions. In the 1824 election, there were several candidates for the presidency: Secretary of State John Quincy Adams of Massachusetts, Secretary of the Treasury William H. Crawford of Georgia, and Congressman Henry Clay of Kentucky. Adams represented northern interests, Crawford southern, and Clay, western. When Andrew Jackson agreed to run, he was the only candidate with a truly na-

tional reputation. At the same time, many states had extended voting rights to an increasing number of citizens. Jackson won the popular vote, with 153,544 votes and had the most electoral votes, with 99, but no candidate received a majority of elector votes. In accordance with the Twelfth Amendment, the House of Representatives would select the president from the top three finishers—Jackson, Adams, and Crawford—with each state having one vote. The election in the House took place on February 9, 1825. Clay threw his support behind Adams, a critical factor in Adams's victory. Upon taking office, Adams appointed Henry Clay Secretary of State. Immediately, Clay was accused of trading his support for a cabinet position and charges of a "corrupt bargain" would overshadow Adams's term in office and would hang over Clay for the rest of his career. This letter, from Jackson to Henry Lee, was written later in 1825, after the dust from the election had settled and suspicions of Adams's and Clay's supposed corruption had become embedded in the minds of Jackson's supporters. The

Author Biography

Andrew Jackson was born March 15, 1767 in the Waxhaws region of the western Carolinas, but historians do not know for sure if he was born in North or South Carolina. Jackson served as a courier during the Revolutionary War and was captured by British forces in 1781, at the age of 14. Following the war, he became a lawyer in Tennessee, at that point part of the western frontier of the United States. He served in the House of Representatives in 1796 and then as a U.S. Senator starting in 1797 but resigned before the end of his term. He returned home, becoming a state Supreme Court judge as well as being elected to a leadership position in the Tennessee militia. It was as a military leader that Jackson first attained national prominence, first against Native American forces in the Creek War of 1813–1814 and then against British forces at the Battle of New Orleans in January, 1815, for which he was awarded the Congressional Medal of Honor. In 1818, he led troops in the First Seminole War, his actions precipitating the U.S. seizure of western Florida from Spain. In 1824, as we will see, he was not successful in his presidential campaign. He would win in 1828, however, and serve two terms as president. His presidency was not only known for incidents like the conflict over Indian Removal in the Southeastern U.S., the Bank War, and the South Carolina Nullification crisis but also the for the development of the Democratic Party, organized

to elect Jackson supporters to Congress in 1826 and, ultimately, to elect Jackson president in 1828. An additional crucial development during Jackson's term in office was the expansion of the political patronage system, in which loyal party supporters would be rewarded with political appointments by successful candidates. Jackson left the presidency in 1837 and lived the rest of his life at his plantation, the Hermitage, in Tennessee until his death at age 78, on June 8, 1845.

HISTORICAL DOCUMENT

. . . . I much regret the attack made upon you in the Nashville Republican which you have detailed in your letter before me. Altho, the editor of that paper, Mr Murray, was friendly to my election as President, and is esteemed as a private friend, still I assure you I have never been in his printing office in my life, nor on any occasion have I suggested, or attempted to regulate, the course pursued by him as public printer. In that capacity like ourselves, he is amenable to the tribunal of the public, where he ought to be adjudged upon his own merits. It is to be lamented that of late this tribunal is a mask from which too much slander and abuse are directed against the character, public and private, of almost all those who are brought before it. Such however seems to be the morals of the times, to which source I assure you, I at once attributed the aspersions to which you called my attention, and not to any change of principle inferable from the acceptance of the appointment now held by you. Since the receipt of your letter I have made some enquiry of a friend on the subject, and find that Mr Murray had received the letter referred to in his publication, and withheld it from the public until the one made its appearance in the Richmond enquirer with comments, when he gave the one he had recd a place in his paper.

I am pleased to read your sentiments with regard to the support due to the administration so far as its measures may redound to the prosperity of our common country. Mr Adams is the Constitutional President and as such I would myself be the last man in the Commonwealth to oppose him upon any other ground than that of principle. How he reached the office is an enquiry for the succeeding canvass, when the principles of the constitu-

tion, apart from his ministerial acts, or at least without necessary opposition to them, will sanction the investigation. As to his character also, it is hardly necessary for me to observe, that I had esteemed him as a virtuous, able and honest man; and when rumour was stamping the sudden union of his and the friends of Mr Clay with intrigue, barter and bargain I did not, nay, I could not believe that Mr Adams participated in a management deserving such epithets. Accordingly when the election was terminated, I manifested publicly a continuation of the same high opinion of his virtue, and of course my disbelief of his having had knowledge of the pledges, which many men of high standing boldly asserted to be the price of his election. But when these strange rumours became facts, when the predicted stipulation was promptly fulfilled, and Mr Clay was Secretary of State, the inference was irresistible—I could not doubt the facts. It was well known that during the canvass Mr Clay had denounced him as an apostate, as one of the most dangerous men in the union, and the last man in it that ought to be brought into the executive chair. This denunciation was made publicly as I was informed by Govr Duval, and taken into view with the publication relative to the treaty of Ghent, when the nomination was made to the Senate. I do not think the human mind can resist the conviction that the whole prediction was true, and that Mr Adams by the redemption of the pledge stood at once before the American people as a participant in the disgraceful traffic of Congressional votes for executive office. From that moment I withdrew all intercourse with him, not however to oppose his administration when I think it useful to the country—here feeble as my aid may be it will always be freely given. But I withdrew in accordance with another principle not at all in conflict with such a course. It is that which regulating the morals of society, to superior office would invite virtue unrespected, and in the private relations of life forbids an association with those whom we believe corrupt or capable of cherishing vice when it ministers to selfish aggrandizement.

Still Sir, I am too charitable to believe that the acceptance of an Office under Mr Adams is either evidence of a. change of principle, or of corruption, and I entertain the same opinion of you now, and of your adherence to political honesty that I ever did. Every freeman has a right to his opinion of both men and things, and it is his bounden duty to exercise it fearlessly and candidly. This liberty of opinion is the best boon of freemen, and he that makes it the agent of the greatest good establishes the most unquestionable claims upon the gratitude and love of his country.

GLOSSARY

aspersions: negative remarks about one's character

intrigue: secret plans, conspiracies

redound: to reflect

stipulation: a requirement that needs to be fulfilled

traffic: trade or exchange

tribunal: a court or trial

Document Analysis

Jackson begins his letter to Lee by expressing dismay that the Nashville *Republican* newspaper portrayed him as disloyal to Jackson's cause or candidacy due to Lee's acceptance of a Post Office position from the John Quincy Adams administration. He also assures Lee that while the paper's editor (Mr. Murphy) was a Jackson supporter in the 1824 election, Jackson did not have any control or influence over the paper's operation. Jackson then argues that the editor, like everyone in a prominent position, is subject to "the tribunal of the public, where he ought to be adjudged upon his own merits." This brief phrase encompasses much of the "democratic" ideals that were rising in American politics during the 1820s, including an emphasis on the will of the people and on the importance of public figures' merits (rather than wealth, education, or social status) being the deciding factor in their rise to prominence. This tribunal, however, has problems, Jackson notes, due to the habit of the people to direct "much slander and abuse" toward these figures. It is this popular desire to undermine pubic figures that was responsible for the editorial attack on Lee, Jackson argues, rather than any evidence of lee's disloyalty to Andrew Jackson.

The second paragraph comprises the bulk of he letter as well as the clearest explication of Jackson's attitude toward the new Adams administration. This paragraph begins with Jackson praising Lee's attitude toward the Adams administration; an attitude of support "so far as its measures may redound to the prosperity of our common country." This is a carefully qualified endorsement as, of course, policies that may bring prosperity to the "common country" depend greatly on one's political viewpoint. In an era of increasing sectionalism (conflict between different regions of the United States, particularly the north and the south), there was great disagreement over which policies—if any—benefited the whole nation. In the aftermath of the contentious 1824 election, Jackson is very careful to present himself—as well as his supporters—as being scrupulously loyal to the government. In another distinctly qualified statement, Jackson affirms that John Quincy Adams "is the **Constitutional** President" [emphasis added]. It would be reasonable to interpret this phrasing as Jackson reserving to himself (in an unspoken way) the position of the American voters' choice for president. Adams was president, yes, but on a technicality rather than because of the will of the people.

As Jackson continues, however, we see clear evidence of the suspicion that he and his supporters felt about the resolution of the 1824 electoral deadlock. Jackson makes it clear that he respected Adams as "a virtuous, able, and honest man" and that he did not initially believe the rumors that Adam's and Clay's supporters had conspired against Jackson to deliver the presidency to Adams. However "when these strange rumours became facts, when the predicted stipulation was promptly fulfilled, and Mr Clay was Secretary of State, the inference was irresistible" and these "facts" compelled Jackson to acknowledge that Adams had knowledge of the corrupt bargain. Adams "stood at once before the American people as a participant in the disgraceful traffic of Congressional votes for executive office." Despite his animosity toward Adams, Jackson reiterates that he would not "oppose his administration" in instances where it was "useful to the country." On a personal basis, however, Jackson would be unable to associate with someone was "corrupt or capable of cherishing vice" as Adams appeared to be.

Jackson concludes his letter to Lee by reassuring him that merely serving in a post at the appointment of the present does not prove that he is personally corrupt and, rather generously, proclaims that every "freeman" has a right and a responsibility to express their political opinions "freely and candidly." The use of the term "freeman" is also an important reminder that the political system—and the emerging "democracy" of the time—was not open to all Americans. Slaves, women, and others were not part of that system. While the expansion of voting rights going on at the time was, in many ways, unprecedented, rights would continue to expand throughout the nineteenth and twentieth centuries.

Essential Themes

This letter from Andrew Jackson to Henry Lee encapsulates several themes that dominated public affairs in the mid-1820s and would continue to shape American politics for decades to come. One of these themes is Jackson's endorsement of the "corrupt bargain" explanation for Clay's endorsement of John Quincy Adams and Adams's subsequent appointment of Clay as Secretary of State. While the outcome of the process is unimpeachable (hence Jackson's acknowledgement of Adams as "the Constitutional President), Jackson is clear in his disdain for the corruption involved. Jackson's careful phrasing of "Constitutional President" and support for the Adams administration "so far as its measures may redound to

the prosperity of our common country" are calculated to position Jackson as doggedly supportive of the Constitution and of the integrity of the nation's institutions, even when those institutions and procedures did not work in his favor. It also allows Jackson to continue building the narrative that he was the true choice of the American voters in 1824 and, conceivably, could be again in 1828. In opposition to the image of political elites like Clay and Adams trading votes, favors, and offices, Jackson and his supporters would position themselves as being placed into power by—and, subsequently, being beholden to—the will of the people. This idea of a broad "democratic" movement rising up and forcing the American political system to conform to an enlarged notion of popular sovereignty would transform American political culture in the 1820s and 1830 and lay the groundwork for a populist flavor to American presidential politics.

The initial subject of Jackson's letter to Lee, to reassure Lee that he did not support the accusations of corruption and disloyalty published in the Nashville newspaper, illustrate a second theme that would loom large in American politics in the nineteenth century: the question of political patronage. The appointment of citizens to government posts (such as Postmasters) would, in the Jackson administration, be transformed into a tool to motivate and reward political supporters in a new model of a national political party.

—*Aaron Gulyas, MA*

Bibliography and Additional Reading

Brands, H.W. *Andrew Jackson: His Life and Times*. New York: Doubleday, 2005.

Cheathem, Mark R. *Andrew Jackson and the Rise of the Democrats: A Reference Guide*. Santa Barbara: ABC-CLIO, 2015.

Presidential Election of 1824: A Resource Guide. The Library of Congress. https://www.loc.gov/rr/program/bib/elections/election1824.html

Ratcliffe, Donald J. *The One-Party Presidential Contest: Adams, Jackson, and 1824's Five-Horse Race*. Lawrence, Kansas: University Press of Kansas, 2015.

Remini, Robert. *Henry Clay: A Statesman for the Union*. New York: WW Norton, 1991.

Wilentz, Sean, *The Rise of American Democracy: Jefferson to Lincoln*. New York: Horton, 2008.

■ "The South in Danger"

Date: September 25, 1844
Author: Democratic Association of Washington, D.C.
Genre: Speech

Summary Overview

During the 1840s, sectional animosity between northern and southern states began to increase at a feverish pitch. Much of this animosity revolved around the place of slavery in the expanding United States and the controversy over the annexation of Texas threatened to expose rifts that many thought had been healed with the Missouri compromise of the early 1820s. This document, "The South in Danger" emerged during the presidential campaign of 1844 and was an attempt to exploit those sectional fears and animosity in order to split southern members of the Whig party from their northern comrades, ensuring defeat for Whig candidate Henry Clay and victory for the Democrat, James K. Polk. The anonymous address—suspected to have been written and distributed by Robert J. Walker, a U.S. Senator from Mississippi and supporter of Texas annexation—attempts to link the Whig party in the northern states and Henry Clay to the Abolitionist movement. Opponents of slavery, by the mid-1840s, were moving away from moderate proposals to eliminate slavery gradually or relocate freed slaves to Africa and were, instead, demanding immediate emancipation for slaves and an end to the institution of slavery.

Defining Moment

In 1836, American-born residents in Texas rose up in rebellion against the government of Mexico, eventually establishing the independent Republic of Texas. Soon afterward, the Texas government expressed an interest in becoming part of the United States through a process called *annexation*. American politicians, however, were leery of upsetting the careful balance of slave-states and free-states that had been the rule since the Missouri Compromise of 1820. As slave owners streamed into Texas, the issue of annexing the region became a political nightmare. President Martin van Buren avoided the issue but his successor John Tyler (who became President when William Henry Harrison died after only a month

in office) brought the issue to the forefront, calling for annexation as a way to create supporting southern states in the hope of running on his own for the presidency in 1844. Letters between Tyler and Secretary of State John Calhoun, however, leaked to newspapers. This letter presented the Texas annexation in terms of bolstering and extending the institution of slavery in the United States. This drew outrage from many in free states and Tyler's presidential hopes evaporated.

In his place, Democrats floated the idea of running former President Martin Van Buren. Van Buren and Whig party candidate Henry Clay agree to jointly denounce the immediate annexation of Texas, claiming that it might instigate a war with Mexico (which disputed Texas's independent status). The push for annexation in southern states, however, proved too powerful and Van Buren was denied the Democratic nomination in favor of Tennessee's James K. Polk, a staunch expansionist whose platform called not only for the annexation of Texas but also the expansion of American control of the "Oregon Country" in the Pacific Northwest as a way of getting northern Democrats to support his candidacy. The campaign became a referendum on national expansion and, for northern abolitionists, a concern that national expansion carried with it a danger that the institution of slavery would expand as well. The perceived danger was so great, that Abolitionists established their own political party, the Liberty Party, running Kentucky abolitionist James G. Birney as its presidential candidate. The Whig party found itself in a situation where it had to maintain unity between its northern and southern wings. The document below expressly attempts to exploit that northern–southern divide in the party.

Author Biography

This address, from the Democratic Association of Washington, D.C., is not attributed to a particular author, although the chair and secretary of the organization are listed at the end. One edition of this talk contained an afterword by Willis Green, the chair of the National Whig committee in which he argues that the address was authored by Robert J. Walker, at the time serving as a U.S. Senator from Mississippi. His evidence for argument is that Walker was found to be carrying copies of the address, with the intention "to circulate it only in the South, and to prevent, if possible, its appearance in the North." Green asserts that Walker is promoting the address in the South, and denouncing it in the North as being a forgery. Regardless of the truth of Green's conspiracy theory, the contents of the address do match well with Walker's political views. In the Senate, Walker was a vocal supporter of the An-

nexation of Texas, first introducing a measure to bring it into the union as early as 1837. Walker also feared that the failure to absorb Texas into the United States would open the door for Great Britain to take the territory as part of its empire, spelling doom for the United States. Walker, as we see in the address, was a strong defender of slavery but he also opposed the importation of new slaves and supported gradual, eventual emancipation. For someone with Walker's views, the radicalism of the Abolitionist movement in the north threatened to undermine national stability.

While the authorship of this document is clouded in mystery, it fits well with Walker's fears and anxieties over a possible Whig victory in 1844.

HISTORICAL DOCUMENT

THE SOUTH IN DANGER
READ BEFORE YOU VOTE.
ADDRESS OF THE DEMOCRATIC ASSOCIATION OF WASHINGTON, D.C.

There never was a period when the South was in so much danger as at this moment. To procure the Abolition vote for Henry Clay, we will show that the Whig party of the North, their leading presses, legislative bodies, and statesmen, have denounced the South, they have held up slavery as a crime, they have promised a speedy union to effect its overthrow with the Abolitionists, and have joined with them in holding up the South to obloquy and reproach. The means used by this new coalition are to represent the people of the South to their sister States and to the world as disgraced and degraded by the institution of slavery, and as unworthy of Christian communion and social intercourse. Already this demoniac feeling has dissolved the Methodist church, and other American churches are threatened with a similar fate. The object is to *taboo the South*, to render us infamous, to put the mark of Cain upon our forehead, and to deprive us of character first, as the means of despoiling us of our property afterwards. Men of the South, the effort is to disgrace and degrade you and your children forever. That such a party exists in the North, is conceded. They denounce you in their presses, petitions, and speeches, as man-stealers, as robbers, as flesh-jobbers, as slave-breeders, as convict criminals, as vile and infamous, as unworthy of Chris-

tian or social communion, and, finally, as existing only by sufferance as a part of the Union. Now if, as we shall demonstrate, the party which thus denounces the South is courted by the Whig party of the North, if they are assured, as we shall show, by the Whigs of the North, that their views are identical with those of the Abolitionists, that they are only using different means to accomplish the same object, and that the abolition of slavery will be more certainly effected by the election of Clay than that of Birney, surely you cannot continue united as a party with the Whigs of the North, who thus join with your enemies to disgrace and degrade you. If the leading Whig statesmen of the North denounce you as culprits and criminals, and, immediately succeeding this denunciation, these your avowed enemies are nominated and elected as Governors, as members of Congress and of the State Legislatures, by the Whig party of the North, can you continue united with such a party; and if you do, are not your own votes joined with those of your enemies in subjecting you to disgrace and degradation? But let us to the proof; and we extract from the National Intelligencer, republished in the Liberty Legion, the following address on the subject of Texas, by twenty-one members of Congress, *all* friends of Mr. Clay, *all* of whom, since their condemnation of you, have been sustained by the united vote of the Whigs of the North:

"We hesitate not to say, that annexation, effected by any act or proceeding of the Federal Government, or any of its departments, would be identical with dissolution. It would be a violation of our national compact, its objects, designs, and the great elementary principles which entered into its formation, of a character so deep und fundamental, and would be an attempt to eternize an institution and a power of a nature so unjust in themselves, so injurious to the interests and abhorrent to the feelings of the people of the free States, as, in our opinion, not only inevitably to result in a dissolution of the Union, but fully to justify it; and we not only assert that the people of the free States 'ought not submit to it,' but we say, with confidence, they would not submit to it. We know their present temper and spirit on this subject too well to believe for a moment that they would become *particeps criminis* in any such subtle contrivance for the irremediable perpetuation of an institution which the wisest and best men who formed our Federal Constitution, as well from the slave as well as the free States, *regarded as an evil and a curse,* soon to become extinct under the operation of laws to be passed prohibiting the slave trade, and the progressive influence of the principles of the Revolution.". . . .

Of the Whig members of Congress who signed this address, (for it was scorned and denounced by the Democrats,) each one was elected by the Whig party, each of them is still a Whig, an ardent friend of Henry Clay, and each of them has been sustained since this denunciation of the South by his Whig constituents of the North, thus endorsing these libels upon us and our institutions. These Whig members of Congress denounced slavery "as an evil and curse," as an institution "unjust, injurious to the interests and *abhorrent* lo the feelings of the people of the free States;" and, finally, they declared that the attempt to sustain it by the annexation of Texas would "fully justify a dissolution of the Union." If these charges are true, they disgrace and degrade the South. Yet they were made by 21 leading Whig friends of Mr. Clay in Congress, and endorsed subsequently by their Whig constituents. Nearly all of the twenty-one members wore

sustained for re-election by their Whig constituents, or those who did not return again to Congress they elevated to higher stations. . .

In his speech of 13th July, 1814, to the great Whig Syracuse Convention of New York, and received by them with unbounded applause, Governor Seward says to that portion present who were Abolitionists: "I have always behaved and trusted that the Whigs of America would come up to the ground you have so nobly assumed; not that I supposed or believed they would all at once, or from the same impulses, reach that ground; but that the progress of events would surely bring them there, and they would assume it cheerfully. That consummation has come. All that is dear to the Whigs of the United States, in regard to policy, to principle, and to administration, is now involved with your own favorite cause, in the present issue, upon the admission of Texas into the Union. You have now this great, generous, and triumphant party on the very ground to which you have invited them, and for not assuming which prematurely you have so often denounced them;" and he adds: "The security, the duration, the extension of slavery, all depend on the annexation of Texas. How, then, can any friend of emancipation vote for (Polk) the Texas candidate, or withhold his vote from (Clay) the Whig candidate, without exhibiting the mere caprice of faction." Such are the open appeals of the Whigs of the North, through their meetings, presses, and leaders, to the Abolitionists, to vote for Mr. Clay, and overthrow slavery. . . .

The *New York Tribune* of August contains the letter of John Quincy Adams, dated July 29, 1844, in which, speaking of what he calls "the slave mongering Texas treaty," and the determination of England to abolish slavery in Texas and throughout the world, he says: "We are yet to learn with what ears the sound of the trumpet of slavery was listened to by the British Queen and her ministers. We are yet to learn whether the successor of Elizabeth on the throne of England, and her Burleighs and Walsinghams, upon hearing that their avowed purpose to promote universal emancipation and the extinction of slavery upon the earth is to be met by the man robbers of our own country with exterminating war, will, like craven cowards, turn their backs and flee, or eat their own words, or disclaim the purpose which they have avowed."
. . .

At the great Whig mass meeting at Springfield, Massachusetts. . . . Mr. Webster, the great Whig leader in the North, addressed the same meeting, and thus appealed directly to the Abolitionists in favor of Mr. Clay : "If the third party, as it is called, (*the Abolitionists!*) will but *unite with the Whigs* in defeating a measure which both alike condemn, then, indeed, the voice of Massachusetts will be heard throughout the Union." "If there he one person belonging to that third party here, of him I would ask, what he intends to do in this crisis? If there be none, let me request each one of you who may know such a man, to put the question to him when you return home. No one can deny, that to vote for Mr. Polk is to vote for the annexation of Texas; or if he should deny, it is no less true. I tell you that if Polk is elected, annexation follows inevitably!" And Mr. Webster adds: "The great fundamental everlasting objection to the annexation of Texas is, that it is a scheme for the extension of the slavery of the African race." But in a still later speech to the great Whig mass meeting at Boston Common, on the 19th September, 1844, Mr. Webster said: "There is no disguising it. It is either Polk and Texas, or neither Polk nor Texas. On the other side is Henry Clay. His opinions have been expressed on this subject of Texas." "Well, then, gentlemen, I, for one, say that, under the present circumstances of the case, I give my vote heartily for Mr. Clay; and I say I give it, among other reasons, because he is pledged against Texas. With his opinions on mere incidental points I do not now mean to hold any controversy. I hold, unquestionably, that the annexation of Texas does tend and will tend to the existence and perpetuation of African slavery and the tyranny of race over race on this continent, and therefore I will not go for it." "Henry Clay has said that he is against annexation unless it is called for by *the common consent of the country*, and that he is against Texas being made a new province, against the wishes of any *considerable number* of these States. Till then he holds himself bound to oppose annexation. Here is his pledge, and upon it I take my stand. He is a man of honor and truth, and will redeem his pledge. Yes, gentlemen, we take him at his word, and he dare not forfeit that word." . . .

The Legislatures of the Whig States of Massachusetts and Vermont pass resolutions against the annexation of Texas upon the very strongest anti-slavery and Abolition grounds, and Mr. Clay approves, endorses, adopts, and sustains them, by referring to these resolutions as a sufficient reason of itself against the annexation of Texas. The doctrine of the Whig Legislatures of the North is, that slavery is a crime and a disgrace, and that the slaveholding States are not fit associates for the free States of the North; and Mr. Clay adopts unequivocally these resolutions, by giving them as an insuperable objection to the annexation. And now how stands the case? By the last census, the North has 135 Representatives in Congress, and the South but 88, being a majority of 47 in favor of the North, which it still increases at every census.

The Senate is still equally divided, but Wisconsin and Iowa are both to be admitted as free States; and if Florida wore admitted at the same time, it would make a majority against us in the Senate. The only hope of South, then, is in the annexation of Texas, which would give the South a majority in the Senate, whilst the North maintained its preponderance in the House, and thus give effectual security to the South, and greatly tend to preserve and perpetuate the Union, which, with the growing spirit of abolition in the North, would be greatly endangered by giving to the North the unrestrained majority in both Houses of Congress. Even if Mr. Clay were not opposed to annexation, the whole Whig party of the North are, and their success would be the defeat of annexation, whatever the views of Mr. Clay might be. . . .

On the 2[d] of June, 1836, he voted against the engrossment of the bill preventing the transmission of incendiary Abolition documents through the mail: and on the 8th June, 1836, he voted against the passage of that bill, so important to the safety of the South... In his speech at Lexington. Ky., in September, 1836, printed under his own eye, in one of his friendly presses, the Lexington Intelligencer, and also printed in Niles's Register of the 17th September 1836, Mr. Clay says: "I consider slavery as a curse—a curse to the master; a wrong, a grievous wrong to the slave In the abstract it is all wrong, and no possible contingency can make it right." ... What stronger encouragement can Abolition ask than this? Men of the South, do you consider that you, as charged by Mr. Clay, are offering "a grievous wrong to the slave?" If so, write the irrevocable sentence of your own acknowledged guilt and self-degradation, by electing to the highest office in your gift the very man who has thus condemned, rebuked, and denounced you. And when you have done the deed, and the rejoicing shouts of Vermont, and Massachusetts, and the other Whig States of the North, triumphant, by your aid, over your friends, the prostrate Democracy of the North, shall proclaim to you, in the language of your President, ABOLISH SLAVERY, which you yourselves will thus have declared "A GRIEVOUS WRONG TO THE SLAVE," "AND NO POSSIBLE CONTINGENCY CAN MAKE IT RIGHT," what will be your answer, and how will you ESCAPE the sentence of your own self-condemnation? Reflect, then, Whigs of the South, our brethren and fellow-citizens, pause and consider well all the dreadful consequences, before you sink us all together into one common abyss of ruin and degradation.

JAMES TOWLES, *Chairman*.

C. P. SENGSTACK, *Secretary*.

Washington City, September 25, 1844.

GLOSSARY

craven: dishonorable, lacking courage

incendiary: designed to create or promote conflict

mark of Cain: From the Hebrew Bible, a permanent sign of wrong-doing and a warning to others

obloquy: public criticism or a verbal attack

particeps criminis: Latin, "partner in crime"; accomplice

Document Analysis

The speech begins by emphasizing that the current danger to the South is unprecedented. This danger stems from the Whig party's apparent courting of northern Abolitionists. The author argues that Whig politicians and supporters have insulted the South by presenting slavery as a crime. Further, the Whigs are, the author claims, actively working with Abolitionists to "overthrow" the institution of slavery. The work of Abolitionists and their allies in the Whig Party go beyond simply denouncing slavery. Rather, these forces are attempting to "represent the people of the South to their sister States and to the world as disgraced and degraded by the institution of slavery," meaning that they are trying to persuade voters in northern states that the people of the southern states have been fundamentally corrupted by the practice of owning slaves and, perhaps, are not truly equal to other Americans. Certainly, the author argues, this sentiment has begun to take hold, and he cites the split between northern and southern wings of the Methodist church and other churches as an example. The author speaks in some fairly extreme terms, warning of a plot to "taboo the South"—to render it completely unacceptable to decent people. This is part of a larger plot to "despoil" the people of the south of their property. The author then lays out the argument that this view of the south, held by Abolitionists, is the same as the view held by the northern wing of the Whig party and that slavery will be attacked much more successfully upon the victory of the Whig candidate, Henry Clay, than if the Abolitionists' Liberty Party candidate, James Birney, were elected. This long first paragraph ends by asking southern Whigs why they would remain supporters of a party whose northern members subject them "to disgrace and degradation" and launches into the remainder of the address, which focuses on the "proof" that the northern wing of the Whig party was allied to the abolitionist cause. Much of this evidence revolves around the Whigs' position against the rapid annexation of Texas.

The first piece of evidence cited is a statement by members of Congress ("all friends of Henry Clay"). In this statement, the opponents of annexation argue that to absorb Texas would be "identical with dissolution" of the Union because it would perpetuate the institution of slavery. Citizens of the free states "would not submit" to such an annexation, since it would make them partners in crime with the slave owners. The statement also invokes the memory of the American founders ("the wisest and best men who formed our Federal Constitution"), explaining that they viewed slavery as evil and believed it would fade away, as evidenced by the passage of laws against he slave trade. This statement was endorsed by twenty-one Whigs, the author argues, who were all either re-elected or received higher offices. Thus, both the Whig party and northern Whig voters agree with the equation of Texas annexation (and the extension of slavery) with the dissolution of the union as well as sharing the opinion of slavery as "evil."

The evidence continues with selections from speeches, letters, or other statements by William Seward, John Quincy Adams, and Daniel Webster, all of whom were northerners and prominent Whigs. At that time Seward governor of New York (and later Senator and Secretary of State under the Lincoln and Johnson administrations), Adams was a former President (and bitter enemy of Polk's mentor, Andrew Jackson) as well as a member of Congress from Massachusetts, and Webster was a Senator from Massachusetts. The thrust of Seward's speech—or, at least, the excerpt selected by the author—is that abolitionists can trust that the Whig party shares their ambitions for limiting the extension of slavery, tying that extension to the annexation of Texas. The author highlights Seward's claim that anyone who favors the emancipation (freeing) of slaves must vote for Clay. Adams's comments come from a letter to a New York newspaper in which he refers to the Texas annexation agreement as "slave mongering" and refers to British efforts ("the successor of Elizabeth" is a reference to Queen Victoria) to end slavery. The letter from Adams suggests that American efforts to expand slavery may lead to conflict with Britain. One could argue that the selection from Adams's writings on the subject were specifically chosen to present Adams as almost hoping that Britain would intervene was specifically tailored to paint the abolition movement not only as a dispute between sections of the United States but, potentially, as an opportunity for foreign meddling in the nation's political life. Walker, in non-anonymous writings, had expressed fear that if the United States did not annex Texas, Great Britain may attempt to colonize it, undermining the United States. Daniel Webster, is described addressing a Whig meeting in Massachusetts, supporting Henry Clay and urging supporters of the Abolitionist party to join forces with the Whigs, since both parties sought to prevent the annexation of Texas ("a measure which both alike condemn").

Following these excerpts from prominent Whigs, Walker turns his attention to action the Whigs had taken in various states that Clay supported, such as resolutions from the Massachusetts and Vermont state governments opposing annexation. This leads into a discussion of the balance of power in Congress at the Federal level. Walker argues that without the annexation of Texas, southern, slave-holding states would be in the minority in the Senate as well as the House of Representatives.

Walker's address closes with more evidence that Clay opposes the interests of slave-owners and supports the radicalism of the Abolitionists, using his vote against measures to ban abolitionist materials from the mail as well as speeches in which he condemned slavery in the same harsh terms as the Abolitionists and northern Whigs like Webster and Seward. In the final sentences, Walker calls upon Whig party supporters in the south to consider whether or not they can support a candidate like Henry Clay, asserting that a Clay victory may sink the region "into one common abyss of ruin and degradation."

Essential Themes

Polk won the election, receiving 170 electoral votes (with 138 needed to secure victory) but the popular vote was one of the closest of the nineteenth century, with Polk receiving 49.5%, Clay 48.1%, and Birney 2.3%. The presence of Birney, the Abolitionist, Liberty party candidate in addition to being a talking point in this address, has provided a great deal of fodder for historians and political scientists over the years. Birney received 15,812 votes in New York and 3632 votes in Michigan—mostly attributable to his very clear stance against the annexation of Texas. Despite what the address above claims, Clay was much less solid on this issue than Birney and in Michigan and—especially—New York, the support Birney received may have kept Clay from winning the presidency. The margins by which Polk won in those two states could have been overcome by Polk without Birney being on the ballot.

This address, in its attempts to drive a wedge between Whigs of the north and the south, provides an excellent illustration of the growing animosity between north and south—especially the increasing fear on the part of slavery's supporters.

—*Aaron Gulyas, MA*

Bibliography and Additional Reading

Borneman, Walter R. *Polk: The Man Who Transformed the Presidency and America.* New York: Random House, 2009.

Holt, Michael F. *The Rise and Fall of the American Whig Party: Jacksonian Politics and the Onset of Civil War.* Oxford: Oxford University Press, 1999.

Presidential Election of 1844, A Resource Guide. Library of Congress, https://www.loc.gov/rr/program/bib/elections/election1844.html.

Remini, Robert. *Henry Clay: A Statesman for the Union.* New York: WW Norton, 1991.

Silbey, Joel H. *Storm over Texas: The Annexation Controversy and the Road to Civil War.* Oxford: Oxford University Press, 2005.

■ Kansas–Nebraska Act

Date: May 30, 1854
Author: Stephen A. Douglas
Genre: Law

Summary Overview

The Kansas–Nebraska Act created two new territories in an effort to organize white settlement in the rich farmland of the central United States. Democratic Senator Stephen A. Douglas of Illinois introduced this legislation in part to advance his state's interest in a transcontinental railroad, but also as an attempt to reduce national tension over the spread of slavery. A key provision in the bill, known as popular sovereignty, allowed settlers in the Kansas and Nebraska territories to vote on whether to allow slavery or not. Yet this only inflamed the sectional crisis, as competing factions battled to take political control of the territories in what became known as Bleeding Kansas. The act is widely seen as a major step in the run-up to the U.S. Civil War.

Defining Moment

By the 1850s, expansionist politicians and settlers were eyeing the lands west of Missouri and Iowa. Parts of present-day Nebraska, Kansas, and Oklahoma made up the Indian Territory, where many American Indians had been resettled on lands they were promised would be theirs forever. Opening any of this land to non-Indian settlement would require the negotiation of new treaties. Another issue connected to the desire for expanding settlement was the possibility of building a railroad to the Pacific coast. After the negotiation of the Oregon Treaty with Great Britain in 1846 and the conclusion of the war with Mexico in 1848, U.S. territory stretched across the continent, and there was much speculation about a transcontinental railroad. One proposal for financing such a venture was for the federal government to make land grants to the railroads, including massive parcels the railroad companies could sell to settlers to recoup some of the construction costs. Such land grants, however, could not be made without reorganizing the Indian Territory.

A major question surrounding the reorganization and opening of new lands to settlement was whether slav-

ery would be allowed in the new areas. The Missouri Compromise of 1820 had prohibited slavery north of the 36°30′ line of latitude in lands obtained in the Louisiana Purchase of 1803, except in the proposed state of Missouri. The situation grew more complicated with the addition of Western lands beyond the Louisiana Purchase after the Mexican–American War, and in 1849 California requested status as a free state. The Compromise of 1850 temporarily resolved the issue by admitting California while creating the territories of New Mexico and Utah with undeclared slavery status. The notion that settlers in these territories would decide the question of slavery by vote—popular sovereignty—took hold.

Stephen A. Douglas, a Democratic senator from Illinois, firmly believed that the United States was destined to expand across the continent. He also desired to see Chicago, Illinois, become the eastern terminus of a new railroad across the West. Therefore, he proposed legislation to create the territories of Nebraska and Kansas, opening these lands to non-Indian settlement and beginning the process of forming new states. After lengthy and heated debate in Congress, the Kansas–Nebraska Act, amended to more clearly replace the Missouri Compromise with popular sovereignty, was passed and signed by President Franklin Pierce on May 30, 1854.

Author Biography

Stephen A. Douglas was born on April 23, 1813, in Brandon, Vermont. He moved to Illinois in 1834 to seek new opportunities and became an attorney. He quickly rose to prominence in the Illinois Democratic Party. He served in the state legislature before being elected to the U.S. House of Representatives in 1843 and to the U.S. Senate in 1846. A forceful politician and a champion of popular sovereignty, he was highly influential in the Compromise of 1850 and the Kansas–Nebraska Act.

In 1858, Douglas held a series of famous debates with Abraham Lincoln, then the Republican challenger for his Senate seat. Douglas was reelected but would face Lincoln again in 1860, when Douglas was one of the presidential candidates of the divided Democratic Party and Lincoln was the Republican nominee. After Lincoln was elected, Douglas undertook a speaking tour in support of preserving the Union. He died of typhoid fever in Chicago on June 3, 1861.

HISTORICAL DOCUMENT

Transcript of Kansas–Nebraska Act (1854)

An Act to Organize the Territories of Nebraska and Kansas.

Be it enacted by the Senate and House of Representatives of the United States of America in Congress assembled, That all that part of the territory of the United States included within the following limits, except such portions thereof as are hereinafter expressly exempted from the operations of this act, to wit: beginning at a point in the Missouri River where the fortieth parallel of north latitude crosses the same; then west on said parallel to the east boundary of the Territory of Utah, the summit of the Rocky Mountains; thence on said summit northwest to the forty-ninth parallel of north latitude; thence east on said parallel to the western boundary of the territory of Minnesota; thence southward on said boundary to the Missouri River; thence down the main channel of said river to the place of beginning, be, and the same is hereby, created into a temporary government by the name of the Territory Nebraska; and when admitted as a State or States, the said Territory or any portion of the same, shall be received into the Union with without slavery, as their constitution may prescribe at the time of the admission: Provided, That nothing in this act contained shall be construed to inhibit the government of the United States from dividing said Territory into two or more Territories, in such manner and at such tin as Congress shall deem convenient and proper, or from attaching a portion of said Territory to any other State or Territory of the United States: Provided further, That nothing in this act contained shall construed to impair the rights of person or property now pertaining the Indians in said Territory so long as such rights shall remain unextinguished by treaty between the United States and such Indians, or include any territory which, by treaty with any Indian tribe, is not, without the consent of said tribe, to be included within the territorial line or jurisdiction of any State or Territory; but all such territory shall excepted out of the boundaries, and constitute no part of the Territory of Nebraska, until said tribe shall signify their assent to the President of the United States to be included within the said Territory of Nebraska. or to affect the authority of the government of the United States make any regulations respecting such Indians, their lands, property, or other rights, by treaty, law, or otherwise, which it would have been competent to the government to make if this act had never passed.

SEC. 2. *And be it further enacted*, That the executive power and authority in and over said Territory of Nebraska shall be vested in a Governor who shall hold his office for four years, and until his successor shall be appointed and qualified, unless sooner removed by the President of the United States. The Governor shall reside within said Territory, and shall be commander-in-chief of the militia thereof. He may grant pardons and respites for offences against the laws of said Territory, and reprieves for offences against the laws of the United States, until the decision of the President can be made known thereon; he shall commission all officers who shall be appointed to office under the laws of the aid Territory, and shall take care that the laws be faithfully executed.

SEC. 3. *And be it further enacted*, That there shall be a Secretary of said Territory, who shall reside therein, and hold his office for five years, unless sooner removed by the President of the United States; he shall record and preserve all the laws and proceedings of the Legislative Assembly hereinafter constituted, and all the acts and proceedings of the Governor in his executive department; he shall transmit one copy of the laws and journals of the Legislative Assembly within thirty days after the end of each session, and one copy of the executive proceedings and official correspondence semi-annually, on the first days of January and July in each year to the President of the United States, and two copies of the laws to the President of the Senate and to the Speaker of the House of Representatives, to be deposited in the libraries of Congress, and in or case of the death, removal, resignation, or absence of the Governor from the Territory, the Secretary shall be, and he is hereby, authorized and required to execute and perform all the powers and duties of the Governor during such vacancy or absence, or until another Governor shall be duly appointed and qualified to fill such vacancy.

SEC 4. *And be it further enacted*, That the legislative power and authority of said Territory shall be vested in the Governor and a Legislative Assembly. The Legislative Assembly shall consist of a Council and House of Representatives. The Council shall consist of thirteen members, having the qualifications of voters, as hereinafter prescribed, whose term of service shall continue two years. The House of Representatives shall, at its first session, consist of twenty-six members, possessing the same qualifications as prescribed for members of the Council, and whose term of service shall continue one year. The number of representatives may be increased by the Legislative Assembly, from time to time, in proportion to the increase of qualified voters: *Provided*, That the whole number shall never exceed thirty-nine. An apportionment shall be made, as nearly equal as practicable, among the several counties or districts, for the election of the council and representatives, giving to each section of the Territory representation in the ratio of its qualified voters as nearly as may be. And the members of the Council and of the House of Representatives shall reside in, and be inhabitants of, the district or county, or counties for which they may be elected, respectively. Previous to the first election, the Governor shall cause a census, or enumeration of the inhabitants and qualified voters of the several counties and districts of the Territory, to be taken by such persons and in such mode as the Governor shall designate and appoint; and the persons so appointed shall receive a reasonable compensation therefor. And the first election shall be held at such time and places, and be conducted in such manner, both as to the persons who shall superintend such election and the returns thereof, as the Governor shall appoint and direct; and he shall at the same time declare the number of members of the Council and House of Representatives to which each of the counties or districts shall be entitled under this act. The persons having the highest number of legal votes in each of said council districts for members of the Council, shall be declared by the Governor to be duly elected to the Council; and the persons having the highest number of legal votes for the House of Representatives, shall be declared by the Governor to be duly elected members of said house: *Provided*, That in case two or more persons voted for shall have an equal number of votes, and in case a vacancy shall otherwise occur in either branch of the Legislative Assembly, the Governor shall order a new election; and the persons thus elected to the Legislative Assembly shall meet at such place and on such day as the Governor shall appoint; but thereafter, the time, place, and manner of holding and conducting all elections by the people, and the apportioning the representation in the several counties or districts to the Council and House of Representatives, according to the number of qualified voters, shall be prescribed by law, as well as the day of the commencement of the regular sessions of the Legislative Assembly: *Provided*, That no session in any one year shall exceed the term of forty days, except the first session, which may continue sixty days.

SEC. 5. *And be it further enacted*, That every free white male inhabitant above the age of twenty-one years who shall be an actual resident of said Territory, and shall possess the qualifications hereinafter prescribed, shall be entitled to vote at the first election, and shall be eligible to any office within the said Territory; but the qualifications of voters, and of holding office, at all subsequent elections, shall be such as shall be prescribed by the Legislative Assembly: *Provided*, That the right of suffrage and of holding office shall be exercised only by citizens of the United States and those who shall have declared on oath their intention to become such, and shall have taken an oath to support the Constitution of the United States and the provisions of this act: And provided further, That no officer, soldier, seaman, or marine, or other person in the army or navy of the United States, or attached to troops in the service of the United States, shall be allowed to vote or hold office in said Territory, by reason of being on service therein.

SEC. 6. *And be it further enacted*, That the legislative power of the Territory shall extend to all rightful subjects of legislation consistent with the Constitution of the United States and the provisions of this act; but no law shall be passed interfering with the primary disposal of the soil; no tax shall be imposed upon the property of the United States; nor shall the lands or other property of non-residents be taxed higher than the lands or other property of residents. Every bill which shall have passed the Council and House of Representatives of the said Territory shall, before it become a law, be presented to the Governor of the Territory; if he approve, he shall sign it; but if not, he shall return it with his objections to the house in which it originated, who shall enter the objections at large on their journal, and proceed to reconsider it. If, after such reconsideration two thirds of that house shall agree to pass the bill, it shall be sent, together with the objections, to the other house, by which it shall likewise be reconsidered, and if approved by two thirds of that house, it shall become a law. But in all such cases the votes of both houses shall be determined by yeas and nays, to be entered on the journal of each house respectively. If any bill shall not be returned by the Governor within three days (Sundays excepted) after it shall have been presented to him, the same shall be a law in like manner as if he had signed it, unless the Assembly, by adjournment, prevents its return, in which case it shall not be a law.

SEC. 7. *And be it further enacted*, That all township, district, and county officers, not herein otherwise provided for, shall be appointed or elected, as the case may be, in such manner as shall be provided by the Governor and Legislative Assembly of the Territory of Nebraska. The Governor shall nominate, and, by and with the advice and consent of the Legislative Council, appoint all officers not herein otherwise provided for; and in the first instance the Governor alone may appoint all said officers, who shall hold their offices until the end of the first session of the Legislative Assembly; and shall lay off the necessary districts for members of the Council and House of Representatives, and all other officers.

SEC. 8. *And be it further enacted*, That no member of the Legislative Assembly shall hold, or be appointed to, any office which shall have been created, or the salary or emoluments of which shall have been increased, while he was a member, during the term for which he was elected, and for one year after the expiration of such term; but this restriction shall not be applicable to members of the first Legislative Assembly; and no person holding a commission or appointment under the United States, except Postmasters, shall be a member of the Legislative Assembly, or hold any office under the government of said Territory.

SEC. 9. *And be it further enacted*, That the judicial power of said Territory shall be vested in a Supreme Court, District Courts, Probate Courts, and in Justices of the Peace. The Supreme Court shall consist of a chief justice and two associate justices, any two of whom shall constitute a quorum, and who shall hold a term at the seat of government of said Territory annually, and they shall hold their offices during the period of four years, and until their successor shall be appointed and qualified. The said Territory shall be divided into three judicial districts, and a district court shall be held in each of said districts by one of the justices of the Supreme Court, at such times and places as may be prescribed by of law; and the said judges shall, after their appointments, respectively, reside in the districts which shall be assigned them. The jurisdiction of the several courts herein provided for, both appellate and original, and that of the probate courts and of justices of the peace, shall be as limited by law: *Provided*, That justices of the peace shall not have jurisdiction of any matter in controversy when the title or boundaries of land may be in dispute, or where the debt or sum claimed shall exceed one hundred dollars; and the said supreme and districts courts, respectively, shall possess chancery as well as common law jurisdiction. Each District Court, or the judge thereof, shall appoint its clerk, who shall also be the register in chancery, and shall keep his office at the place where the court may, be held. Writs of error, bills of exception, and appeals, shall be allowed in all cases from the final decisions of said district courts to the Supreme Court, under such regulations as may be prescribed by law; but in no case removed to the Supreme Court shall trial by jury be allowed in said court. The Supreme Court, or the justices thereof, shall appoint its own clerk, and every clerk shall hold his office at the pleasure of the court for which he shall have been appointed. Writs of error, and appeals from the final decisions of said Supreme Court, shall be allowed, and may be taken to the Supreme Court of the United States, in the same manner and under the same regulations as from the circuit courts of the United States, where the value of the property, or the amount in controversy, to be ascertained by the oath or affirmation of either party, or other competent witness, shall exceed one thousand dollars; except only that in all cases involving title to slaves, the said writs of error, or appeals shall be allowed and decided by the said Supreme Court, without regard to the value of the matter, property, or title in controversy; and except also that a writ of error or appeal shall also be allowed to the Supreme Court of the United States, from the decision of the said Supreme Court created by this act, or of any judge thereof, or of the district courts created by this act, or of any judge thereof, upon any writ of habeas corpus, involving the question of personal freedom: *Provided*, that nothing herein contained shall be construed to apply to or affect the provisions to the "act respecting fugitives from justice, and persons escaping from the service of their masters," approved February twelfth, seventeen hundred and ninety-three, and the "act to amend and supplementary to the aforesaid act," approved September eighteen, eighteen hundred and fifty; and each of the said district courts shall have and exercise the same jurisdiction in all cases arising under the Constitution and Laws of the United States as is vested in the Circuit and District Courts of the United States; and the said Supreme and District Courts of the said Territory, and the respective judges thereof, shall and may grant writs of habeas corpus in all cases in which the same are granted by the judges of the United States in the District of Columbia; and the first six days of every term of said courts, or so much thereof as shall be necessary, shall be appropriated to the trial of causes arising under the said constitution and laws, and writs of error and appeal in all such cases shall be made to the Supreme Court of said Territory, the same as in other cases. The said clerk shall receive in all such cases the same fees which the clerks of the district courts of Utah Territory now receive for similar services.

SEC. 10. *And be it further enacted*, That the provisions of an act entitled "An act respecting fugitives from justice, and persons escaping from the service of their masters," approved February twelve, seventeen hundred and ninety-three, and the provisions of the act entitled "An act to amend, and supplementary to, the aforesaid act, approved September eighteen, eighteen hundred

and fifty, be, and the same are hereby, declared to extend to and be in full force within the limits of said Territory of Nebraska."

SEC. 11. *And be it further enacted*, That there shall be appointed an Attorney for said Territory, who shall continue in office for four years, and until his successor shall be appointed and qualified, unless sooner removed by the President, and who shall receive the same fees and salary I as the Attorney of the United States for the present Territory of Utah. There shall also be a Marshal for the Territory appointed, who shall hold his office for four years, and until his successor shall be appointed and qualified, unless sooner removed by the President, and who shall execute all processes issuing from the said courts when exercising their jurisdiction as Circuit and District Courts of the United States; he shall perform the duties, be subject to the same regulation and penalties, and be entitled to the same fees, as the Marshal of the District Court of the United States for the present Territory of Utah, and shall, in addition, be paid two hundred dollars annually as a compensation for extra services.

SEC. 12. *And be it further enacted*, That the Governor, Secretary, Chief Justice, and Associate Justices, Attorney and Marshal, shall be nominated, and, by and with the advice and consent of the Senate, appointed by the President of the United States. The Governor and a Secretary to be appointed as aforesaid, shall, before they act as such, respectively take an oath or affirmation before the District Judge or some Justice of the Peace in the limits of said Territory, duly authorized to administer oaths and affirmations by the laws now in force therein, or before the Chief Justice, or some Associate Justice of the Supreme Court of the United States, to support the Constitution of the United States, and faithfully to discharge the duties of their respective offices, which said oaths, when so taken, shall be certified by the person by whom the same shall have been taken; and such certificates shall be received and recorded by the said Secretary among the Executive proceedings; and the Chief Justice and Associate Justices, and all other civil officers in said Territory, before they act as such, shall take a like oath or affirmation before the said Governor or Secretary, or some Judge or Justice of the Peace of the Territory, who may be duly commissioned and qualified, which said oath or affirmation shall be certified and transmitted by the person taking the same to the Secretary, to be by him recorded as aforesaid; and, afterwards, the like oath or affirmation shall be taken, certified, and recorded, in such manner and form as may be prescribed by law. The Governor shall receive an annual salary of two thousand five hundred dollars. The Chief Justice and Associate Justices shall each receive an annual salary of two thousand dollars. The Secretary shall receive an annual salary of two thousand dollars. The said salaries shall be paid quarter-yearly, from the dates of the respective appointments, at the Treasury of the United States; but no such payment shall be made until said officers shall have entered upon the duties of their respective appointments. The members of the Legislative Assembly shall be entitled to receive three dollars each per day during their attendance at the sessions thereof, and three dollars each for every twenty miles' travel in going to and returning from the said sessions, estimated according to the nearest usually travelled route; and an additional allowance of three dollars shall be paid to the presiding officer of each house for each day he shall so preside. And a chief clerk, one assistant clerk, a sergeant-at-arms, and doorkeeper, may be chosen for each house; and the chief clerk shall receive four dollars per day, and the said other officers three dollars per day, during the session of the Legislative Assembly; but no other officers shall be paid by the United States: *Provided*, That there shall be but one session of the legislature annually, unless, on an extraordinary occasion, the Governor shall think proper to call the legislature together. There shall be appropriated, annually, the usual sum, to be expended by the Governor, to defray the contingent expenses of the Territory, including the salary of a clerk of the Executive Department; and there shall also be appropriated, annually, a sufficient sum, to be expended by the Secretary of the Territory, and upon an estimate to be made by the Secretary of the Treasury of the United States, to defray the expenses of the Legislative Assembly, the printing of the laws, and other incidental expenses; and the Governor and Secretary of the Territory shall, in the disbursement of all moneys intrusted to them, be governed solely by the instructions of the Secretary of the Treasury of the United States, and shall, semi-annually, account to the said Secretary for the manner in which the aforesaid moneys shall have been expended; and no expenditure shall be made by said Legislative Assembly for objects not specially authorized by the acts of Congress, making the appropriations, nor beyond the sums thus appropriated for such objects.

SEC. 13. *And be it further enacted,* That the Legislative Assembly of the Territory of Nebraska shall hold its first session at such time and place in said Territory as the Governor thereof shall appoint and direct; and at said first session, or as soon thereafter as they shall deem expedient, the Governor and Legislative Assembly shall proceed to locate and establish the seat of government for said Territory at such place as they may deem eligible; which place, however, shall thereafter be subject to be changed by the said Governor and Legislative Assembly.

SEC. 14. *And be it further enacted,* That a delegate to the House of Representatives of the United States, to serve for the term of two years, who shall be a citizen of the United States, may be elected by the voters qualified to elect members of the Legislative Assembly, who shall be entitled to the same rights and privileges as are exercised and enjoyed by the delegates from the several other Territories of the United States to the said House of Representatives, but the delegate first elected shall hold his seat only during the term of the Congress to which he shall be elected. The first election shall be held at such time and places, and be conducted in such manner, as the Governor shall appoint and direct; and at all subsequent elections the times, places, and manner of holding the elections, shall be prescribed by law. The person having the greatest number of votes shall be declared by the Governor to be duly elected; and a certificate thereof shall be given accordingly. That the Constitution, and all Laws of the United States which are not locally inapplicable, shall have the same force and effect within the said Territory of Nebraska as elsewhere within the United States, except the eighth section of the act preparatory to the admission of Missouri into the Union approved March sixth, eighteen hundred and twenty, which, being inconsistent with the principle of non-intervention by Congress with slaves in the States and Territories, as recognized by the legislation of eighteen hundred and fifty, commonly called the Compromise Measures, is hereby declared inoperative and void; it being the true intent and meaning of this act not to legislate slavery into any Territory or State, nor to exclude it therefrom, but to leave

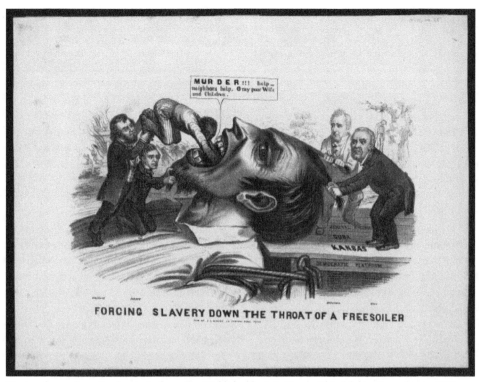

Forcing slavery down the throat of a freesoiler. (Published by J. L. Magee, Philadelphia, Pennsylvania, 1856; Library of Congress)

the people thereof perfectly free to form an regulate their domestic institutions in their own way, subject only to the Constitution of the United States: *Provided*, That nothing herein contained shall be construed to revive or put in force any law or regulation which may have existed prior to the act of sixth March, eighteen hundred and twenty, either protecting, establishing, prohibiting, or abolishing slavery.

SEC. 15. *And be it further enacted*, That there shall hereafter be appropriated, as has been customary for the Territorial governments, sufficient amount, to be expended under the direction of the said Governor of the Territory of Nebraska, not exceeding the sums heretofore appropriated for similar objects, for the erection of suitable public buildings at the seat of government, and for the purchase of a library, to be kept at the seat of government for the use of the Governor, Legislative Assembly, Judges of the Supreme Court, Secretary, Marshal, and

Attorney of said Territory, and such other persons, and under such regulations as shall be prescribed by law.

SEC. 16. *And be it further enacted*, That when the lands in the said Territory shall be surveyed under the direction of the government of the United States, preparatory to bringing the same into market, section; numbered sixteen and thirty-six in each township in said Territory shall be, and the same are hereby, reserved for the purpose of being applied to schools in said Territory, and in the States and Territories hereafter to be erected out of the same.

SEC. 17. *And be it further enacted*, That, until otherwise provided by law, the Governor of said Territory may define the Judicial Districts of said Territory, and assign the judges who may be appointed for said Territory to the several districts; and also appoint the times and places for holding courts in the several counties or subdivisions in each of said Judicial Districts by proclamation, to be issued by him; but the Legislative Assembly, at their first or any subsequent session, may organize, alter, or modify such Judicial Districts, and assign the judges, and alter the times and places of holding the courts, as to them shall seem proper and convenient.

SEC. 18. *And be it further enacted*, That all officers to be appointed by the President, by and with the advice and consent of the Senate, for the Territory of Nebraska, who, by virtue of the provisions of any law now existing, or which may be enacted during the present Congress, are required to give security for moneys that may be intrusted with them for disbursement, shall give such security, at such time and place, and in such manner, as the Secretary of the Treasury may prescribe.

SEC. 19. *And be it further enacted*, That all that part of the Territory of the United States included within the following limits, except such portions thereof as are hereinafter expressly exempted from the operations of this act, to wit, beginning at a point on the western boundary of the State of Missouri, where the thirty-seventh parallel of north latitude crosses the same; thence west on said parallel to the eastern boundary of New Mexico; thence north on said boundary to latitude thirty-eight; thence following said boundary westward to the east boundary of the Territory of Utah, on the summit of the Rocky Mountains; thence northward on said summit to the fortieth parallel of latitude, thence east on said parallel to the western boundary of the State of Missouri; thence south with the western boundary of said State to the place of beginning, be, and the same is hereby, created into a temporary government by the name of the Territory of Kansas; and when admitted as a State or States, the said Territory, or any portion of the same, shall be received into the Union with or without slavery, as their Constitution may prescribe at the time of their admission: *Provided*, That nothing in this act contained shall be construed to inhibit the government of the United States from dividing said Territory into two or more Territories, in such manner and at such times as Congress shall deem convenient and proper, or from attaching any portion of said Territory to any other State or Territory of the United States: *Provided* further, That nothing in this act contained shall be construed to impair the rights of person or property now pertaining to the Indians in said Territory, so long as such rights shall remain unextinguished by treaty between the United States and such Indians, or to include any territory which, by treaty with any Indian tribe, is not, without the consent of said tribe, to be included within the territorial limits or jurisdiction of any State or Territory; but all such territory shall be excepted out of the boundaries, and constitute no part of the Territory of Kansas, until said tribe shall signify their assent to the President of the United States to be included within the said Territory of Kansas, or to affect the authority of the government of the United States to make any regulation respecting such Indians, their lands, property, or other rights, by treaty, law, or otherwise, which it would have been competent to the government to make if this act had never passed.

SEC. 20. *And be it further enacted*, That the executive power and authority in and over said Territory of Kansas shall be vested in a Governor, who shall hold his office for four years, and until his successor shall be appointed and qualified, unless sooner removed by the President of the United States. The Governor shall reside within said Territory, and shall be commander-in-chief of the militia thereof. He may grant pardons and respites for offences against the laws of said Territory, and reprieves for offences against the laws of the United States, until the decision of the President can be made known thereon; he shall commission all officers who shall be appointed to office under the laws of the said Territory, and shall take care that the laws be faithfully executed.

SEC. 21. *And be it further enacted*, That there shall be a Secretary of said Territory, who shall reside therein, and hold his office for five years, unless sooner removed by the President of the United States; he shall record and preserve all the laws and proceedings of the Legislative Assembly hereinafter constituted, and all the acts and proceedings of the Governor in his Executive Department; he shall transmit one copy of the laws and journals of the Legislative Assembly within thirty days after the end of each session, and one copy of the executive proceedings and official correspondence semi-annually, on the first days of January and July in each year, to the President of the United States, and two copies of the laws to the President of the Senate and to the Speaker of the House of Representatives, to be deposited in the libraries of Congress; and, in case of the death, removal, resignation, or absence of the Governor from the Territory, the Secretary shall be, and he is hereby, authorized and required to execute and perform all the powers and duties of the Governor during such vacancy or absence, or until another Governor shall be duly appointed and qualified to fill such vacancy.

SEC. 22. *And be it further enacted*, That the legislative power and authority of said Territory shall be vested in the Governor and a Legislative Assembly. The Legislative Assembly shall consist of a Council and House of Representatives. The Council shall consist of thirteen members, having the qualifications of voters, as hereinafter prescribed, whose term of service shall continue two years. The House of Representatives shall, at its first session, consist of twenty-six members possessing the same qualifications as prescribed for members of the Council, and whose term of service shall continue one year. The number of representatives may be increased by the Legislative Assembly, from time to time, in proportion to the increase of qualified voters: *Provided*, That the whole number shall never exceed thirty-nine. An apportionment shall be made, as nearly equal as practicable, among the several counties or districts, for the election of the Council and Representatives, giving to each section of the Territory representation in the ratio of its qualified voters as nearly as may be. And the members of the Council and of the House of Representatives shall reside in, and be inhabitants of, the district or county, or counties, for which they may be elected, respectively. Previous to the first election, the Governor shall cause a census, or enumeration of the inhabitants and qualified voters of the several counties and districts of the Territory, to be taken by such persons and in such mode as the Governor shall designate and appoint; and the persons so appointed shall receive a reasonable compensation therefor. And the first election shall be held at such time and places, and be conducted in such manner, both as to the persons who shall superintend such election and the returns thereof, as the Governor shall appoint and direct; and he shall at the same time declare the number of members of the Council and House of Representatives to which each of the counties or districts shall be entitled under this act. The persons having the highest number of legal votes in each of said Council Districts for members of the Council, shall be declared by the Governor to be duly elected to the Council; and the persons having the highest number of legal votes for the House of Repre-

sentatives, shall be declared by the Governor to be duly elected members of said house: Provided, That in case two or more persons voted for shall have an equal number of votes, and in case a vacancy shall otherwise occur in either branch of the Legislative Assembly, the Governor shall order a new election; and the persons thus elected to the Legislative Assembly shall meet at such place and on such day as the Governor shall appoint; but thereafter, the time, place, and manner of holding and conducting all elections by the people, and the apportioning the representation in the several counties or districts to the Council and House of Representatives, according to the number of qualified voters, shall be prescribed by law, as well as the day of the commencement of the regular sessions of the Legislative Assembly: *Provided*, That no session in any one year shall exceed the term of forty days, except the first session, which may continue sixty days.

SEC. 23. *And be it further enacted*, That every free white male inhabitant above the age of twenty-one years, who shall be an actual resident of said Territory, and shall possess the qualifications hereinafter prescribed, shall be entitled to vote at the first election, and shall be eligible to any office within the said Territory; but the qualifications of voters, and of holding office, at all subsequent elections, shall be such as shall be prescribed by the Legislative Assembly: *Provided*, That the right of suffrage and of holding office shall be exercised only by citizens of the United States, and those who shall have declared, on oath, their intention to become such, and shall have taken an oath to support the Constitution of the United States and the provisions of this act: And, provided further, That no officer, soldier, seaman, or marine, or other person in the army or navy of the United States, or attached to troops in the service of the United States, shall be allowed to vote or hold office in said Territory by reason of being on service therein.

SEC. 24. *And be it further enacted*, That the legislative power of the Territory shall extend to all rightful subjects of legislation consistent with the Constitution of the United States and the provisions of this act; but no law shall be passed interfering with the primary disposal of the soil; no tax shall be imposed upon the property of the United States; nor shall the lands or other property of non-residents be taxed higher than the lands or other properly of residents. Every bill which shall have passed the Council and House of Representatives of the said Territory shall, before it become a law, be presented to the Governor of the Territory; if he approve, he shall sign it; but if not, he shall return it with his objections to the house in which it originated, who shall enter the objections at large on their journal, and proceed to reconsider it. If, after such reconsideration, two thirds of that house shall agree to pass the bill, it shall be sent, together with the objections, to the other house, by which, it shall likewise be reconsidered, and, if approved by two thirds of that house, it shall become a law. But in all such cases the votes of both houses shall be determined by yeas and nays, to be entered on the journal of each house, respectively. If any bill shall not be returned by the Governor within three days (Sundays excepted) after it shall have been presented to him, the same shall be a law in like manner as if he had signed it, unless the Assembly, by adjournment, prevent its return, in which case it shall not be a law.

SEC. 25. *And be it further enacted*, That all township, district, and; county officers, not herein otherwise provided for, shall be appointed or elected as the case may be, in such manner as shall be provided by the Governor and Legislative Assembly of the Territory of Kansas. The Governor shall nominate, and, by and with the advice and consent of the Legislative Council, appoint all officers not herein otherwise provided for; and, in the first instance, the Governor alone may appoint all said officers, who shall hold their offices until the end of the first session of the Legislative Assembly; and shall lay off the necessary districts for members of the Council and House of Representatives, and all other officers.

SEC. 26. *And be it further enacted*, That no member of the Legislative Assembly shall hold, or be appointed to, any office which shall have been created, or the salary or emoluments of which shall have been increased, while he was a member, during the term for which he was elected, and for one year after the expiration of such term; but this restriction shall not be applicable to members of the first Legislative Assembly; and no person holding a commission or appointment under the United States, except postmasters, shall be a member of the Legislative Assembly, or shall hold any office under the government of said Territory.

SEC. 27. *And be it further enacted*, That the judicial power of said Territory shall be vested in a supreme court, district courts, probate courts, and in justices of the peace. The Supreme Court shall consist of chief justice and two associate justices, any two of whom shall constitute a quorum, and who shall hold a term at the seat of government of said Territory annually; and they shall hold their offices during the period of four years, and until their successors shall be appointed and qualified. The said Territory shall be divided into three judicial districts, and a district court shall be held in each of said districts by one of the justices of the Supreme Court, at such times and places as may be prescribed by law; and the said judges shall, after their appointments, respectively, reside in the districts which shall be assigned them. The jurisdiction of the several courts herein provided for, both appellate and original, and that of the probate courts and of justices of the peace, shall be as limited by law: *Provided*, That justices of the peace shall not have jurisdiction of any matter in controversy when the title or boundaries of land may be in dispute, or where the debt or sum claimed shall exceed one hundred dollars; and the said supreme and district courts, respectively, shall possess chancery as well as common law jurisdiction. Said District Court, or the judge thereof, shall appoint its clerk, who shall also be the register in chancery, and shall keep his office at the place where the court may be held. Writs of error, bills of exception, and appeals shall be allowed in all cases from the final decisions of said district courts to the Supreme Court, under such regulations as may be prescribed by law; but in no case removed to the Supreme Court shall trial by jury be allowed in said court. The Supreme Court, or the justices thereof, shall appoint its own clerk, and every clerk shall hold his office at the pleasure of the court for which he shall have been appointed. Writs of error, and appeals from the final decisions of said supreme court, shall be allowed, and may be taken to the Supreme Court of the United States, in the same manner and under the same regulations as from the Circuit Courts of the United States, where the value of the property, or the amount in controversy, to be ascertained by the oath or affirmation of either party, or other competent witness, shall exceed one thousand dollars; except only that in all cases involving title to slaves, the said writ of error or appeals shall be allowed and decided by said supreme court, without regard to the value of the matter, property, or title in controversy; and except also that a writ of error or appeal shall also be allowed to the Supreme Court of the United States, from the decision of the said supreme court created by this act, or of any judge thereof, or of the district courts created by this act, or of any judge thereof, upon any writ of habeas corpus, involving the question of personal freedom: *Provided*, That nothing herein contained shall be construed to apply to or affect the provisions of the "act respecting fugitives from justice, and persons escaping from the service of their masters," approved February twelfth, seventeen hundred and ninety-three, and the "act to amend and supplementary to the aforesaid act," approved September eighteenth, eighteen hundred and fifty; and each of the said district courts shall have and exercise the same jurisdiction in all cases arising under the Constitution and laws of the United States as is vested in the Circuit and District Courts of the United States; and the said supreme and district courts of the said Territory, and the respective judges thereof, shall and may grant writs of habeas corpus in all cases in which the same are granted by the judges of the United States in the District of Columbia; and the first six days of every term of said courts, or so much thereof as may be necessary, shall be appropriated to the trial of causes arising under the said Constitution and laws, and writs of error and appeal in all such cases shall-be made to the Supreme Court of said Territory, the same as in other cases. The said clerk shall receive the same fees in all such cases, which the clerks of the district courts of Utah Territory now receive for similar services.

SEC. 28. *And be it further enacted*, That the provisions of the act entitled "An act respecting fugitives from justice, and persons escaping from, the service of their masters," approved February twelfth, seventeen hundred and ninety-three, and the provisions of the act entitled "An act to amend, and supplementary to, the aforesaid act," approved September eighteenth, eighteen hundred and fifty, be, and the same are hereby, declared to extend to and be in full force within the limits of the said Territory of Kansas.

SEC. 29. *And be it further enacted*, That there shall be appointed an attorney for said Territory, who shall continue in office for four years, and until his successor shall be appointed and qualified, unless sooner removed by the President, and who shall receive the same fees and salary as the Attorney of the United States for the present Territory of Utah. There shall also be a marshal for the Territory appointed, who shall hold his office for four years, and until his successor shall be appointed and qualified, unless sooner removed by the President, and who shall execute all processes issuing from the said courts where exercising their jurisdiction as Circuit and District Courts of the United States; he shall perform the duties, be subject to the same regulations and penalties, and be entitled to the same fees, as the Marshal of the District Court of the United States for the present Territory of Utah, and shall, in addition, be paid two hundred dollars annually as a compensation for extra services.

SEC. 30. *And be it further enacted*, That the Governor, Secretary, Chief Justice, and Associate Justices, Attorney, and Marshal, shall be nominated, and, by and with the advice and consent of the Senate, appointed by the President of the United States. The Governor and Secretary to be appointed as aforesaid shall, before they act as such, respectively take an oath or affirmation before the district judge or some justice of the peace in the limits of said Territory, duly authorized to administer oaths and affirmations by the laws now in force therein, or before the Chief Justice or some Associate Justice of the Supreme Court of the United States, to support the Constitution of the United States, and faithfully to discharge the duties of their respective offices, which said oaths, when so taken, shall be certified by the person by whom the same shall have been taken; and such certificates shall be received and recorded by the said secretary among the executive proceedings; and the Chief Justice and Associate Justices, and all other civil officers in said Territory, before they act as such, shall take a like oath or affirmation before the said Governor or Secretary, or some Judge or Justice of the Peace of the Territory who may be duly commissioned and qualified, which said oath or affirmation shall be certified and transmitted by the person taking the same to the Secretary, to be by him recorded as aforesaid; and, afterwards, the like oath or affirmation shall be taken, certified, and recorded, in such manner and form as may be prescribed by law. The Governor shall receive an annual salary of two thousand five hundred dollars. The Chief Justice and Associate Justices shall receive as an annual salary of two thousand dollars. The Secretary shall receive an annual salary of two thousand dollars. The said salaries shall be paid quarter-yearly, from the dates of the respective appointments, at the Treasury of the United States; but no such payment shall be made until said officers shall have entered upon the duties of their respective appointments. The members of the Legislative Assembly shall be entitled to receive three dollars each per day during their attendance at the sessions thereof, and three dollars each for every twenty miles' travel in going to and returning from the said sessions, estimated according to the nearest usually travelled route; and an additional allowance of three dollars shall be paid to the presiding officer of each house for each day he shall so preside. And a chief clerk, one assistant clerk, a sergeant at-arms, and door-keeper, may be chosen for each house; and the chief clerk shall receive four dollars per day, and the said other officers three dollars per day, during the session of the Legislative Assembly; but no to other officers shall be paid by the United States: Provided, That there shall be but one session of the Legislature annually, unless, on an extraordinary occasion, the Governor shall think proper to call the Legislature together. There shall be appropriated, annually, the usual sum, to be expended by the Governor, to defray the contingent expenses of the Territory, including the salary of a clerk of the Executive Department and there shall also be appropriated, annually, a sufficient sum, to be expended by the Secretary of the Territory, and upon an estimate to be made by the Secretary of the Treasury of the United States, to defray the expenses of the Legislative Assembly, the printing of the laws, and other incidental expenses; and the Governor and Secretary of the Territory shall, in the disbursement of all moneys intrusted to them, be governed solely by the instructions of the secretary of the Treasury of the United States, and shall, semi-annually, account to the said secretary for lit the manner in which the aforesaid moneys shall have been expended; and no expenditure shall be made by said Legislative Assembly for objects not specially authorized by the acts of Congress making the appropriations, nor beyond the sums thus appropriated for such objects.

SEC. 31. *And be it further enacted*, That the seat of government of said Territory is hereby located temporarily at Fort Leavenworth; and that such portions of the public buildings as may not be actually used and needed for military purposes, may be occupied and used, under the direction of the Governor and Legislative Assembly, for such public purposes as may be required under the provisions of this act.

SEC. 32. *And be it further enacted*, That a delegate to the House of Representatives of the United States, to serve for the term of two years, who shall be a citizen of the United States, may be elected by the voters qualified to elect members of the Legislative Assembly, who shall be entitled to the same rights and privileges as are exercised and enjoyed by the delegates from the several other Territories of the United States to the said House of Representatives, but the delegate first elected shall hold his seat only during the term of the Congress to which he shall be elected. The first election shall be held at such time and places, and be conducted in such manner, as the Governor shall appoint and direct; and at all subsequent elections, the times, places, and manner of holding the elections shall be prescribed by law. The person having the greatest number of votes shall be declared by the Governor to be duly elected, and a certificate thereof shall be given accordingly. That the Constitution, and all laws of the United States which are not locally inapplicable, shall have the same force and effect within the said Territory of Kansas as elsewhere within the United States, except the eighth section of the act preparatory to the admission of Missouri into the Union, approved March sixth, eighteen hundred and twenty, which, being inconsistent with the principle of non-intervention by Congress with slavery in the States and Territories, as recognized by the legislation of eighteen hundred and fifty, commonly called the Compromise Measures, is hereby declared inoperative and void; it being the true intent and meaning of this act not to legislate slavery into any Territory or State, nor to exclude it therefrom, but to leave the people thereof perfectly free to form and regulate their domestic institutions in their own way, subject only to the Constitution of the United States: *Provided*, That nothing herein contained shall be construed to revive or put in force any law or regulation which may have existed prior to the act of sixth of March, eighteen hundred and twenty, either protecting, establishing, prohibiting, or abolishing slavery.

SEC. 33. *And be it further enacted*; That there shall

hereafter be appropriated, as has been customary for the territorial governments, a sufficient amount, to be expended under the direction of the said Governor of the Territory of Kansas, not exceeding the sums heretofore appropriated for similar objects, for the erection of suitable public buildings at the seat of government, and for the purchase of a library, to be kept at the seat of government for the use of the Governor, Legislative Assembly, Judges of the Supreme Court, Secretary, Marshal, and Attorney of said Territory, and such other persons, and under such regulations, as shall be prescribed by law.

SEC. 34. *And be it further enacted*, That when the lands in the said Territory shall be surveyed under the direction of the government of the United States, preparatory to bringing the same into market, sections numbered sixteen and thirty-six in each township in said Territory shall be, and the same are hereby, reserved for the purpose of being applied to schools in said Territory, and in the States and Territories hereafter to be erected out of the same.

SEC. 35. *And be it further enacted*, That, until otherwise provided by law, the Governor of said Territory may define the Judicial Districts of said Territory, and assign the judges who may be appointed for said Territory to the several districts; and also appoint the times and places for holding courts in the several counties or subdivisions in each of said judicial districts by proclamation, to be issued by him; but the Legislative Assembly, at their first or any subsequent session, may organize, alter, or modify such judicial districts, and assign the judges, and alter the times and places of holding the courts as to them shall seem proper and convenient.

SEC. 36. *And be it further enacted*, That all officers to be appointed by the President, by and with the advice and consent of the Senate, for the Territory of Kansas, who, by virtue of the provisions of any law now existing, or which may be enacted during the present Congress, are required to give security for moneys that may be intrusted with them for disbursement, shall give such security, at such time and place, and in such manner as the Secretary of the Treasury may prescribe.

SEC. 37. *And be it further enacted*, That all treaties, laws, and other, engagements made by the government of the United States with the Indian tribes inhabiting the territories embraced within this act, shall be faithfully and rigidly observed, notwithstanding any thing contained in this act; and that the existing agencies and superintendencies of said Indians be continued with the same powers and duties which are now prescribed by law, except that the President of the United States may, at his discretion, change the location of the office of superintendent.

Approved, May 30, 1854.

Document Analysis

The significance of the Kansas-Nebraska Act is not easily discerned in the document itself. Like most legislation it is long and somewhat dry, technical reading. The bill is lengthy because it creates two separate territories and repeats the same terms as they apply to Nebraska and then to Kansas. Most of the provisions are the standard language Congress uses when setting up any territory—defining the borders, setting up the executive offices that will be filled by presidential appointments, and specifying the type of legislature the territory will have.

One more notable section of the act deals with Indian lands. Some of the region under consideration had been made into reservations for Indians moved out of the eastern parts of the United States in the 1830s and 1840s. The bill states that those lands will not be part of the new territories until the Indians have given up their rights to the land "by treaty, law, or otherwise." In effect, however, the act does indeed open the territory of various tribes to white settlers, as the government has the power to exert its will and break treaties with impunity.

The real significance of the Kansas-Nebraska Act lies in a short but controversial provision applied to both territories. The act declares that when either territory applies for statehood they "shall be received into the Union with or without slavery, as their Constitution may prescribe at the time of admission." This is the doctrine of popular sovereignty—that the residents of these territories will decide for themselves whether to ban or allow slavery. Crucially, this controversial policy essentially overturns the Missouri Compromise that had previously banned slavery in the area that would become Kansas and Nebraska. Popular sovereignty was supported by many Southerners and its inclusion was critical for the bill to gain enough support to be passed. While some Northerners also supported the policy, most strongly opposed it.

This 1856 map shows slave states (gray), free states (pink), U.S. territories (green), and Kansas in center (white). (Library of Congress Geography and Map Division)

Essential Themes

The Kansas-Nebraska Act further inflamed the already tense national debate over the expansion of slavery and widened the growing division between the North and South. Activists and settlers from both sides poured into the new territories, especially Kansas, in an effort to build a majority for or against slavery. The struggle over Kansas resulted in a localized civil war there from about 1854 to 1859 known as Bleeding Kansas. "Free-soiler" immigrants from Northern states battled pro-slavery "Border Ruffians" from Missouri and violence and voter fraud ran rampant. The conflict distracted from the fact that the federal government broke or forcefully renegotiated its treaties with the Native American tribes living in the region to allow for expanded settlement, forcing many tribes to new reservations in Oklahoma or less desirable parts of Kansas.

Stephen Douglas, an advocate of compromise and national unity, could not have foreseen the consequences of the act and the popular sovereignty policy he championed. His own Democratic Party was divided over the issue and suffered greatly in the subsequent elections. The Whig party also split into northern and southern factions and ultimately dissolved altogether. In the aftermath, some former Whigs, some northern Democrats, and members of the Liberty Party and the Free Soil Party came together to form the new Republican Party.

Douglas's presidential ambitions were also damaged by the controversy of the Kansas-Nebraska Act. When he ran for the Democratic presidential nomination in 1860, many northerners turned against him, and when he was nominated many of the convention delegates from the South walked out and eventually nominated another Democratic candidate. This division of the Democrats in 1860 opened the way for the election of Republican Abraham Lincoln, who had gained recognition in part by debating Douglas in the 1858 Senate campaign in their shared home state of Illinois. The election of the anti-slavery Lincoln provided the final push for several Southern states to secede from the Union as the Confederate States of America.

In January 1861, Kansas was admitted to the Union as a free state, but by then it was too late to prevent the culmination of North-South tensions with the outbreak of the U.S. Civil War in April of that year. Nebraska became a state in 1867, after the Union victory in the Civil War outlawed slavery everywhere in the United States.

—*Mark S. Joy, PhD*

Bibliography and Additional Reading

Etcheson, Nicole. *Bleeding Kansas: Contested Liberty in the Civil War Era*. Lawrence: UP of Kansas, 2004. Print.

Huston, James L. *Stephen A. Douglas and the Dilemmas of Democratic Equality*. Lanham: Rowman, 2007. Print.

Morrison, Michael A. *Slavery and the American West: The Eclipse of Manifest Destiny and the Coming of the Civil War*. Chapel Hill: U of North Carolina P, 1997. Print.

Potter, David M., and Don E. Fehrenbacher. *The Impending Crisis, 1848–1861*. New York: Harper Perennial, 2011. Print.

THE THIRD PARTY SYSTEM, 1854-96

Covering the period 1854 to 1896, the third party system—or third phase of American political history—was defined by issues of nationalism, sectionalism (leading to civil war), slavery/race, and modernization and industrialization. The great battles over abolishing slavery raged in the first decade of this period, expressed in 1860-64 in the form of the Civil War between the North and the South. The period was dominated, for the most part, by the newly established Republican Party, with Abraham Lincoln as its first standard-bearer.

The Republicans drew the bulk of their support from Northern businessmen, merchants, skilled tradespersons, property owners, commercial farmers, and various Protestant groups; in the South, Republicans also won the support of Freedmen. Democrats, on the other hand, drew their support from Southern plantation owners, conservative businessmen, Northern city "bosses," Catholic immigrants, unskilled laborers, and a variety of small farmers. During this third phase of the American party system, the Whigs dropped out of the picture, even though some of their programs such as national banks and railroad development were promoted by Republicans.

Reconstruction following the war was another major theme of this period. The Radical Republicans, an anti-slavery, anti-secessionist faction within the Republican Party, sought to punish the South for its actions before and during the war by, among other things, continuing to maintain an army there, and by ensuring that many state legislatures were Republican (or Republican friendly) and had a fair number of Freedmen on them. To many white Southerners, such measures were anathema. One of the most contentious and controversial presidential election occurred near the end of Reconstruction, that between Republican Rutherford B. Hayes of Ohio and Democrat Samuel J. Tilden of New York, in 1876. The vote was very close, and disputes arose over the tallying of votes in a few states. Thus emerged the Compromise of 1877, a political deal between the parties whereby Democrats conceded the election to Hayes in exchange for Republicans agreeing to withdraw federal troops from the South, thereby ending Reconstruction.

Although the Republicans governed at the national level for much of this third phase of U.S. political history, many of the presidential races were close, and Democrats did manage to win the 1884 and 1892 elections. During the later part of the period, growing wealth—much of it from the railroads—ushered in the Gilded Age and the era of the "robber barons." The election of 1896, between Republican William McKinley and Democrat William Jennings Bryan, marks both the end of the third party system and the beginning of the fourth. The Democrats under Bryan repudiated their own Southern "Bourbon" business faction, thereby ensuring McKinley's win and the start of a new, modern business era in the nation as a whole.

■ "House Divided" Speech

Date: June 16, 1858
Author: Abraham Lincoln
Genre: Speech

Summary Overview

Slavery dominated the political landscape of the United States in 1858. The emerging Republican Party was focused on this issue. In one of the most visible races of 1858, the Illinois Republicans nominated Abraham Lincoln as their candidate for the United States Senate. His acceptance speech, now know as the House Divided Speech, was a strong statement about how slavery put the future of the United States at risk. Although most saw this speech as too radical, hurting Lincoln's electability, it clearly stated Lincoln's beliefs. It was this speech that many in the South looked to when making their decision to secede from the Union only a few years later.

Defining Moment

Addressing the core of the Illinois Republican Party, Abraham Lincoln not only reminded them of his position on slavery but also staked out what was an extreme stance for the Republicans. The Republican Party had just come into existence a few years prior to this speech, because the Democratic Party generally supported the institution of slavery, while the Whig Party was disintegrating over it. Although these two main parties were far from identical, Northern abolitionists pushed hard for an alternative which clearly opposed slavery. The Republican Party was that institution and was feeling its way forward, being pulled in one direction by those who wanted to win elections in contested areas and in the other by those who wanted to maintain a clear, strong anti-slavery position. In this speech, given at Springfield, Lincoln placed himself in this latter camp, making a clear statement about the need to end the institution of slavery.

As a former Congressman and member of the Illinois legislature, Abraham Lincoln was aware of the feelings of the people of Illinois on the issue of slavery. He made this speech, which not only clearly separated him from his opponent, Stephen A. Douglas, but which he knew placed him outside the mainstream political thought of the people of the state. However, he had become active in the Republican Party to fight for the end of slavery, and in his campaign for the U.S. Senate he wanted to do so forcefully. Although not victorious in this campaign, Lincoln was successful in moving the people toward his point of view.

This speech, in conjunction with the debates during the campaign, made Lincoln a national figure in the Republican Party and beyond. Lincoln's senatorial campaign was one of the reasons he was selected to be the Republican nominee for president in 1860. This speech was one of the primary reasons the South seceded after Lincoln won that election. Lincoln's views, as illustrated in this speech, can be seen as a major reason that slavery finally ended in the United States during the 1860's. Lincoln lost the election, but because of this speech he eventually was able to bring about his goal, the end of slavery.

Author Biography

Abraham Lincoln was born February, 12, 1809. He was born in Kentucky to Thomas and Nancy Hanks Lincoln. His family moved to Indiana and then to Illinois. Mainly self-educated, Lincoln first worked as a manual laborer. Moving to New Salem, Illinois, Lincoln worked for a year and then became co-owner of a business. His business took him south on the Mississippi River, and during these trips he witnessed the Southern culture based on slavery. He was in the Illinois Militia during the Black Hawk War and then returned to New Salem. He continued his studies, entering the legal profession in 1836. Elected to the Illinois General Assembly, Lincoln pushed for the expansion of voting rights to all men. He rejected slavery, but did not see himself as an abolitionist because he thought their extreme position only made the pro-slavery people try harder to keep slavery. In 1842, he married Mary Todd, and they had four children, two of whom survived Lincoln.

Lincoln was a member of the Whig Party, serving eight years in the General Assembly. In 1846, he was the only Whig elected to Congress from Illinois, the rest being Democrats. He vowed to serve only one term, and during that term he worked unsuccessfully to pass several anti-slavery bills, while also criticizing the ongoing Mexican-American War as American expansionism.

With the essential demise of the Whig Party in Illinois, Lincoln dropped out of politics. However, Douglas' support of the Kansas-Nebraska Act caused Lincoln to try for a senate seat in 1854. He dropped out, supporting the eventual winner. In 1858, he accepted the nomination of the Republican Party for the U.S. Senate. Although losing the election, this speech and his performance in the debates made him a national figure. He ran for president on the Republican ticket in 1860, and won against a splintered opposition. Most leaders of the Southern states believed they would have no future in the Union, leading to those states seceding, which resulted in the Civil War. He was an active president, in terms of how the war was conducted. During the War, he took steps to end slavery on federal land and in the states which had seceded. While planning steps to unify the country in the post-war period, Lincoln was assassinated by John Wilkes Booth, a Southern sympathizer. He died on April 15, 1865.

HISTORICAL DOCUMENT

Mr. President and Gentlemen of the Convention: If we could first know where we are and whither we are tending, we could better judge what to do and how to do it. We are now far into the fifth year since a policy was initiated with the avowed object and confident promise of putting an end to slavery agitation. Under the operation of that policy, that agitation has not only not ceased but has constantly augmented. In my opinion, it will not cease until a crisis shall have been reached and passed. "A house divided against itself cannot stand." I believe this government cannot endure, permanently, half slave and half free. I do not expect the Union to be dissolved; I do not expect the house to fall; but I do expect it will cease to be divided. It will become all one thing, or all the other. Either the opponents of slavery will arrest the further spread of it and place it where the public mind shall rest in the belief that it is in the course of ultimate extinction, or its advocates will push it forward till it shall become alike lawful in all the states, old as well as new, North as well as South.

Have we no tendency to the latter condition?

Let anyone who doubts carefully contemplate that now almost complete legal combination—piece of machinery, so to speak—compounded of the Nebraska doctrine and the Dred Scott decision. Let him consider, not only what work the machinery is adapted to do, and how well adapted, but also let him study the history of its construction and trace, if he can, or rather fail, if he can, to trace the evidences of design and concert of action among its chief architects, from the beginning. The new year of 1854 found slavery excluded from more than half the states by state constitutions and from most of the national territory by congressional prohibition. Four days later commenced the struggle which ended in repealing that congressional prohibition. This opened all the national territory to slavery and was the first point gained.

But, so far, Congress *only* had acted; and an endorsement by the people, real or apparent, was indispensable to save the point already gained and give chance for more. This necessity had not been overlooked, but had been provided for, as well as might be, in the notable argument of "squatter sovereignty," other-wise called "sacred right of self-government," which latter phrase, though expressive of the only rightful basis of any government, was so perverted in this attempted use of it as to amount to just this: That if any *one* man choose to enslave *another,* no *third* man shall be allowed to object. That argument was incorporated into the Nebraska Bill itself, in the language which follows:

It being the true intent and meaning of this act not to legislate slavery into a territory or state, nor to exclude it therefrom, but to leave the people there-of perfectly free to form and regulate their domestic institutions in their own way, subject only to the Constitution of the United States.

Then opened the roar of loose declamation in favor of "squatter sovereignty" and "sacred right of self-government." "But," said opposition members, "let us amend the bill so as to expressly declare that the people of the territory may exclude slavery." "Not we," said the friends of the measure; and down they voted the amendment. While the Nebraska Bill was passing through Congress, a law case, involving the question of a Negro's freedom, by reason of his owner having voluntarily taken him first into a free state and then into a territory covered by the congressional prohibition, and held him as a slave for a long time in each, was passing through the United States Circuit Court for the district of Missouri; and both Nebraska Bill and lawsuit were brought to a decision in the same month of May 1854. The Negro's name was Dred Scott, which name now designates the decision finally made in the case. Before the then next presidential election, the law case came to, and was argued in, the Supreme Court of the United States; but the decision of it was deferred until after the election. Still, before the election, Senator Trumbull, on the floor of the Senate, requested the leading advocate of the Nebraska Bill to state his opinion whether the people of a territory can constitutionally exclude slavery from their limits; and the latter answers: "That is a question for the Supreme Court."

The election came. Mr. Buchanan was elected, and the endorsement, such as it was, secured. That was the second point gained. The endorsement, however, fell short of a clear popular majority by nearly 400,000 votes, and so, perhaps, was not overwhelmingly reliable and satisfactory. The outgoing President, in his last annual message, as impressively as possible echoed back upon the people the weight and authority of the endorsement. The Supreme Court met again, did not announce their decision, but ordered a reargument.

The presidential inauguration came, and still no decision of the Court; but the incoming President, in his inaugural address, fervently exhorted the people to abide by the forthcoming decision, whatever it might be. Then, in a few days, came the decision.

The reputed author of the Nebraska Bill finds an early occasion to make a speech at this capital endorsing the Dred Scott decision, and vehemently denouncing all opposition to it. The new President, too, seizes the early occasion of the Silliman letter to endorse and strongly construe that decision, and to express his astonishment that any different view had ever been entertained!

At length a squabble springs up between the President and the author of the Nebraska Bill, on the mere question of fact, whether the Lecompton constitution was or was not in any just sense made by the people of Kansas; and in that quarrel the latter declares that all he wants is a fair vote for the people, and that he cares not whether slavery be voted down or voted up. I do not understand his declaration, that he cares not whether slavery be voted down or voted up, to be intended by him other than as an apt definition of the policy he would impress upon the public mind—the principle for which he declares he has suffered so much and is ready to suffer to the end. And well may he cling to that principle! If he has any parental feeling, well may he cling to it. That principle is the only shred left of his original Nebraska doctrine.

Under the Dred Scott decision, "squatter sovereignty"

squatted out of existence, tumbled down like temporary scaffolding; like the mold at the foundry, served through one blast and fell back into loose sand; helped to carry an election and then was kicked to the winds. His late joint struggle with the Republicans against the Lecompton constitution involves nothing of the original Nebraska doctrine. That struggle was made on a point—the right of a people to make their own constitution—upon which he and the Republicans have never differed.

The several points of the Dred Scott decision, in connection with Senator Douglas' "care not" policy, constitute the piece of machinery in its present state of advancement. This was the third point gained. The working points of that machinery are:

First, that no Negro slave, imported as such from Africa, and no descendant of such slave can ever be a citizen of any state in the sense of that term as used in the Constitution of the United States. This point is made in order to deprive the Negro, in every possible event, of the benefit of that provision of the United States Constitution which declares that "the citizens of each state shall be entitled to all the privileges and immunities of citizens in the several states."

Second, that, "subject to the Constitution of the United States," neither Congress nor a territorial legislature can exclude slavery from any United States territory. This point is made in order that individual men may fill up the territories with slaves, without danger of losing them as property, and thus enhance the chances of permanency to the institution through all the future.

Third, that whether the holding a Negro in actual slavery in a free state makes him free, as against the holder, the United States courts will not decide, but will leave to be decided by the courts of any slave state the Negro may be forced into by the master. This point is made, not to be pressed immediately but, if acquiesced in for awhile, and apparently endorsed by the people at an election, then to sustain the logical conclusion that what Dred Scott's master might lawfully do with Dred Scott in the free state of Illinois, every other master may lawfully do with any other one, or 1,000 slaves, in Illinois or in any other free state. Auxiliary to all this, and working hand in hand with it, the Nebraska doctrine, or what is left of it, is to educate and mold public opinion, at least Northern public opinion, not to care whether slavery is voted down or voted up. This shows exactly where we now are; and partially, also, whither we are tending.

It will throw additional light on the latter to go back and run the mind over the string of historical facts already stated. Several things will now appear less dark and mysterious than they did when they were transpiring. The people were to be left "perfectly free," "subject only to the Constitution." What the Constitution had to do with it, outsiders could not then see. Plainly enough, now, it was an exactly fitted niche for the Dred Scott decision to afterward come in and declare the perfect freedom of the people to be just no freedom at all.

Why was the amendment expressly declaring the right of the people voted down? Plainly enough, now, the adoption of it would have spoiled the niche for the Dred Scott decision. Why was the Court decision held up? Why even a senator's individual opinion withheld till after the presidential election? Plainly enough, now, the speaking out then would have damaged the "perfectly free" argument upon which the election was to be carried. Why the outgoing President's felicitation on the endorsement? Why the delay of a reargument? Why the incoming President's advance exhortation in favor of the decision? These things look like the cautious patting and petting of a spirited horse preparatory to mounting him when it is dreaded that he may give the rider a fall. And why the hasty after-endorsement of the decision by the President and others?

We cannot absolutely know that all these exact adaptations are the result of preconcert. But when we see a lot of framed timbers, different portions of which we know have been gotten out at different times and places and by different workmen—Stephen, Franklin, Roger, and James, for instance—and when we see these timbers joined together and see they exactly make the frame of a house or a mill, all the tenons and mortises exactly fitting, and all the lengths and proportions of the different pieces exactly adapted to their respective places, and not a piece too many or too few, not omitting even scaffolding, or, if a single piece be lacking, we see the place in the frame exactly fitted and prepared yet to bring such piece in—in such a case, we find it impossible not to believe that Stephen and Franklin and Roger and James all understood one another from the beginning, and all worked upon a common plan or draft drawn up before the first blow was struck.

GLOSSARY

Buchanan: James Buchanan, the Fifteenth President of the United States from 1857 to 1861

indorsement: an archaic spelling of endorsement

Lecompton Constitution: a fraudulent effort by supporters of slavery to adopt a pro-slavery constitution for Kansas as the foundation for admission to the union; it was rejected by Congress

Nebraska Doctrine/Nebraska Bill: original name of the Kansas-Nebraska Act which changed the territorial law to allow the settlers to choose whether to enter the Union as a Free or Slave state

Republicans . . . mustered over thirteen hundred thousand: number of votes the Republican candidate received in the 1856 presidential election

Senator Trumbull: the other senator from Illinois

Document Analysis

The people of Illinois were generally opposed to slavery. In line with much of nineteenth century society, many did not necessarily see it as a moral evil, although a strong minority did. For most citizens of Illinois, slavery was an economic institution which gave an unfair advantage to those who were in the position to own this source of low cost labor. Just as Lincoln's family had ended up in Illinois because his father could not compete against plantations employing slave labor, this was the case for many in the state. They had no desire to allow the institution into Illinois, even if they did not find slavery morally reprehensible. Lincoln and the Republican Party were in line with mainstream thought in Illinois by opposing the spread of slavery. Politically, Lincoln was attempting to depict his opponent, Stephen A. Douglas, as the one on the fringe. While not specifically pro-slavery, Douglas had worked hard to broker compromises in Congress which might allow new states to come in as either free or slave, depending upon the views of the inhabitants. By illustrating that Douglas had worked to keep the South happy, rather than holding a hard line against slavery, Lincoln hoped the people of Illinois would not support Douglas. However, in reality, Lincoln's assertion that ultimately slavery had to be abolished placed him on the fringe and was not acceptable to a majority of Illinois voters. Many were not as optimistic as Lincoln that the abolition of slavery could be achieved without the nation being "dissolved."

Lincoln's strong opposition to the institution of slavery, including his belief that slavery was morally wrong, placed him within the mainstream of the Republican Party. From his business experience on the Mississippi River, he could relate to the fact that it not only gave economic advantages to a small group of people, but it had created two very divergent cultures within the United States. It was clear to Lincoln that if the United States were going to remain united, there had to be political and social unity on what had become a central and divisive issue throughout the first seven decades of the republic. Using a Biblical quotation, which would have been known by most of his audience, Lincoln said "A house divided against itself cannot stand." Applying this to slavery in the United States, Lincoln went on to say, "this government cannot endure, permanently half slave and half free." For Lincoln, slavery had to end as soon as possible; there was no other acceptable option.

What he feared, and what he emphasized in the speech, was that politically the unification of the nation was moving in the opposite direction; Lincoln saw the entire country becoming open to slavery. Because anti-slavery views were at the heart of the Republican Party, Lincoln claimed that they, and only they, were in the position to stop the growth of slavery.

Looking back to 1854, the year the Republican Party was formed, Lincoln outlined the drastic changes which had occurred as regarded the issue of slavery. Without explicitly mentioning Douglas in his opening argument, Lincoln used Douglas' phrases to describe the debate which had taken place on the Kansas-Nebraska Act (referred to by Lincoln as the Nebraska bill). This law allowed the people who created states in the territory which became the states of Kansas and Nebraska, to decide whether to have slavery or to exclude it. Previously, under the Missouri Compromise of 1820, slavery had been excluded from this territory. Douglas had been one of the Northern Democratic leaders who had helped guide the Kansas-Nebraska Act through the Senate. Douglas had asserted that the Act would lead to stronger ties between North and South. Although mentioning Douglas' work on this bill was a major part of the speech, it was not until almost halfway through the speech that Lincoln mentioned Douglas by name.

In using this rhetorical tactic, Lincoln was better able focus on recent events rather than the person. Once he mentioned Douglas, Lincoln then tried to show how Douglas' views in conjunction with the 1857 Dred Scott decision by the Supreme Court would make the extension of slavery almost mandatory. Lincoln's reference to "Douglas' 'care-not' policy" was intended to excite the Republican base. Douglas had used this phrase in the Kansas-Nebraska Act debate, essentially saying he did not care if the territories became free or slave states. This, Douglas asserted, should be left to the people establishing the states. Lincoln, and the Republican Party, did care about this issue, which was what had caused the party to be formed. Toward the end of this speech, Lincoln rejected the idea which some in Illinois advanced, that Douglas, as both a Democrat (the strongest party in the South) and an experienced legislative leader, would be the best person to work to limit future proposed legislation which might assist slave owners. Lincoln rejected this, since, according to Lincoln, Douglas had spent a great deal of effort to show that it was "a sacred right of white men to take negro slaves into the new territories." Having done this, Lincoln rejected any assumption that Douglas would take a strong stand against the Southern Democrats in the future.

Just as Lincoln focused his speech on one issue, slavery, and ignored all the other social and economic issues facing Illinois and the United States, he went beyond what Douglas himself had specifically done on this issue. Much of the speech focused on the Dred Scott decision, including references to the timing of the court's decision, as well as semi-veiled references to the Democratic Party's behind-the-scenes efforts their desired decision. At various times in the history of the United States there have been landmark Supreme Court decisions which have galvanized both supporters and opponents of the ruling. The Dred Scott case fell into this category. At issue was whether a slave taken into a Free State, or a federally mandated slave-free territory, could gain his freedom. Among the points of the majority opinion, the court ruled that Africans who were brought into the United States as slaves, or if their ancestors had been brought in as slaves, could not be U.S. citizens, and as such, they were always slaves, even in territories which had been designated as free by Congress. In addition, federal laws designating territories as free were unconstitutional and judicial jurisdiction regarding slaves who had traveled through free states was given to the home state of the slave owner.

As with the Kansas-Nebraska Act, Chief Justice Taney, writing the majority opinion, believed that this ruling would ease tensions on the issue of slavery within the country. The effect was actually the opposite. Lincoln seized upon this discontent to challenge the ruling and its implications. Lincoln charged that the Supreme Court's decision had been held up until after the 1856 presidential election in order to assist the Democratic candidate, James Buchanan. In fact, while a candidate and president- elect, Buchanan had contacted members of the Supreme Court regarding the timing of the decision. While Lincoln was not able to give specifics on this, he did raise the timing issue directly in the speech. The timing of the ruling was important, because it was a close election with three parties fielding candidates who won electoral votes. Buchanan, as a Democrat, easily carried all the Southern states and secured victory by winning his home state of Pennsylvania and, with the strong support of Douglas, Illinois. Buchanan also carried Indiana, New Jersey, and California among the free states. Fremont, the Republican candidate, won the other Northern states, with Fillmore winning Maryland. If the ruling had come prior to the election, it is possible that more support for Freemont might have developed or that the Republicans might have won more seats in Congress.

Hinted at in the speech by Lincoln's references to Democratic leaders ideas fitting so well with the Court's ruling, was the fact that some Democrats, including President-elect Buchanan had contacted a member of the court from a Northern state, pushing him to join with the majority of Southern justices in order that the ruling not be seen as based on the regional affiliation of the justices. Although the Supreme Court had been vague in dealing with the issue of slaves in free states, in Lincoln's opinion the result of the Dred Scott case was that the process had been started whereby "the Supreme Court has made Illinois a slave State." All that was needed was to have the "little niche" bringing this about by "another Supreme Court decision, declaring that the Constitution of the United States does not permit a state to exclude slavery." Lincoln aggressively raised this issue because it was one which was important to most of the people in Illinois. Douglas' popular references to self-determination and self-government would be contradicted if Illinois had to allow slavery within its borders. Even though it had not yet happened, Lincoln emphasized this possibility in order to try to broaden the basis of his support.

Lincoln closed his speech by extending an olive branch to Douglas. Lincoln stated that he hoped that in the future he and Douglas could "come together on principle so that our great cause may have assistance from his great ability." However, Lincoln stated, "he is not now with us." Whether he eventually would join the anti-slavery movement or not, Lincoln told his fellow Republicans, "If we stand firm, we shall not fail." His closing words were, "sooner or later the victory is sure to come." Lincoln hammered hard on the issue of slavery and the role which Douglas had played in allowing it to spread. Lincoln pushed the idea that the Democrats were responsible for recent decisions which called into question the ability of people to keep slavery out of their territories, and maybe even their states. Lincoln did not hesitate to clearly speak his beliefs in a manner which all could appreciate. While, in part because of this speech, he was unable to unseat the incumbent senator, his views gave direction to the Republican Party and ultimately led to his election as president two years later. For this reason, if for no other, Lincoln's House Divided Speech was an important point in American political history.

Essential Themes

Abraham Lincoln presented a very liberal view of what American society could become through juxtaposing his dream with the events of the 1850s. During the four years prior to this speech, Lincoln believed that the pro-slavery movement had made major gains through the Kansas-Nebraska Act and the Dred Scott decision. However, this made Lincoln more determined to end the American institution of slavery in order that his vision of a truly united United States of America might come into existence. At the end of his speech, Lincoln stated that "wise councils may accelerate or mistakes delay it," but he was certain that slavery would end. This certainty regarding change is a part of his legacy. In this speech, he made it clear that, win or lose, he was one of the individuals who would push to bring about this change. What type of political evolution might have led to the peaceful end of slavery in the United States is unknown; since just over two years after Lincoln made this speech, he was elected president, the South seceded, and the Civil War ensued. His views on slavery and his later political success not only led to the Civil War, but they started the United States on the path toward full equality for all persons. This speech was a sign pointing in that direction. Clearly, vocalizing

the problems confronting the United States was only a small step forward, but it was an important one. Lincoln's rejection of the idea that people were superior or inferior, based on the color of their skin, was an important statement for a political leader to make.

Lincoln was correct that slavery was morally wrong. He was correct that a nation must be united on issues of central importance, or face a diminished ability to be united on other fronts. This speech was not only a record of the initial beliefs of the Republican Party; it was a call to see the common humanity of all people. It was an attempt to help everyone see this in such a way that it drew the country together. Although unsuccessful in his bid for the U.S. Senate, Lincoln's questioning of the status quo pushed the debate on slavery to a new level.

—Donald A. Watt, PhD

Bibliography and Additional Reading

Abraham Lincoln Online. *House Divided Speech*. Abraham Lincoln Online, 2013. Web. 6 Oct. 2013.

C-SPAN. *American Presidents: Life Portraits: Abraham Lincoln*. Washington: National Cable Satellite Corporation, 2012. Web. 6 Oct 2013.

Foner, Eric. *The Fiery Trial: Abraham Lincoln and American Slavery*. New York: Norton, 2010. Print.

Jaffa, Harry V. *A New Birth of Freedom: Abraham Lincoln and the Coming of the Civil War*. Lanham: Rowman & Littlefield, 2000. Print.

Miller Center of Public Affairs. *American President: Abraham Lincoln (1809-1865)*. Charlottesville: U of Virginia, 2012. Web. 15 Oct 2012.

National Park Service. *House Divided Speech*. Springfield: Lincoln National Historic Site, 2013. Web. 30 Sept. 2013.

Sandburg, Carl. *Abraham Lincoln: The Prairie Years and the War Years*. New York: Harcourt Brace, 1954. Print.

White, Ronald C. *Abraham Lincoln: A Biography*. New York: Random House, 2009. Print.

Winkle, Kenneth J. *The Young Eagle: The Rise of Abraham Lincoln*. Dallas: Taylor, 2001. Print.

Rival presidential nominees Lincoln and Douglas are matched in a footrace, in which Lincoln's long stride is a clear advantage. (Library of Congress)

■ The Lincoln-Douglas Debates

Date: August 27 and October 7, 1858
Authors: Stephen A. Douglas; Abraham Lincoln
Genre: Speech

Summary Overview

Stephen A. Douglas was a national figure and leader in the Senate, having helped pass compromises on slavery. Abraham Lincoln was well known within Illinois as an anti-slavery advocate. As they were running for the Senate, these speeches communicated what was at the heart of each man's position about the key issue of slavery. While touching on a few other subjects, slavery was the issue of the day. The texts of the speeches were published nationwide and helped to galvanize public opinion on both sides of the slavery issue. The positions each man took not only determined the outcome of the Senatorial election, but of the presidential election of 1860.

Defining Moment

From the time the Constitutional Convention met in Philadelphia, slavery had been a major factor in American politics. During the 1850's, divisions over the issue of slavery had reached critical proportions. Prior to the senatorial contest of 1858, Abraham Lincoln, the Republican candidate, had made clear his strong anti-slavery stance. Although Stephen Douglas, the Democrat, held a moderate position on slavery, he sought to keep the United States united, by such efforts as pushing the Senate to pass the Compromise of 1850 and the Kansas-Nebraska Act in 1854. The Dred Scott case in 1857, forced the issue of slavery into an even brighter spotlight, and everyone knew that the national government would be called upon to once again deal with this issue. Thus, Lincoln and Douglas focused on this issue rather than what might be considered issues of importance only to the people of Illinois.

In 1858, senators were selected by the state legislatures, not by popular vote. In November, 1858, elections would be held statewide to choose members of the state legislature. The U.S. Senate election would be held the following January, by those elected in November. Thus, while the two men were appealing to the general public for support of their ambitions, Lincoln and Douglas did this by seeking support for their parties in the elections for the state legislature. With the Democratic Party winning in the south, and the Republican Party in the north, the result was that there were fifty-four Democrats and forty-six Republics in the Illinois General Assembly and State Senate. The January vote for senator was strictly along party lines. However, both Lincoln and Douglas gained such national support from these debates that their respective parties looked to them as presidential candidates in 1860.

Author Biographies

Stephen A. Douglas was born on April 23, 1813 in Brandon, Vermont. In 1833, he moved to Illinois, where he taught school for a year. Going into politics, by age twenty-seven, he had already been a State's Attorney, representative in the State House, the Illinois Secretary of State, and a judge on the state Supreme Court. In 1843 he became a member of the United States House of Representatives. In 1846 Douglas was elected to the U.S. Senate for the first of his three terms.

As a Representative, he supported the Mexican-American War. As a Senator, he worked hard to preserve the Union by compromise on the issue of slavery and by developing stronger inter-regional economic ties. Douglas supported several key legislative items which reflected this. Thus, on slavery, he worked hard to pass the Compromise of 1850 and the Kansas-Nebraska Act, and worked to expand the railroads. After two previous tries, in 1860, he was finally nominated to be president, but the Democratic Party was badly split. After Lincoln was elected, Douglas worked with him to try to stop the Southern secession, until Douglas died in Chicago on June 3, 1861.

Abraham Lincoln was born on February 12, 1809 in Kentucky. In 1816, his family moved to Indiana, and in 1830 they moved to Illinois. He co-owned a small business and was unsuccessful in his first few attempts to win elected office. While teaching himself law, he won his first of four terms as a representative in the Illinois House. In 1846, he was the only Whig elected from Illinois to the U.S. House of Representatives, with the pledge to serve only one term. He was opposed to the Mexican-American War and tried, but failed, to end slavery in the District of Columbia.

Lincoln stayed out of politics until Douglas' support of the Kansas-Nebraska Act drew him back. As the Whig Party disintegrated, Lincoln helped found the Republican Party. In this 1858 campaign, Lincoln gave the famous "House Divided" speech when accepting the nomination. Although losing to Douglas, he gained enough fame to be nominated by the Republicans for president in 1860, easily winning the four-way race. His victory caused the Southern states to secede, resulting in the Civil War. During the war he freed the slaves in the Southern states and gave strong leadership to the war effort. As the war drew to a close, he was assassinated, dying on April 15, 1865.

HISTORICAL DOCUMENT

August 27, 1858

Second Debate: Freeport, Illinois

Mr. Douglas' Speech

[Note: Remarks in parentheses are comments from the audience.]

Ladies and Gentlemen—The silence with which you have listened to Mr. Lincoln during his hour is creditable to this vast audience, composed of men of various political parties. Nothing is more honorable to any large mass of people assembled for the purpose of a fair discussion, than that kind and respectful attention that is yielded not only to your political friends, but to those who are opposed to you in politics.

I am glad that at last I have brought Mr. Lincoln to the conclusion that he had better define his position on certain political questions to which I called his attention at Ottawa. He there showed no disposition, no inclination, to answer them. I did not present idle questions for him to answer merely for my gratification. I laid the foundation for those interrogatories by showing that they constituted the platform of the party whose nominee he is for the Senate. I did not presume that I had the right to catechise him as I saw proper, unless I showed that his party, or a majority of it, stood upon the platform and were in favor of the propositions upon which my questions were based. I desired simply to know, inasmuch as he had been nominated as the first, last, and only choice of his party, whether he concurred in the platform which that party had adopted for its government. In a few moments

I will proceed to review the answers which he has given to these interrogatories; but in order to relieve his anxiety I will first respond to these which he has presented to me. Mark you, he has not presented interrogatories which have ever received the sanction of the party with which I am acting, and hence he has no other foundation for them than his own curiosity. (Voice: "That's a fact.")

First, he desires to know if the people of Kansas shall form a Constitution by means entirely proper and unobjectionable and ask admission into the Union as a State, before they have the requisite population for a member of Congress, whether I will vote for that admission. Well, now, I regret exceedingly that he did not answer that interrogatory himself before he put it to me, in order that we might understand, and not be left to infer, on which side he is. ("Good, good.") Mr. Trumbull, during the last session of Congress, voted from the beginning to the end against the admission of Oregon, although a free State, because she had not the requisite population for a member of Congress. ("That's it.") Mr. Trumbull would not consent, under any circumstances, to let a State, free or slave, come into the Union until it had the requisite population. As Mr. Trumbull is in the field, fighting for Mr. Lincoln, I would like to have Mr. Lincoln answer his own question and tell me whether he is fighting Trumbull on that issue or not. ("Good, put it to him," and cheers.)

But I will answer his question. In reference to Kansas, it is my opinion, that as she has population enough to constitute a slave State, she has people enough for a free State. (Cheers.) I will not make Kansas an exceptional case to the other States of the Union. (Sound, and "hear,

hear.") I hold it to be a sound rule of universal application to require a Territory to contain the requisite population for a member of Congress, before it is admitted as a State into the Union. I made that proposition in the Senate in 1856, and I renewed it during the last session, in a bill providing that no Territory of the United States should form a Constitution and apply for admission until it had the requisite population. On another occasion I proposed that neither Kansas, or any other Territory, should be admitted until it had the requisite population. Congress did not adopt any of my propositions containing this general rule, but did make an exception of Kansas. I will stand by that exception. (Cheers.) Either Kansas must come in as a free State, with whatever population she may have, or the rule must be applied to all the other Territories alike. (Cheers.) I therefore answer at once, that it having been decided that Kansas has people enough for a slave State, I hold that she has enough for a free State. ("Good," and applause.) I hope Mr. Lincoln is satisfied with my answer; ("he ought to be," and cheers,) and now I would like to get his answer to his own interrogatory—whether or not he will vote to admit Kansas before she has the requisite population. ("Hit him again.") I want to know whether he will vote to admit Oregon before that Territory has the requisite population. Mr. Trumbull will not, and the same reason that commits Mr. Trumbull against the admission of Oregon, commits him against Kansas, even if she should apply for admission as a free State. ("You've got him," and cheers.) If there is any sincerity, any truth, in the argument of Mr. Trumbull in the Senate, against the admission of Oregon because she had not 93,420 people, although her population was larger than that of Kansas, he stands pledged against the admission of both Oregon and Kansas until they have 93,420 inhabitants. I would like Mr. Lincoln to answer this question.

I would like him to take his own medicine. (Laughter.) If he differs with Mr. Trumbull, let him answer his argument against the admission of Oregon, instead of poking questions at me. ("Right, good, good," laughter and cheers.)

The next question propounded to me by Mr. Lincoln is, can the people of a Territory in any lawful way, against the wishes of any citizen of the United States, exclude slavery from their limits prior to the formation of a State Constitution? I answer emphatically, as Mr. Lincoln has heard me answer a hundred times from every stump in Illinois, that in my opinion the people of a Territory can, by lawful means, exclude slavery from their limits prior to the formation of a State Constitution. Mr. Lincoln knew that I had answered that question over and over again. He heard me argue the Nebraska bill on that principle all over the State in 1854, in 1855, and in 1856, and he has no excuse for pretending to be in doubt as to my position on that question. It matters not what way the Supreme Court may hereafter decide as to the abstract question whether slavery may or may not go into a Territory under the Constitution, the people have the lawful means to introduce it or exclude it as they please, for the reason that slavery cannot exist a day or an hour anywhere, unless it is supported by local police regulations. ("Right, right.") Those police regulations can only be established by the local legislature, and if the people are opposed to slavery they will elect representatives to that body who will by unfriendly legislation effectually prevent the introduction of it into their midst. If, on the contrary, they are for it, their legislation will favor its extension. Hence, no matter what the decision of the Supreme Court may be on that abstract question, still the right of the people to make a slave Territory or a free Territory is perfect and complete under the Nebraska bill. I hope Mr. Lincoln deems my answer satisfactory on that point.

[Deacon Bross spoke.]

In this connection, I will notice the charge which he has introduced in relation to Mr. Chase's amendment. I thought that I had chased that amendment out of Mr. Lincoln's brain at Ottawa; (laughter) but it seems that still haunts his imagination, and he is not yet satisfied. I had supposed that he would be ashamed to press that question further. He is a lawyer, and has been a member of Congress, and has occupied his time and amused you by telling you about parliamentary proceedings. He ought to have known better than to try to palm off his miserable impositions upon this intelligent audience. ("Good," and cheers.) The Nebraska bill provided that the legislative power, and authority of the said Territory, should extend to all rightful subjects of legislation consistent with the organic act and the Constitution of the United States. It did not make any exception as to slavery, but gave all the power that it was possible for Congress to give, without

violating the Constitution to the Territorial Legislature, with no exception or limitation on the subject of slavery at all. The language of that bill which I have quoted, gave the full power and the full authority over the subject of slavery, affirmatively and negatively, to introduce it or exclude it, so far as the Constitution of the United States would permit. What more could Mr. Chase give by his amendment? Nothing. He offered his amendment for the identical purpose for which Mr. Lincoln is using it, to enable demagogues in the country to try and deceive the people. ("Good, hit him again," and cheers.)
[Deacon Bross spoke.]

His amendment was to this effect. It provided that the Legislature should have the power to exclude slavery: and General Cass suggested, "why not give the power to introduce as well as exclude?" The answer was, they have the power already in the bill to do both. Chase was afraid his amendment would be adopted if he put the alternative proposition and so make it fair both ways, but would not yield. He offered it for the purpose of having it rejected. He offered it, as he has himself avowed over and over again, simply to make capital out of it for the stump. He expected that it would be capital for small politicians in the country, and that they would make an effort to deceive the people with it, and he was not mistaken, for Lincoln is carrying out the plan admirably. ("Good, good.") Lincoln knows that the Nebraska bill, without Chase's amendment, gave all the power which the Constitution would permit. Could Congress confer any more? ("No, no.") Could Congress go beyond the Constitution of the country? We gave all a full grant, with no exception in regard to slavery one way or the other. We left that question as we left all others, to be decided by the people for themselves, just as they pleased. I will not occupy my time on this question. I have argued it before all over Illinois. I have argued it in this beautiful city of Freeport; I have argued it in the North, the South, the East, and the West, avowing the same sentiments and the same principles. I have not been afraid to avow my sentiments up here for fear I would be trotted down into Egypt. (Cheers and laughter.)

The third question which Mr. Lincoln presented is, if the Supreme Court of the United States shall decide that a State of this Union cannot exclude slavery from its own limits, will I submit to it? I am amazed that Lincoln should ask such a question. ["A school boy knows better."] Yes, a school-boy does know better. Mr. Lincoln's object is to cast an imputation upon the Supreme Court. He knows that there never was but one man in America, claiming any degree of intelligence or decency, who ever for a moment pretended such a thing. It is true that the *Washington Union*, in an article published on the 17th of last December, did put forth that doctrine, and I denounced the article on the floor of the Senate, in a speech which Mr. Lincoln now pretends was against the President. The Union had claimed that slavery had a right to go into the free States, and that any provision in the Constitution or laws of the free States to the contrary were null and void. I denounced it in the Senate, as I said before, and I was the first man who did. Lincoln's friends, Trumbull, and Seward, and Hale, and Wilson, land the whole Black Republican side of the Senate, were silent. They left it to me to denounce it. (Cheers.) And what was the reply made to me on that occasion? Mr. Toombs, of Georgia, got up and undertook to lecture me on the ground that I ought not to have deemed the article worthy of notice, and ought not to have replied to it; that there was not one man, woman or child south of the Potomac, in any slave State, who did not repudiate any such pretension. Mr. Lincoln knows that that reply was made on the spot, and yet now he asks this question. He might as well ask me, suppose Mr. Lincoln should steal a horse, would I sanction it; (laughter) and it would be as genteel in me to ask him, in the event he stole a horse, what ought to be done with him. He casts an imputation upon the Supreme Court of the United States, by supposing that they would violate the Constitution of the United States. I tell him that such a thing is not possible. (Cheers.) It would be an act of moral treason that no man on the bench could ever descend to. Mr. Lincoln himself would never in his partisan feelings so far forget what was right as to be guilty of such an act. ("Good, good.") The fourth question of Mr. Lincoln is, are you in favor of acquiring additional territory, in disregard as to how such acquisition may affect the Union on the slavery questions? This question is very ingeniously and cunningly put.
[Deacon Bross here spoke, sotto voce, — the reporter understanding him to say, "Now we've got him."]

The Black Republican creed lays it down expressly,

that under no circumstances shall we acquire any more territory unless slavery is first prohibited in the country. I ask Mr. Lincoln whether he is in favor of that proposition. Are you (addressing Mr. Lincoln) opposed to the acquisition of any more territory, under any circumstances, unless slavery is prohibited in it? That he does not like to answer. When I ask him whether he stands up to that article in the platform of his party, he turns, Yankee-fashion, and without answering it, asks me whether I am in favor of acquiring territory without regard to how it may affect the Union on the slavery question. ("Good.")

I answer that whenever it becomes necessary, in our growth and progress, to acquire more territory, that I am in favor of it, without reference to the question of slavery, and when we have acquired it, I will leave the people free to do as they please, either to make it slave or free territory, as they prefer.

[Here Deacon Bross spoke, the reporter believes that he said, "That's bold." It was said solemnly.]

It is idle to tell me or you that we have territory enough. Our fathers supposed that we had enough when our territory extended to the Mississippi river, but a few years' growth and expansion satisfied them that we needed more, and the Louisiana territory, from the West branch of the Mississippi to the British possessions, was acquired. Then we acquired Oregon, then California and New Mexico. We have enough now for the present, but this is a young and a growing nation. It swarms as often as a hive of bees, and as new swarms are turned out each year, there must be hives in which they can gather and make their honey. ("Good.") In less than fifteen years, if the same progress that has distinguished this country for the last fifteen years continues, every foot of vacant land between this and the Pacific ocean, owned by the United States, will be occupied. Will you not continue to increase at the end of fifteen years as well as now? I tell you, increase, and multiply, and expand, is the law of this nation's existence. ("Good.") You cannot limit this great Republic by mere boundary lines, saying, "thus far shalt thou go, and no further." Any one of you gentlemen might as well say to a son twelve years old that he is big enough, and must not grow any larger, and in order to prevent his growth put a hoop around him to keep him to his present size. What would be the result? Either the hoop must burst and be rent asunder, or the child

must die. So it would be with this great nation. With our natural increase, growing with a rapidity unknown in any other part of the globe, with the tide of emigration that is fleeing from despotism in the old world to seek refuge in our own, there is a constant torrent pouring into this country that requires more land, more territory upon which to settle, and just as fast as our interests and our destiny require additional territory in the North, in the South, or on the Islands of the ocean, I am for it, and when we acquire it, will leave the people, according to the Nebraska bill, free to do as they please on the subject of slavery and every other question. ("Good, good," hurray for Douglas.)

I trust now that Mr. Lincoln will deem himself answered on his four points. He racked his brain so much in devising these four questions that he exhausted himself, and had not strength enough to invent the others. (Laughter.) As soon as he is able to hold a council with his advisers, Lovejoy, Farnsworth, and Fred Douglass, he will frame and propound others. ["Good, good," etc. Renewed laughter, in which Mr. Lincoln feebly joined, saying that he hoped with their aid to get seven questions, the number asked him by Judge Douglas, and so make conclusions even.] You Black Republicans who say good, I have no doubt think that they are all good men. ("White, white.") I have reason to recollect that some people in this country think that Fred Douglass is a very good man. The last time I came here to make a speech, while talking from the stand to you, people of Freeport, as I am doing to-day, I saw a carriage, and a magnificent one it was, drive up and take a position on the outside of the crowd; a beautiful young lady was sitting on the box-seat, whilst Fred Douglass and her mother reclined inside, and the owner of the carriage acted as driver. (Laughter, cheers, cries of right, what have you to say against it, etc.) I saw this in your own town. ("What of it.") All I have to say of it is this, that if you, Black Republicans, think that the negro ought to be on a social equality with your wives and daughters, and ride in a carriage with your wife, whilst you drive the team, you have perfect right to do so. I am told that one of Fred Douglass' kinsmen, another rich black negro, is now traveling in this part of the State making speeches for his friend Lincoln as the champion of black men. ("White men, white men," and "what have you to say against it?" "That's right," etc.) All

I have to say on that subject is, that those of you who believe that the negro is your equal and ought to be on an equality with you socially, politically, and legally, have a right to entertain those opinions, and of course will vote for Mr. Lincoln. ("Down with the negro," "no, no," etc.)

I have a word to say on Mr. Lincoln's answer to the interrogatories contained in my speech at Ottawa, and which he has pretended to reply to here to-day. Mr. Lincoln makes a great parade of the fact that I quoted a platform as having been adopted by the Black Republican party at Springfield in 1854, which, it turns out, was adopted at another place. Mr. Lincoln loses sight of the thing itself in his ecstacies over the mistake I made in stating the place where it was done. He thinks that that platform was not adopted on the right "spot."

When I put the direct questions to Mr. Lincoln to ascertain whether he now stands pledged to that creed—to the unconditional repeal of the Fugitive Slave law, a refusal to admit any more slave States into the Union even if the people want them, a determination to apply the Wilmot Proviso, not only to all the territory we now have, but all that we may hereafter acquire, he refused to answer, and his followers say, in excuse, that the resolutions upon which I based my interrogatories were not adopted at the "right spot." (Laughter and applause.)

Lincoln and his political friends are great on "spots." (Renewed laughter.) In Congress, as a representative of this State, he declared the Mexican war to be unjust and infamous, and would not support it, or acknowledge his own country to be right in the contest, because he said that American blood was not shed on American soil in the "right spot." ("Lay on to him.") And now he cannot answer the questions I put to him at Ottawa because the resolutions I read were not adopted at the "right spot." It may be possible that I was led into an error as to the spot on which the resolutions I then read were proclaimed, but I was not, and am not in error as to the fact of their forming the basis of the creed of the Republican Party when that party was first organized. [Cheers.] I will state to you the evidence I had, and upon which I relied for my statement that the resolutions in question were adopted at Springfield on the 5th of October, 1854. Although I was aware that such resolutions had been passed in this district, and nearly all the northern Congressional Districts and County Conventions, I had not noticed whether or not they had been adopted by any State Convention. In 1856, a debate arose in Congress between Major Thomas L. Harris, of the Springfield District, and Mr. Norton, of the Joliet District, on political matters connected with our State, in the course of which, Major Harris quoted those resolutions as having been passed by the first Republican State Convention that ever assembled in Illinois. I knew that Major Harris was remarkable for his accuracy, that he was a very conscientious and sincere man, and I also noticed that Norton did not question the accuracy of this statement. I therefore took it for granted that it was so, and the other day when I concluded to use the resolutions at Ottawa, I wrote to Charles H. Lanphier, editor of the State Register, at Springfield, calling his attention to them, telling him that I had been informed that Major Harris was lying sick at Springfield, and desiring him to call upon him and ascertain all the facts concerning the resolutions, the time and the place where they were adopted. In reply, Mr. Lanphier sent me two copies of his paper, which I have here. The first is a copy of the State Register, published at Springfield, Mr. Lincoln's own town, on the 16th of October 1854, only eleven days after the adjournment of the Convention, from which I desire to read the following:

During the late discussions in this city, Lincoln made a speech, to which Judge Douglas replied. In Lincoln's speech he took the broad ground that, according to the Declaration of Independence, the whites and blacks are equal. From this he drew the conclusion, which he several times repeated, that the white man had no right to pass laws for the government of the black man without the nigger's consent. This speech of Lincoln's was heard and applauded by all the Abolitionists assembled in Springfield. So soon as Mr. Lincoln was done speaking, Mr. Codding arose and requested all the delegates to the Black Republican Convention to withdraw into the Senate chamber. They did so, and after long deliberation, they laid down the following Abolition platform as the platform on which they stood. We call the particular attention of all our readers to it.

Then follows the identical platform, word for word, which I read at Ottawa. (Cheers.) Now, that was published in Mr. Lincoln's own town, eleven days after the Convention was held, and it has remained on record up to this day never contradicted.

When I quoted the resolutions at Ottawa and questioned Mr. Lincoln in relation to them, he said that his name was on the committee that reported them, but he did not serve, nor did he think he served, because he was, or thought he was, in Tazewell County at the time the Convention was in session. He did not deny that the resolutions were passed by the Springfield Convention. He did not know better, and evidently thought that they were, but afterward his friends declared that they had discovered that they varied in some respects from the resolutions passed by that Convention. I have shown you that I had good evidence for believing that the resolutions had been passed at Springfield. Mr. Lincoln ought to have known better; but not a word is said about his ignorance on the subject, whilst I, notwithstanding the circumstances, am accused of forgery.

Now, I will show you that if I have made a mistake as to the place where these resolutions were adopted—and when I get down to Springfield I will investigate the matter and see whether or not I have—that the principles they enunciate were adopted as the Black Republican platform (white, white,) in the various counties and Congressional Districts throughout the north end of the State in 1854. This platform was adopted in nearly every county that gave a Black Republican majority for the Legislature in that year, and here is a man (pointing to Mr. Denio, who sat on the stand near Deacon Bross) who knows as well as any living man that it was the creed of the Black Republican party at that time. I would be willing to call Denio as a witness, or any other honest man belonging to that party. I will now read the resolutions adopted at the Rockford Convention on the 30th of August, 1854, which nominated Washburne for Congress. You elected him on the following platform:

Resolved, That the continued and increasing aggressions of slavery in our country are destructive of the best rights of a free people, and that such aggressions cannot be successfully resisted without the united political action of all good men.

Resolved, That the citizens of the United States hold in their hands peaceful, constitutional and efficient remedy against the encroachments of the slave power, the ballot-box, and, if that remedy is boldly and wisely applied, the principles of liberty and eternal justice will be established.

Resolved, That we accept this issue forced upon us by the slave power, and, in defense of freedom, will cooperate and be known as Republicans, pledged to the accomplishment of the following purposes:

To bring the Administration of the Government back to the control of first principles; to restore Kansas and Nebraska to the position of free Territories; to repeal and entirely abrogate the Fugitive Slave law; to restrict slavery to those States in which it exists; to prohibit the admission of any more slave States into the Union; to exclude slavery from all the Territories over which the General Government has exclusive jurisdiction, and to resist the acquisition of any more Territories unless the introduction of slavery therein forever shall have been prohibited.

Resolved, That in furtherance of these principles we will use such constitutional and lawful means as shall seem best adapted to their accomplishment, and that we will support no man for office under the General or State Government who is not positively committed to the support of these principles, and whose personal character and conduct is not a guaranty that he is reliable and shall abjure all party allegiance and ties.

Resolved, That we cordially invite persons of all former political parties whatever in favor of the object expressed in the above resolutions to unite with us in carrying them into effect.

[Senator Douglas was frequently interrupted in reading these resolutions by loud cries of "Good, good," "that's the doctrine," and vociferous applause.]

Well, you think that is a very good platform, do you not? ("Yes, yes, all right," and cheers.) If you do, if you approve it now, and think it is all right, you will not join with those men who say that I libel you by calling these your principles, will you? ("Good, good, hit him again," and great laughter and cheers.) Now, Mr. Lincoln complains; Mr. Lincoln charges that I did you and him injustice by saying that this was the platform of your party. (Renewed laughter.) I am told that Washburne made a speech in Galena last night, in which he abused me awfully for bringing to light this platform, on which he was elected to Congress. He thought that you had forgotten it, as he and Mr. Lincoln desire to. (Laughter.) He did not deny but that you had adopted it, and that he had subscribed to and was pledged by it, but he did not think it was fair to call it up and remind the people that it was their platform.

[Here Deacon Bross spoke.]

But I am glad to find you are more honest in your abolitionism than your leaders, by avowing that it is your platform, and right in your opinion. (Laughter, "you have them, good, good.")

In the adoption of that platform, you not only declared that you would resist the admission of any more slave States, and work for the repeal of the Fugitive Slave law, but you pledged yourselves not to vote for any man for State or Federal offices who was not committed to these principles. You were thus committed. Similar resolutions to those were adopted in your county Convention here, and now with your admissions that they are your platform and embody your sentiments now as they did then, what do you think of Mr. Lincoln, your candidate for the U. S. Senate, who is attempting to dodge the responsibility of this platform, because it was not adopted in the right spot. I thought that it was adopted in Springfield, but it turns out it was not, that it was adopted at Rockford, and in the various counties which comprise this Congressional District. When I get into the next district, I will show that the same platform was adopted there, and so on through the State, until I nail the responsibility of it upon the back of the Black Republican party throughout the State. ("White, white," three cheers for Douglas.)

[A voice— "Couldn't you modify and call it brown?" (Laughter)]

Mr. Douglas—Not a bit. I thought that you were becoming a little brown when your members in Congress voted for the Crittenden-Montgomery bill, but since you have backed out from that position and gone back to Abolitionism, you are black and not brown. (Shouts of laughter, and a voice, "Can't you ask him another question?") Gentlemen, I have shown you what your platform

was in 1854. You still adhere to it. The same platform was adopted by nearly all the counties where the Black Republican party had a majority in 1854. I wish now to call your attention to the action of your representatives in the Legislature when they assembled together at Springfield. In the first place, you must remember that this was the organization of a new party. It is so declared in the resolutions themselves, which say that you are going to dissolve all old party ties and call the new party Republican.

The old Whig party was to have its throat cut from ear to ear, and the Democratic Party was to be annihilated and blotted out of existence, whilst in lieu of these parties the Black Republican party was to be organized on this Abolition platform. You know who the chief leaders were in breaking up and destroying these two great parties. Lincoln on the one hand and Trumbull on the other, being disappointed politicians, and having retired or been driven to obscurity by an outraged constituency because of their political sins, formed a scheme to abolitionize the two parties and lead the old line Whigs and old line Democrats captive, bound hand and foot, into the Abolition camp. Giddings, Chase, Fred Douglass and Lovejoy were here to christen them whenever they were brought in. Lincoln went to work to dissolve the old line Whig party. Clay was dead, and although the sod was not yet green on his grave, this man undertook to bring into disrepute those great Compromise measures of 1850, with which Clay and Webster were identified. Up to 1854 the old Whig party and the Democratic Party had stood on a common platform so far as this slavery question was concerned. You Whigs and we Democrats differed about the bank, the tariff, distribution, the specie circular and the sub-treasury, but we agreed on this slavery question and the true mode of preserving the peace and harmony of the Union. The Compromise measures of 1850 were introduced by Clay, were defended by Webster, and supported by Cass, and were approved by Fillmore, and sanctioned by the National men of both parties.

They constituted a common plank upon which both Whigs and Democrats stood. In 1852 the Whig party, in its last National Convention at Baltimore, indorsed and approved these measures of Clay, and so did the National Convention of the Democratic party, held that same year. Thus the old line Whigs and the old line Democrats stood pledged to the great principle of self-government, which guaranties to the people of each Territory the right to decide the slavery question for themselves. In 1854, after the death of Clay and Webster, Mr. Lincoln, on the part of the Whigs, undertook to abolitionize the Whig party, by dissolving it, transferring the members into the Abolition camp and making them train under Giddings, Fred Douglass, Lovejoy, Chase, Farnsworth, and other Abolition leaders. Trumbull undertook to dissolve the Democratic Party by taking old Democrats into the Abolition camp. Mr. Lincoln was aided in his efforts by many leading Whigs throughout the State. Your member of Congress, Mr. Washburne, being one of the most active. Trumbull was aided by many renegades from the Democratic Party, among whom were John Wentworth, Tom Turner, and others, with whom you are familiar. *[Mr. Turner, who was one of the moderators, here interposed and said that he had drawn the resolutions which Senator Douglas had read.]*

Mr. Douglas—Yes, and Turner says that he drew these resolutions. ["Hurray for Turner," "Hurray for Douglas."] That is right, give Turner cheers for drawing the resolutions if you approve them. If he drew those resolutions he will not deny that they are the creed of the Black Republican party.

Mr. Turner—"They are our creed exactly."

Mr. Douglas—And yet Lincoln denies that he stands on them. Mr. Turner says that the creed of the Black Republican party is the admission of no more slave States, and yet Mr. Lincoln declares that he would not like to be placed in a position where he would have to vote for them. All I have to say to friend Lincoln is, that I do not think there is much danger of his being placed in such a position. As Mr. Lincoln would be very sorry to be placed in such an embarrassing position as to be obliged to vote on the admission of any more slave States, I propose, out of mere kindness, to relieve him from any such necessity.

When the bargain between Lincoln and Trumbull was completed for abolitionizing the Whig and Democratic parties, they "spread" over the State, Lincoln still pretending to be an old line Whig, in order to "rope in" the Whigs, and Trumbull pretending to be as good a Democrat as he ever was, in order to coax the Democrats over into the Abolition ranks. They played the part that

"decoy ducks" play down on the Potomac River. In that part of the country they make artificial ducks and put them on the water in places where the wild ducks are to be found, for the purpose of decoying them. Well, Lincoln and Trumbull played the part of these "decoy ducks" and deceived enough old line Whigs and old line Democrats to elect a Black Republican Legislature. When that Legislature met, the first thing it did was to elect as Speaker of the House, the very man who is now boasting that he wrote the Abolition platform on which Lincoln will not stand. I want to know of Mr. Turner whether or not, when he was elected, he was a good embodiment of Republican principles?

Mr. Turner—"I hope I was then and am now."

Mr. Douglas—He swears that he hopes he was then and is now. He wrote that Black Republican platform, and is satisfied with it now. I admire and acknowledge Turner's honesty. Every man of you know that what he says about these resolutions being the platform of the Black Republican party is true, and you also know that each one of these men who are shuffling and trying to deny it are only trying to cheat the people out of their votes for the purpose of deceiving them still more after the election. I propose to trace this thing a little further, in order that you can see what additional evidence there is to fasten this revolutionary platform upon the Black Republican party. When the Legislature assembled, there was an United States Senator to elect in the place of Gen. Shields, and before they proceeded to ballot, Lovejoy insisted on laying down certain principles by which to govern the party. It has been published to the world and satisfactorily proven that there was, at the time the alliance was made between Trumbull and Lincoln to abolitionize the two parties, an agreement that Lincoln should take Shields's place in the United States Senate, and Trumbull should have mine so soon as they could conveniently get rid of me. When Lincoln was beaten for Shields's place, in a manner I will refer to in a few minutes, he felt very sore and restive; his friends grumbled, and some of them came out and charged that the most infamous treachery had been practiced against him; that the bargain was that Lincoln was to have had Shields's place, and Trumbull was to have waited for mine, but that Trumbull having the control of a few abolitionized Democrats, he prevented them from voting for Lincoln, thus keeping him within a few votes of an election until he succeeded in forcing the party to drop him and elect Trumbull. Well, Trumbull having cheated Lincoln, his friends made a fuss, and in order to keep them and Lincoln quiet, the party were obliged to come forward, in advance, at the last State election, and make a pledge that they would go for Lincoln and nobody else. Lincoln could not be silenced in any other way.

Now, there are a great many Black Republicans of you who do not know this thing was done. ["White, white," and great clamor.] I wish to remind you that while Mr. Lincoln was speaking there was not a Democrat vulgar and blackguard enough to interrupt him. But I know that the shoe is pinching you. I am clinching Lincoln now, and you are scared to death for the result. I have seen this thing before. I have seen men make appointments for joint discussions, and the moment their man has been heard, try to interrupt and prevent a fair hearing of the other side. I have seen your mobs before, and defy your wrath. [Tremendous applause.] My friends, do not cheer, for I need my whole time. The object of the opposition is to occupy my attention in order to prevent me from giving the whole evidence and nailing this double dealing on the Black Republican party. As I have before said, Lovejoy demanded a declaration of principles on the part of the Black Republicans of the Legislature before going into an election for United States Senator. He offered the following preamble and resolutions which I hold in my hand:

WHEREAS, Human slavery is a violation of the principles of natural and revealed rights; and whereas, the fathers of the Revolution, fully imbued with the spirit of these principles, declared freedom to be the inalienable birthright of all men; and whereas, the preamble to the Constitution of the United States avers that that instrument was ordained to establish justice, and secure the blessings of liberty to ourselves and our posterity; and whereas, in furtherance of the above principles, slavery was forever prohibited in the old North-west Territory, and more recently in all that Territory lying west and north of the State of Missouri, by the act of the Federal Government; and whereas, the repeal of the prohibition last referred to, was contrary to the wishes of the people of Illinois, a violation of an implied compact, long deemed sacred by the citizens of the United States, and a wide departure from the uniform action of the General Government in relation to the extension of slavery; therefore,

Resolved, by the House of Representatives, the Senate concurring therein, That our Senators in Congress be instructed, and our Representatives requested to introduce, if not otherwise introduced, and to vote for a bill to restore such prohibition to the aforesaid Territories, and also to extend a similar prohibition to all territory which now belongs to the United States, or which may hereafter come under their jurisdiction.

Resolved, That our Senators in Congress be instructed, and our Representatives requested, to vote against the admission of any State into the Union, the Constitution of which does not prohibit slavery, whether the territory out of which such State may have been formed shall have been acquired by conquest, treaty, purchase, or from original territory of the United States.

Resolved, That our Senators in Congress be instructed, and our Representatives requested, to introduce and vote for a bill to repeal an act entitled "an act respecting fugitives from justice and persons escaping from the service of their masters;" and, failing in that, for such a modification of it as shall secure the right of habeas corpus and trial by jury before the regularly-constituted authorities of the State, to all persons claimed as owing service or labor.

(Cries of "good," "good," and cheers.) Yes, you say "good," "good," and I have no doubt you think so. Those resolutions were introduced by Mr. Lovejoy immediately preceding the election of Senator. They declared first, that the Wilmot Proviso must be applied to all territory north of 36 deg. 30 min. Secondly, that it must be applied to all territory south of 36 deg. 30 min. Thirdly, that it must be applied to all the territory now owned by the United

States, and finally, that it must be applied to all territory hereafter to be acquired by the United States. The next resolution declares that no more slave States shall be admitted into this Union under any circumstances whatever, no matter whether they are formed out of territory now owned by us or that we may hereafter acquire, by treaty, by Congress, or in any manner whatever. The next resolution demands the unconditional repeal of the Fugitive Slave law, although its unconditional repeal would leave no provision for carrying out that clause of the Constitution of the United States which guaranties the surrender of fugitives. If they could not get an unconditional repeal, they demanded that that law should be so modified as to make it as nearly useless as possible. Now, I want to show you who voted for these resolutions. When the vote was taken on the first resolution it was decided in the affirmative—yeas 41, nays 32. You will find that this is a strict party vote, between the Democrats on the one hand, and the Black Republicans on the other. [Cries of "White, white," and clamor.] I know your name, and always call things by their right name. The point I wish to call your attention to, is this: that these resolutions were adopted on the 7th day of February, and that on the 8th they went into an election for a United States Senator, and that day every man who voted for these resolutions, with but two exceptions, voted for Lincoln for the United States Senate. ["Give us their names."] I will read the names over to you if you want them, but I believe your object is to occupy my time.

On the next resolution the vote stood—yeas 33, nays 40, and on the third resolution—yeas 35, nays 47. I wish to impress it upon you, that every man who voted for those resolutions, with but two exceptions, voted on the next day for Lincoln for U. S. Senator. Bear in mind that the members who thus voted for Lincoln were elected to the Legislature pledged to vote for no man for office under the State or Federal Government who was not committed to this Black Republican platform. They were all so pledged. Mr. Turner, who stands by me, and who then represented you, and who says that he wrote those resolutions, voted for Lincoln, when he was pledged not to do so unless Lincoln was in favor of those resolutions. I now ask Mr. Turner [turning to Mr. Turner], did you violate your pledge in voting for Mr. Lincoln, or did he commit himself to your platform before you cast your

vote for him?

I could go through the whole list of names here and show you that all the Black Republicans in the Legislature, who voted for Mr. Lincoln, had voted on the day previous for these resolutions. For instance, here are the names of Sargent and Little of Jo Daviess and Carroll, Thomas J. Turner of Stephenson, Lawrence of Boone and McHenry, Swan of Lake, Pinckney of Ogle county, and Lyman of Winnebago. Thus you see every member from your Congressional District voted for Mr. Lincoln, and they were pledged not to vote for him unless he was committed to the doctrine of no more slave States, the prohibition of slavery in the Territories, and the repeal of the Fugitive Slave law. Mr. Lincoln tells you today that he is not pledged to any such doctrine. Either Mr. Lincoln was then committed to those propositions, or Mr. Turner violated his pledges to you when he voted for him. Either Lincoln was pledged to each one of those propositions, or else every Black Republican Representative from this Congressional District violated his pledge of honor to his constituents by voting for him. I ask you which horn of the dilemma will you take? Will you hold Lincoln up to the platform of his party, or will you accuse every Representative you had in the Legislature of violating his pledge of honor to his constituents? There is no escape for you. Either Mr. Lincoln was committed to those propositions, or your members violated their faith. Take either horn of the dilemma you choose. There is no dodging the question; I want Lincoln's answer. He says he was not pledged to repeal the Fugitive Slave law, that he does not quite like to do it; he will not introduce a law to repeal it, but thinks there ought to be some law; he does not tell what it ought to be; upon the whole, he is altogether undecided, and don't know what to think or do. That is the substance of his answer upon the repeal of the Fugitive Slave law. I put the question to him distinctly, whether he indorsed that part of the Black Republican platform which calls for the entire abrogation and repeal of the Fugitive Slave law. He answers no! that he does not indorse that, but he does not tell what he is for, or what he will vote for. His answer is, in fact, no answer at all. Why cannot he speak out and say what he is for and what he will do?

In regard to there being no more slave States, he is not pledged to that. He would not like, he says, to be put in a position where he would have to vote one way or another upon that question. I pray you, do not put him in a position that would embarrass him so much. Gentlemen, if he goes to the Senate, he may be put in that position, and then which way will he vote?

[A Voice—"How will you vote?"]

Mr. Douglas—I will vote for the admission of just such a State as by the form of their Constitution the people show they want; if they want slavery, they shall have it; if they prohibit slavery it shall be prohibited. They can form their institutions to please themselves, subject only to the Constitution; and I for one stand ready to receive them into the Union. Why cannot your Black Republican candidates talk out as plain as that when they are questioned? I do not want to cheat any man out of his vote. No man is deceived in regard to my principles if I have the power to express myself in terms explicit enough to convey my ideas.

Mr. Lincoln made a speech when he was nominated for the United States Senate which covers all these Abolition platforms. He there lays down a proposition so broad in its abolitionism as to cover the whole ground. "In my opinion it [the slavery agitation] will not cease until a crisis shall have been reached and passed. 'A house divided against itself cannot stand.' I believe this Government cannot endure permanently half slave and half free. I do not expect the house to fall—but I do expect it will cease to be divided. It will become all one thing or all the other. Either the opponents of Slavery will arrest the further spread of it, and place it where the public mind shall rest in the belief that it is in the course of ultimate extinction, or its advocates will push it forward till it shall become alike lawful in all the States—old as well as new, North as well as South."

There you find that Mr. Lincoln lays down the doctrine that this Union cannot endure divided as our fathers made it, with free and slave States. He says they must all become one thing, or all the other; that they must all be free or all slave, or else the Union cannot continue to exist. It being his opinion that to admit any more slave States, to continue to divide the Union into free and slave States, will dissolve it. I want to know of Mr. Lincoln whether he will vote for the admission of another slave State.

He tells you the Union cannot exist unless the States are all free or all slave; he tells you that he is opposed to making them all slave, and hence he is for making them all free, in order that the Union may exist; and yet he will not say that he will not vote against another slave State, knowing that the Union must be dissolved if he votes for it. I ask you if that is fair dealing? The true intent and inevitable conclusion to be drawn from his first Springfield speech is, that he is opposed to the admission of any more slave States under any circumstance. If he is so opposed, why not say so? If he believes this Union cannot endure divided into free and slave States, that they must all become free in order to save the Union, he is bound as an honest man, to vote against any more slave States. If he believes it he is bound to do it. Show me that it is my duty in order to save the Union to do a particular act, and I will do it if the Constitution does not prohibit it. (Applause.) I am not for the dissolution of the Union under any circumstances. (Renewed applause.) I will pursue no course of conduct that will give just cause for the dissolution of the Union. The hope of the friends of freedom throughout the world rests upon the perpetuity of this Union. The down-trodden and oppressed people who are suffering under European despotism all look with hope and anxiety to the American Union as the only resting place and permanent home of freedom and self-government.

Mr. Lincoln says that he believes that this Union cannot continue to endure with slave States in it, and yet he will not tell you distinctly whether he will vote for or against the admission of any more slave States, but says he would not like to be put to the test. (Laughter.) I do not think he will be put to the test. (Renewed laughter.) I do not think that the people of Illinois desire a man to represent them who would not like to be put to the test on the performance of a high constitutional duty. (Cries of "good.") I will retire in shame from the Senate of the United States when I am not willing to be put to the test in the performance of my duty. I have been put to severe tests. ("That is so.") I have stood by my principles in fair weather and in foul, in the sunshine and in the rain. I have defended the great principles of self-government here among you when Northern sentiment ran in a torrent against me, (A voice—"that is so") and I have defended that same great principle when Southern sentiment came down like an avalanche upon me. I was not afraid of any test they put to me. I knew I was right—I knew my principles were sound—I knew that the people would see in the end that I had done right, and I knew that the God of Heaven would smile upon me if I was faithful in the performance of my duty. (Cries of "good," cheers, and laughter.)

Mr. Lincoln makes a charge of corruption against the Supreme Court of the United States, and two Presidents of the United States, and attempts to bolster it up by saying that I did the same against the Washington Union. Suppose I did make that charge of corruption against the Washington Union, when it was true, does that justify him in making a false charge against me and others? That is the question I would put. He says that at the time the Nebraska bill was introduced, and before it was passed, there was a conspiracy between the Judges of the Supreme Court, President Pierce, President Buchanan and myself by that bill, and the decision of the court to break down the barrier and establish slavery all over the Union. Does he not know that that charge is historically false as against President Buchanan? He knows that Mr. Buchanan was at that time in England, representing this country with distinguished ability at the Court of St. James, that he was there for a long time before, and did not return for a year or more after. He knows that to be true, and that fact proves his charge to be false as against Mr. Buchanan. (Cheers.) Then again, I wish to call his attention to the fact that at the time the Nebraska bill was passed, the Dred Scott case was not before the Supreme Court at all; it was not upon the docket of the Supreme Court; it had not been brought there, and the Judges in all probability knew nothing of it. Thus the history of the country proves the charge to be false as against them. As to President Pierce , his high character as a man of integrity and honor is enough to vindicate him from such a charge, (laughter and applause,) and as to myself, I pronounce the charge an infamous lie, whenever and wherever made, and by whomsoever made. I am willing that Mr. Lincoln should go and rake up every public act of mine, every measure I have introduced, report I have made, speech delivered, and criticise them, but when he charges upon me a corrupt conspiracy for the purpose of perverting the institutions of the country, I brand it as it deserves. I say the history of the country proves it to be false, and that it could not have been possible at the time. But now he tries to protect himself in this charge, because I made a charge against the Washington Union. My speech in the Senate against the Washington Union was made because it advocated a revolutionary doctrine, by declaring that the free States had not the right to prohibit slavery within their own limits. Because I made that charge against the Washington Union, Mr. Lincoln says it was a charge against Mr. Buchanan. Suppose it was; is Mr. Lincoln the peculiar defender of Mr. Buchanan? Is he so interested in the Federal Administration, and so bound to it, that he must jump to the rescue and defend it from every attack that I may make against it? (Great laughter and cheers.) I understand the whole thing. The Washington Union, under that most corrupt of all men, Cornelius Wendell, is advocating Mr. Lincoln's claim to the Senate. Wendell was the printer of the last Black Republican House of Representatives; he was a candidate before the present Democratic House, but was ignominiously kicked out, and then he took the money which he had made out of the public printing by means of the Black Republicans, bought the Washington Union, and is now publishing it in the name of the Democratic party, and advocating Mr. Lincoln's election to the Senate. Mr. Lincoln therefore considers an attack upon Wendell and his corrupt gang as a personal attack upon him. (Immense cheering and laughter.) This only proves what I have charged, that there is an alliance between Lincoln and his supporters, and the Federal office-holders of this State, and Presidential aspirants out of it, to break me down at home.

[A VOICE.—"That is impossible," and cheering.]

Mr. Lincoln feels bound to come in to the rescue of the Washington Union. In that speech which I delivered in answer to the Washington Union, I made it distinctly against the Union, and against the Union alone. I did not choose to go beyond that. If I have occasion to attack the President's conduct, I will do it in language that will not be misunderstood. When I differed with the President, I spoke out so that you all heard me. ("That you did," and cheers.) That question passed away; it resulted in the triumph of my principle by allowing the people to do as they please, and there is an end of the controversy. Whenever the great principle of self-government—the right of the people to make their own Constitution, and come into the Union with slavery or without it, as they see proper, shall again arise, you will find me standing firm in defense of that principle, and fighting whoever fights it. ("Right, right." "Good, good," and cheers.) If Mr. Buchanan stands, as I doubt not he will, by the recommendation contained in his Message, that hereafter all State Constitutions ought to be submitted to the people before the admission of the State into the Union, he will find me standing by him firmly, shoulder to shoulder, in carrying it out. I know Mr. Lincoln's object; he wants to divide the Democratic Party, in order that he may defeat me and get to the Senate.

Mr. Douglas' time here expired, and he stopped on the moment.

October 7, 1858

Fifth Debate: Galesburg, Illinois

Mr. Lincoln's Speech

Mr. Lincoln was received as he came forward with three enthusiastic cheers, coming from every part of the vast assembly. After silence was restored, Mr. Lincoln said:

MY FELLOW-CITIZENS:—A very large portion of the speech which Judge Douglas has addressed to you has previously been delivered and put in print. [Laughter.] I do not mean that for a hit upon the Judge at all. [Renewed laughter.] If I had not been interrupted, I was going to say that such an answer as I was able to make to a very large portion of it, had already been more than once made and published. There has been an opportunity afforded to the public to see our respective views upon the topics discussed in a large portion of the speech which he has just delivered. I make these remarks for the purpose of excusing myself for not passing over the entire ground that the Judge has traversed. I however desire to take up some of the points that he has attended to, and ask your attention to them, and I shall follow him backwards upon some notes which I have taken, reversing the order by beginning where he concluded.

The Judge has alluded to the Declaration of Independence, and insisted that negroes are not included in that Declaration; and that it is a slander upon the framers of that instrument, to suppose that negroes were meant therein; and he asks you: Is it possible to believe that Mr. Jefferson, who penned the immortal paper, could have

supposed himself applying the language of that instrument to the negro race, and yet held a portion of that race in slavery? Would he not at once have freed them? I only have to remark upon this part of the Judge's speech (and that, too, very briefly, for I shall not detain myself, or you, upon that point for any great length of time), that I believe the entire records of the world, from the date of the Declaration of Independence up to within three years ago, may be searched in vain for one single affirmation, from one single man, that the negro was not included in the Declaration of Independence; I think I may defy Judge Douglas to show that he ever said so, that Washington ever said so, that any President ever said so, that any member of Congress ever said so, or that any living man upon the whole earth ever said so, until the necessities of the present policy of the Democratic party, in regard to slavery, had to invent that affirmation. And I will remind Judge Douglas and this audience, that while Mr. Jefferson was the owner of slaves, as undoubtedly he was, in speaking upon this very subject, he used the strong language that "he trembled for his country when he remembered that God was just;" and I will offer the highest premium in my power to Judge Douglas if he will show that he, in all his life, ever uttered a sentiment at all akin to that of Jefferson.

The next thing to which I will ask your attention is the Judge's comments upon the fact, as he assumes it to be, that we cannot call our public meetings as Republican meetings; and he instances Tazewell county as one of the places where the friends of Lincoln have called a public meeting and have not dared to name it a Republican meeting. He instances Monroe County as another where Judge Trumbull and Jehu Baker addressed the persons whom the Judge assumes to be the friends of Lincoln, calling them the "Free Democracy." I have the honor to inform Judge Douglas that he spoke in that very county of Tazewell last Saturday, and I was there on Tuesday last, and when he spoke there he spoke under a call not venturing to use the word "Democrat." [Turning to Judge Douglas.] What think you of this?

So again, there is another thing to which I would ask the Judge's attention upon this subject. In the contest of 1856 his party delighted to call themselves together as the "National Democracy," but now, if there should be a notice put up any where for a meeting of the "National

Democracy," Judge Douglas and his friends would not come. They would not suppose themselves invited. They would understand that it was a call for those hateful post-masters whom he talks about.

Now a few words in regard to these extracts from speeches of mine, which Judge Douglas has read to you, and which he supposes are in very great contrast to each other. Those speeches have been before the public for a considerable time, and if they have any inconsistency in them, if there is any conflict in them, the public have been unable to detect it. When the Judge says, in speaking on this subject, that I make speeches of one sort for the people of the northern end of the State, and of a different sort for the southern people, he assumes that I do not understand that my speeches will be put in print and read north and south. I knew all the while that the speech that I made at Chicago, and the one I made at Jonesboro and the one at Charleston, would all be put in print and all the reading and intelligent men in the community would see them and know all about my opinions. And I have not supposed, and do not now suppose, that there is any conflict whatever between them. But the Judge will have it that if we do not confess that there is a sort of inequality between the white and black races, which justifies us in making them slaves, we must, then, insist that there is a degree of equality that requires us to make them our wives. Now, I have all the while taken a broad distinction in regard to that matter; and that is all there is in these different speeches which he arrays here, and the entire reading of either of the speeches will show that that distinction was made. Perhaps by taking two parts of the same speech, he could have got up as much of a conflict as the one he has found. I have all the while maintained, that in so far as it should be insisted that there was an equality between the white and black races that should produce a perfect social and political equality, it was an impossibility. This you have seen in my printed speeches, and with it I have said, that in their right to "life, liberty and the pursuit of happiness," as proclaimed in that old Declaration, the inferior races are our equals.

And these declarations I have constantly made in reference to the abstract moral question, to contemplate and consider when we are legislating about any new country which is not already cursed with the actual presence of the evil—slavery. I have never manifested any impatience with the necessities that spring from the actual presence of black people amongst us, and the actual existence of slavery amongst us where it does already exist; but I have insisted that, in legislating for new countries, where it does not exist, there is no just rule other than that of moral and abstract right! With reference to those new countries, those maxims as to the right of a people to "life, liberty and the pursuit of happiness," were the just rules to be constantly referred to. There is no misunderstanding this, except by men interested to misunderstand it. I take it that I have to address an intelligent and reading community, who will peruse what I say, weigh it, and then judge whether I advance improper or unsound views, or whether I advance hypocritical, and deceptive, and contrary views in different portions of the country. I believe myself to be guilty of no such thing as the latter, though, of course, I cannot claim that I am entirely free from all error in the opinions I advance.

The Judge has also detained us awhile in regard to the distinction between his party and our party. His he assumes to be a national party—ours a sectional one. He does this in asking the question whether this country has any interest in the maintenance of the Republican Party? He assumes that our party is altogether sectional—that the party to which he adheres is national; and the argument is, that no party can be a rightful party—can be based upon rightful principles—unless it can announce its principles every where. I presume that Judge Douglas could not go into Russia and announce the doctrine of our national Democracy; he could not denounce the doctrine of kings and emperors and monarchies in Russia; and it may be true of this country, that in some places we may not be able to proclaim a doctrine as clearly true as the truth of Democracy, because there is a section so directly opposed to it that they will not tolerate us in doing so. Is it the true test of the soundness of a doctrine, that in some places people won't let you proclaim it? Is that the way to test the truth of any doctrine? Why, I understood that at one time the people of Chicago would not let Judge Douglas preach a certain favorite doctrine of his. I commend to his consideration the question, whether he takes that as a test of the unsoundness of what he wanted to preach.

There is another thing to which I wish to ask attention

for a little while on this occasion. What has always been the evidence brought forward to prove that the Republican Party is a sectional party? The main one was that in the Southern portion of the Union the people did not let the Republicans proclaim their doctrines amongst them. That has been the main evidence brought forward—that they had no supporters, or substantially none, in the slave States. The South have not taken hold of our principles as we announce them; nor does Judge Douglas now grapple with those principles. We have a Republican State Platform, laid down in Springfield in June last, stating our position all the way through the questions before the country. We are now far advanced in this canvass. Judge Douglas and I have made perhaps forty speeches apiece, and we have now for the fifth time met face to face in debate, and up to this day I have not found either Judge Douglas or any friend of his taking hold of the Republican platform or laying his finger upon anything in it that is wrong. I ask you all to recollect that. Judge Douglas turns away from the platform of principles to the fact that he can find people somewhere who will not allow us to announce those principles. If he had great confidence that our principles were wrong, he would take hold of them and demonstrate them to be wrong. But he does not do so. The only evidence he has of their being wrong is in the fact that there are people who won't allow us to preach them. I ask again is that the way to test the soundness of a doctrine?

I ask his attention also to the fact that by the rule of nationality he is himself fast becoming sectional. I ask his attention to the fact that his speeches would not go as current now south of the Ohio River as they have formerly gone there. I ask his attention to the fact that he felicitates himself to-day that all the Democrats of the free States are agreeing with him, while he omits to tell us that the Democrats of any slave State agree with him. If he has not thought of this, I commend to his consideration the evidence in his own declaration, on this day, of his becoming sectional too. I see it rapidly approaching. Whatever may be the result of this ephemeral contest between Judge Douglas and myself, I see the day rapidly approaching when his pill of sectionalism, which he has been thrusting down the throats of Republicans for years past, will be crowded down his own throat.

Now in regard to what Judge Douglas said (in the beginning of his speech) about the Compromise of 1850, containing the principle of the Nebraska bill, although I have often presented my views upon that subject, yet as I have not done so in this canvass, I will, if you please, detain you a little with them. I have always maintained, so far as I was able, that there was nothing of the principle of the Nebraska bill in the Compromise of 1850 at all—nothing whatever. Where can you find the principle of the Nebraska bill in that Compromise? If any where, in the two pieces of the Compromise organizing the Territories of New Mexico and Utah. It was expressly provided in these two acts, that, when they came to be admitted into the Union, they should be admitted with or without slavery, as they should choose, by their own Constitutions. Nothing was said in either of those acts as to what was to be done in relation to slavery during the territorial existence of those Territories, while Henry Clay constantly made the declaration (Judge Douglas recognizing him as a leader) that, in his opinion, the old Mexican laws would control that question during the territorial existence, and that these old Mexican laws excluded slavery. How can that be used as a principle for declaring that during the territorial existence as well as at the time of framing the Constitution, the people, if you please, might have slaves if they wanted them? I am not discussing the question whether it is right or wrong; but how are the New Mexican and Utah laws patterns for the Nebraska bill? I maintain that the organization of Utah and New Mexico did not establish a general principle at all. It had no feature of establishing a general principle. The acts to which I have referred were a part of a general system of Compromises. They did not lay down what was proposed as a regular policy for the Territories; only an agreement in this particular case to do in that way, because other things were done that were to be a compensation for it. They were allowed to come in in that shape, because in another way it was paid for—considering that as a part of that system of measures called the Compromise of 1850, which finally included half a dozen acts. It included the admission of California as a free State, which was kept out of the Union for half a year because it had formed a free Constitution. It included the settlement of the boundary of Texas, which had been undefined before, which was in itself a slavery question; for, if you pushed the line farther west, you made Texas larger, and made more slave Territory; while, if you drew the line toward the east, you narrowed the boundary and diminished the domain of slavery, and by so much increased free Territory. It included the abolition of the slave-trade in the District of Columbia. It included the passage of a new Fugitive Slave law. All these things were put together, and though passed in separate acts, were nevertheless in legislation (as the speeches at the time will show), made to depend upon each other. Each got votes, with the understanding that the other measures were to pass, and by this system of Compromise, in that series of measures, those two bills—the New Mexico and Utah bills—were passed; and I say for that reason they could not be taken as models, framed upon their own intrinsic principle, for all future Territories. And I have the evidence of this in the fact that Judge Douglas, a year afterward, or more than a year afterward, perhaps, when he first introduced bills for the purpose of framing new Territories, did not attempt to follow these bills of New Mexico and Utah; and even when he introduced this Nebraska bill, I think you will discover that he did not exactly follow them. But I do not wish to dwell at great length upon this branch of the discussion. My own opinion is, that a thorough investigation will show most plainly that the New Mexico and Utah bills were part of a system of Compromise, and not designed as patterns for future territorial legislation; and that this Nebraska bill did not follow them as a pattern at all.

The Judge tells, in proceeding, that he is opposed to making any odious distinctions between free and slave States. I am altogether unaware that the Republicans are in favor of making any odious distinctions between the free and slave States. But there still is a difference, I think, between Judge Douglas and the Republicans in this. I suppose that the real difference between Judge Douglas and his friends, and the Republicans on the contrary, is, that the Judge is not in favor of making any difference between slavery and liberty—that he is in favor of eradicating, of pressing out of view, the questions of preference in this country for free or slave institutions; and consequently every sentiment he utters discards the idea that there is any wrong in slavery. Every thing that emanates from him or his coadjutors in their course of policy, carefully excludes the thought that there is any thing wrong in slavery. All their arguments, if you will con-

sider them, will be seen to exclude the thought that there is any thing whatever wrong in slavery. If you will take the Judge's speeches, and select the short and pointed sentences expressed by him—as his declaration that he "don't care whether slavery is voted up or down"— you will see at once that this is perfectly logical, if you do not admit that slavery is wrong. If you do admit that it is wrong, Judge Douglas cannot logically say he don't care whether a wrong is voted up or voted down. Judge Douglas declares that if any community want slavery they have a right to have it. He can say that logically, if he says that there is no wrong in slavery; but if you admit that there is a wrong in it, he cannot logically say that any body has a right to do wrong. He insists that, upon the score of equality, the owners of slaves and owners of property—of horses and every other sort of property—should be alike and hold them alike in a new Territory. That is perfectly logical, if the two species of property are alike and are equally founded in right. But if you admit that one of them is wrong, you cannot institute any equality between right and wrong. And from this difference of sentiment— the belief on the part of one that the institution is wrong, and a policy springing from that belief which looks to the arrest of the enlargement of that wrong; and this other sentiment, that it is no wrong, and a policy sprung from that sentiment which will tolerate no idea of preventing that wrong from growing larger, and looks to there never being an end of it through all the existence of things,— arises the real difference between Judge Douglas and his friends on the one hand, and the Republicans on the other. Now, I confess myself as belonging to that class in the country who contemplate slavery as a moral, social and political evil, having due regard for its actual existence amongst us and the difficulties of getting rid of it in any satisfactory way, and to all the Constitutional obligations which have been thrown about it; but, nevertheless, desire a policy that looks to the prevention of it as a wrong, and looks hopefully to the time when as a wrong it may come to an end.

Judge Douglas has again, for, I believe, the fifth time, if not the seventh, in my presence, reiterated his charge of a conspiracy or combination between the National Democrats and Republicans. What evidence Judge Douglas has upon his subject I know not, inasmuch as he never favors us with any. I have said upon a former occasion, and I do not choose to suppress it now, that I have no objection to the division in the Judge's party. He got it up himself. It was all his and their work. He had, I think, a great deal more to do with the steps that led to the Lecompton Constitution than Mr. Buchanan had; though at last, when they reached it, they quarreled over it, and their friends divided upon it. I am very free to confess to Judge Douglas that I have no objection to the division; but I defy the Judge to show any evidence that I have in any way promoted that division, unless he insists on being a witness himself in merely saying so. I can give all fair friends of Judge Douglas here to understand exactly the view that Republicans take in regard to that division.

Don't you remember how two years ago the opponents of the Democratic Party were divided between Fremont and Fillmore? I guess you do. Any Democrat who remembers that division, will remember also that he was at the time very glad of it, and then he will be able to see all there is between the National Democrats and the Republicans. What we now think of the two divisions of Democrats, you then thought of the Fremont and Fillmore divisions. That is all there is of it.

But, if the Judge continues to put forward the declaration that there is an unholy and unnatural alliance between the Republican and the National Democrats, I now want to enter my protest against receiving him as an entirely competent witness upon that subject. I want to call to the Judge's attention an attack he made upon me in the first one of these debates, at Ottawa, on the 21st of August. In order to fix extreme Abolitionism upon me, Judge Douglas read a set of resolutions which he declared had been passed by a Republican State Convention, in October, 1854, at Springfield, Illinois, and he declared I had taken part in that Convention. It turned out that although a few men calling themselves an anti-Nebraska State Convention had sat at Springfield about that time, yet neither did I take any part in it, nor did it pass the resolutions or any such resolutions as Judge Douglas read.

So apparent had it become that the resolutions which he read had not been passed at Springfield at all, nor by a State Convention in which I had taken part, that seven days afterward, at Freeport, Judge Douglas declared that he had been misled by Charles H. Lanphier, editor of the State Register, and Thomas L. Harris, member of Congress in that District, and he promised in that speech that when he went to Springfield he would investigate the matter. Since then Judge Douglas has been to Springfield, and I presume has made the investigation; but a month has passed since he has been there, and so far as I know, he has made no report of the result of his investigation. I have waited as I think sufficient time for the report of that investigation, and I have some curiosity to see and hear it. A fraud—an absolute forgery was committed, and the perpetration of it was traced to the three—Lanphier, Harris and Douglas. Whether it can be narrowed in any way so as to exonerate any one of them, is what Judge Douglas's report would probably show.

It is true that the set of resolutions read by Judge Douglas were published in the Illinois State Register on the 16th of October, 1854, as being the resolutions of an anti-Nebraska Convention, which had sat in that same month of October, at Springfield. But it is also true that the publication in the Register was a forgery then, and the question is still behind, which of the three, if not all of them, committed that forgery? The idea that it was done by mistake, is absurd. The article in the Illinois State Register contains part of the real proceedings of that Springfield Convention, showing that the writer of the article had the real proceedings before him, and purposely threw out the genuine resolutions passed by the Convention, and fraudulently substituted the others. Lanphier then, as now, was the editor of the Register, so that there seems to be but little room for his escape. But then it is to be borne in mind that Lanphier has less interest in the object of that forgery than either of the other two. The main object of that forgery at that time was to beat Yates and elect Harris to Congress, and that object was known to be exceedingly dear to Judge Douglas at that time. Harris and Douglas were both in Springfield when the Convention was in session, and although they both left before the fraud appeared in the Register, subsequent events show that they have both had their eyes fixed upon that Convention.

The fraud having been apparently successful upon the occasion, both Harris and Douglas have more than once since then been attempting to put it to new uses. As the fisherman's wife, whose drowned husband was brought home with his body full of eels, said when she was asked, "What was to be done with him?" "Take the eels out and set him again"; so Harris and Douglas have shown a disposition to take the eels out of that stale fraud by which they gained Harris's election, and set the fraud again more than once. On the 9th of July, 1856, Douglas attempted a repetition of it upon Trumbull on the floor of the Senate of the United States, as will appear from the appendix of the Congressional Globe of that date. On the 9th of August, Harris attempted it again upon Norton in the House of Representatives, as will appear by the same documents—the appendix to the Congressional Globe of that date. On the 21st of August last, all three—Lanphier, Douglas and Harris—reattempted it upon me at Ottawa. It has been clung to and played out again and again as an exceedingly high trump by this blessed trio. And now that it has been discovered publicly to be a fraud, we find that Judge Douglas manifests no surprise at it at all. He makes no complaint of Lanphier, who must have known it to be a fraud from the beginning.

He, Lanphier and Harris, are just as cozy now, and just as active in the concoction of new schemes as they were before the general discovery of this fraud. Now all this is very natural if they are all alike guilty in that fraud, and it is very unnatural if any one of them is innocent. Lanphier perhaps insists that the rule of honor among thieves does not quite require him to take all upon himself, and consequently my friend Judge Douglas finds it difficult to make a satisfactory report upon his investigation. But meanwhile the three are agreed that each is "a most honorable man."

Judge Douglas requires an indorsement of his truth and honor by a re-election to the United States Senate, and he makes and reports against me and against Judge Trumbull, day after day, charges which we know to be utterly untrue, without for a moment seeming to think that this one unexplained fraud, which he promised to investigate, will be the least drawback to his claim to belief. Harris ditto. He asks a re-election to the lower House of Congress without seeming to remember at all that he is involved in this dishonorable fraud! The Illinois State Register, edited by Lanphier, then, as now, the central organ of both Harris and Douglas, continues to din the public ear with this assertion without seeming to suspect that these assertions are at all lacking in title to belief.

After all, the question still recurs upon us, how did that fraud originally get into the State Register? Lanphier then, as now, was the editor of that paper. Lanphier knows. Lanphier cannot be ignorant of how and by whom it was originally concocted. Can he be induced to tell, or if he has told, can Judge Douglas be induced to tell how it originally was concocted? It may be true that Lanphier insists that the two men for whose benefit it was originally devised, shall at least bear their share of it! How that is, I do not know, and while it remains unexplained, I hope to be pardoned if I insist that the mere fact of Judge Douglas making charges against Trumbull and myself is not quite sufficient evidence to establish them! While we were at Freeport, in one of these joint discussions, I answered certain interrogatories which Judge Douglas had propounded to me, and there in turn propounded some to him, which he in a sort of way answered. The third one of these interrogatories I have with me and wish now to make some comments upon it. It was in these words: "If the Supreme Court of the United States shall decide that the States cannot exclude slavery from their limits, are you in favor of acquiescing in, adhering to and following such decision, as a rule of political action?"

To this interrogatory Judge Douglas made no answer in any just sense of the word. He contented himself with sneering at the thought that it was possible for the Supreme Court ever to make such a decision. He sneered at me for propounding the interrogatory. I had not propounded it without some reflection, and I wish now to address to this audience some remarks upon it. In the second clause of the sixth article, I believe it is, of the Constitution of the United States, we find the following language: "This Constitution and the laws of the United States which shall be made in pursuance thereof; and all treaties made, or which shall be made under the authority of the United States, shall be the supreme law of the land; and the judges in every State shall be bound thereby, any thing in the Constitution or laws of any State to the contrary notwithstanding."

The essence of the Dred Scott case is compressed into the sentence which I will now read: "Now, as we have already said in an earlier part of this opinion, upon a different point, the right of property in a slave is distinctly and expressly affirmed in the Constitution." I repeat it, "The right of property in a slave is distinctly and expressly affirmed in the Constitution!" What is it to be "affirmed" in the Constitution? Made firm in the Constitution —so made that it cannot be separated from the Constitution without breaking the Constitution—durable as the Constitution, and part of the Constitution. Now, remembering the provision of the Constitution which I have read, affirming that that instrument is the supreme law of the land; that the Judges of every State shall be bound by it, any law or Constitution of any State to the contrary notwithstanding; that the right of property in a slave is affirmed in that Constitution, is made, formed into, and cannot be separated from it without breaking it; durable as the instrument; part of the instrument; —what follows as a short and even syllogistic argument from it? I think it follows, and I submit to the consideration of men capable of arguing, whether as I state it, in syllogistic form, the argument has any fault in it?

Nothing in the Constitution or laws of any State can destroy a right distinctly and expressly affirmed in the Constitution of the United States.

The right of property in a slave is distinctly and expressly affirmed in the Constitution of the United States.

Therefore, nothing in the Constitution or laws of any State can destroy the right of property in a slave. I believe that no fault can be pointed out in that argument; assuming the truth of the premises, the conclusion, so far as I have capacity at all to understand it, follows inevitably. There is a fault in it as I think, but the fault is not in the reasoning; but the falsehood in fact is a fault of the premises. I believe that the right of property in a slave is not distinctly and expressly affirmed in the Constitution, and Judge Douglas thinks it is. I believe that the Supreme Court and the advocates of that decision may search in vain for the place in the Constitution where the right of a slave is distinctly and expressly affirmed. I say, therefore, that I think one of the premises is not true in fact. But it is true with Judge Douglas. It is true with the Supreme Court who pronounced it. They are estopped from denying it, and being estopped from denying it, the conclusion follows that the Constitution of the United States being the supreme law, no constitution or law can interfere with it. It being affirmed in the decision that the right of property in a slave is distinctly and expressly affirmed in the Constitution, the conclusion inevitably follows that

no State law or constitution can destroy that right. I then say to Judge Douglas and to all others, that I think it will take a better answer than a sneer to show that those who have said that the right of property in a slave is distinctly and expressly affirmed in the Constitution, are not prepared to show that no constitution or law can destroy that right. I say I believe it will take a far better argument than a mere sneer to show to the minds of intelligent men that whoever has so said, is not prepared, whenever public sentiment is so far advanced as to justify it, to say the other. This is but an opinion, and the opinion of one very humble man; but it is my opinion that the Dred Scott decision, as it is, never would have been made in its present form if the party that made it had not been sustained previously by the elections. My own opinion is, that the new Dred Scott decision, deciding against the right of the people of the States to exclude slavery, will never be made, if that party is not sustained by the elections. I believe, further, that it is just as sure to be made as to-morrow is to come, if that party shall be sustained. I have said, upon a former occasion, and I repeat it now, that the course of argument that Judge Douglas makes use of upon this subject (I charge not his motives in this), is preparing the public mind for that new Dred Scott decision. I have asked him again to point out to me the reasons for his first adherence to the Dred Scott decision as it is. I have turned his attention to the fact that General Jackson differed with him in regard to the political obligation of a Supreme Court decision. I have asked his attention to the fact that Jefferson differed with him in regard to the political obligation of a Supreme Court decision. Jefferson said, that "Judges are as honest as other men, and not more so." And he said, substantially, that "whenever a free people should give up in absolute submission to any department of government, retaining for themselves no appeal from it, their liberties were gone." I have asked his attention to the fact that the Cincinnati platform, upon which he says he stands, disregards a time-honored decision of the Supreme Court, in denying the power of Congress to establish a National Bank. I have asked his attention to the fact that he himself was one of the most active instruments at one time in breaking down the Supreme Court of the State of Illinois, because it had made a decision distasteful to him—a struggle ending in the remarkable circumstance of his sitting down as one of the new

Judges who were to overslaugh that decision—getting his title of Judge in that very way.

So far in this controversy I can get no answer at all from Judge Douglas upon these subjects. Not one can I get from him, except that he swells himself up and says, "All of us who stand by the decision of the Supreme Court are the friends of the Constitution; all you fellows that dare question it in any way, are the enemies of the Constitution."

Now, in this very devoted adherence to this decision, in opposition to all the great political leaders whom he has recognized as leaders—in opposition to his former self and history, there is something very marked. And the manner in which he adheres to it—not as being right upon the merits, as he conceives (because he did not discuss that at all), but as being absolutely obligatory upon every one simply because of the source from whence it comes—as that which no man can gainsay, whatever it may be—this is another marked feature of his adherence to that decision. It marks it in this respect, that it commits him to the next decision, whenever it comes, as being as obligatory as this one, since he does not investigate it, and won't inquire whether this opinion is right or wrong. So he takes the next one without inquiring whether it is right or wrong. He teaches men this doctrine, and in so doing prepares the public mind to take the next decision when it comes, without any inquiry. In this I think I argue fairly (without questioning motives at all), that Judge Douglas is more ingeniously and powerfully preparing the public mind to take that decision when it comes; and not only so, but he is doing it in various other ways. In these general maxims about liberty—in his assertions that he "don't care whether slavery is voted up or voted down;" that "whoever wants slavery has a right to have it;" that "upon principles of equality it should be allowed to go every where;" that "there is no inconsistency between free and slave institutions." In this he is also preparing (whether purposely or not) the way for making the institution of slavery national! I repeat again, for I wish no misunderstanding, that I do not charge that he means it so; but I call upon your minds to inquire, if you were going to get the best instrument you could, and then set it to work in the most ingenious way, to prepare the public mind for this movement, operating in the free States, where there is now an abhorrence of the institution of slavery, could you find an instrument so capable of doing it as Judge Douglas? or one employed in so apt a way to do it?

I have said once before, and I will repeat it now, that Mr. Clay, when he was once answering an objection to the Colonization Society, that it had a tendency to the ultimate emancipation of the slaves, said that "those who would repress all tendencies to liberty and ultimate emancipation must do more than put down the benevolent efforts of the Colonization Society—they must go back to the era of our liberty and independence, and muzzle the cannon that thunders its annual joyous return—they must blot out the moral lights around us—they must penetrate the human soul, and eradicate the light of reason and the love of liberty!" And I do think—I repeat, though I said it on a former occasion—that Judge Douglas, and whoever like him teaches that the negro has no share, humble though it may be, in the Declaration of Independence, is going back to the era of our liberty and independence, and, so far as in him lies, muzzling the cannon that thunders its annual joyous return; that he is blowing out the moral lights around us, when he contends that whoever wants slaves has a right to hold them; that he is penetrating, so far as lies in his power, the human soul, and eradicating the light of reason and the love of liberty, when he is in every possible way preparing the public mind, by his vast influence, for making the institution of slavery perpetual and national.

There is, my friends, only one other point to which I will call your attention for the remaining time that I have left me, and perhaps I shall not occupy the entire time that I have, as that one point may not take me clear through it.

Among the interrogatories that Judge Douglas propounded to me at Freeport, there was one in about this language: "Are you opposed to the acquisition of any further territory to the United States, unless slavery shall first be prohibited therein?" I answered as I thought, in this way, that I am not generally opposed to the acquisition of additional territory, and that I would support a proposition for the acquisition of additional territory, according as my supporting it was or was not calculated to aggravate this slavery question amongst us. I then proposed to Judge Douglas another interrogatory, which was correlative to that: "Are you in favor of acquiring additional territory in disregard of how it may affect us upon the slavery question?" Judge Douglas answered, that is, in his own way he answered it. I believe that, although he took a good many words to answer it, it was a little more fully answered than any other. The substance of his answer was, that this country would continue to expand—that it would need additional territory—that it was as absurd to suppose that we could continue upon our present territory, enlarging in population as we are, as it would be to hoop a boy twelve years of age, and expect him to grow to man's size without bursting the hoops. [Laughter.] I believe it was something like that. Consequently he was in favor of the acquisition of further territory, as fast as we might need it, in disregard of how it might affect the slavery question. I do not say this as giving his exact language, but he said so substantially, and he would leave the question of slavery where the territory was acquired, to be settled by the people of the acquired territory. ["That's the doctrine."] May be it is; let us consider that for a while. This will probably, in the run of things, become one of the concrete manifestations of this slavery question. If Judge Douglas's policy upon this question succeeds and gets fairly settled down, until all opposition is crushed out, the next thing will be a grab for the territory poor Mexico, an invasion of the rich lands of South America, then the adjoining islands will follow, each one of which promises additional slave fields. And this question is to be left to the people of those countries for settlement. When we shall get Mexico, I don't know whether the Judge will be in favor of the Mexican people that we get with it settling that question for themselves and all others; because we know the Judge has a great horror for mongrels, and I understand that the people of Mexico are most decidedly a race of mongrels. I understand that there is not more than one person there out of eight who is pure white, and I suppose from the Judge's previous declaration that when we get Mexico or any considerable portion of it, that he will be in favor of these mongrels settling the question, which would bring him somewhat into collision with his horror of an inferior race.

It is to be remembered, though, that this power of acquiring additional territory is a power confided to the President and Senate of the United States. It is a power not under the control of the representatives of the people any further than they, the President and the Senate, can be considered the representatives of the people. Let me illustrate that by a case we have in our history. When we acquired the territory from Mexico in the Mexican war, the House of Representatives, composed of the immediate representatives of the people, all the time insisted that the territory thus to be acquired should be brought in upon condition that slavery should be forever prohibited therein, upon the terms and in the language that slavery had been prohibited from coming into this country. That was insisted upon constantly, and never failed to call forth an assurance that any territory thus acquired should have that prohibition in it, so far as the House of Representatives was concerned. But at last the President and Senate acquired the territory without asking the House of Representatives any thing about it, and took it without that prohibition. They have the power of acquiring territory without the immediate representatives of the People being called upon to say any thing about it, and thus furnishing a very apt and powerful means of bringing new territory into the Union, and when it is once brought into the country, involving us anew in this slavery agitation. It is, therefore, as I think, a very important question for the consideration of the American people, whether the policy of bringing in additional territory, without considering at all how it will operate upon the safety of the Union in reference to this one great disturbing element in our national politics, shall be adopted as the policy of the country. You will bear in mind that it is to be acquired, according to the Judge's view, as fast as it is needed, and the indefinite part of this proposition is that we have only Judge Douglas and his class of men to decide how fast it is needed. We have no clear and certain way of determining or demonstrating how fast territory is needed by the necessities of the country. Whoever wants to go out filibustering, then, thinks that more territory is needed. Whoever wants wider slave fields, feels sure that some additional territory is needed as slave territory. Then it is as easy to show the necessity of additional slave territory as it is to assert any thing that is incapable of absolute demonstration. Whatever motive a man or a set of men may have for making annexation of property or territory, it is very easy to assert, but much less easy to disprove, that it is necessary for the wants of the country.

And now it only remains for me to say that I think

it is a very grave question for the people of this Union to consider whether, in view of the fact that this slavery question has been the only one that has ever endangered our Republican institutions—the only one that has ever threatened or menaced a dissolution of the Union—that has ever disturbed us in such a way as to make us fear for the perpetuity of our liberty—in view of these facts, I think it is an exceedingly interesting and important question for this people to consider, whether we shall engage in the policy of acquiring additional territory, discarding altogether from our consideration, while obtaining new territory, the question how it may affect us in regard to this the only endangering element to our liberties and national greatness. The Judge's view has been expressed. I, in my answer to his question, have expressed mine. I think it will become an important and practical question.

Our views are before the public. I am willing and anxious that they should consider them fully—that they should turn it about and consider the importance of the question, and arrive at a just conclusion as to whether it is or is not wise in the people of this Union, in the acquisition of new territory, to consider whether it will add to the disturbance that is existing amongst us—whether it will add to the one only danger that has ever threatened the perpetuity of the Union or our own liberties. I think it is extremely important that they shall decide, and rightly decide, that question before entering upon that policy. And now, my friends, having said the little I wish to say upon this head, whether I have occupied the whole of the remnant of my time or not, I believe I could not enter upon any new topics so as to treat it fully without transcending my time, which I would not for a moment think of doing. I give way to Judge Douglas.

GLOSSARY

abolitionist: one who wanted to totally do away with slavery

Deacon Bross: the presiding officer for the debate in Freeport

Fred Douglass: Fredrick Douglass, the famous African-American leader and social reformer

inferior races: a nineteenth-century view and term for non-whites

Lecompton Constitution: a pro-slavery state constitution illegally drawn up for Kansas but never accepted by the national government

Nebraska Bill: original name of the Kansas-Nebraska Act allowing a local vote on slavery

Trumbull, Lyman: the man for whom Lincoln stepped aside in the 1854 senatorial election; at that time Trumbull was a Democrat

Document Analysis

In political campaigns, each candidate tries to use tactics which will be advantageous for himself/herself. During the 1858 senatorial campaign, this was very much the case. Douglas, as the incumbent, did not want to give Lincoln any additional stature by appearing with him. Lincoln wanted joint speeches, but if that were not possible then he planned to follow Douglas around the state and give a speech the day after Douglas spoke. When Douglas saw the advantage this was giving Lincoln, since Douglas could not refute anything Lincoln said, Douglas agreed to seven joint appearances which were termed debates. The format was for one person to speak for an hour, the second to speak for an hour and a half, and then the first person to speak again for half an hour. It was not a modern-style debate, but it did give the people an opportunity to see and hear both men. The speeches used for this article are Douglas' speech at Freeport, the second debate, and Lincoln's speech at Galesburg, the fifth debate. As was always the case prior to people having the ability to make audio recordings of speeches, there are slightly different versions which have come down from that time. The Republicans and Democrats had stenographers transcribe the speeches, but in the copies which were ultimately printed, each party often "improved" their candidate's speech while leaving the other's in a rough form. This did not alter the ideology, just the style.

In the first debate, Douglas went first and put Lincoln on the defensive raising several questions about to Lincoln's anti-Mexican-American War stance, and the radical anti-slavery platform of the Republicans in the 1854 senatorial election. At this second debate, Lincoln spoke first, and among his remarks finally explicitly responded to the questions Douglas had raised, while raising four of his own dealing with the territories of the United States, slavery, and the recent Supreme Court ruling (Dred Scott Case). Douglas began by giving false praise to Lincoln for being led (by Douglas) to finally "define his position on certain political questions to which I called his attention at Ottawa." He then disparaged Lincoln's questions as not based on the Republican Party platform, but Lincoln's "own curiosity." Some people think that Lincoln asked these questions looking beyond this election, to the future of the two political parties. Whatever the reason, Douglas responded to them in a way which generally was in line with the opinions of Illinois voters in 1858, but not necessarily with the broader Democratic Party.

Lincoln had asked whether Douglas would vote to admit Kansas, which according to some did not have enough people to normally qualify for admission. After dwelling at length on the fact that the Republican Congressman from Freeport's district had voted against admitting Oregon due to population concerns, Douglas went on to say he would vote for its admission, whether slave or free. In light of the Dred Scott ruling stating that Congress could not make laws regulating slavery in the territories, Lincoln asked if Douglas if the people of the territory could ban slavery prior to statehood. Douglas was best known for his advocacy of popular sovereignty, which normally applied at the state level, but here applied it to a territory. Douglas stated that voters in a territory could "exclude slavery from their limits prior to the formation of a State Constitution." Ever since the Dred Scott ruling, Douglas had been trying to walk a fine line between ignoring the Supreme Court ruling and allowing slavery to spread throughout the nation's western territories. In light of that ruling, Lincoln asked if Douglas would support the Supreme Court if it ruled that slavery was legal everywhere. Douglas did not really answer this, but stated that the Supreme Court would never do anything unconstitutional and therefore, Douglas supported its rulings.

The fourth question was whether Douglas would support the territorial expansion of the United States, regardless of the slavery question. Douglas estimated that it would be fifteen years before any more territory would be needed, but he would support further expansion with the understanding that the local people would make the final decision regarding slavery. Even in a free state such as Illinois most whites looked down on blacks. Thus, in answering this final question Douglas used the phrase Black Republicans to refer to Lincoln's party. He sought to gain further advantage by disparaging Lincoln's views, as Douglas pretended to be open minded on the issue of race by stating, "All I have to say on that subject is, that those of you who believe that the negro is your equal and ought to be on an equality with you socially, politically, and legally, have a right to entertain those opinions."

After responding to Lincoln's questions, Douglas then moved onto points which he made repeatedly throughout all the debates. This was to paint the Republican Party and Abraham Lincoln as extremists on the issue of slavery and against Douglas' doctrine of popular sovereignty. The first Illinois Republican Convention in 1854 had adopted a very strong stand against slavery and against the expansion of slavery into new areas whether new territories or states. Although the 1858 Convention had not adopted as strong a stand, they did not repudiate it. Lincoln's House Divided speech was seen by all as a strong statement against slavery. Previously, Lincoln had tried to partially evade the ramifications of the 1854 Convention's statement by saying Douglas was wrong as to where it had been adopted. Douglas used this and tied it in with Lincoln's objections to the Mexican-American War, in which Lincoln had asked President Polk to show him the spot on American soil where the Mexicans had attacked Americans. Douglas then read the 1854 founding document for the Republican Party, which clearly stated that slavery should be restricted to the current fifteen Southern states with legal sanctions against taking slaves elsewhere, including repeal of the Fugitive Slave Law. For Douglas, whose party was the majority party in most Southern states, this was taking rejection of slavery too far.

Douglas, in the remainder of his speech, kept up this constant attack that Lincoln and the "Black Republicans" were extremists on slavery, having moved completely into the abolitionist's camp. He also attacked Lincoln for lack of consistency, since during this campaign Douglas asserted that Lincoln had not said if he would support the entry of additional slave States into the Union. The Illinois Republican Party's founding documents, and the charge to those selecting a nominee for senator both made it clear that all their elected leaders must work to stop any spread of slavery. The preamble to the state's Republican declaration of principles stated, "Human slavery is a violation of the principles of natural and revealed rights." It called on anyone elected to vote to restore what had been the situation prior to the Dred Scott ruling. Douglas charged that Lincoln had been one of the individuals who had intentionally sabotaged the Whig Party, which had a moderate stance on slavery, in order to create the Republican Party with the more extreme anti-slavery stance. Douglas understood that the people of Illinois, a free state, were not strong advocates of slavery. The key to his position was that the people in a territory, or state, should make the decision regarding slavery and not the national government or courts. He believed that local officials and magistrates held the key as to whether or not slavery could survive in a particular locality. Sometimes called his Freeport Doctrine, Douglas throughout the campaign pushed local popular sovereignty as the answer to any question about slavery, rather than taking a firm stand on one side or the other. However, this ended up putting him on the side of accepting slavery,

which while it did not hurt him in the 1858 senatorial election, was devastating to his candidacy in the 1860 presidential election.

By the Fifth Debate, the pattern of the speeches and the major points which each man emphasized had been fairly well set. Lincoln, who spoke second, began his speech with the assertion that Douglas was saying the same old thing in speech after speech. Since much of the same could have been said about Lincoln, Lincoln took this opportunity to take a slightly new approach based on a reference which Douglas had made to the Declaration of Independence. Douglas had begun his speech with his usual refrain of popular sovereignty and then dealt extensively with the issue of Kansas and the various proposals which had been put forward for its statehood. Then he referred to a statement, made by Lincoln in Chicago, about the Declaration of Independence applying to everyone. Then Douglas stated that when Lincoln was seeking votes and speaking in the southern part of the state, he contradicted himself by saying whites were superior. In presenting his own views, Douglas stated that the American government "was made by white men for the benefit of white men and their posterity forever." As for people of African descent, Douglas stated "it does not follow by any means that he should be a slave." Douglas saw them as inferiors, who could not be citizens but should be given basic rights. Douglas ended by criticizing Lincoln's desire that the national government mandate the country "become all one thing or all the other," knowing that Lincoln meant that slavery should end. Having listened to Douglas' remarks, Lincoln began by clearly stating that he believed the Declaration of Independence did apply to everyone. Lincoln denied that his speeches were different, in his remarks on race, in different parts of the state. Rather Lincoln charged that Douglas tried to avoid being linked with the Democrats in the South. Lincoln denied any major differences among his speeches, but affirmed that politically "the inferior races are our equals." This indicates that Lincoln was a man of the nineteenth century, not the twenty-first. Lincoln accepted that there were differences between blacks and whites, but was open to new possibilities—as he stated, "I have never manifested any impatience with the necessities that spring from the actual presence of black people amongst us." He was willing to let slavery continue in the South, but stated that in other states and territories it should not be introduced, but that freedom and liberty should be the norm, based upon the historical precedent of seeking "life, liberty, and the pursuit of happiness." For 1858, this interpretation of the Declaration of Independence was very liberal. Looking a few years into the future, this point was the most important one within the speech, as it was seen by the Southern states as an indicator that when president, Lincoln would work to totally end slavery, even though he had said it could remain in the South.

Douglas had also charged that the Republican Party was a sectional party, with strength only in the North. Lincoln did not dispute that, but made the claim it was because the people in the South did not allow the Republicans to organize, and also stated that in the near future the Democratic Party would be a sectional party, meaning it would be basically only in the South. Lincoln also disputed with Douglas that the bills establishing the New Mexico and Utah Territories were a pattern which was, or even should have been, followed in the Kansas-Nebraska Act. Lincoln asserted that since New Mexico and Utah were set up as part of a compromise, they were a special case. Also, the bills said the territories could vote to apply as a slave or Free State, but said nothing about them as a territory. The Kansas-Nebraska Act did make the territories open for slavery. Lincoln continued to attack Douglas on the statement Douglas had made many times: Douglas did not "care whether slavery is voted up or down." This meant, Lincoln charged, that Douglas did not see slavery as something which was wrong. Lincoln, on the other hand, made it clear that he was one who saw "slavery as a moral, social and political evil." Lincoln also denied that the Illinois Republicans were working with the National Democratic Party, as was believed by some because of the 1854 Senate race. This was part of the reason some people would believe Douglas' charge. Lincoln completed his speech by dealing with the source of the radical 1854 statements on slavery and then commenting upon the Dred Scott case in such a way as to make it clear that he did not accept the verdict. Lincoln said that the reasoning used in the case was not wrong; rather, the premise that the Constitution guaranteed the right to own slaves was incorrect.

Lincoln charged that Douglas' openness to slavery was more than just letting people choose, Douglas' acceptance of slavery and his support of the Dred Scott decision meant, in Lincoln's opinion that Douglas was "preparing . . . the way for making the institution of slavery national!" In addition, Lincoln depicted Douglas as supporting the enlargement of the United States into Mexico and beyond, not just to meet the needs of its citizens but, more important, to gain "additional slave fields." Lincoln depicted Douglas as upholding slavery in such a way that even Illinois, as a free state, would not be safe from slaveholders moving into the state in the future. He asserted that allowing Douglas to return to the Senate and continue to implement his political views, would not only hinder attempts to limit slavery, but could lead to the destruction of the nation.

Essential Themes

Lincoln concluded his speech at Galesburg with the statement, "this slavery question has been the only one that has ever endangered our Republican institutions—the only one that has ever threatened or menaced a dissolution of the Union—that has ever disturbed us in such a way as to make us fear for the perpetuity of our liberty." Because this issue was the focus of national politics, it was also the focus for the races to be a part of the national government. Stephen A. Douglas had been a leader not only in the Democratic Party, but also among those who had tried to seek out compromises on the issue in order to keep the nation unified. Throughout the debates he continually asserted that the people in each individual territory or state should make their own decision about slavery. He believed that in this way the recent Dred Scott ruling could be ignored and the North and South could remain together. In this way, he also believed that he could be victorious in his bid to return to the Senate. Lincoln saw slavery as a "moral evil" which ultimately should be banned. Although he was enough of a realist to know that nothing could be done about it in the current slave states, he was insistent that it should not be allowed to spread any further. His message of the equality of all people, framed within the words of the Declaration of Independence, was one which he hoped would resonate with voters and allow him to enter the Senate. Although Douglas, and his supporters, won this contest, the publication of the debates and their national distribution gave the two men the stature which would enable them to both be nominated for president two years later.

—*Donald A. Watt, PhD*

Bibliography and Additional Reading

C-SPAN American History TV. *Lincoln-Douglas Debate Reenactment*. Washington, D.C.: National Cable Satellite Corporation, 2011. Web.

Civil War Research Engine. *House Divided: Lincoln-Douglas Debates Digital Classroom*. Carlisle, Penn.: Dickinson College, 2010. Web. 6 Oct. 2013.

Guelzo, Allen C. *Lincoln and Douglas: The Debates that Defined America*. New York: Simon & Schuster, 2008. Print.

Holzer, Harold, ed. *The Lincoln-Douglas Debates: The First Complete, Unexpurgated Text*. New York: Fordham UP, 2004. Print.

Johannsen, Robert Walter. *Stephen A. Douglas*. New York: Oxford UP, 1997 ed. Print.

LincolnNet. *The Lincoln/Douglas Debates of 1858*. Lincoln Library, Northern Illinois U, 2002. Web. 6 Oct. 2013.

National Park Service. *The Lincoln-Douglas Debates of 1858*. Washington: Department of the Interior, 2013. Web. 30 Sept. 2013.

Winkle, Kenneth J. *The Young Eagle: The Rise of Abraham Lincoln*. Dallas: Taylor, 2001. Print.

THE SENATORIAL TAPSTER.

CUSTOMER.—I NOTICE YOU DRAW YOUR ALE VERY MILD NOW, WILLIAM.

LANDLORD SEWARD.—YES, THIS IS A NEW TAP, SOME I BREWED MYSELF LAST WEDNESDAY ; MY CUSTOMERS THOUGHT THE ROCHESTER ALE WAS RATHER TOO STRONG.

In this March 1860 cartoon, Seward brews "mild beer" in his February 29, 1860 address to position himself as a moderate after the "irrepressible conflict" speech. Henry Louis Stephens, The Senatorial Tapster. Vanity Fair Volume 1, 1860

■ On the Irrepressible Conflict

Date: October 25, 1858
Author: William H. Seward
Genre: Speech

Summary Overview

This document is an excerpt from a speech the Republican Senator William H. Seward delivered in Rochester, New York, on October 25, 1858. He portrayed the United States as a nation divided between regions based on free and slave systems of labor, regions he predicted would inevitably clash. In what quickly became known as his "On the Irrepressible Conflict" speech, Seward voiced the fears of Northern Republicans who were wary of the expansion of the Southern Slave Power, articulated the free-labor worldview that had developed in the North by the 1850s, and even posed the opening argument in the later debate among historians over the inevitability of the American Civil War.

Defining Moment

By the 1850s, Seward was more radical on the issue of slavery than most Northerners, who typically only wanted to ban slavery in the territories. For instance, during the debate over the Compromise of 1850, which extended the line of the 1820 Missouri Compromise between slave and free territories all the way to California, Seward delivered an inflammatory speech on the floor of the Senate. He declared that the Constitution opposed slavery, believed Congress should ban slavery in the territories, and portrayed slavery as a threat to democracy. One of his statements, delivered in his March 11, 1850, speech "Freedom in the New Territories," that "there is a higher law than the Constitution," especially triggered Southern animosity since, as historian Sean Wilentz notes, a Northerner seemed to be invoking extralegal religious sentiment as justification for a potential end to slavery. Moving through the National Republican, Anti-Masonic, Whig, and Republican parties throughout the antebellum period, Seward consistently sought to combat immorality and aristocracy in politics. Furthermore, in his eyes, the system of slavery corrupted American politics, specifically through the Democratic Party. When deep fissures over the opening of further territories to the ex-pansion of slavery under the 1854 Kansas-Nebraska Act destroyed the Whig Party, Seward enthusiastically helped the nascent Republican Party establish itself in New York in late 1855. Long before his most famous speech, "On the Irrepressible Conflict," Seward's readiness to combat slavery formed from his involvement in the Protestant religious fervor of the Second Great Awakening, the subsequent Protestant reform societies, and the political parties that favored stronger government intervention in economic and social matters. As an indication of his consistent and in fact deepening antislavery sentiments, when he learned of the Supreme Court's 1857 decision in *Dred Scott v. Sandford*, which in part declared the Missouri Compromise of 1820 unconstitutional and opened up the entire West to slavery, Seward delivered a blistering harangue against the decision in the Senate.

Thus, by 1858, Northerners loved Seward for his consistent antislavery stance and his remarkably articulate and passionate speeches. Unsurprisingly, Southerners despised him. Therefore, after winning a new six-year term in the Senate in 1854, he went on the campaign trail in the North in 1858 to bolster support for his fellow Republican candidates. At the front of a packed Corinthian Hall in Rochester, New York, on October 25, 1858, Seward delivered what would become his most famous speech against what Republicans by then termed the "Slave Power." As usual, many Northern Republicans embraced the speech and Democrats in both the North and South lambasted Seward as a warmonger, an agitator who would cause slaves to rise in rebellion, and a threat to slavery itself. For instance, the *New York Herald-Tribune* labeled him an "arch agitator" and said he was one of the "more dangerous" abolitionists. Antislavery abolitionists praised the speech, but moderate papers such as the *New York Times* suggested his language was dangerous. Southerners viewed Seward's speech as further evidence that the central objective of the new Republican Party was the elimination of slavery. While Seward had not explicitly mentioned ending slavery where it existed, his portrayal of an inevitable conflict suggested that soon slavery itself would become the target of the Republican Party. In the minds of Southerners, the Republicans would only need to take a small step from objecting to the expansion of slavery into the territories, which they openly did in the late 1850s, to seeking to destroy slavery everywhere in the United States. Indeed, the primary trigger to South Carolinian, and broadly Southern, secession was that in 1860, Republican leader Abraham Lincoln won the presidency without a single Southern electoral vote. With the slaveholding states now a permanent minority in the United States, Southerners believed they could no longer protect themselves from a North dominated by the Republican Party, led by men such as Seward, that would likely, Southerners believed, target their peculiar institution for elimination.

Author Biography

After Abraham Lincoln, William Seward was one of the most important Northern Republicans of the Civil War era. Seward was born in 1801 into a wealthy family in rural Orange County, New York. Although his family initially owned a few slaves, he came to dislike slavery, and the family's slaves gained their freedom as New York slowly ended the institution during the early 1800s. After graduating from Union College in Schenectady, he became a lawyer and settled in Auburn, New York, where he joined a law practice and married Frances Miller, the daughter of the senior partner in his firm.

Seward soon became involved in the rough-and-tumble politics of antebellum New York, leaving the short-lived National Republican Party for the Anti-Masonic Party when the latter formed in the late 1820s. Despite his wealthy upbringing and comfortable income, Seward was attracted to any movement he deemed moral at its

core, as the Anti-Masons seemed to be in their determination to combat what they saw as the corrupt influence of Freemasons in politics and government. By the mid-1830s, however, Seward moved to the Whig Party because, as Wilentz writes, he "envisaged government as a lever for commercial improvement and as a weapon to combat social ills, from crime in the cities to inadequate schooling in the countryside" (482–83). Thus, Seward's belief in the utility of government both to expand economic opportunity and to reform society placed him firmly on an ideological trajectory that during the antebellum period would find him in the National Republican, Anti-Mason, Whig, and then Republican parties. These political movements generally believed government should aid in the construction of infrastructure such as canals, railroads, and national roads and should also provide funds and legislation to aid the social-reform movements emerging from the Second Great Awakening of the early nineteenth century. The latter included the temperance movement, poor relief, and abolitionism, among others.

Running as a Whig, Seward was elected governor of New York in 1838 and reelected two years later, but he faced opposition from both the Democratic Party and conservatives in his own party who did not like his reform agenda. Next, Seward was elected to the U.S. Senate in the tumultuous year of 1849 when the nation was deciding how to treat the vast new territory acquired from Mexico. He would remain in Congress first as a Whig and then a Republican, until Lincoln appointed him secretary of state in early 1861. In that position, he presided over the purchase of Alaska from Russia in 1867. He also constructed a grand vision for the expansion of American power into the Pacific and the Caribbean that would not be realized until the very end of the nineteenth century. He retired in 1869 and died on October 10, 1872.

HISTORICAL DOCUMENT

The unmistakable outbreaks of zeal which occur all around me show that you are earnest men—and such a man am I. Let us, therefore, at least for a time, pass all secondary and collateral questions, whether of a personal or of a general nature, and consider the main subject of the present canvass. The Democratic Party, or, to speak

more accurately, the party which wears that attractive name—is in possession of the federal government. The Republicans propose to dislodge that party, and dismiss it from its high trust.

The main subject, then, is whether the Democratic Party deserves to retain the confidence of the American people. In attempting to prove it unworthy, I think that I am not actuated by prejudices against that party, or by prepossessions in favor of its adversary; for I have learned, by some experience, that virtue and patriotism, vice and selfishness, are found in all parties, and that they differ less in their motives than in the policies they pursue.

Our country is a theatre, which exhibits, in full operation, two radically different political systems; the one resting on the basis of servile or slave labor, the other on voluntary labor of freemen. The laborers who are enslaved are all negroes, or persons more or less purely of African derivation. But this is only accidental. The principle of the system is, that labor in every society, by whomsoever performed, is necessarily unintellectual, groveling and base; and that the laborer, equally for his own good and for the welfare of the State, ought to be enslaved. The white laboring man, whether native or foreigner, is not enslaved, only because he cannot, as yet, be reduced to bondage . . .

The slave system is one of constant danger, distrust, suspicion, and watchfulness. It debases those whose toil alone can produce wealth and resources for defense, to the lowest degree of which human nature is capable, to guard against mutiny and insurrection, and thus wastes energies which otherwise might be employed in national development and aggrandizement. The free-labor system educates all alike, and by opening all the fields of industrial employment and all the departments of authority, to the unchecked and equal rivalry of all classes of men, at once secures universal contentment, and brings into the highest possible activity all the physical, moral, and social energies of the whole state. In states where the slave system prevails, the masters, directly or indirectly, secure all political power, and constitute a ruling aristocracy. In states where the free-labor system prevails, universal suffrage necessarily obtains, and the state inevitably becomes, sooner or later, a republic or democracy . . .

Hitherto, the two systems have existed in different States, but side by side within the American Union. This has happened because the Union is a confederation of States. But in another aspect the United States constitute only one nation. Increase of population, which is filling the States out to their very borders, together with a new and extended network of railroads and other avenues, and an internal commerce which daily becomes more intimate, is rapidly bringing the States into a higher and more perfect social unity or consolidation. Thus, these antagonistic systems are continually coming into closer contact, and collision results . . .

Unlike too many of those who in modern time invoke their authority, they had a choice between the two. They preferred the system of free labor, and they determined to organize the government, and so direct its activity, that that system should surely and certainly prevail. For this purpose, and no other, they based the whole structure of the government broadly on the principle that all men are created equal, and therefore free—little dreaming that, within the short period of one hundred years, their descendants would bear to be told by any orator, however popular, that the utterance of that principle was merely a rhetorical rhapsody; or by any judge, however venerated, that it was attended by mental reservation, which rendered it hypocritical and false . . .

It remains to say on this point only one word, to guard against misapprehension. If these States are to again become universally slaveholding, I do not pretend to say with what violations of the constitution that end shall be accomplished. On the other hand, while I do confidently believe and hope that my country will yet become a land of universal freedom, I do not expect that it will be made so otherwise than through the action of the several States co-operating with the federal government, and all acting in strict conformity with their respective constitutions.

The strife and contentions concerning slavery, which gently disposed persons so habitually deprecate, are nothing more than the ripening of the conflict which the fathers themselves not only thus regarded with favor, but which they may be said to have instituted.

It is not to be denied, however, that thus far the course of that contest has not been according to their humane anticipations and wishes. In the field of federal politics, slavery, deriving unlooked-for advantages from commercial changes, and energies unforeseen from the facilities of combination between members of the slaveholding class and between that class and other property classes, early rallied, and has at length made a stand, not merely to retain its original defensive position, but to extend its sway throughout the whole Union. It is certain that the slaveholding class of American citizens indulge this high ambition, and that they derive encouragement for it from the rapid and effective political successes which they have already obtained. The plan of operation is this: By continued appliances of patronage and threats of disunion, they will keep a majority favorable to these designs in the Senate, where each State has an equal representation.

Through that majority they will defeat, as they best can, the admission of free States and secure the admission of slave States. Under the protection of the judiciary, they will, on the principle of the Dred Scott case, carry slavery into all the territories of the United States now existing and hereafter to be organized. By the action of the President and Senate, using the treaty-making power, they will annex foreign slaveholding States. In a favorable conjuncture they will induce Congress to repeal the act of 1808 which prohibits the foreign slave trade, and so they will import from Africa, at a cost of only twenty dollars a head, slaves enough to fill up the interior of the continent. Thus relatively increasing the number of slave States, they will allow no amendment to the constitution prejudicial to their interest; and so, having permanently established their power, they expect the federal judiciary to nullify all State laws which shall interfere with internal or foreign commerce in slaves. When the free States shall be sufficiently demoralized to tolerate these designs, they reasonably conclude that slavery will be accepted by those States themselves.

I shall not stop to show how speedy or how complete would be the ruin which the accomplishment of these slaveholding schemes would bring upon the country. For one, I should not remain in the country to test the sad experiment. Having spent my manhood, though not my whole life, in a free State, no aristocracy of any kind, much less an aristocracy of slaveholders, shall ever make the laws of the land in which I shall be content to live. Having seen the society around me universally engaged in agriculture, manufactures, and trade, which were innocent and beneficent, I shall never be a denizen of a State where men and women are reared as cattle, and bought and sold as merchandise.

When that evil day shall come, and all further effort at resistance shall be impossible, then, if there shall be no better hope for redemption than I can now foresee, I shall say with Franklin, while looking abroad over the whole earth for a new and more congenial home, "Where

liberty dwells, there is my country."

You will tell me that these fears are extravagant and chimerical. I answer, they are so; but they are so only because the designs of the slaveholders must and can be defeated. But it is only the possibility of defeat that renders them so. They cannot be defeated by inactivity. There is no escape from them compatible with nonresistance. How, then, and in what way, shall the necessary resistance be made? There is only one way. The Democratic Party must be permanently dislodged from the government.

The reason is, that the Democratic Party is inextricably committed to the designs of the slaveholders, which I have described. Let me be well understood. I do not charge that the Democratic candidates for public office now before the people are pledged to—much less that the Democratic masses who support them really adopt—those atrocious and dangerous designs. Candidates may, and generally do, mean to act justly, wisely, and patriotically, when they shall be elected; but they become the ministers and servants, not the dictators, of the power which elects them. The policy which a party shall pursue at a future period is only gradually developed, depending on the occurrence of events never fully foreknown. The motives of men, whether acting as electors or in any other capacity, are generally pure.

Nevertheless, it is not more true that "hell is paved with good intentions," than it is that earth is covered with wrecks resulting from innocent and amiable motives.

The very constitution of the Democratic Party commits it to execute all the designs of the slaveholders, whatever they may be. It is not a party of the whole Union, of all the free States and of all the slave States; nor yet is it a party of the free States in the North and in the Northwest; but it is a sectional and local party, having practically its seat within the slave States, and counting its constituency chiefly and almost exclusively there. Of all its representatives in Congress and in the electoral colleges, two-thirds uniformly come from these States. Its great element of strength lies in the vote of the slaveholders, augmented by the representation of three-fifths of the slaves. Deprive the Democratic party of this strength, and it would be a helpless and hopeless minority, incapable of continued organization. The Democratic Party, being thus local and sectional, acquires new strength from the admission of ever new slave State, and loses relatively by the admission of every new free State into the Union . . .

This dark record shows you, fellow-citizens, what I was unwilling to announce at an earlier stage of this argument, that of the whole nefarious schedule of slave-holding designs which I have submitted to you, the Democratic Party has left only one yet to be consummated—the abrogation of the law which forbids the African slave-trade.

I know—few, I think, know better than I—the resources and energies of the Democratic Party, which is identical with the slave power. I do ample justice to its traditional popularity. I know further—few, I think, know better than I—the difficulties and disadvantages of organizing a new political force, like the Republican Party, and the obstacles it must encounter in laboring without prestige and without patronage. But, understanding all this, I know that the Democratic Party must go down, and that the Republican Party must rise into its place. The Democratic Party derived its strength, originally, from its adoption of the principles of equal and exact justice to all men. So long as it practiced this principle faithfully it was invulnerable.

It became vulnerable when it renounced the principle, and since that time it has maintained itself, not by virtue of its own strength, or even of its traditional merits, but because there as yet had appeared in the political field no other party that had the conscience and the courage to take up, and avow, and practice the life-inspiring principle which the Democratic party had surrendered. At last, the Republican Party has appeared.

It avows, now, as the Republican party of 1800 did, in one word, its faith and its works, "Equal and exact justice to all men." Even when it first entered the field, only half organized, it struck a blow which only just failed to secure complete and triumphant victory. In this, its second campaign, it has already won advantages which render that triumph now both easy and certain.

The secret of its assured success lies in that very characteristic which, in the mouth of scoffers, constitutes its great and lasting imbecility and reproach. It lies in the fact that it is a party of one idea; but that is a noble one—an idea that fills and expands all generous souls; the idea of equality—the equality of all men before human tribunals and human laws, as they all are equal before the divine tribunal and divine laws.

I know, and you know, that a revolution has begun. I know, and all the world knows, that revolutions never go backward. Twenty senators and a hundred representatives proclaim boldly in Congress to-day sentiments and opinions and principles of freedom which hardly so many men, even in this free State, dared to utter in their own homes twenty years ago. While the government of the United States, under the conduct of the Democratic party, has been all that time surrendering one plain and castle after another to slavery, the people of the United States have been no less steadily and perseveringly gathering together the forces with which to recover back again all the fields and all the castles which have been lost, and to confound and overthrow, by one decisive blow, the betrayers of the constitution and freedom forever.

GLOSSARY

aggrandizement: an increase in size or stature

chimerical: illusory

derivation: descent, lineage

Dred Scott case: *Dred Scott v. Sandford* (1857), a Supreme Court decision that favored the rights of slave owners

fathers: in this case, the Founding Fathers of the United States slave power: term used by Northerners to describe what they saw as the threatening political power of Southern slaveholders

universal suffrage: voting rights for all adult citizens

Document Analysis

To Seward, two completely divergent societies had come into being in the United States. Opposite sources of labor had created "two radically different political systems," one free and the other slave. This was quite a drastic portrayal of the increasingly sharp and violent sectional divide that was plaguing the United States. Most American leaders in the 1850s, both in the North and the South, still emphasized the ideals Americans had in common, including belief in the Constitution, liberty, private property, individual rights, and the voting franchise, for white men at least. Of course, some abolitionists argued the Constitution was in fact an evil, proslavery document, but such voices constituted a minority of Northerners even up to the advent of the Civil War. Seward, however, viewed the situation differently. He portrayed the North and the South as two different societies based on two different economic systems, constituted by two different systems of labor, and that would soon clash. His arguments echoed the warnings of other Republicans that the expansion of the Slave Power threatened Northern white rights, but his clear, hard-hitting style and clever phrasing helped his words stick in the minds of his audience. In addition, the inevitability of a coming conflict seemed alarmingly new to both Northerners and Southerners.

While setting up the initial framework for his argument, Seward described Southern slavery in an interesting way. He noted its racial character but also claimed that "this is only accidental." He argued that the very nature of the slave system required workers, of any race, to be enslaved for the good of society and then hinted this meant that whites could soon find themselves under the yoke of slavery as well. Claiming the white man "cannot, as yet, be reduced to bondage," indicated his fear that the slave-owning aristocracy of the South might one day place whites in chains to serve their own purposes. Seward saw slavery as fundamentally unconcerned with race. He believed the South had only adopted African slaves because of the particular nature of American history. Therefore, Seward was subtly warning his white audience that the Slave Power and the system of slavery in the South could one day threaten their rights. By claiming this threat to white rights, Seward was contributing to the already well-established Republican argument that the Slave Power threatened the rights of Northern white men. Expansion of slavery into the territories, Republicans argued, would keep whites from the opportunity and freedom they sought. Events such as the gag rule in Congress during the late 1830s and early 1840s, when speaking of slavery was officially prohibited, and the Fugitive Slave Act of 1850, which required Northerners to help Southern slave catchers or face fines or imprisonment, seemed to threaten Northern whites' freedom, claimed Republicans throughout the 1850s. Thus, Seward's speech tapped into the ongoing Republican argument that slavery was not merely an issue contained in the South. The system threatened to expand nationally and trample white rights.

In addition to warning of the threats to white freedom, Seward argued that slavery undermined the economic opportunity of individual whites and slowed the economic growth of the nation as a whole. Seward pointed out that to maintain the system of slavery, whites had "to guard against mutiny and insurrection, and thus [slavery] wastes energies which otherwise might be employed in national development and aggrandizement." The slave system not only threatened to trample on the rights of whites but also made whites into guardsmen and robbed the entire nation of their potential economic productivity. For Seward, the free labor system he and the Republican Party advocated was far superior. In such a system, individual farmers and workers gained direct profit from their hard work and simultaneously contributed to national wealth and development. In such a free-labor system, human capacities were unleashed for good purposes and all men, in theory, could receive equal education and be equal in politics. On the contrary, in the slave system, according to Seward, "the masters, directly or indirectly, secure all political power, and constitute a ruling aristocracy." Seward was not completely correct, because while large landowners often held political office, most white men in the South from any class did have the franchise and therefore could vote for their desired candidate. Returning the Southern elite to office repeatedly indicated that the rest of the Southern white male population often agreed with the goals, arguments, and views of their slaveholding neighbors. For instance, the Southern states would declare secession in 1860 and 1861 through special conventions to which delegates were democratically elected. In some places in the South, property-holding requirements for voting remained in place, and more commonly, owning land was required to hold office; however, compared to the rest of the world in the mid-nineteenth century, the South was a relatively democratic political system, for white men at least. Thus, Seward's attempt to portray a conflict between a democracy and an aristocracy was not entirely accurate, although it played well to Northern audiences. In addition, while the South was democratic in nature, this simply meant the entire white population, even non-slave-holders, supported the institution of slavery.

For Seward, the conflict between two fundamentally divergent social systems had reached a decision point. Because of a growing populace, the economic expansion the United States had experienced in the previous decades, and the internal improvements that Whigs and then Republicans championed (such as national roads, railroads, and canals), "these antagonistic systems are continually coming into closer contact, and collision results." Although slavery and free labor had existed separately for a while, the two systems were interacting more closely. For Seward, the remarkable growth the United States had experienced during the first half of the nineteenth century in terms of the development of infrastructure, the expansion and integration of regional and national markets, and new achievements in travel and communications, including the train and the telegraph, was creating a crisis situation in which the slave and free-labor societies were beginning to clash and to maneuver for expansion into the newly acquired territories from Mexico and to gain control, at each other's expense, of states that already existed. The market, communications, and transportation revolutions of the antebellum period, identified and given causal strength by various historians, seemed to Seward to be forcing the American population to make a decision about what type of society the United States would be in the future.

Seward then enlisted the original founders of the United States in support of his arguments. Seward seemed to believe that the Constitution was antislavery in nature. Thus, the Founding Fathers had intended that slavery would wither away and die. He even noted that the deep divisions over slavery Americans witnessed during the 1850s were actually a logical extension of the "conflict which the fathers themselves not only thus regarded with favor, but which they may be said to have instituted." Did Seward mean the first generation of American statesmen had intended to create such deep sectional strife? On the contrary, Seward believed the Founding Fathers had assumed that by constructing a Constitution and a political system based on equality, slavery would die a natural death. Unfortunately, said Seward, "thus far the course of that contest has not been according to their humane anticipations and wishes." Without noting the actual crop, cotton, that produced the deepening hold of slavery in the South during the antebellum decades, Seward spoke

of the "commercial changes" that had created the cotton empire in the southern United States. Indeed, few Americans in the late eighteenth century had predicted the switch from tobacco to cotton in the South that subsequently produced an agricultural system centered on one of the most profitable raw materials in the world at the time. Seward's point, however, was that the Founding Fathers' intention for slavery was for it to end slowly and quietly through the extension of the ideals of freedom and free labor. Economic changes, however, had helped prevent such an extinction of the peculiar institution.

Seward pointed out that those who benefited from the slave system also actively protected it. Seward first mentioned "the rapid and effective political successes which they have already obtained," which invoked a number of Northern resentments against the South that stemmed from the nation's antebellum political history. The three-fifths clause of the Constitution, whereby a slave counted as three-fifths of a person for purposes of state representation in the House of Representatives and the Electoral College, had long given the Southern states, especially Virginia, a political advantage in national elections. For instance, between 1788 and 1828, only one non-Virginian held the presidency: John Adams of Massachusetts, from 1796 to 1800. Such Southern control of the White House, and often of Congress, had created animosity among Northerners because of the way the South used the people they oppressed to further their own political control.

Seward then voiced the increasing fear held by Republicans and Northerners throughout the 1850s that the Slave Power would extend its sway into all the western territories. In fact, blocking the extension of slavery into the territories was the central organizing principle of the Republican Party in the 1850s. While the Compromise of 1850 had extended westward the line between slave and free states of the original Missouri Compromise of 1820, the 1854 Kansas-Nebraska Act had opened up vast areas in the northern plains and northern Rockies to the possibility of slavery. Seward also condemned "the principle of the Dred Scott case." In 1857, the Supreme Court had not only declared the former slave Dred Scott to not be a person but also had also ruled that the original Missouri Compromise was unconstitutional, thus threatening to, as Seward put it, "carry slavery into all the territories of the United States now existing and hereafter to be organized." Throughout the 1850s, Northerners came to believe that the Slave Power of the South intended to expand slavery into the entire area of the old Louisiana

Purchase and the newly acquired regions from Mexico. Halting such expansion was a core goal of the Republican Party, and Seward warned his constituents that dire consequences would result if they were unsuccessful in that objective.

Seward went on to warn that the slaveholders would reopen the international slave trade and abuse the power of the federal and state courts to allow slavery wherever they wanted. He even claimed that one day "when the free States shall be sufficiently demoralized to tolerate these designs, they reasonably conclude that slavery will be accepted by those States themselves." Thus, Seward went even farther than most Republican leaders and tried to convince his listeners that even their very freedom in their own home states was at stake in blocking the Democrats and the Slave Power. Seward then passionately declared that he would never live in a place controlled by an "aristocracy of any kind, much less an aristocracy of slaveholders" and claimed he would travel the world in search of such a free place. He was hinting that there actually was no such place in the world at the time other than the United States and was thus portraying the liberty found in the United States, at least in the North, according to him, as an experiment of historical importance for humanity. Indeed, in the mid-nineteenth century, few places in the world valued individual and property rights as highly as the United States, and most Americans, while they continued to be wary of direct involvement in the affairs of nations across the oceans, wanted the world to see the country as a beacon of liberty and freedom. Seward was suggesting that slavery undermined the historical importance of the United States.

Much of what Seward said during his speech seemed alarmist. He had accused the slaveholders of subverting the Constitution, of wanting to reopen the Atlantic slave trade, of oppressing their fellow white citizens, and of threatening to extend slavery even into the free states. When he addressed the charge that "these fears are extravagant and chimerical," he openly admitted "they are so." He did not hide the fact he was trying to scare his audience, but he was doing so, he claimed, "because the designs of the slaveholders must and can be defeated." In order to combat such a powerful enemy, Seward believed, he had to warn of the potentially dire consequences that could result from further electoral victories by the Democrats. He claimed "inactivity" and "non-resistance" were not options, since such courses of action would only aid in the Slave Power's oppression of Northern whites. The solution for Seward was Republican electoral victory. He

mentioned that many Democratic officeholders and the population who supported the Democrats were not at fault, although this seemed to contradict much of what he had already said in his speech. He claimed the elite slaveholders had hijacked the Democratic Party for their own evil designs. He argued the Democrats were a "sectional and local party" and needed to be confined to the South and not permitted to expand elsewhere. If slavery expanded into the western territories, new slave states would be added to the nation, which would augment the power of the slave states in Congress. To Seward, the Democrats had "renounced the principle" of "equal and exact justice to all men" that had been the original central idea of the party. According to Seward, the Republicans should carry the banner of "the idea of equality—the equality of all men before human tribunals and human laws, as they are all equal before the divine tribunal and divine laws." Seward declared this idea a "revolution" and claimed the Republicans would emerge victorious because "revolutions never go backward." The above excerpt ended with heated words against the Democrats. Seward believed the clash between the slave states and free states, between the Republicans and Democrats, indeed between freedom and equality on one hand and aristocracy and oppression on the other, was now an inevitable "irrepressible conflict."

Essential Themes

One of the central debates in the study of the Civil War focuses on whether or not the United States could have avoided such a bloody showdown. Seward issued the opening salvo in that debate even before the Civil War occurred. Historian Kenneth M. Stampp, in *The Imperiled Union* (1980), has noted, "After the Civil War Seward's concept of an irrepressible conflict involving issues of fundamental importance became, in various forms, the predominant view among historians of the sectional crisis" (193). While some historians and politicians argued the tragedy could have been averted, many more adopted Seward's view that, because of the central moral issues involved in slavery, the war had been unavoidable. While modern historians hold mixed views on the inevitability of the war, Seward's conception of the sectional struggle cast a long shadow over the work of historians into the early part of the twentieth century. Although Stampp, in *And the War Came* (1964), notes that Seward "himself vigorously denied the inevitability of the war when the final crisis came" (2–3), his 1858 speech has remained a classic statement of the position that the Civil War would one day arrive, and was always going to happen, as long as slavery remained in the United States.

Thus, Seward's speech not only contributed to Republican electoral victories in 1858 but also helped frame one of the debates about the coming of the Civil War. In addition, the excerpt above provides a window into the minds of many Northern Republicans during the 1850s, as they feared the expansion of the Slave Power into the territories and worried what the expansion of slavery meant for Northern white rights. While Seward was a bit more radical than the average Northerner, he nevertheless addressed many of their concerns when he rose to speak in Rochester in October 1858. Therefore, his speech was either widely praised or condemned in his contemporary context because he clearly spelled out the Northern Republican worldview. His speech remains an important part of the discussion of the onset of the Civil War, because of his clear stance on the "irrepressible" and inevitable nature of a coming conflict between economic, social, and political systems based on either slave labor or free labor. Thus, he was a part of the events surrounding the Civil War, and his views and speech have contributed to the ongoing discussion of those events up to the present.

—*Kevin E. Grimm, PhD*

Bibliography and Additional Reading

Bancroft, Frederic. *The Life of William Henry Seward.* Vol. 1. New York: Harper, 1900. Print.

Foner, Eric. *Free Soil, Free Labor, Free Men: The Ideology of the Republican Party before the Civil War.* New York: Oxford UP, 1995. Print.

Goodwin, Doris Kearns. *Team of Rivals: The Political Genius of Abraham Lincoln.* New York: Simon & Schuster, 2005. Print.

Herring, George C. *From Colony to Superpower: US Foreign Relations since 1776.* New York: Oxford UP, 2008. Print.

Howe, Daniel Walker. *What Hath God Wrought: The Transformation of America, 1815–1848.* New York: Oxford UP, 2007. Print.

McPherson, James M. *Battle Cry of Freedom: The Civil War Era.* New York: Oxford UP, 1988. Print.

Rozwenc, Edwin C. *The Causes of the American Civil War.* 2nd ed. Lexington, MA: Heath, 1972. Print.

Sellers, Charles S. *The Market Revolution: Jacksonian America, 1815–1846.* New York: Oxford UP, 1991. Print.

Stampp, Kenneth M. *And the War Came: The North and the Secession Crisis, 1860–61.* Chicago: U of Chicago P, 1964. Print.

———., ed. *The Causes of the Civil War.* Englewood Cliffs, NJ: Prentice, 1965. Print.

———. *The Imperiled Union: Essays on the Background of the Civil War.* New York: Oxford UP, 1980. Print.

Wilentz, Sean. *The Rise of American Democracy: Jefferson to Lincoln.* New York: Norton, 2005. Print.

■ Cooper Union Address

Date: February 27, 1860
Author: Abraham Lincoln
Genre: Speech; political sermon

Summary Overview

February 27, 1860, was a cold, snowy day in New York City. Still, many spectators enthusiastically braved the weather to come to the Cooper Union for the Advancement of Science and Art, also called the Cooper Institute. Their object was to hear a speaker from Illinois, Abraham Lincoln, known as a spellbinding western orator who had bested Stephen Douglas in debates for the Senate two years before. Now these sophisticated New Yorkers wanted to see Lincoln in action. More than just private individuals, there were newspaper reporters and publishers present, and their impressions would shape how many in the North came to view Lincoln.

Lincoln recognized the significance of this moment. He had traveled from Springfield, had purchased a new suit for the occasion, and earlier in the day, he had sat for a picture to be taken by the famous photographer Mathew Brady, an image that could be copied and disseminated far and wide. Lincoln's speech at Cooper Union would include historical analysis about the founding generation's view of slavery expansion, direct addresses to both Southerners and his fellow Republicans, and a ringing defense of the moral rightness—and hence moral power—of opposition to the expansion of slavery.

Defining Moment

Lincoln's address came at a time of growing sectional conflict, contentions within political parties, and tensions in public attitudes. The ongoing question revolved around the treatment of slavery, both in states where it already existed and especially in the new western territories. The Missouri Compromise of 1820 had largely kept this issue off of the table, but in 1854, Senator Stephen A. Douglas's Kansas-Nebraska Act changed how new territories determined the legality of slavery, attempting to base the decision on popular sovereignty, which would allow the settlers in each territory to vote on the issue. When applied in Kansas, the result was disastrous, leading to the violent clash known as Bleeding Kansas, po-

litical disputes over what was truly the popular will, and even violence in Congress, with Democratic representative Preston Brooks caning Republican senator Charles Sumner almost to death. The expansion of slavery into the territories seemed even more certain with the 1857 Supreme Court decision in *Dred Scott v. Sandford*. The court, led by Chief Justice Roger Taney, declared that masters could take slaves into any territory, essentially opening all western territories to slavery. The ruling sparked outrage across the North.

With tensions running high, conditions became even more delicate in the wake of John Brown's raid in October 1859. Brown believed himself divinely inspired to lead a slave revolt and liberate Virginia's slaves through violence. Having practiced violent attacks in Kansas at Pottawatomie Creek, Brown now looked eastward, adopting as his target the federal arsenal at Harpers Ferry, Virginia (now West Virginia). Brown believed that by seizing weapons and arming slaves he would spark a widespread revolt. Brown's plan failed, and he was captured, tried, and executed. To Northern antislavery advocates, Brown was a martyr. To Southerners, he was a madman, inspired by the violent language of abolitionists and "Black Republicans."

Amidst these sectional tensions, discord was also fracturing the national parties. Stephen Douglas still hoped for the Democratic nomination for the 1860 presidential election, which he had been eyeing for years. His candidacy, however, would run into Southern Democratic objections that his popular-sovereignty position was not proslavery enough. By trying to stay neutral, Douglas had alienated Southern radicals, leaving him open to a Southern challenge. Seeing these discords, Republicans might take encouragement for the upcoming election, but their party suffered from the ambitions of many men who might make a claim to the nomination. The leading candidate was William Seward of New York, but some thought him too radical an opponent of slavery to win.

Other politicians, such as Salmon P. Chase of Ohio, Simon Cameron of Pennsylvania, and Edward Bates of Missouri, all had regional followings and could make a claim to lead the Republican Party. Any other challengers would have to prove both articulate and compelling to a diverse Republican base throughout the country.

Author Biography

Abraham Lincoln may be remembered as one of the United States' greatest presidents, but few would have foreseen that future as 1860 began. Lincoln was born in Kentucky on February 12, 1809, and moved with his family to Indiana at age eight. When he was twenty-one, his family moved again, to Illinois. As a young man, he worked a number of physical jobs to build his personal capital, including assembling a flatboat and sailing it to New Orleans. In what would later earn him one of his political nicknames—the Railsplitter—Lincoln and a friend split hundreds of logs to create rails for split-rail fences. After a limited military career during the Black Hawk War, Lincoln owned and worked in a general store in New Salem, Illinois. When the store failed, Lincoln took up law, joining the Illinois bar in 1836. He relocated to Springfield and built a successful legal practice working on both local cases and cases for railroad companies. He married Mary Todd in 1842 and started a family.

During this time, Lincoln began practicing politics. He served multiple terms in the Illinois House of Representatives. Identifying as a Whig—and lionizing Henry Clay—Lincoln even earned one term in the U.S. House of Representatives, serving from 1847 to 1849. He lost support because of his opposition to President James K. Polk's Mexican-American War, which was popular in Illinois. After his one term, he believed he would retire from politics; instead, he was energized by the passage of the Kansas-Nebraska Act, shepherded through Congress by fellow Illinoisan Stephen Douglas, which sought to nullify the Missouri Compromise and open more territory to slavery. Lincoln soon affiliated with the emerging Republican Party.

Lincoln emerged as a national figure in the 1858 Illinois senatorial election, in which he carried the Republican banner against Douglas, who was seeking reelection as preparation for running for president in 1860. Lincoln kicked off the campaign with his fiery "House Divided" speech and soon provoked Douglas into participating in seven debates throughout Illinois. These Lincoln-Douglas debates not only proved important for the Illinois campaign but also sparked national interest. Lincoln's full speeches from the debates were reprinted in newspapers and, when gathered together, became a best-selling booklet. Although Lincoln lost the election— he won a majority of votes but lost because the decision was made by the Democratic-majority Illinois legislature—he saw it as only a momentary setback. In 1859, Lincoln campaigned for Republican candidates throughout the Midwest, including Iowa and Wisconsin. In Ohio, he once again challenged Douglas, who was stumping for Democrats in the state, and gave significant speeches in both Cincinnati and Columbus.

Lincoln's actions in 1858–59 brought him to the attention of eastern Republicans and garnered him the invitation to speak in New York City in February 1860. He was initially scheduled to speak at Henry Ward Beecher's Plymouth Church in Brooklyn, but with the growing interest in Lincoln, the venue was shifted to the auditorium of Cooper Union in Manhattan.

HISTORICAL DOCUMENT

Mr. President and fellow-citizens of New-York:

The facts with which I shall deal this evening are mainly old and familiar; nor is there anything new in the general use I shall make of them. If there shall be any novelty, it will be in the mode of presenting the facts, and the inferences and observations following that presentation. In his speech last autumn, at Columbus, Ohio, as reported in "The New-York Times," Senator Douglas said:

"Our fathers, when they framed the Government under which we live, understood this question just as well, and even better, than we do now."

I fully indorse this, and I adopt it as a text for this discourse. I so adopt it because it furnishes a precise and an agreed starting point for a discussion between Republicans and that wing of the Democracy headed by Senator Douglas. It simply leaves the inquiry: "What was the understanding those fathers had of the question mentioned?"

What is the frame of Government under which we live?

The answer must be: "The Constitution of the United States." That Constitution consists of the original, framed in 1787, (and under which the present government first went into operation,) and twelve subsequently framed amendments, the first ten of which were framed in 1789.

Who were our fathers that framed the Constitution? I suppose the "thirty-nine" who signed the original instrument may be fairly called our fathers who framed that part of the present Government. It is almost exactly true to say they framed it, and it is altogether true to say they fairly represented the opinion and sentiment of the whole nation at that time. Their names, being familiar to nearly all, and accessible to quite all, need not now be repeated.

I take these "thirty-nine" for the present, as being "our fathers who framed the Government under which we live."

What is the question which, according to the text, those fathers understood "just as well, and even better than we do now?"

It is this: Does the proper division of local from federal authority, or anything in the Constitution, forbid *our Federal Government* to control as to slavery in *our Federal Territories?*

Upon this, Senator Douglas holds the affirmative, and Republicans the negative. This affirmation and denial form an issue; and this issue—this question—is precisely what the text declares our fathers understood "better than we."

Let us now inquire whether the "thirty-nine," or any of them, ever acted upon this question; and if they did, how they acted upon it—how they expressed that better understanding?

In 1784, three years before the Constitution—the United States then owning the Northwestern Territory, and no other, the Congress of the Confederation had before them the question of prohibiting slavery in that Territory; and four of the "thirty-nine" who afterward framed the Constitution, were in that Congress, and voted on that question. Of these, Roger Sherman, Thomas Mifflin, and Hugh Williamson voted for the prohibition, thus showing that, in their understanding, no line dividing local from federal authority, nor anything else, properly forbade the Federal Government to control as to slavery in federal territory. The other of the four—James M'Henry—voted against the prohibition, showing that, for some cause, he thought it improper to vote for it. In 1787, still before the Constitution, but while the Convention was in session framing it, and while the Northwestern Territory still was the only territory owned by the United States, the same question of prohibiting slavery in the territory again came before the Congress of the Confederation; and two more of the "thirty-nine" who afterward signed the Constitution, were in that Congress, and voted on the question. They were William Blount and William Few; and they both voted for the prohibition—thus showing that, in their understanding, no line dividing local from federal authority, nor anything else, properly forbids the Federal Government to control as to slavery in Federal territory. This time the prohibition became a law, being part of what is now well known as the Ordinance of '87.

The question of federal control of slavery in the territories, seems not to have been directly before the Convention which framed the original Constitution; and hence it is not recorded that the "thirty-nine," or any of them, while engaged on that instrument, expressed any opinion on that precise question.

In 1789, by the first Congress which sat under the Constitution, an act was passed to enforce the Ordinance of '87, including the prohibition of slavery in the Northwestern Territory. The bill for this act was reported by one of the "thirty-nine," Thomas Fitzsimmons, then a member of the House of Representatives from Pennsylvania. It went through all its stages without a word of opposition, and finally passed both branches without yeas and nays, which is equivalent to an unanimous passage. In this Congress there were sixteen of the thirty-nine fathers who framed the original Constitution. They were John Langdon, Nicholas Gilman, Wm. S. Johnson, Roger Sherman, Robert Morris, Thos. Fitzsimmons, William Few, Abraham Baldwin, Rufus King, William Paterson, George Clymer, Richard Bassett, George Read, Pierce Butler, Daniel Carroll, James Madison.

This shows that, in their understanding, no line dividing local from federal authority, nor anything in the Constitution, properly forbade Congress to prohibit slavery in the federal territory; else both their fidelity to correct principle, and their oath to support the Constitution, would have constrained them to oppose the prohibition . . . . In 1803, the Federal Government purchased the Louisiana country. Our former territorial acquisitions came from certain of our own States; but this Louisiana country was acquired from a foreign nation. In 1804, Congress gave a territorial organization to that part of it which now constitutes the State of Louisiana. New Orleans, lying within that part, was an old and comparatively large city. There were other considerable towns and settlements, and slavery was extensively and thoroughly intermingled with the people. Congress did not, in the Territorial Act, prohibit slavery; but they did interfere with it—take control of it—in a more marked and extensive way than they did in the case of Mississippi. The substance of the provision therein made, in relation to slaves, was:

First. That no slave should be imported into the territory from foreign parts.

Second. That no slave should be carried into it who had been imported into the United States since the first day of May, 1798.

Third. That no slave should be carried into it, except by the owner, and for his own use as a settler; the penalty in all the cases being a fine upon the violator of the law, and freedom to the slave.

This act also was passed without yeas and nays. In the Congress which passed it, there were two of the "thirty-nine." They were Abraham Baldwin and Jonathan Dayton. As stated in the case of Mississippi, it is probable they both voted for it. They would not have allowed it to pass without recording their opposition to it, if, in their understanding, it violated either the line properly dividing local from federal authority, or any provision of the Constitution.

In 1819–20, came and passed the Missouri question. Many votes were taken, by yeas and nays, in both branches of Congress, upon the various phases of the general question. Two of the "thirty-nine"—Rufus King and Charles Pinckney—were members of that Congress. Mr. King steadily voted for slavery prohibition and against all compromises, while Mr. Pinckney as steadily voted against slavery prohibition and against all compromises. By this, Mr. King showed that, in his understanding, no line dividing local from federal authority, nor anything in the Constitution, was violated by Congress prohibiting slavery in federal territory; while Mr. Pinckney, by his votes, showed that, in his understanding, there was some sufficient reason for opposing such prohibition in that case.

The cases I have mentioned are the only acts of the "thirty-nine," or of any of them, upon the direct issue, which I have been able to discover. . . .

The sum of the whole is, that of our thirty-nine fathers who framed the original Constitution, twenty-one—a clear majority of the whole—certainly understood that no proper division of local from federal authority, nor any part of the Constitution, forbade the Federal Government to control slavery in the federal territories; while all the rest probably had the same understanding. Such, unquestionably, was the understanding of our fathers who framed the original Constitution; and the text affirms that they understood the question "better than we."

But, so far, I have been considering the understanding of the question manifested by the framers of the original Constitution. In and by the original instrument, a mode was provided for amending it; and, as I have already stated, the present frame of "the Government under which we live" consists of that original, and twelve amendatory articles framed and adopted since. Those who now insist that federal control of slavery in federal territories violates the Constitution, point us to the provisions which they suppose it thus violates; and, as I understand, they all fix upon provisions in these amendatory articles, and not in the original instrument. The Supreme Court, in the Dred Scott case, plant themselves upon the fifth amendment, which provides that no person shall be deprived of "life, liberty or property without due process of law;" while Senator Douglas and his peculiar adherents plant themselves upon the tenth amendment, providing that "the powers not delegated to the United States by the Constitution," "are reserved to the States respectively, or to the people."

Now, it so happens that these amendments were framed by the first Congress which sat under the Constitution— the identical Congress which passed the act already mentioned, enforcing the prohibition of slavery in the Northwestern Territory. Not only was it the same Congress, but they were the identical, same individual men who, at the same session, and at the same time within the session, had under consideration, and in progress toward maturity, these Constitutional amendments, and this act prohibiting slavery in all the territory the nation then owned. The Constitutional amendments were introduced before, and passed after the act enforcing the Ordinance of '87; so that, during the whole pendency of the act to enforce the Ordinance, the Constitutional amendments were also pending.

The seventy-six members of that Congress, including sixteen of the framers of the original Constitution, as before stated, were pre-eminently our fathers who framed that part of "the Government under which we live," which is now claimed as forbidding the Federal Government to control slavery in the federal territories.

Is it not a little presumptuous in any one at this day to affirm that the two things which that Congress deliberately framed, and carried to maturity at the same time, are absolutely inconsistent with each other? And does not such affirmation become impudently absurd when coupled with the other affirmation from the same mouth, that those who did the two things, alleged to be inconsistent, understood whether they really were inconsistent better than we—better than he who affirms that they are inconsistent?

It is surely safe to assume that the thirty-nine framers of the original Constitution, and the seventy-six members of the Congress which framed the amendments thereto, taken together, do certainly include those who may be fairly called "our fathers who framed the Government under which we live." And so assuming, I defy any man to show that any one of them ever, in his whole life, declared that, in his understanding, any proper division of local from federal authority, or any part of the Constitution, forbade the Federal Government to control as to slavery in the federal territories. I go a step further. I defy any one to show that any living man in the whole world ever did, prior to the beginning of the present century, (and I might almost say prior to the beginning of the last half of the present century,) declare that, in his understanding, any proper division of local from federal authority, or any part of the Constitution, forbade the Federal Government to control as to slavery in the federal territories. To those who now so declare, I give, not only "our fathers who framed the Government under which we live," but with them all other living men within the century in which it was framed, among whom to search, and they shall not be able to find the evidence of a single man agreeing with them.

Now, and here, let me guard a little against being misunderstood. I do not mean to say we are bound to follow implicitly in whatever our fathers did. To do so, would be to discard all the lights of current experience—to reject all progress—all improvement. What I do say is, that if we would supplant the opinions and policy of our fathers in any case, we should do so upon evidence so conclusive, and argument so clear, that even their great authority, fairly considered and weighed, cannot stand; and most surely not in a case whereof we ourselves declare they understood the question better than we.

If any man at this day sincerely believes that a proper division of local from federal authority, or any part of the Constitution, forbids the Federal Government to control as to slavery in the federal territories, he is right to say so, and to enforce his position by all truthful evidence and fair argument which he can. But he has no right to mislead others, who have less access to history, and less leisure to study it, into the false belief that "our fathers, who framed the Government under which we live," were of the same opinion—thus substituting falsehood and deception for truthful evidence and fair argument. If any man at this day sincerely believes "our fathers who framed the Government under which we live," used and applied principles, in other cases, which ought to have led them to understand that a proper division of local from federal authority or some part of the Constitution, forbids the Federal Government to control as to slavery in the federal territories, he is right to say so. But he should, at the same time, brave the responsibility of declaring that, in his opinion, he understands their principles better than they did themselves; and especially should he not shirk that responsibility by asserting that they "understood the question just as well, and even better, than we do now."

But enough! *Let all who believe that "our fathers, who framed the Government under which we live, understood this question just as well, and even better, than we do now," speak as they spoke, and act as they acted upon it. This is all Republicans ask—all Republicans desire—in relation to slavery. As those fathers marked it, so let it be again marked, as an evil not to be extended, but to be tolerated and protected only because of and so far as its actual presence among us makes that toleration and protection a necessity. Let all the guarantees those fathers gave it, be, not grudgingly, but fully and fairly maintained.* For this Republicans contend, and with this, so far as I know or believe, they will be content. . . .

Your purpose, then, plainly stated, is that you will destroy the Government, unless you be allowed to construe and enforce the Constitution as you please, on all points in dispute between you and us. You will rule or ruin in all events.

This, plainly stated, is your language. Perhaps you will say the Supreme Court has decided the disputed Constitutional question in your favor. Not quite so. But waiving the lawyer's distinction between dictum and decision, the Court have decided the question for you in a sort of way. The Court have substantially said, it is your Constitutional right to take slaves into the federal territories, and to hold them there as property. When I say the decision was made in a sort of way, I mean it was made in a divided Court, by a bare majority of the Judges, and they not quite agreeing with one another in the reasons for making it; that it is so made as that its avowed supporters disagree with one another about its meaning, and that it was mainly based upon a mistaken statement of fact—the statement in the opinion that "the right of property in a slave is distinctly and expressly affirmed in the Constitution."

An inspection of the Constitution will show that the right of property in a slave is not *"distinctly* and *expressly"* affirmed" in it. Bear in mind, the Judges do not pledge their judicial opinion that such right is *impliedly* affirmed in the Constitution; but they pledge their veracity that it is *"distinctly* and *expressly"* affirmed there—"distinctly," that is, not mingled with anything else—"expressly," that is, in words meaning just that, without the aid of any

inference, and susceptible of no other meaning.

If they had only pledged their judicial opinion that such right is affirmed in the instrument by implication, it would be open to others to show that neither the word "slave" nor "slavery" is to be found in the Constitution, nor the word "property" even, in any connection with language alluding to the things slave, or slavery, and that wherever in that instrument the slave is alluded to, he is called a "person;"— and wherever his master's legal right in relation to him is alluded to, it is spoken of as "service or labor which may be due,"—as a debt payable in service or labor. Also, it would be open to show, by contemporaneous history, that this mode of alluding to slaves and slavery, instead of speaking of them, was employed on purpose to exclude from the Constitution the idea that there could be property in man.

To show all this, is easy and certain.

When this obvious mistake of the Judges shall be brought to their notice, is it not reasonable to expect that they will withdraw the mistaken statement, and reconsider the conclusion based upon it?

And then it is to be remembered that "our fathers, who framed the Government under which we live"—the men who made the Constitution—decided this same Constitutional question in our favor, long ago—decided it without division among themselves, when making the decision; without division among themselves about the meaning of it after it was made, and, so far as any evidence is left, without basing it upon any mistaken statement of facts. . . .

The question recurs, what will satisfy them? Simply this: We must not only let them alone, but we must, somehow, convince them that we do let them alone. This, we know by experience, is no easy task. We have been so trying to convince them from the very beginning of our organization, but with no success. In all our platforms and speeches we have constantly protested our purpose to let them alone; but this has had no tendency to convince them. Alike unavailing to convince them, is the fact that they have never detected a man of us in any attempt to disturb them.

These natural, and apparently adequate means all failing, what will convince them? This, and this only: cease to call slavery *wrong*, and join them in calling it *right*. And this must be done thoroughly—done in *acts* as well as in *words.* Silence will not be tolerated—we must place our-selves avowedly with them. Senator Douglas's new sedition law must be enacted and enforced, suppressing all declarations that slavery is wrong, whether made in politics, in presses, in pulpits, or in private. We must arrest and return their fugitive slaves with greedy pleasure. We must pull down our Free State constitutions. The whole atmosphere must be disinfected from all taint of opposition to slavery, before they will cease to believe that all their troubles proceed from us.

I am quite aware they do not state their case precisely in this way. Most of them would probably say to us, "Let us alone, *do* nothing to us, and *say* what you please about slavery." But we do let them alone—have never disturbed them—so that, after all, it is what we say, which dissatisfies them. They will continue to accuse us of doing, until we cease saying.

I am also aware they have not, as yet, in terms, demanded the overthrow of our Free-State Constitutions. Yet those Constitutions declare the wrong of slavery, with more solemn emphasis, than do all other sayings against it; and when all these other sayings shall have been silenced, the overthrow of these Constitutions will be demanded, and nothing be left to resist the demand. It is nothing to the contrary, that they do not demand the whole of this just now. Demanding what they do, and for the reason they do, they can voluntarily stop nowhere short of this consummation. Holding, as they do, that slavery is morally right, and socially elevating, they cannot cease to demand a full national recognition of it, as a legal right, and a social blessing.

Nor can we justifiably withhold this, on any ground save our conviction that slavery is wrong. If slavery is right, all words, acts, laws, and constitutions against it, are themselves wrong, and should be silenced, and swept away. If it is right, we cannot justly object to its nationality—its universality; if it is wrong, they cannot justly insist upon its extension—its enlargement. All they ask,

we could readily grant, if we thought slavery right; all we ask, they could as readily grant, if they thought it wrong. Their thinking it right, and our thinking it wrong, is the precise fact upon which depends the whole controversy. Thinking it right as they do, they are not to blame for desiring its full recognition, as being right; but, thinking it wrong, as we do, can we yield to them? Can we cast our votes with their view, and against our own? In view of our moral, social, and political responsibilities, can we do this?

Wrong as we think slavery is, we can yet afford to let it alone where it is, because that much is due to the necessity arising from its actual presence in the nation; but can we, while our votes will prevent it, allow it to spread into the National Territories, and to overrun us here in these Free States? If our sense of duty forbids this, then let us stand by our duty, fearlessly and effectively. Let us be diverted by none of those sophistical contrivances wherewith we are so industriously plied and belabored—contrivances such as groping for some middle ground between the right and the wrong, vain as the search for a man who should be neither a living man nor a dead man—such as a policy of "don't care" on a question about which all true men do care—such as Union appeals beseeching true Union men to yield to Disunionists, reversing the divine rule, and calling, not the sinners, but the righteous to repentance—such as invocations to Washington, imploring men to unsay what Washington said, and undo what Washington did.

Neither let us be slandered from our duty by false accusations against us, nor frightened from it by menaces of destruction to the Government nor of dungeons to ourselves.

LET US HAVE FAITH THAT RIGHT MAKES MIGHT, AND IN THAT FAITH, LET US, TO THE END, DARE TO DO OUR DUTY AS WE UNDERSTAND IT.

GLOSSARY

decision: in law, the binding ruling of a court

dictum: in law, comments supporting a decision, of varying weight, depending on the agreement or disagreement of a divided court

Louisiana country: land drained by the Mississippi River, purchased by Thomas Jefferson from Napoleonic France in 1803

Document Analysis

Lincoln opens his address in an unusual, understated way, claiming, "The facts with which I shall deal this evening are mainly old and familiar." It is almost as if Lincoln is trying to lower expectations from the outset. The only "novelty," he promises his hearers, may lie "in the mode of presenting the facts, and the inferences and observations following that presentation." Lincoln is rhetorically preparing his hearers, genteel New Yorkers, for a closely argued speech, a lawyer's brief, warning that they should not expect a soaring rhetorical performance. This strategy will serve Lincoln well. He will begin the first and longest section of the speech by detailing a history of the Founding Fathers' attitudes to slavery's expansion. As the speech progresses, its tone and power will rise. In the second section, as he addresses Southerners, he will add sarcasm to his logic, while still retaining a moderate voice. Only at the end, while addressing his fellow Republicans—and, ultimately, the nation—will Lincoln unleash his clearest statement about the moral issue of slavery and challenge his hearers to a commitment to a moral crusade. The emotional payoff at the end is the direct result of the deliberate, calculated beginning.

Lincoln begins his first section with a quote from his old senatorial rival and future presidential rival, Stephen Douglas. Lincoln reports to his hearers, "In his speech last autumn, at Columbus, Ohio, as reported in 'The New-York Times,' Senator Douglas said: 'Our fathers, when they framed the Government under which we live, understood this question just as well, and even better, than we do now.'" Rather than directing an attack against Douglas, Lincoln uses this quote as the launching pad for his entire talk, skillfully turning the very words of his primary opponent against him by demonstrating that his understanding of this statement is superior to Douglas's. Further, Lincoln will invest this statement with even more meaning than Douglas intended. One clue to this is the way Lincoln says he is going to "adopt" the claim "as a text for this discourse." In speaking of such a text, Lincoln is comparing this statement to a biblical passage. His style is reminiscent of a minister proposing a biblical text to expound in a sermon. Thus, although this is a secular speech, it carries with it the form and cadence of the sermons Lincoln's audience would have been familiar with from many Sundays spent in church services. Lincoln will take this principle—"Our fathers . . . understood this question just as well, and even better, than we do now"—and elucidate it in a type of political sermon.

How, then, to understand how the "fathers," as Lincoln repeatedly calls them throughout the speech, viewed the issue of slavery's expansion? Lincoln claims it is a useful question, furnishing a "precise and an agreed starting point." From a philosophical perspective, this becomes an exercise in determining the founders' attitude on the subject and then giving them the benefit of the doubt that their way was correct. Lincoln is doing his best to be filiopietistic—revering his (political) ancestors. His politics would be predicated on a respect for the political fathers. He is trying to determine an original intent.

Lincoln's approach is built upon a certain type of conservative outlook that he reveals later in the speech. In a section of the speech not reproduced here, defending his approach, he asks, "What is conservatism? Is it not adherence to the old and tried, against the new and untried?" Lincoln claims the conservative mantle, against Southern charges of his radicalism, by aligning his position with that of the founders. Lincoln's was not an unthinking, reactionary position. He did not want to "discard all the lights of current experience—to reject all progress—all improvement." Rather, he believed that the logic of the founders' position needed to be understood and given due weight, especially if all sides agreed they understood the question better that people in Lincoln's day.

To examine this question, Lincoln could have gone in a variety of directions, as many historians have done subsequently. Lincoln, however, proves his historical and legal research—which he did for hours in the capitol's law library in Springfield—through painstaking explanation.

First, he considers how to define the frame of government in the nation. His answer is the Constitution and its subsequent amendments. This allows him to take as his sample of the Founding Fathers the thirty-nine signatories of the Constitution. Then Lincoln frames the question still further: did these fathers believe the "Federal Government" had power to control slavery in "our Federal Territories"? In this, Lincoln is not asking a broader question about what the framers of the Constitution thought about the morality of the slave trade or slavery in general. He observes, again in a section not reproduced here, that sixteen of the founders who left no legislative mark on the question were still known as "noted anti-slavery men," including Benjamin Franklin and Alexander Hamilton. Yet Lincoln looks only to the congressional votes left behind by the twenty-three of thirty-nine fathers who had opportunity to indicate their opinion.

Lincoln then marches through a number of legislative moments that might have given rise to objections to federal determinations about slavery in territories. One of his key examples is the Northwest Ordinance, drafted under the Articles of Confederation but signed into law by George Washington in 1789, which demonstrates congressional prohibition of slavery in new territory. Other examples that at least partially support his claim are the Territorial Act—an act passed in 1804 that divided the Louisiana Purchase into the Territory of Orleans and the District of Louisiana—and the debates over Missouri statehood in 1820. In totaling up attitudes, Lincoln sidesteps the two counterexamples he mentions: James M'Henry (McHenry) of Maryland and Charles Pinckney of South Carolina. Both voted against prohibiting slavery in a given territory. Lincoln does not deny this, but he claims their opposition was to the specific context, not Congress's overall power to limit slavery. Lincoln's conclusion, then, is that of the original thirty-nine founders, twenty-one, "a clear majority of the whole," saw no hindrance to Congress's limiting slavery in territories. Lincoln claims that "such, unquestionably, was the understanding of our fathers who framed the original Constitution."

If this was the case, then Lincoln had both a negative and a positive conclusion. The negative conclusion is directed against Democrats such as Douglas who wanted to deny what Lincoln claims the founders had affirmed. In the face of this evidence, Lincoln claims that counterarguments are "a little presumptuous" and indeed "impudently absurd." Anyone arguing against Lincoln—and Douglas is the implied disputant—is said to be welcome to bring forth other evidence. "But he has no right to mislead others, who have less access to history, and less leisure to study it, into the false belief that 'our fathers . . .' were of the same opinion—thus substituting falsehood and deception for truthful evidence and fair argument."

The positive conclusion that Lincoln comes to is that Republicans stand in line with the founders, and this policy should become again the policy of the land. He wants Americans to "speak as they spoke, and act as they acted." His final conclusion in this section is that "this is all Republicans ask—all Republicans desire—in relation to slavery. As those fathers marked it, so let it be again marked, as an evil not to be extended, but to be tolerated and protected only because of and so far as its actual presence amongst us makes that toleration and protection a necessity." Thus, Lincoln's Republican position is radical only insofar as it goes to the root of the nation's political history. He does not demand more; he does not want to change the terms of slavery where it exists. He wishes to mark it as an evil, tolerating it where necessary but not giving it carte blanche to spread.

After making that significant policy point, Lincoln turns to address Southerners. He signals this by saying, "And now, if they would listen—as I suppose they will not—I would address a few words to the Southern people." (In the section of the excerpt that begins, "Your purpose, then, plainly stated," the *your* refers to Southerners.) Lincoln uses this technique of directly addressing those he disagrees with in several speeches; perhaps his most famous usage came near the end of his first inaugural address, when he said, "In *your* hands, my dissatisfied fellow countrymen, and not in *mine*, is the momentous issue of civil war" (271). In this section of the Cooper Union speech, Lincoln indicates his frustration that Southerners almost certainly will not listen.

Still, Lincoln tries to communicate across the sectional divide. One way he does so is by interpreting the recent *Dred Scott* case. Lincoln had been attacking the *Dred Scott* ruling for years, as was evident in both his "House Divided" speech and his debates with Douglas. Here, he challenges Southerners' desire to claim the *Dred Scott* decision as having constitutionally settled the issue of slavery in the territories. He brings up two points against the ruling. First, he claims it was decided based on a mistaken reading of the Constitution, as demonstrated by the opinion's argument that "the right of property in a slave is distinctly and expressly affirmed in the Constitution." Lincoln argues that this is not the case, since slavery is never mentioned explicitly in the Constitution, and whenever slaves are "alluded to," they are described as "person[s]" rather than property. Second, he claims the witness of "our fathers," who "made the Constitution" and allowed the federal government to prohibit slavery in the Northwest Territory.

Even with this explanation, Lincoln does not believe Southerners will respond well, because, he charges, Southerners are refusing to join the debate with good faith or open minds. Lincoln thus has some strong words for the South. He charges Southerners with threatening to destroy the Union if their view of the Constitution is not validated. "You will rule or ruin in all events," he tells them. Against Southern threats of secession, Lincoln points out that they are endangering the Union, not him. Within the year, the Southern states would begin to carry out their threats.

In his final section, Lincoln addresses Republicans, both those assembled at Cooper Union and all those who he knew would later read his address. In the excerpt, this section starts with, "The question recurs, what will satisfy them?" Of course, *them* refers to the same Southerners he previously addressed as *you*; now, the unreasonable Southerners are the problem to be addressed. And the problem is dramatic indeed, because the proslavery Southerners are demanding that Republicans "cease to call slavery *wrong*, and join them in calling it *right*. And this must be done thoroughly— done in *acts* as well as in *words*." As Lincoln observes, neither silence about the subject nor leaving slavery alone where it exists is enough for such Southerners.

Lincoln worries that in both word and deed, this will lead to the negation of "our Free State constitutions." The reason for the Southerners' intransigence is their belief "that slavery is morally right, and socially elevating," so "they cannot cease to demand a full national recognition of it, as a legal right, and a social blessing." The proslavery South, following the lead of John C. Calhoun, had decided that slavery was not a necessary evil but a positive good. If it was a positive good, it needed not only to be protected but to be expanded, and without criticism.

And so, by his final paragraphs, Lincoln has reached the nub of the conflict, not only between Southerners and Republicans, but ultimately between the states: the morality of slavery. As Lincoln presents the choice, slavery is either morally right or morally wrong, and he comes down on the side of it being a moral wrong. Lincoln had already made this point in his 1859 speech in Cincinnati, saying, "I think Slavery is wrong, morally, and politically. I desire that it should be no further spread in these United States, and I should not object if it should gradually terminate in the whole Union." He believed there should be "a national policy in regard to the institution of slavery, that acknowledges and deals with that institution as being wrong" (qtd. in Carwardine 123). Lincoln reiterates this position in his penultimate paragraph, which he begins by saying, "Wrong as we think slavery is"— that is, identifying it as a wrong. If this is the case, he argues, then Republicans cannot acquiesce to Southern demands that they treat it as a right, and they also must oppose Stephen Douglas's policy of moral indifference.

Lincoln concludes with a stirring peroration, its force reflected in its expression in all capitals: "LET US HAVE FAITH THAT RIGHT MAKES MIGHT, AND IN THAT FAITH, LET US, TO THE END, DARE TO DO OUR DUTY AS WE UNDERSTAND IT." Moral duty, he says, flows from moral rectitude, and Lincoln is thus rallying all those who saw slavery as a moral evil and refused to let it expand beyond its current borders. From a stolid beginning, Lincoln ends with a crescendo, trumpeting not just a superior policy but the only moral one, and the only one that could promote positive action.

Essential Themes

The speech had significant effects in 1860 and afterward. Politically, it showed Northern Republicans that Lincoln was a serious thinker, and a moderate one. The speech catapulted him into the limelight, and his popularity rose significantly. It also launched him on a speaking tour of New England, where he met similarly positive responses. By raising Lincoln's national profile, the speech prepared the way for him to garner the Republican nomination at the party convention in Chicago in May. Although several state delegations had their favorites, Lincoln was a second choice of many states, and he picked up their votes in subsequent rounds of voting. During the campaign itself, the Cooper Union speech was reprinted as evidence of Lincoln's responsible Republican outlook.

After Lincoln received the nomination, the election dynamics were in his favor. The Democrats fractured. Their convention in Charleston, South Carolina, ended in a Southern walkout and failed to nominate a candidate. Later, Douglas earned the support of the Northern Democrats, while sitting vice president John C. Breckinridge became the Southerners' choice. Meanwhile, a Constitutional Union Party formed with John Bell at the head to appeal to the border states and some old-line Whigs. With the vote fragmented, Lincoln won the popular vote and dominated the Electoral College vote, although he did so without any support from the South.

In Harold Holzer's view, Lincoln's speech at Cooper Union was "the speech that made Abraham Lincoln president." Further, themes that he developed in the speech would shape subsequent American development. Lincoln's condemnation of slavery would increasingly be picked up by Northerners, and his claim that "right makes might" contributed to the vision of a moral and religious crusade against slavery. Once secession occurred, Northerners could fight passionately, first for the Union and then, after the Emancipation Proclamation, for the Union and the liberation of the slaves.

Additionally, Lincoln's concern for American patterns derived from the Founding Fathers would continue to inform his leadership. His precise accounting of the founders' attitudes on slavery expansion reflected his strong sense of the need to follow their advice. He demonstrated his desire for "adherence to the old and tried, against the new and untried." Although the Civil War would introduce unimaginable new circumstances, Lincoln as president would govern in a way he believed consistent with the original founding vision.

—*Jonathan Den Hartog, PhD*

Bibliography and Additional Reading

Carwardine, Richard. *Lincoln: A Life of Purpose and Power.* New York: Vintage, 2006. Print.

Corry, John. *Lincoln at Cooper Union.* New York: Xlibris, 2003. Print.

Ecelbarger, Gary. *The Great Comeback: How Abraham Lincoln Beat the Odds to Win the 1860 Republican Nomination.* New York: Dunne, 2008. Print.

Egerton, Douglas. *Year of Meteors: Stephen Douglas, Abraham Lincoln, and the Election That Brought On the Civil War.* New York: Bloomsbury, 2010. Print.

Foner, Eric. *The Fiery Trial: Abraham Lincoln and American Slavery.* New York: Norton, 2010. Print.

Guelzo, Allen. *Abraham Lincoln: Redeemer President.* Grand Rapids: Eerdmans, 1999. Print.

———. *Abraham Lincoln as a Man of Ideas.* Carbondale: Southern Illinois UP, 2009. Print.

———. *Fateful Lightning: A New History of the Civil War and Reconstruction.* New York: Oxford UP, 2012. Print.

Holzer, Harold. *Lincoln at Cooper Union: The Speech That Made Abraham Lincoln President.* New York: Simon, 2004. Print.

Jaffa, Harry, and Robert Johannsen, eds. *In the Name of the People: Speeches and Writings of Lincoln and Douglas in the Ohio Campaign of 1859.* Columbus: Ohio State UP, 1959. Print.

Lincoln, Abraham. "First Inaugural Address—Final Text." *The Collected Works of Abraham Lincoln.* Ed. Roy Prentice Basler. Vol. 4. New Brunswick: Rutgers UP, 1953. Print. 262–71.

McPherson, James. *Battle Cry of Freedom: The Civil War Era.* New York: Oxford UP, 2003. Print.

Oakes, James. *The Radical and the Republican: Frederick Douglass, Abraham Lincoln, and the Triumph of Antislavery Politics.* New York: Norton, 2007. Print.

Potter, David. *The Impending Crisis, 1848–1861.* New York: Harper, 1977. Print.

■ Abraham Lincoln's First Inaugural Address

Date: March 4, 1861
Author: Abraham Lincoln
Genre: Speech

Summary Overview

Newly elected president Abraham Lincoln had one opportunity to try to convince the Southern slave-holding states not to force the issue of secession from the United States. Although seven states had already declared that they were forming the Confederate States of America, in his first inaugural speech, Lincoln sought to alleviate their concerns regarding the issues of slavery and states' rights. The entire speech was focused on these issues, as was the attention of the entire country. While Lincoln had easily won the necessary votes in the Electoral College, defeating three other candidates to claim the presidency, his victory came with the support of only about 40 percent of voters, primarily from the North. Although Lincoln claimed that he would not push for legislation abolishing slavery, it was clear from his time in Congress that he opposed the institution. In the South this caused great anxiety, which Lincoln sought to assuage in his inaugural address to the nation. However, the moderate tone he struck in this speech was not accepted by Southern leaders, who would ultimately move forward with their plans for secession.

Defining Moment

By the time Lincoln took office in early 1861, the United States government had been working for decades to find a way of dealing with slavery that would satisfy Americans on both ends of the political spectrum, implementing various compromises that proved largely ineffective. Following the disintegration of the Whig Party, Lincoln decided to join the emerging Republican Party, which had initially formed to combat slavery. Although he ran for president as a moderate, the Republican label made Lincoln appear a much stronger antislavery candidate than the Southern leaders could accept. However, the Republican Party was the only unified party in the 1860 presidential election, which allowed Lincoln to capture 180 electoral votes and nearly 40 percent of the popular vote. The other three major candidates split the remainder of the popular vote and 123 electoral votes. Because of this outcome, seven states took steps to form the Confederate States of America, beginning about three months before Lincoln's inauguration.

As of March 4, the date of Lincoln's inauguration, the secession of the Southern states had been carried out peacefully, which suggested to Lincoln that a compromise could still be achieved. Thus, after outlining his understanding of the situation and the Constitution, Lincoln speaks directly to the Southern leaders, telling them, "You can have no conflict without being yourselves the aggressors." Extending the possibility of a peaceful resolution, he promises that the United States could return to normal if the Southern states returned to the Union. However, Lincoln warns that he would take the necessary steps to preserve the United States if this did not occur.

Although slavery could be considered the central cause of the division between North and South, there was a second issue that had emerged over the past decade: the South was losing control of American politics. Because of the Three-Fifths Compromise (1787), which stipulated that three-fifths of the slave population of a slave state would be counted toward that state's total population, even though slaves were unable to vote, the South for decades had more representation in Congress and the Electoral College than the number of actual voters would normally justify. Of the first fifteen presidents, only six were born in the North, and each served only one term. However, in 1860 Lincoln became the third consecutive Northerner to be elected as well as the first successful candidate who did not receive any Southern electoral votes. It was clear to Southern leaders that without radical steps, slavery, and the traditional Southern way of life would soon come to an end.

Author Biography

Abraham Lincoln was born on February 12, 1809. His parents, Thomas and Nancy Hanks Lincoln, lived in Hardin County, Kentucky, when Lincoln was born. During his childhood his family moved to Indiana, and they later relocated to Illinois. Lincoln's formal education was limited; however, he taught himself to read and other basic skills. Desiring to do more than be a manual laborer, Lincoln left home when he was twenty-two, worked for a businessman, and a year later bought a store with an associate. He served as an officer in the Illinois militia during the Black Hawk War and then became postmaster of New Salem, Illinois. Lincoln next decided to study law and was admitted to the bar in 1836. As he had won an election to the Illinois General Assembly in 1834, he practiced law in Springfield, where he met and married Mary Todd, with whom he had four children.

Elected as a Whig, Lincoln served four terms in the general assembly. In 1846, again as a Whig, he was elected to the United States House of Representatives. During his term, he sponsored several bills that would have limited slavery. Lincoln did not run for reelection, but his opposition to slavery drew him back into politics in 1854, when he sought, but lost, a seat in the U.S. Senate. The continuing issue of slavery splintered the Whig Party, and Lincoln was drawn to the emerging Republican Party in 1856. In 1858, he ran for the Senate for the second time. Lincoln again lost, but his debates against Stephen A. Douglas and powerful "House Divided" speech made him a national figure. He was nominated for president by the Republican Party in 1860 and ran against a splintered Democratic Party, easily securing the necessary number of electoral votes.

With the attack on the federal garrison at Fort Sumter in South Carolina, Lincoln became a wartime president. He forcefully took control of the national government and became very involved with the major aspects of the military campaigns. During the war, he supported legislation to do away with slavery on federal land and also issued the Emancipation Proclamation, which freed all slaves in the Confederacy. Lincoln was reelected in 1864, losing only three states. As the war approached its end and politicians began to develop plans for Reconstruction, Lincoln was assassinated by actor and Confederate sympathizer John Wilkes Booth. He died on April 15, 1865.

HISTORICAL DOCUMENT

In compliance with a custom as old as the Government itself, I appear before you to address you briefly and to take in your presence the oath prescribed by the Constitution of the United States to be taken by the President "before he enters on the execution of this office." I do not consider it necessary at present for me to discuss those matters of administration about which there is no special anxiety or excitement.

Apprehension seems to exist among the people of the Southern States that by the accession of a Republican Administration their property and their peace and personal security are to be endangered. There has never been any reasonable cause for such apprehension. Indeed, the most ample evidence to the contrary has all the while existed and been open to their inspection. It is found in nearly all the published speeches of him who now addresses you. I do but quote from one of those speeches when I declare that—

I have no purpose, directly or indirectly, to interfere with the institution of slavery in the States where it exists. I believe I have no lawful right to do so, and I have no inclination to do so.

Those who nominated and elected me did so with full knowledge that I had made this and many similar declarations and had never recanted them; and more than this, they placed in the platform for my acceptance, and as a law to themselves and to me, the clear and emphatic resolution which I now read:

Resolved, That the maintenance inviolate of the rights of the States, and especially the right of each State to order and control its own domestic institutions according to its own judgment exclusively, is essential to that balance of power on which the perfection and endurance of our political fabric depend; and we denounce the lawless invasion by armed force of the soil of any State or Territory,

Photograph shows participants and crowd at the first inauguration of President Abraham Lincoln, at the U.S. Capitol, Washington, D.C. Lincoln is standing under the wood canopy, at the front, midway between the left and center posts. The 1861 inauguration is believed to be the first ever photographed, and some sources credit it to Scottish photographer, Alexander Gardner. (Library of Congress)

no matter what pretext, as among the gravest of crimes.

I now reiterate these sentiments, and in doing so I only press upon the public attention the most conclusive evidence of which the case is susceptible that the property, peace, and security of no section are to be in any wise endangered by the now incoming Administration. I add, too, that all the protection which, consistently with the Constitution and the laws, can be given will be cheerfully given to all the States when lawfully demanded, for whatever cause—as cheerfully to one section as to another.

There is much controversy about the delivering up of fugitives from service or labor. The clause I now read is as plainly written in the Constitution as any other of its provisions:

No person held to service or labor in one State, under the laws thereof, escaping into another, shall in consequence of any law or regulation therein be discharged from such service or labor, but shall be delivered up on claim of the party to whom such service or labor may be due.

It is scarcely questioned that this provision was intended by those who made it for the reclaiming of what we call fugitive slaves; and the intention of the lawgiver is the law. All members of Congress swear their support to the whole Constitution—to this provision as much as to any other. To the proposition, then, that slaves whose cases come within the terms of this clause "shall be delivered up" their oaths are unanimous. Now, if they would make the effort in good temper, could they not with nearly equal unanimity frame and pass a law by means of which to keep good that unanimous oath?

There is some difference of opinion whether this clause should be enforced by national or by State authority, but surely that difference is not a very material one. If the slave is to be surrendered, it can be of but little consequence to him or to others by which authority it is done. And should anyone in any case be content that his oath shall go unkept on a merely unsubstantial controversy as to how it shall be kept?

Again: In any law upon this subject ought not all the safeguards of liberty known in civilized and humane jurisprudence to be introduced, so that a free man be not in any case surrendered as a slave? And might it not be well at the same time to provide by law for the enforcement of that clause in the Constitution which guarantees that "the citizens of each State shall be entitled to all privileges and immunities of citizens in the several States"?

I take the official oath to-day with no mental reservations and with no purpose to construe the Constitution or laws by any hypercritical rules; and while I do not choose now to specify particular acts of Congress as proper to be enforced, I do suggest that it will be much safer for all, both in official and private stations, to conform to and abide by all those acts which stand unrepealed than to violate any of them trusting to find impunity in having them held to be unconstitutional.

It is seventy-two years since the first inauguration of a President under our National Constitution. During that period fifteen different and greatly distinguished citizens have in succession administered the executive branch of the Government. They have conducted it through many perils, and generally with great success. Yet, with all this scope of precedent, I now enter upon the same task for the brief constitutional term of four years under great and peculiar difficulty. A disruption of the Federal Union, heretofore only menaced, is now formidably attempted. I hold that in contemplation of universal law and of the Constitution the Union of these States is perpetual. Perpetuity is implied, if not expressed, in the fundamental law of all national governments. It is safe to assert that no government proper ever had a provision in its organic law for its own termination. Continue to execute all the express provisions of our National Constitution, and the Union will endure forever, it being impossible to destroy it except by some action not provided for in the instrument itself.

Again: If the United States be not a government proper, but an association of States in the nature of contract merely, can it, as a contract, be peaceably unmade by less than all the parties who made it? One party to a contract may violate it—break it, so to speak—but does it not require all to lawfully rescind it?

Descending from these general principles, we find the proposition that in legal contemplation the Union is perpetual confirmed by the history of the Union itself. The Union is much older than the Constitution. It was formed, in fact, by the Articles of Association in 1774. It was matured and continued by the Declaration of Independence in 1776. It was further matured, and the faith of all the then thirteen States expressly plighted and engaged that it should be perpetual, by the Articles of Confederation in 1778. And finally, in 1787, one of the declared objects for ordaining and establishing the Constitution was "to form a more perfect Union."

But if destruction of the Union by one or by a part only of the States be lawfully possible, the Union is less perfect than before the Constitution, having lost the vital element of perpetuity.

It follows from these views that no State upon its own mere motion can lawfully get out of the Union; that resolves and ordinances to that effect are legally void, and that acts of violence within any State or States against the authority of the United States are insurrectionary or revolutionary, according to circumstances.

I therefore consider that in view of the Constitution and the laws the Union is unbroken, and to the extent of my ability, I shall take care, as the Constitution itself expressly enjoins upon me, that the laws of the Union be faithfully executed in all the States. Doing this I deem to be only a simple duty on my part, and I shall perform it so far as practicable unless my rightful masters, the American people, shall withhold the requisite means or in some authoritative manner direct the contrary. I trust this will not be regarded as a menace, but only as the declared purpose of the Union that it will constitutionally defend and maintain itself.

In doing this there needs to be no bloodshed or violence, and there shall be none unless it be forced upon the national authority. The power confided to me will be used to hold, occupy, and possess the property and places belonging to the Government and to collect the duties and imposts; but beyond what may be necessary for these objects, there will be no invasion, no using of force against or among the people anywhere. . . .

The mails, unless repelled, will continue to be furnished in all parts of the Union. So far as possible the people everywhere shall have that sense of perfect security which is most favorable to calm thought and reflection. The course here indicated will be followed unless current events and experience shall show a modification or change to be proper, and in every case and exigency

my best discretion will be exercised, according to circumstances actually existing and with a view and a hope of a peaceful solution of the national troubles and the restoration of fraternal sympathies and affections.

That there are persons in one section or another who seek to destroy the Union at all events and are glad of any pretext to do it I will neither affirm nor deny; but if there be such, I need address no word to them. To those, however, who really love the Union may I not speak?

Before entering upon so grave a matter as the destruction of our national fabric, with all its benefits, its memories, and its hopes, would it not be wise to ascertain precisely why we do it? Will you hazard so desperate a step while there is any possibility that any portion of the ills you fly from have no real existence? Will you, while the certain ills you fly to are greater than all the real ones you fly from, will you risk the commission of so fearful a mistake?

All profess to be content in the Union if all constitutional rights can be maintained. Is it true, then, that any right plainly written in the Constitution has been denied? I think not. Happily, the human mind is so constituted that no party can reach to the audacity of doing this. Think, if you can, of a single instance in which a plainly written provision of the Constitution has ever been denied. If by the mere force of numbers a majority should deprive a minority of any clearly written constitutional right, it might in a moral point of view justify revolution; certainly would if such right were a vital one. But such is not our case. All the vital rights of minorities and of individuals are so plainly assured to them by affirmations and negations, guaranties and prohibitions, in the Constitution that controversies never arise concerning them. But no organic law can ever be framed with a provision specifically applicable to every question which may occur in practical administration. No foresight can anticipate nor any document of reasonable length contain express provisions for all possible questions. Shall fugitives from labor be surrendered by national or by State authority? The Constitution does not expressly say. May Congress prohibit slavery in the Territories? The Constitution does not expressly say. Must Congress protect slavery in the Territories? The Constitution does not expressly say.

From questions of this class spring all our constitutional controversies, and we divide upon them into majorities and minorities. If the minority will not acquiesce, the majority must, or the Government must cease. There is no other alternative, for continuing the Government is acquiescence on one side or the other. If a minority in such case will secede rather than acquiesce, they make a precedent which in turn will divide and ruin them, for a minority of their own will secede from them whenever a majority refuses to be controlled by such minority. For instance, why may not any portion of a new confederacy a year or two hence arbitrarily secede again, precisely as portions of the present Union now claim to secede from it? All who cherish disunion sentiments are now being educated to the exact temper of doing this. Is there such perfect identity of interests among the States to compose a new union as to produce harmony only and prevent renewed secession?

Plainly the central idea of secession is the essence of anarchy. A majority held in restraint by constitutional checks and limitations, and always changing easily with deliberate changes of popular opinions and sentiments, is the only true sovereign of a free people. Whoever rejects it does of necessity fly to anarchy or to despotism. Unanimity is impossible. The rule of a minority, as a permanent arrangement, is wholly inadmissible; so that, rejecting the majority principle, anarchy or despotism in some form is all that is left.

I do not forget the position assumed by some that constitutional questions are to be decided by the Supreme Court, nor do I deny that such decisions must be binding in any case upon the parties to a suit as to the object of that suit, while they are also entitled to very high respect and consideration in all parallel cases by all other departments of the Government. And while it is obviously possible that such decision may be erroneous in any given case, still the evil effect following it, being limited to that particular case, with the chance that it may be overruled and never become a precedent for other cases, can better be borne than could the evils of a different practice. At the same time, the candid citizen must confess that if the policy of the Government upon vital questions affecting the whole people is to be irrevocably fixed by decisions of the Supreme Court, the instant they are made in ordinary litigation between parties in personal actions the people will have ceased to be their own rulers, having to that extent practically resigned their Government into

the hands of that eminent tribunal. Nor is there in this view any assault upon the court or the judges. It is a duty from which they may not shrink to decide cases properly brought before them, and it is no fault of theirs if others seek to turn their decisions to political purposes.

One section of our country believes slavery is right and ought to be extended, while the other believes it is wrong and ought not to be extended. This is the only substantial dispute. The fugitive-slave clause of the Constitution and the law for the suppression of the foreign slave trade are each as well enforced, perhaps, as any law can ever be in a community where the moral sense of the people imperfectly supports the law itself. The great body of the people abide by the dry legal obligation in both cases, and a few break over in each. This, I think, can not be perfectly cured, and it would be worse in both cases after the separation of the sections than before.

The foreign slave trade, now imperfectly suppressed, would be ultimately revived without restriction in one section, while fugitive slaves, now only partially surrendered, would not be surrendered at all by the other. Physically speaking, we can not separate. We can not remove our respective sections from each other nor build an impassable wall between them. A husband and wife may be divorced and go out of the presence and beyond the reach of each other, but the different parts of our country can not do this. They can not but remain face to face, and intercourse, either amicable or hostile, must continue between them. Is it possible, then, to make that intercourse more advantageous or more satisfactory after separation than before? Can aliens make treaties easier than friends can make laws? Can treaties be more faithfully enforced between aliens than laws can among friends? Suppose you go to war, you can not fight always; and when, after much loss on both sides and no gain on either, you cease fighting, the identical old questions, as to terms of intercourse, are again upon you.

This country, with its institutions, belongs to the people who inhabit it. Whenever they shall grow weary of the existing Government, they can exercise their constitutional right of amending it or their revolutionary right to dismember or overthrow it. I can not be ignorant of the fact that many worthy and patriotic citizens are desirous of having the National Constitution amended. While I make no recommendation of amendments, I fully recognize the rightful authority of the people over the whole subject, to be exercised in either of the modes prescribed in the instrument itself; and I should, under existing circumstances, favor rather than oppose a fair opportunity being afforded the people to act upon it. I will venture to add that to me the convention mode seems preferable, in that it allows amendments to originate with the people themselves, instead of only permitting them to take or reject propositions originated by others, not especially chosen for the purpose, and which might not be precisely such as they would wish to either accept or refuse.

I understand a proposed amendment to the Constitution—which amendment, however, I have not seen—has passed Congress, to the effect that the Federal Government shall never interfere with the domestic institutions of the States, including that of persons held to service. To avoid misconstruction of what I have said, I depart from my purpose not to speak of particular amendments so far as to say that, holding such a provision to now be implied constitutional law, I have no objection to its being made express and irrevocable.

The Chief Magistrate derives all his authority from the people, and they have referred none upon him to fix terms for the separation of the States. The people themselves can do this if also they choose, but the Executive as such has nothing to do with it. His duty is to administer the present Government as it came to his hands and to transmit it unimpaired by him to his successor. Why should there not be a patient confidence in the ultimate justice of the people? Is there any better or equal hope in the world? In our present differences, is either party without faith of being in the right? If the Almighty Ruler of Nations, with His eternal truth and justice, be on your side of the North, or on yours of the South, that truth and that justice will surely prevail by the judgment of this great tribunal of the American people.

By the frame of the Government under which we live this same people have wisely given their public servants but little power for mischief, and have with equal wisdom provided for the return of that little to their own hands at very short intervals. While the people retain their virtue and vigilance no Administration by any extreme of wickedness or folly can very seriously injure the Government in the short space of four years.

My countrymen, one and all, think calmly and well upon this whole subject. Nothing valuable can be lost by taking time. If there be an object to hurry any of you in hot haste to a step which you would never take deliberately, that object will be frustrated by taking time; but no good object can be frustrated by it. Such of you as are now dissatisfied still have the old Constitution unimpaired, and, on the sensitive point, the laws of your own framing under it; while the new Administration will have no immediate power, if it would, to change either. If it were admitted that you who are dissatisfied hold the right side in the dispute, there still is no single good reason for precipitate action. Intelligence, patriotism, Christianity, and a firm reliance on Him who has never yet forsaken this favored land are still competent to adjust in the best way all our present difficulty.

In your hands, my dissatisfied fellow-countrymen, and not in mine, is the momentous issue of civil war. The Government will not assail you. You can have no conflict without being yourselves the aggressors. You have no oath registered in heaven to destroy the Government, while I shall have the most solemn one to "preserve, protect, and defend it."

I am loath to close. We are not enemies, but friends. We must not be enemies. Though passion may have strained it must not break our bonds of affection. The mystic chords of memory, stretching from every battlefield and patriot grave to every living heart and hearthstone all over this broad land, will yet swell the chorus of the Union, when again touched, as surely they will be, by the better angels of our nature.

GLOSSARY

anarchy: a political theory, or state of being, in which there is no political authority

chief magistrate: in this context, the president

fugitive slaves: individuals who had escaped from slavery to a state where slavery was illegal

plighted: pledged

recant: to take back or retract a statement

Southern States: the slave states that were in the process of seceding from the Union

---

Document Analysis

On March 4, 1861, Lincoln arrived in Washington, DC, to be sworn into office and to deliver his inaugural address. After he had been formally elected by the Electoral College on December 5, 1860, the first seven states to secede quickly began the process. During the next two months, Lincoln worked on his speech in Springfield while watching the events unfold. In February, he began his journey by rail to Washington. Because of credible threats to his life uncovered by railroad and government officials, the trip between Baltimore, Maryland, and Washington was taken in secret.

As the newly elected president, Lincoln was tasked with confronting the secessionist movement and convincing the Southern states that had seceded to return to the Union. Lincoln sought to outline his proposed policy on slavery and make it clear that the United States was an entity that could not be divided. Lincoln took seriously the founding documents of the United States, such as the Declaration of Independence and the Constitution, and believed that once formed, the United States was forever. Thus, for the sake of peace, he was willing to undertake policies that were more moderate than his personal position on slavery. However, Lincoln was not willing to decrease the power of the national government or extend the institution of slavery beyond the states in which it was already legal. In writing his speech, Lincoln consulted with other leading Republicans and made several changes based on their input. The most important recommended change was suggested by New York senator (and soon to be Lincoln's secretary of state) William Seward, who encouraged Lincoln to close with one last plea to the South for peace. Following this advice, Lincoln rewrote the two closing paragraphs to the now-

famous speech, which he delivered on March 4 before an audience of more than thirty thousand.

Lincoln opens the speech with a formal nod to the essential actions of the day. Taking the oath of office was the only action the Constitution mandated, but following the precedent instituted by George Washington, Lincoln spoke to the people who had gathered as well. Unlike those of his predecessors, Lincoln's inaugural speech focuses on only one topic, the one that was causing "special anxiety" within the country. This was the "property, peace, and security" of citizens in the Southern part of the United States. In this way, Lincoln courteously introduces the issue of slaves and the institution of slavery, with the related issue of the steps the national government would take to enforce its policies and responsibilities, as the main focus of the speech.

He then boldly speaks out on the issue of slavery, explaining, "I have no purpose, directly or indirectly, to interfere with the institution of slavery in the States where it exists." Based on Lincoln's reading of the federal laws at that time, he sought to preserve the status quo in the South; however, he was firmly opposed to the extension of slavery to any federal territory and the admission of any new states that allowed slavery within their borders. For Southern leaders, the status quo was not enough. For the future of the institution, and for their political survival, the leaders of the South believed that slavery should be extended into the American West. The phrase "where it exists," at the opening of the speech, was enough, for Southerners, to negate anything further that Lincoln said.

Next, Lincoln reiterates his moderate position, in terms of the Republican Party, on slavery. Even though the party platform included strong language against it,

Lincoln points out that he had specifically requested that the platform also incorporate a statement that each state could "order and control its own domestic institutions." The issue of fugitive slaves was of great concern to many Southern politicians, and Lincoln attempts to reassure them by quoting from the portion of the Constitution specifying that states must return to another state anyone "held to service or labor." A strong supporter of the Constitution, Lincoln proclaims that those charged with upholding the document must enforce its policy on fugitive slaves just as they enforce sections on other matters. These statements demonstrate that Lincoln was attempting to walk a fine line between allowing slavery and trying to limit it. In this inaugural address, Lincoln was clearly speaking as the president of the nation, charged with upholding the laws and Constitution, not as a private citizen who at times disagreed with the prevailing laws.

Lincoln then moves on to the status of the United States as a nation. He explains that the United States was created as an ongoing institution and notes that this was consistent with both universal law and the intentions of the Founding Fathers. Lincoln understood that what was happening in 1861 was different from anything that had occurred in the history of the United States. There had been discussions of splitting the Union in the past, but dissatisfied regional leaders had never moved beyond discussion. The actions taken first by South Carolina and then by six additional states went far beyond discussion. Lincoln argues that the Union was intended to last forever, as the founders included no provision in the Constitution for its termination. Secondly, he suggests that if the Constitution was to be considered a contract, then all states would have to agree to any changes, as was the case in civil contracts. Lincoln next states that the United States is more than the Constitution and a set of laws, since it existed for thirteen years prior to the writing of the Constitution. Thus, Lincoln explains, "It follows from these views that no State upon its own mere motion can lawfully get out of the Union."

Having set forward his main points, Lincoln goes on to expand on these and call for calm consideration of what was happening. Continuing to discuss the issue of secession, Lincoln states that "the central idea of secession is the essence of anarchy," suggesting that once the process of secession has begun, it will be difficult to stop. Once one group had broken off from a larger one, a smaller group could break away from the secessionist group, and the process could continue until each unit (state) was

completely separate from all others. Lincoln does admit that if a constitutional right had been denied, "it might in a moral point of view justify revolution." However, he asserts that no such right had been or was at that time being denied to any group. He had faith that the constitutional checks and balances would keep the majority from illegally imposing its will on the minority. Lincoln promises that as president, he would uphold the Constitution, which included providing government services such as the post office, collecting taxes, and following the laws passed by Congress and Supreme Court rulings. However, it also meant enforcing federal laws and Supreme Court rulings in all states and territories.

The enforcement of federal laws and the protection of federal property, in Lincoln's mind, did not necessitate the end of slavery or any type of armed conflict. Lincoln was willing to let the political process work through the issues of the day and was confident that "a peaceful solution" could be found. That being said, if "calm thought and reflection" failed to result in an agreement, and if an insurrection prevented the government from enforcing the laws of the United States in all parts of the country, "bloodshed or violence" could result. Lincoln warns, "The certain ills you fly to are greater than all the real ones you fly from." As president, he was ready to do whatever it might take to preserve the Union and to implement and enforce the laws of the nation. Reflecting further upon slavery, Lincoln notes that the Constitution offers little guidance in this area. Although there are a few statements related to slavery in the Constitution, the lack of unity on the issue among the Founding Fathers meant that the document is silent on many things. In addition, those attending the Constitutional Convention could not have imagined every possible situation. They chose instead to write what is often called a brief constitution, one that addresses the major structural issues of government but leaves the details to be developed as needed. Thus, Lincoln lists several areas of controversy, including the enforcement of fugitive slave laws and the legality of slavery within federal territories, and asserts that the Constitution says nothing about any of them.

If the nation accepted the rulings of the Supreme Court on cases related to slavery and fugitive slaves, Lincoln states that the only issue separating the South from the North would therefore be whether slavery "ought to be extended" into new parts of the nation. While Lincoln had previously stated his position that slavery should only be allowed in the current slave states, he did recognize his duty to follow the will of the nation as a whole and of the Supreme Court. Thus, if the people wanted to extend slavery by constitutional means or sought to pass an amendment guaranteeing slavery forever (as had been discussed toward the end of previous president James Buchanan's term), he would not oppose any action by Congress or by a constitutional convention. He had "patient confidence in the ultimate justice of the people." Thus, peaceful changes made by amending the system of government would be appropriate. Lincoln tells the people that if the leaders of the South "hold the right side in the dispute," then a peaceful, deliberate discussion of the situation would bring about appropriate changes that would guarantee the continuation of slavery. However, if hasty actions were taken, leading to war, at the end of the war the South would face "the identical old questions."

Lincoln closes his speech with an earnest plea to the South. He states, "In your hands, my dissatisfied fellow-countrymen, and not in mine, is the momentous issue of civil war." This is Lincoln's first use of the term "civil war," and his direct statement, at the close of the speech, indicates that he understood the extent of the issues confronting him as president. Having promised not to invade any region of the country so long as federal laws were observed and federal property was not assaulted, Lincoln notes that the choice, then, lay with the dissatisfied Southern leaders. Those leaders had not taken any "oath registered in heaven to destroy the Government," but Lincoln reminds them that he has taken one to "preserve, protect, and defend" the United States and will not shirk his duty.

In closing, Lincoln expresses his desire to be "not enemies, but friends." He cites the common heritage of the North and the South, "stretching from every battlefield and patriot grave." Lincoln hoped that this common heritage and reasonable leaders on both sides would allow the continuation of peace and the development of a solution to the problems through constitutional means. However, as eloquent as this speech was, Lincoln's views were not accepted by leaders in the South, and just over a month later, the Civil War began with the Confederate attack on the Union-occupied Fort Sumter.

Essential Themes

For decades, Lincoln has consistently been named one of the two top presidents of the United States in academic as well as popular surveys. His vision of the United States, and his willingness to stand by that vi-

sion in a time of crisis, has been the key component in these judgments. While the tragedy of his assassination added to people's belief in his dedication to the nation, it was Lincoln's willingness to reach out to others while standing firm that endeared him to many. In his first inaugural address, Lincoln demonstrates this quality while outlining the major issues of his day.

The unity of the United States, for Lincoln, was not in name only. He firmly believed that nothing should destroy that union. As its president, Lincoln vowed to see that "the laws of the Union be faithfully executed in all the States." His understanding was that no one and no region was above the law. Therefore, no matter how strongly one disagreed with a law or a ruling of the Supreme Court, the only remedy was to work to have the law changed or the Constitution amended. While Lincoln was not the first to believe in the sanctity of the Constitution, his forceful pronouncement of this ideal has been reflected in political statements ever since. Although he was the first president elected by the Republican Party, Lincoln's view that the "the Union of these States is perpetual" has since been incorporated into all mainstream American parties.

Lincoln also set an example regarding the political ideal that all branches of the government must work together. For more than two decades before being elected president, Lincoln had spoken against slavery, including against rulings by the Supreme Court. However, as president, Lincoln understood his oath of office to include upholding all federal laws and Supreme Court rulings, no matter his personal opinion. While he might have supported some legislative changes to bring certain laws more in line with his personal views had war not broken out, Lincoln primarily sought to uphold federal laws and regulations that had been created in accordance with the Constitution. His emphasis on this also had an influence on his presidential successors, assisting those who faced pressure to ignore federal laws to stand firm in upholding the Constitution.

—Donald A. Watt, PhD

Bibliography and Additional Reading

"American President: Abraham Lincoln (1809–1865)." *The Miller Center.* U of Virginia, 2013. Web. 24 Apr. 2013.

"American Presidents Life Portraits: Abraham Lincoln." *AH: American History TV.* National Cable Satellite Corporation, 2013. Web. 24 Apr. 2013.

Beschloss, Michael, and Hugh Sidey. *The Presidents of the United States of America.* Washington: White House Historical Assn., 2009. Print.

Goodwin, Doris Kearns. *Team of Rivals: The Political Genius of Abraham Lincoln.* New York: Simon, 2005. Print.

Jaffa, Harry V. *A New Birth of Freedom: Abraham Lincoln and the Coming of the Civil War.* Lanham: Rowman, 2000. Print.

"Lincoln's First Inaugural Address." *American Treasures of the Library of Congress.* Lib. of Cong., 27 July 2010. Web. 24 Apr. 2013.

Sandburg, Carl. *Abraham Lincoln: The Prairie Years and the War Years.* New York: Harcourt, 1954. Print.

White, Ronald C. *A. Lincoln: A Biography.* New York: Random, 2009. Print.

Fellow Countrymen:

At this second appearing to take the oath of the presidential office, there is less occasion for an extended address than there was at the first. Then a statement, somewhat in detail, of a course to be pursued, seemed fitting and proper. Now, at the expiration of four years, during which public declarations have been constantly called forth on every point and phase of the great contest which still absorbs the attention, and engrosses the energies of the nation, little that is new could be presented. The progress of our arms, upon which all else chiefly depends, is as well known to the public as to myself; and it is, I trust, reasonably satisfactory and encouraging to all. With high hope for the future, no prediction in regard to it is ventured.

On the occasion corresponding to this four years ago, all thoughts were anxiously directed to an impending civil war. All dreaded it— all sought to avert it. While the inaugeral address was being delivered from this place, devoted altogether to saving the Union without war, insurgent agents were in

◼ Abraham Lincoln's Second Inaugural Address

Date: March 4, 1865
Author: Abraham Lincoln
Genre: Speech; political sermon

Summary Overview

On March 4, 1865, with the American Civil War nearing its end and the defeat of the Confederacy a foregone conclusion, Abraham Lincoln used the occasion of his second inaugural address to present his vision of what the nation should do and what it could become in the years that followed a war that had been a tragedy for both sides.

In a brief speech, Lincoln consciously chose not to highlight Union military victories nor blame Confederate leaders for leading the nation down the path to war. Rather, he struck a distinctly conciliatory note, speaking of binding the wounds of the war and renewing the unity of the nation. He did not talk of punishing the South but rather of renewing the ties of national brotherhood. Lincoln set the tone for the policies he hoped to pursue in the period that followed, known as Reconstruction. The United States, in Lincoln's estimation, could learn from the tragedy of the prior four years and use that knowledge to finally fulfill the vision that the Founding Fathers had some ninety years before.

Defining Moment

It is hard to think of a more contentious time in the history of the United States than the four years of the Civil War. Brothers fought against brothers, with both armies claiming to defend the legacy of the Founding Fathers. What lit the fuse of civil war was the election of President Abraham Lincoln in 1860, who won by a landslide in the North yet did not carry a single state in the South. In December 1860, South Carolina passed an ordinance of secession, citing the encroachment of state rights by the federal government. Six other slave-holding states followed suit by February 1861. Lincoln had warned in 1858 that "a house divided against itself cannot stand," and by 1864 the war was finally drawing to a close. At the conclusion of his re-election campaign, Lincoln had won 212 of the 233 electoral votes. But however large his support was in the Union, he was faced with the herculean task of taking what had been two separate and warring countries for four years and reuniting them.

Over the course of the war, the American people had witnessed unimaginable carnage. More than 620,000 people, roughly 2 percent of the American population, died in the conflict. Although Lincoln enjoyed widespread support in the North, there were significant ideological divisions. Though many Northerners agreed on the justice of the Union cause, much of the population was weary of the constant carnage and sacrifice of war. The campaign of Lincoln's 1864 Democratic opponent, former general in chief of the Union Army, George B. McClellan, had run on the promise that he would negotiate with the Confederate government to bring an end to the war as quickly as possible. However, as the campaign and year of 1864 progressed, it became increasingly clear that the Confederate armies were nearing defeat. In March 1864 Lincoln had appointed Ulysses S. Grant as general in chief of the Armies of the United States. General William T. Sherman was leading his army through the South, blazing a trail of destruction that ended in Atlanta, which he captured on September 2, 1864, just two months before the presidential election.

In the nearly four months between Lincoln's re-election and his second inauguration in March 1865, the string of Union victories continued. Sherman continued beyond Atlanta on his "march to the sea," capturing the city of Savannah in December. Peace talks with the Confederacy had begun, though many in the South refused to surrender. By early March it was clear that the Confederate Army could not withstand the Union forces much longer, and Lincoln and his advisers were working to determine their postwar policies. Many of his fellow Republicans, such as Pennsylvania congressman Thaddeus Stevens, wanted a punitive policy that would punish Southern rebels for seceding from the Union and starting such a destructive war. However, Lincoln had already begun to give indications that he viewed things quite differently. During his re-election campaign, Andrew Johnson, a Democrat from Tennessee, was chosen as Lincoln's vice presidential running mate, and as he approached his inaugural address, it was clear that Lincoln planned to present a vision for the period following the war.

Author Biography

Abraham Lincoln was born on February 12, 1809, in Hardin County, Kentucky. He served eight years in the Illinois legislature and practiced law. He lost an 1858 election bid for the U.S. Senate but won the Republican nomination for president two years later. He was elected president in 1860.

At the outset of the Civil War, Lincoln did not pursue the war with the end of slavery in mind. Rather, the preservation of the Union was foremost in his mind. Throughout the early years of the war, while Union Army struggled with leadership and strategy, Lincoln's thoughts on race and slavery evolved. In 1862, Lincoln changed his policy to allow African Americans to join the Union Army. On January 1, 1863, he issued the Emancipation Proclamation, which declared that all slaves in the Confederacy were to be freed forever. This evolution of thought, however, never overwhelmed his desire to restore the Union, including its Southern white secessionists. In November 1863, he gave his most famous speech: The Gettysburg Address laid out a vision of restoration that included the South. Though he pursued complete victory over the South, when the conflict ended it was clear that Lincoln's attitude was conciliatory.

HISTORICAL DOCUMENT

Fellow-Countrymen:

At this second appearing to take the oath of the Presidential office there is less occasion for an extended address than there was at the first. Then a statement somewhat in detail of a course to be pursued seemed fitting and proper. Now, at the expiration of four years, during which public declarations have been constantly called forth on every point and phase of the great contest which still absorbs the attention and engrosses the energies of the nation, little that is new could be presented. The progress of our arms, upon which all else chiefly depends, is as well known to the public as to myself, and it is, I trust, reasonably satisfactory and encouraging to all. With high hope for the future, no prediction in regard to it is ventured.

On the occasion corresponding to this four years ago all thoughts were anxiously directed to an impending civil war. All dreaded it, all sought to avert it. While the inaugural address was being delivered from this place, devoted altogether to saving the Union without war, insurgent agents were in the city seeking to destroy it without war—seeking to dissolve the Union and divide effects by negotiation. Both parties deprecated war, but one of them would make war rather than let the nation survive, and the other would accept war rather than let it perish, and the war came.

One-eighth of the whole population were colored slaves, not distributed generally over the Union, but localized in the southern part of it. These slaves constituted a peculiar and powerful interest. All knew that this interest was somehow the cause of the war. To strengthen, perpetuate, and extend this interest was the object for which the insurgents would rend the Union even by war, while the Government claimed no right to do more than to restrict the territorial enlargement of it. Neither party expected for the war the magnitude or the duration which it has already attained. Neither anticipated that the cause of the conflict might cease with or even before the conflict itself should cease. Each looked for an easier triumph, and a result less fundamental and astounding. Both read the same Bible and pray to the same God, and each invokes His aid against the other. It may seem strange that any men should dare to ask a just God's assistance in wringing their bread from the sweat of other men's faces, but let us judge not, that we be not judged. The prayers of both could not be answered. That of neither has been answered fully. The Almighty has His own purposes. "Woe unto the world because of offenses; for it must needs be that offenses come, but woe to that man by whom the offense cometh." If we shall suppose that American slavery is one of those offenses which, in the providence of God, must needs come, but which, having continued through His appointed time, He now wills to remove, and that He gives to both North and South this terrible war as the woe due to those by whom the offense came, shall we discern therein any departure from those divine attributes which the believers in a living God always ascribe to Him? Fondly do we hope, fervently do we pray, that this mighty scourge of war may speedily pass away. Yet, if God wills that it continue until all the wealth piled by the bondsman's two hundred and fifty years of unrequited toil shall be sunk, and until every drop of blood drawn with the lash shall be paid by

another drawn with the sword, as was said three thousand years ago, so still it must be said "the judgments of the Lord are true and righteous altogether."

With malice toward none, with charity for all, with firmness in the right as God gives us to see the right, let us strive on to finish the work we are in, to bind up the nation's wounds, to care for him who shall have borne the battle and for his widow and his orphan, to do all which may achieve and cherish a just and lasting peace among ourselves and with all nations.

Document Analysis

As Abraham Lincoln began to speak at his second inauguration in March 1865, his agenda was clear. Though his constituency was only made up of the Union states that had remained loyal to the United States during the Civil War, it became apparent that his address was aimed at both the Union and the Confederacy and was meant to present his vision of the reunified nation in the years to follow. Continuing on the themes he began just over a year earlier in his Gettysburg Address, he spoke of reconciliation and reunion with the Confederate states, which were still in rebellion.

Lincoln sets the stage for his remarks by noting the differences between the state of the country at his first and second inaugural addresses. By 1865, the end of the war was imminent, a stark contrast to the apprehension and sense of impending conflict that characterized his first inauguration, four years earlier. Although he acknowledges that both side of the conflict deprecated war, Lincoln is clear on whom he blames for the war, stating that while both parties pursued war, only the South placed making war above the survival of the nation. Another important difference between Lincoln's two inaugural addresses is how he discusses the topic of slavery. In his first inaugural address, Lincoln, still seeking to quell the brewing rebellion, spoke of not interfering with slavery where it already existed. Four years later, he spoke of the slaves as "a peculiar and powerful interest" and a cause of the war.

The president then changes his focus, spending the bulk of the brief address talking of the commonalities that remain between the South and North. He speaks of their common religious views, noting that both prayed for easy victory, but neither had their prayers answered. He spoke of slavery as a sort of national sin that the war

was acting to remove, but one so grievous that if it took "every drop of blood" it would be God's righteous judgment that it was so.

Lincoln concludes with one of his best-known statements, which sums up his views on Reconstruction concisely: "With malice toward none, with charity for all, with firmness in the right as God gives us to see the right, let us strive on to finish the work we are in, to bind up the nation's wounds." In this address, Lincoln clearly conveys his desire for reconciliation and his disinterest in pursuing punitive measures against the Confederates following the war.

Essential Themes

The lasting impact of Lincoln's second inaugural address can be seen in what was actually accomplished during the period known as Reconstruction, as well as what was not achieved. Nothing that happened during Reconstruction can be analyzed without reference to what happened only forty-one days later, on April 14, 1865, when Virginia actor John Wilkes Booth shot and killed Lincoln at Ford's Theatre in Washington, DC. As the president who saw the Union through its most tumultuous four years of existence, Lincoln would have had significant influence over Reconstruction during his second term. However, what that influence would have looked like cannot be known, as his vice president, Andrew Johnson—a Southern Democrat—took office, and Johnson held much less influence over the congressional Republicans.

Certainly, the three "Reconstruction Amendments"—the Thirteenth Amendment, which outlawed slavery; the Fourteenth Amendment, which guaranteed equal protection under the law; and the Fifteenth Amendment, which guaranteed the right to vote regardless of race—

represent a fundamental shift in the definition of the Constitution's "We the People." Lincoln had already alluded to these concepts, and their ratification was likely no matter who was president. However, it is the will with which these amendments were implemented that might have been different were Lincoln to have survived. As it was, Johnson clashed early and often with congressional Radical Republicans, led by Congressman Thaddeus Stevens, over the extent to which Southern secessionists would be punished for the war and to which the federal government would intervene to protect the rights of former slaves through the Freedmen's Bureau. By the end of Reconstruction in 1877, the South had developed the Jim Crow system of segregation and discrimination that would characterize the country well into the twentieth century.

But even if Lincoln's second inaugural address did not lay out a roadmap for the leaders who followed him, it did set a standard to which later generations would aspire. His words were echoed during the civil rights movement of the 1950s and 1960s by leaders such as Martin Luther King Jr. The "just and lasting peace" Lincoln envisioned would prove difficult to achieve. But as a national aspiration, Lincoln's words still carry the same power more than 150 years later as they did when they were spoken.

—*Steven L. Danver, PhD*

Bibliography and Additional Reading

Du Bois, W. E. B. *Black Reconstruction in America: Toward a History of the Part of Which Black Folk Played in the Attempt to Reconstruct Democracy in America, 1860–1880.* Rev. ed. New Brunswick: Transaction, 2012.

Foner, Eric. *Reconstruction: America's Unfinished Revolution, 1863–1877.* New York: Harper, 1988. Print.

McPherson, James M. *Battle Cry of Freedom: The Civil War Era.* New York: Ballantine, 1989. Print.

White, Ronald C., Jr. *Lincoln's Greatest Speech: The Second Inaugural.* New York: Simon, 2002. Print.

■ President Grant's First Inaugural Address

Date: March 4, 1869
Author: Ulysses S. Grant
Genre: Speech

Summary Overview

Ulysses S. Grant was elected president of the United States in November 1868 and took office on March 4, 1869. In his inaugural address, he did not lay out any detailed plans for his administration, but promised to do his best in meeting the responsibilities of the office. Most of his address focused on three major problems. One was the need to pay off the enormous debt incurred by fighting the Civil War. Secondly, during the Civil War, the government had issued paper currency and suspended the practice of redeeming paper money in gold, and Grant believed the government must resume the redemption of paper money with gold coins as soon as possible. Grant expressed concern about "the original occupants of the land"—the Native Americans and promised to support policies aimed at their "civilization" and making them citizens of the United States. He also addressed the restoration of civil law in the former states of the Confederacy, including the issue of voting rights for the freed slaves.

Defining Moment

When Ulysses Grant became president in March 1869, it was less than four years since the Civil War had ended. The impact of the war was still being felt in the struggle over race relations and the civil rights of the freed slaves in the South, and in the enormous debt the federal government had incurred to conduct the war. Additionally, while the Republican Party had controlled the White House and both houses of Congress since Abraham Lincoln's election in 1860, the party was in serious disarray by 1869. When Lincoln had run for re-election in 1864, the Republicans had put Andrew Johnson, a former Democrat, on the ticket as a show of national support for the Union war effort. Johnson had been a U.S. senator from Tennessee before the Civil War, but had opposed secession. But to the dismay of the Republican Party, when Johnson succeeded to the presidency upon Lincoln's death, he pursued a very lenient policy toward the former Confederate states and seemed determined to block any attempt to guarantee the rights of the freed slaves. An attempt to remove Johnson from office by impeachment had failed by a narrow vote, and Johnson had, in fact, tried unsuccessfully to secure the Democratic nomination for president in 1868.

Although speculation about Grant as a presidential candidate had started during the Civil War, Grant was not an automatic choice for the Republican Party in 1868. Before the Civil War, he had seemed to lean toward the Democrats in politics, and for a time, he had identified with Johnson's repudiated Reconstruction policies. His chief opponent for the Republican nomination was Salmon P. Chase, who had served as Secretary of the Treasury in Lincoln's cabinet and was the current Chief Justice of the U.S. Supreme Court. But during Johnson's impeachment trial, Republicans came to believe that Chase favored acquittal of the president, and this cost him support in the 1868 convention. In a vote that followed sectional lines, except for Southern blacks voting Republican in areas where they were allowed to vote, Grant had defeated the Democratic candidate, Horatio Seymour, a former governor of New York. Grant won by a 400,000-vote margin in the popular vote, out of roughly 5.7 million votes cast; but in the Electoral College, his victory margin was more than 134 votes. As Grant took office, he knew two major problems facing the nation were the treatment of the freed slaves in the South—especially the right to vote for adult black males—and the tremendous federal debt caused by the Civil War. In his inaugural address, he promised to address both of these issues.

Author Biography

Ulysses S. Grant was the eighteenth president of the United States, but he had first risen to fame as the pre-eminent Union general in the American Civil War. He was born in Point Pleasant, Ohio on April 27, 1822. He graduated from West Point in 1843. Grant served with distinction in the U.S. war with Mexico (1846 to 1848), but after the war, personal troubles led him to resign from the army in 1854. When the Civil War broke out, Grant became an officer in the Illinois volunteer troops. Due to his success as a commander, he rose steadily through the ranks. In the spring of 1864, Grant was promoted to the newly revived rank of lieutenant general and made the general-in-chief of the Union Army. He was elected president of the United States in November 1868, and re-elected in November 1872. Grant's presidency was marked by corruption and scandal, although it does not appear he was part of any of the scandals. After leaving the presidency, a bad business investment left Grant impoverished. He wrote his Personal Memoirs while dying of throat cancer, hoping to leave a legacy to provide financially for his family. He died at his family home near Saratoga, NY, on July 23, 1885.

First inauguration of Ulysses S. Grant, Capitol building steps, March 4, 1869 by Mathew Brady(U.S. National Archives and Records Administration)

HISTORICAL DOCUMENT

Your suffrages having elected me to the office of President of the United States, I have, in conformity to the Constitution of our country, taken the oath of office prescribed therein. I have taken this oath without mental reservation and with the determination to do to the best of my ability all that is required of me. The responsibilities of the position I feel, but accept them without fear. The office has come to me unsought; I commence its duties untrammeled. I bring to it a conscious desire and determination to fill it to the best of my ability to the satisfaction of the people.

On all leading questions agitating the public mind I will always express my views to Congress and urge them according to my judgment, and when I think it advisable will exercise the constitutional privilege of interposing a veto to defeat measures which I oppose; but all laws will be faithfully executed, whether they meet my approval or not.

I shall on all subjects have a policy to recommend, but none to enforce against the will of the people. Laws are to govern all alike—those opposed as well as those who favor them. I know no method to secure the repeal of bad or obnoxious laws so effective as their stringent execution.

The country having just emerged from a great rebellion, many questions will come before it for settlement in the next four years which preceding Administrations have never had to deal with. In meeting these it is desirable that they should be approached calmly, without prejudice, hate, or sectional pride, remembering that the greatest good to the greatest number is the object to be attained.

This requires security of person, property, and free religious and political opinion in every part of our common country, without regard to local prejudice. All laws to secure these ends will receive my best efforts for their enforcement.

A great debt has been contracted in securing to us and our posterity the Union. The payment of this, principal and interest, as well as the return to a specie basis as soon as it can be accomplished without material detriment to the debtor class or to the country at large, must be provided for. To protect the national honor, every dollar of Government indebtedness should be paid in gold, unless otherwise expressly stipulated in the contract. Let it be understood that no repudiator of one farthing of our public debt will be trusted in public place, and it will go far toward strengthening a credit which ought to be the best in the world, and will ultimately enable us to replace the debt with bonds bearing less interest than we now pay. To this should be added a faithful collection of the revenue, a strict accountability to the Treasury for every dollar collected, and the greatest practicable retrenchment in expenditure in every department of Government.

When we compare the paying capacity of the country now, with the ten States in poverty from the effects of war, but soon to emerge, I trust, into greater prosperity than ever before, with its paying capacity twenty-five years ago, and calculate what it probably will be twenty-five years hence, who can doubt the feasibility of paying every dollar then with more ease than we now pay for useless luxuries? Why, it looks as though Providence had bestowed upon us a strong box in the precious metals locked up in the sterile mountains of the far West, and which we are now forging the key to unlock, to meet the very contingency that is now upon us.

Ultimately it may be necessary to insure the facilities to reach these riches and it may be necessary also that the General Government should give its aid to secure this access; but that should only be when a dollar of obligation to pay secures precisely the same sort of dollar to use now, and not before. Whilst the question of specie payments is in abeyance the prudent business man is careful about contracting debts payable in the distant future. The nation should follow the same rule. A prostrate commerce is to be rebuilt and all industries encouraged.

The young men of the country—those who from their age must be its rulers twenty-five years hence—have a peculiar interest in maintaining the national honor. A moment's reflection as to what will be our commanding influence among the nations of the earth in their day, if they are only true to themselves, should inspire them with national pride. All divisions—geographical, political, and religious—can join in this common sentiment. How the public debt is to be paid or specie payments resumed is not so important as that a plan should be adopted and acquiesced in. A united determination to do is worth more than divided counsels upon the method of doing. Legislation upon this subject may not be necessary now, or even advisable, but it will be when the civil law is more fully restored in all parts of the country and trade resumes its wonted channels.

It will be my endeavor to execute all laws in good faith, to collect all revenues assessed, and to have them properly accounted for and economically disbursed. I will to the best of my ability appoint to office those only who will carry out this design.

In regard to foreign policy, I would deal with nations as equitable law requires individuals to deal with each other, and I would protect the law-abiding citizen, whether of native or foreign birth, wherever his rights are jeopardized or the flag of our country floats. I would respect the rights of all nations, demanding equal respect for our own. If others depart from this rule in their deal-ings with us, we may be compelled to follow their precedent.

The proper treatment of the original occupants of this land, the Indians, is one deserving of careful study. I will favor any course toward them which tends to their civilization and ultimate citizenship.

The question of suffrage is one which is likely to agitate the public so long as a portion of the citizens of the nation are excluded from its privileges in any State. It seems to me very desirable that this question should be settled now, and I entertain the hope and express the desire that it may be by the ratification of the fifteenth article of amendment to the Constitution.

In conclusion I ask patient forbearance one toward another throughout the land, and a determined effort on the part of every citizen to do his share toward cementing a happy union; and I ask the prayers of the nation to Almighty God in behalf of this consummation.

GLOSSARY

abeyance: lapse or temporary suspension; undetermined

civilization: in this case, assimilation or enculturation

sectional pride: geographical or regional bias—particularly, in this case, North versus South

specie: coin money, as against paper; gold as the basis for paper currency

suffrages: votes

wonted: likely, preferred, or most common

Document Analysis

Grant began his inaugural address noting that, although he had not sought the presidency, he was entering the office ready to fulfill the responsibilities it entailed. He did not lay out any detailed policy objectives, but promised to express his views on issues before Congress, to urge legislation in line with his views, and to use the presidential veto over laws that he opposed.

The bulk of Grant's address deals with the need to address financial and monetary issues resulting from the Civil War. The federal government had borrowed roughly three billion dollars to finance the war effort. Also, in December 1861, the U.S. Treasury had suspended the policy of redeeming paper currency for gold, and early the following year, began printing paper money. Grant believed that the debt had to be repaid, but did not lay out any plan for how to do this, and even said the particular method was not as important as simply the determination to do so and getting the process started. Grant also called for the resumption of "specie redemption" as soon as possible—that is, the practice of the U.S. Treasury redeeming paper money with gold coin. Grant believed that addressing these two problems would restore both the credit-worthiness of the nation and the confidence of the business community.

Grant commented briefly on foreign affairs, promising to treat foreign nations fairly and also to protect the rights of American citizens overseas. He warned that the

United States might respond in kind if any nation failed to respect our rights.

Grant also mentioned his concern for the American Indians, who he referred to as "the original occupants of this land." Since spending time on the West Coast in the Army, after the Mexican War, Grant had been impressed with the needs of the Indians. He favored policies that would tend to their "civilization," meaning their assimilation into the general American culture, and he also supported extending U.S. citizenship to the Indians.

Problems involving Reconstruction issues in the former Confederate states received little notice in this address. Grant specifically addressed "suffrage"—the right to vote. Many Southern states were trying to restrict the rights of the freed slaves to vote. Grant believed this issue must be settled quickly, and he hoped it soon would be by the ratification of the Fifteenth Amendment, which forbade any state from using "race, color, or previous condition of servitude" as a basis for denying the right to vote.

Essential Themes

A major emphasis in Grant's inaugural address was the financial responsibility of the federal government, and related to this, the question of what kind of money the nation should use. Throughout early U.S. history, it was generally assumed that the nation should incur debt only in emergency situations, and once the emergency was passed, the debt should be paid off as quickly as possible. Grant believed that the debt incurred fighting the Civil War must be addressed immediately. He also believed that the nation should, as soon as possible, resume the practice of redeeming paper money with gold coins— meaning that people could turn paper money in at the U.S. Treasury and receive gold coinage in return. The government had issued the "greenbacks" during the Civil War as an emergency measure, and many who believed in a "sound money" policy would have agreed with Grant that a return to using only money made from (or clearly backed by) precious metal should be a first priority. Grant believed that the future credit-worthiness of the nation, and the confidence of the business community, required immediate steps to address the debt issue and the resumption of currency redemption. Monetary policy would be a political issue for the next thirty years, as the Greenbacker Party in the 1870s called for continued use of paper money, and the Populist Party in the 1890s demanded the coinage of silver dollars to expand the money supply.

Grant also addressed the issue of civil disorder in the former Confederate states, and the right to vote of the freed slaves. He hoped that the Fifteenth Amendment would soon be adopted. That amendment would prohibit any use of "race, color, or previous condition of servitude" as grounds for denying the right to vote. The Fifteenth Amendment was passed by Congress in March 1869 and ratified in February 1870. The record of Grant's two presidential administrations on Reconstruction and the civil rights of African Americans was mixed. At times, strong action was taken to protect these rights, but in general, the commitment of the Republican Party and Northern voters generally to Reconstruction issues was waning during the 1870s.

—*Mark S. Joy, PhD*

Bibliography and Additional Reading

McFeely, William S. *Grant: A Biography*. New York: W. W. Norton, 1981. Print.

Scaturro, Frank J. *President Grant Reconsidered*. Latham, MD: Rowman & Littlefield, 1999. Print.

Smith, Jean Edward. *Grant*. New York: Simon and Schuster, 2001. Print.

■ A Contested Election: Report to Congress on the Activities of the Ku Klux Klan

Date: February 11, 1870
Author: United States House of Representatives
Genre: Report

Summary Overview

The activities of the newly organized Ku Klux Klan in Tennessee so disrupted the 1868 election in the Fourth Congressional District that Governor William Brownlow invalidated the election results and declared Republican candidate Lewis Tillman the winner. Conservative candidate C. A. Sheafe, who received the majority of votes, contested the decision and petitioned the U.S. House of Representatives to reverse Brownlow's ruling. The House committee tasked with investigating the matter took extensive testimony, which revealed the nature and extent of the Klan's efforts to intimidate African Americans and their white supporters. As a result, the House of Representatives decided that Tillman should be awarded the seat in Congress. The committee's inquiry prompted widespread interest in Klan activities and was instrumental in the establishment of a joint committee of Congress to investigate the Klan's influence across the South.

Defining Moment

In August 1868 the Tennessee state legislature had initiated its own investigation into the activities of the Ku Klux Klan as part of an ongoing campaign by Radical Republican Governor William Brownlow to reactivate the Tennessee State Guard, a militia under his control. The Guard was established in 1867 and used effectively to keep peace during elections that year; however, early in 1868 it was deactivated. Reports during the spring of 1868 of growing violence against African Americans and white Americans who supported Republicans made Brownlow fearful that congressional elections in November would be disrupted. Convinced that federal troops would be unavailable to stop Klan violence, Brownlow called a special session of the Tennessee legislature in July 1868 to push through legislation reactivating the Guard.

During the session, a joint military committee conducted an inquiry into Klan activities. Led by Tennessee state senator William J. Smith and state representative William F. Prosser, former Union officers and staunch supporters of Reconstruction, the committee took testimony from dozens of witnesses who told horrifying stories of intimidation, physical abuse, rape, and murder. The committee's report was printed in September 1868. To Brownlow's dismay, however, the bill authorizing reestablishment of the Guard did not pass in time for him to deploy troops to areas where Klan violence was likely to be highest during the November election.

Initial results in Tennessee's Fourth Congressional District indicated that conservative C. A. Sheafe defeated Republican Lewis Tillman by a comfortable majority. Governor Brownlow was convinced that Klan intimidation kept many of the district's nearly eight thousand African Americans from voting; he declared the results invalid and certified Tillman as the winner. Sheafe contested the decision, and in 1869 the matter was taken up in the U.S. House of Representatives, which has the power to seat its members.

The House committee adjudicating Sheafe's claim heard testimony from individuals who had been subject to Klan intimidation. Also testifying was Tennessee state senator William J. Wisener, another member of the state legislature's joint military committee. Through him, extracts from the joint military committee's report were made part of the House investigation. The House committee also incorporated into its report information from an 1868 account of Klan activities in Tennessee submitted by Major General William P. Carlin, assistant commissioner of the Tennessee Freedmen's Bureau, to Major General Oliver O. Howard, commissioner of the Freedmen's Bureau in Washington, DC, as well as accounts from other bureau agents. Their reports confirmed the testimony of witnesses to both the Tennessee legislature in 1868 and the House committee in 1869 that the Ku Klux Klan was a growing menace, posing a serious threat to the restoration of democracy and the guarantee of equal rights in former Confederate states.

About the Document

The principals in the 1868 election in Tennessee's Fourth Congressional District were little more than pawns in the chess game between Southerners intent on restoring the social and political order as it had existed before the war and Radicals bent on reconstructing the state in the image of its Northern neighbors. Ironically, Republican candidate Lewis Tillman was a Tennessee native who had spent his career in the state's court system and as a newspaper editor, while his conservative opponent, C. A. Sheafe, was an Ohioan who had served in the federal army before moving to Tennessee.

That the Ku Klux Klan played a role in keeping Tillman's supporters from the polls seems indisputable, yet it is in some ways remarkable. Founded in 1866, the Klan had no strong formal organization; many bands of miscreants rode through the countryside calling themselves Klansmen. While the perpetrators of violence were most often members of the working classes, a number of prominent Southerners had ties to the Klan, helping to protect other Klansmen accused of crimes. The Klan remained active throughout the South until the mid-1870s.

In Tennessee the fight against the Klan was led by William G. Brownlow. Born in 1805 in Virginia, Brownlow became a minister and was a traveling preacher throughout Appalachia before settling in Elizabethton, Tennessee, in 1836. Before the Civil War he was editor of a pro-Union newspaper. He left the state after Tennessee seceded but returned in 1863 when Union troops established an occupation force there. He was elected governor in 1865 and was reelected in 1867, largely on votes of his new constituency, freed slaves. Shortly after the 1868 elections, he began lobbying the legislature to appoint him U.S. senator for Tennessee, a position he assumed in March 1869. After serving one term, he returned to Tennessee and resumed his newspaper career until his death in 1877.

Among the groups that gathered information on atrocities committed by the Ku Klux Klan and other reactionary groups in the South, none was more important than the Bureau of Refugees, Freedmen, and Abandoned Lands. Established by Congress in 1865, the Freedmen's Bureau, as it was popularly known, assisted freed slaves with a variety of economic and political issues. Led by Union General Oliver O. Howard, a native of Maine, the Bureau placed agents throughout the South to carry out its mission. These agents were often targets of Klan violence themselves, and their reports to the Bureau's headquarters in Washington, DC, provided further evidence of the difficulties African Americans faced in becoming fully integrated into postwar society.

HISTORICAL DOCUMENT

This pertains to the deposition of William H. Wisener in case of C. A. *Sheafe vs. Lewis Tillman*, contested election.

WM. GALBREATH, Mayor.

Report of the joint military committee of the two houses in relation to the organization of the militia of the State of Tennessee, submitted to the extra session of the thirty-fifth general assembly, September 2, 1868.

Mr. Speaker: Your committee to whom was referred that part of the governor's message relating to outrages perpetrated by an organization known as the Ku-Klux Klan, and the necessity of organizing the militia for the protection of the loyal people of the State of Tennessee,

have had the same under consideration; and after summoning a great many witnesses before them, are satisfied that there exists an organization of armed men going abroad disguised, robbing poor negroes of their fire-arms, taking them out of their houses at night, hanging, shooting, and whipping them in a most cruel manner, and driving them from their homes. Nor is this confined to the colored men alone. Women and children have been subjected to the torture of the lash, and brutal assaults have been committed upon them by these night-prowlers, and in many instances, the persons of females have been violated, and when the husband or father complained, he has been obliged to flee to save his own life.

Nor has this been confined to one county or one section of the State alone. Your committee find, that, after a careful investigation of all the facts, that these depredations have been committed all over Middle and West Tennessee, and in some parts of East Tennessee; particularly has this been the case in Maury, Lincoln, Giles, Marshall, Obion, Hardeman, Fayette and Gibson Counties. In Lincoln County, they took Senator Wm. Wyatt from his house in the night, and inflicted all sorts of indignities upon him. They beat him over the head with their pistols, cutting a frightful gash, and saturating his shirt with blood, leaving him insensible. Senator Wyatt is a Christian gentleman, and sixty-five years of age; his only offense being that he is a Union man and a member of the State legislature.

We also find that the same spirit exists in Obion County; that it was rife there, indeed, one year and a half ago, when the disloyalists so inhumanly and brutally murdered Senator Case and his son. Since then, depredations have been committed all over the country that calls loudly for redress. No loyal man is safe in that country at the present time.

Your committee's attention has also been directed to Maury County. We find that a perfect reign of terror exists there; that some two hundred colored men have had to flee from their homes, and take refuge in the city of Nashville; afraid to return, although here they are destitute of food, or any means of subsistence. In this county, school-houses have been burned down, teachers driven away, and colored men shot, whipped, and murdered at will. Hon. S. M. Arnell, congressman from that district, was sought for, when he was at home on a visit, by members of the Ku-Klux Klan, who were thirsting for his blood.

In Fayette County, the teacher of colored children has been assaulted and driven away by the Ku-Klux Klan.

Your committee find, that to enumerate all the outrages committed by this organization of outlaws, would take more time than can be spared. They would most respectfully direct your attention to a synopsis of the evidence taken before your committee; remarking at the same time, that much valuable information is necessarily left out on account of the witnesses fearing to have their names mentioned in this report, lest they should hereafter, on account of their testimony, lose their lives.

One of the most brutal assaults perhaps, that had been committed, was on the person of a school teacher, in Shelbyville, Bedford County, Tennessee. Mr. Dunlap, a white instructor, was taken from his house in the night by the Ku-Klux Klan, and most inhumanly whipped; and for no other reason than he was a white man, teaching a colored school. One witness testified that he was a confederate soldier, a native Tennessean; has been with negroes all his life, and seen them whipped by different persons; but never saw any one beaten as this man, Dunlap, was. It is in evidence that Mr. Dunlap is a member of the Methodist Church, and a very quiet, inoffensive man. Attention is especially directed to the evidence in this case.

Your committee also find that there has been a determined effort and is still a determined purpose all over Middle and West Tennessee, to keep colored men from the polls, and thus secure the election to office of candidates of the Democratic Party. Very many of the outrages committed have been against men who were formerly soldiers in the national army. The proof shows that there is an eternal hatred existing against all men that voted the republican ticket, or who belong to the Loyal League, or are engaged in teaching schools, and giving instruction to the humbler classes of their fellow-men.

The committee are compelled to conclude, from the evidence before them, that the ultimate object of the Ku-Klux Klan is, to intimidate Union men, both black and white, keep them from the polls on election day, and, by a system of anti-lawry and terrorism, carry the State in November next for Seymour and Blair.

Your committee would again call the attention of the general assembly to the following synopsis of testimony, as better calculated to show the true condition of the country than anything your committee could say:

We are permitted to make the following extracts from the report of Major General Carlin to General Howard, for the month of June, 1868:

"General: I have the honor to submit the following report on the condition of affairs pertaining to this department, during the month of June last. It is with deep regret that I am compelled to begin this report with the statement, that, since my connection with the bureau, no such discouraging state of affairs has prevailed in Tennessee, during any one month, as that for the month of June last. I say discouraging, because it is totally beyond the powers of myself and subordinates to remedy evils that cry aloud for redress.

"In the counties of Marshall, Rutherford, Maury, and Giles, it may be said that a reign of terror has been established, and will doubtless remain, unless the State, or United States, should provide a military force to be stationed in those counties.

"The hostility of the implacable pro-slavery people to colored education has manifested itself in numerous instances of violence toward teachers of colored schools.

"Your attention is called especially to the case of Mr. Newton, who was assaulted and badly wounded at Somerville. He would doubtless have been slain if he had not escaped in time. The case was reported by the undersigned to Major General Thomas, commanding the department, and troops were asked for to protect the school and teachers. Mr. Newton was escorted back by them to his school-house, where he has continued to conduct his school.

"This affair is more particularly described in the extracts from the report of Lieutenant Colonel Palmer, sub-assistant commissioner of the subdistrict of Memphis.

"There will doubtless be great excitement and frequent disturbances in the State during the present political canvass for President and State officers. Nearly every day furnishes additional evidence of the determination of the Ku-Klux Klan and their friends to bring about a state of affairs that will preclude the possibility of personal liberty for the colored people, and the active, out-spoken Union men. I doubt if any measure, short of martial law, will preserve peace and insure safety till after the next election."

A. H. Eastman, agent at Columbia, Tennessee, reports the following extracts:

"The Ku-Klux Klan appear to be on the 'war path.' Complaints of visitations by night, all over my district, of the breaking into of houses and assaults upon the inmates, are very frequent. The Klan went to the house of Joshua Ferrell, an old and quiet colored man, on the night of the 12th instant, called him from his bed, and, while he was unfastening the door, they jumped in upon him and beat his head with a pistol, cutting a gash half an inch wide, four inches long, and to the skull. Then they asked him for fire-arms, which he said he had not. They then took him into a field and whipped him so badly that it nearly killed him. They also tore up everything in the house, and then went to his son's house, took him from his bed, smashed a large looking-glass over the head of his sick wife, who was in bed. They then whipped the man with stirrup-straps and buckles, which cut long and deep gashes into the flesh, and all because, they said, he was a 'big-feeling nigger, voted for Brownlow, and belonged to the Union League.'"

J. K. Nelson, agent at Murfreesboro, Tennessee, says the Ku-Klux Klan took from his house, about midnight, Bill Carlton, (colored) living in Middleton district, and beat him very severely, giving him, as he says, one hundred and fifty lashes with a heavy leather strap.

"On Thursday night last, the Klan went to the house of Minor Fletcher, living eight miles from here, on the Shelbyville pike, rode into his front and back porches on their horses, and called him out. They then proceeded to the house of D. Webb, about ten or twelve in number, and, as he reports, called to him to come out. This he refused to do, until they assured him that he should not be hurt, and threatened him with violence in case of his refusal. He went out; they then accused him of being a radical, and a Loyal Leaguer. He denied being a member of the league, but told them that he was a Union man and always had been. They called him a liar, and threatened to hang him, calling at the same time for a halter. His wife, who was in a critical condition, screamed and plead for him, and begged them to spare him on her account. They then told him to go back to his wife. He turned to go, when one of them caught him by the hair, jerked him to the ground, sprang upon him, and beat him in the face in a shocking manner, at the same time holding a pistol to his head, and threatening to shoot him. They then left him in an almost insensible condition, scarcely able to crawl to his house.

"More than half the outrages perpetrated by this Klan are not reported to me. The parties are afraid, or have a want of confidence in the bureau. There is a feeling of insecurity among the people (Unionists) that has not been equaled since 1861. I am so impressed with my own inability to fully understand the exact condition of affairs that I will be excused for not making the same comprehensible to you.

"This I do know, that I have been sleeping for months with a revolver under my pillow, and a double-barreled shot-gun, heavily charged with buck shot, at one hand, and a hatchet at the other, with an inclination to sell the little piece of mortality with which I am entrusted as dearly as possible. I have had to submit to insults, which make a man despise himself for bearing, and which I cannot submit to any longer. Many freedmen are afraid to sleep in their own houses. Many have already been driven from the country." . . .

Rev. H. O. Hoffman, Shelbyville, Tenn.:

"Have never seen any of the Klan, but that it exists in our county no one doubts. Several have been harmed by this secret organization. Mr. Dunlap and a colored man by the name of Jeff were badly whipped on the night of the 4th of July. His person was cut in great gashes, from the middle of his back to his knees. Mr. Dunlap's offense was teaching a colored school. I have been repeatedly threatened, and was told that the Ku-Klux Klan had a list made of men they designed driving from the country. Found the following note in my yard:

"In Ku-Klux Council, July 24, 1868.

"Rev. Mr. Hoffman: Your name is before the council. Beware! We will attend to you. You shall not call us villains—damn you. Ku-Klux."

"I believe the object of the Klan is to whip unarmed negroes, scare timid white men, break up elections, and interfere with the State government, and steal and plunder the goods of the people." . . .

GLOSSARY

Blair: Francis Blair; politician, Union Army general and unsuccessful candidate for vice president of the United States on the Democratic ticket in 1868

Galbreath, William: mayor of Shelbyville, Tennessee, in 1869

Mr. Speaker: DeWitt C. Senter, speaker of the Tennessee State Legislature in 1868

Radical: term generally used by Southerners after the Civil War to describe those who supported Reconstruction policies and equal rights for former slaves

Seymour: Horatio Seymour, two-term governor of New York (1853–1854 and 1863–1864) and unsuccessful Democratic candidate for president of the United States in 1868

stirrup-straps: leather loops attached to a saddle to assist riders in mounting

Thomas, George Henry: U.S. Army major general, a career soldier and in 1868 commander of the Department of the Cumberland (Tennessee and Kentucky)

Document Analysis

The excerpt above is part of an official report of a committee of the U.S. House of Representatives appointed in 1869 to investigate a contested election that took place the previous November in Tennessee's Fourth Congressional District. The committee was charged with making recommendations to the full House regarding a challenge filed by C. A. Sheafe, who had won the popular vote. Governor William Brownlow, determining that voter intimidation had been rampant in the district, certified Sheafe's opponent, Republican candidate Lewis Tillman, as the winner. The committee's report is contained in the Miscellaneous Documents of the Forty-First Congress (1869–71) under the title *Papers in the Contested Election Case of Sheafe vs. Tillman in the Fourth Congressional District of Tennessee*, which has an official printing date of February 11, 1870. The excerpted passages are taken from official reports and witness testimony that describe conditions in Tennessee during the spring and summer of 1868. The initial selection provides a summary and findings from a joint military committee appointed in August 1868 by the Tennessee legislature to investigate activities of the Ku Klux Klan. The Klan was thought to be responsible for an ongoing campaign of intimidation directed at recently freed slaves and their white supporters in order to keep those in the state supportive of Radical Republicans from voting or exercising other civil rights. Reports written by agents or managers of the Freedmen's Bureau provide information to superiors about the conditions of freed slaves in regions for which the agents were responsible. The brief excerpt from testimony by Reverend H. O. Hoffman describes his experience with the Klan.

Like most reports, the document prepared by the House of Representatives has a formal organization that reflects the conduct of the investigation. In the full report, transcripts of questions posed to each witness and witnesses' responses are recorded verbatim. Among those testifying before the House committee was Tennessee state senator William Wisener, who provided information about his own experiences with the Klan as well as infor-

mation from reports he had received while serving as a member of the joint military committee. As a supplement to Wisener's testimony, the congressional committee authorized the printing of an appendix that offers further evidence of the scope and characteristics of activities being conducted by the Klan. The excerpts above are taken from this appendix, which provides graphic details of the Klan's activities throughout Tennessee.

Founded as a social club in Pulaski, Tennessee, the Ku Klux Klan quickly transformed into an agency of white supremacists and former secessionists disgruntled with Radical Republican efforts to give African Americans equal rights. At a meeting held in Nashville in 1867, former Confederate General Nathan Bedford Forrest was selected as national head of the organization. Despite some attempt to create a structure and hierarchy (complete with mysterious titles for leaders such as "Grand Wizard," "Grand Dragon," and "Grand Cyclops," to name a few), the Klan remained only loosely organized and its leaders had little control over individual groups operating locally under its aegis. In keeping with the secretive nature of the organization, Klan members tended to act at night and nearly always wore disguises. Many Southerners insisted that the Ku Klux Klan did not exist at all. Supporters claimed that much of the violence attributed to the Klan was imagined by its supposed victims, and that night riders who might have caused injury on occasion were simply vigilantes or misguided fun-seeking youth who meant no real harm.

The excerpts from the House of Representatives report represent a sampling of firsthand testimony describing encounters between the Ku Klux Klan and its many victims, and secondhand accounts from officials who routinely received reports of acts of violence. In the first passage, the authors of the joint military committee's report to the Tennessee legislature make clear that, despite protests from many white citizens that the Klan was not really dangerous, this "organization of armed men" posed a serious threat to the safety and well-being of the state's African American population. The summary statement that "poor negroes" were being robbed of their firearms, whipped, hanged, shot, and driven from their homes is based on testimony from numerous African American victims and from white Americans who either witnessed the atrocities or learned of them shortly after they occurred.

The committee seems to go out of its way to stress the widespread nature of the Klan's reign of terror. Traditionally, Tennesseans viewed their state as being divided into three broad regions. When talk of secession grew in 1861, West and Middle Tennessee, areas with many slaveholders, sided with the newly forming Confederacy. East Tennessee, populated by small farmers, was inclined to remain in the Union. While one might have expected trouble in the western and middle regions of the state, the authors of the report make it explicit that all three sections were experiencing an upsurge of Klan violence. After claiming that the "depredations" caused by the Klan extended across the entire state, the committee lists specific counties in which violence was especially prevalent. This list actually served a second purpose: it provided Governor Brownlow a reason for declaring martial law in particularly troubled areas and for deploying troops from the Tennessee State Guard there. Although the governor was unable to send troops in before the November election, after the State Guard was finally reactivated early in 1869, Brownlow declared martial law in nine counties in February.

Particularly noteworthy, too, is the report's stress on the violence committed against white Americans in Tennessee who were working to advance the improvement of the African American population. Virtually every person identified in the excerpt from the joint military committee report is white, including numerous individuals teaching in African American schools who had been intimidated, beaten, or otherwise threatened simply for wanting to educate former slaves. The report's authors also play upon a fear common among Southerners, the desecration of the family ("women and children have been subjected to the torture of the lash") and especially of women ("the persons of females have been violated"). Though perhaps not intentional, there is a note of irony in this behavior. One of the principal arguments of white supremacists was that, if not checked, African Americans would take advantage of white women and adulterate the purity of the race.

Because the joint military committee report was being submitted to colleagues in the legislature, the authors include incidents in which elected officials have suffered at the hands of Klansmen who have no respect for the law or those sworn to uphold it. The extensive description of the treatment of the aging Senator William Wyatt is intended to make fellow legislators realize that the danger posed by the Klan could easily be visited upon them. The allusion to State Senator Almon Case and his son would have also caused consternation among Radical legislators. Case was murdered in January 1867, his son four months earlier. Case's assailant was known but escaped prosecution because he enjoyed the protection of white Americans sympathetic to the Klan's activities. The committee may have been looking toward the upcoming congressional elections when they cited the case of Samuel M. Arnell, who had been elected to the U.S. House of Representatives in a contested election a year earlier. Arnell's experience makes it clear that even members of Congress had much to fear from Klansmen "thirsting" for their blood.

Reports from various officials of the Freedmen's Bureau corroborate the testimony of witnesses before the joint military committee and the congressional committee investigating the contested election. The Freedmen's Bureau was established as the Civil War was coming to a close by President Abraham Lincoln, who foresaw that former slaves would need assistance in becoming independent citizens. Designed to provide legal, medical, educational, and economic aid, the Bureau established offices and deployed agents throughout the South. Their efforts met with stiff resistance from the white population, and many agents found themselves subjected to harassment and intimidation similar to that suffered by the clients they were supposed to be serving. Major General William Carlin's report on conditions in West Tennessee highlights several cases of brutality that had occurred recently in this region, among them the ongoing hostility toward education for African Americans exhibited by "pro-slavery people," by which he means former secessionists who had adopted the mantle of white supremacists. Throughout the South, many white Americans were fearful that, once educated, African Americans would become a powerful political force in communities where they outnumbered white people, and therefore posed a threat to their former masters. Few in the South believed that the races could coexist harmoniously; white Americans especially feared that educating and arming the African American population would inevitably lead to a revolution aimed at wiping out all white people.

Undoubtedly many of the attacks on African Americans perpetrated by the Klan were launched randomly against any African American unfortunate enough to be spotted by night riders out to cause mayhem and create terror. As the reports by agents A. H. Eastman and J. K. Nelson indicate, however, some African Americans were targeted for their political activity. Both Joshua Ferrell and D. Webb were told they were chosen by the Klan because they supported the Union League or the Loyal League, held Radical sympathies, or voted for the Radical Republican candidate for governor in the most recent election. The activities of the Union League (sometimes called the Loyal League) were particularly vexing to former secessionists and white supremacists. Founded in 1862 in Northern cities to support the Union cause, the Union League organized chapters in the South after the war to promote the Republican political agenda and to encourage African Americans to vote and become involved in politics. Many former slaves joined the Union League even if they were not political activists.

As every witness testifies, the Klan's actions ranged from simple intimidation to significant physical violence, sometimes resulting in murder. In many cases threats alone were enough to cause white and African Americans alike to submit to the Klan's will. One intimidation technique typical of many groups of Klansmen is described by the Reverend H. O. Hoffman, who reports having received threats himself, including one delivered in a fashion typical of Klansmen at the time: a note left in his yard warning him that his "name is before the Council" and that the Klan "will attend to you." Such notes alone were often sufficient to deter whites from continuing to support African Americans, and in some cases caused them to leave the region rather than face the prospect of reprisal for their actions.

A number of whites were forced to submit to public insult, which, coupled with secondhand reports of violence, caused them to behave like agent J. K. Nelson, who slept with firearms nearby. Many African Americans, fearing for their lives and wishing to keep themselves and their families safe from Klan attacks, simply fled to what they perceived to be safer regions. As the joint military committee report indicates, this posed new problems: the "two hundred colored men" who fled to Nashville ended up "destitute of food, or any means of subsistence." This early instance of African American flight to urban centers is a harbinger of what would come for many who left the harsh life of the segregated rural South only to end up no better off in crowded cities, where they remained victims of inequality and prejudice.

Some of the hyperbolic language in these excerpts can be attributed to a general tendency during the nineteenth

century for Americans to assume an oratorical posture in their writing. A comparison of these reports with contemporary sermons might reveal striking similarities. Words such as "outrage," "depredation," and "reign of terror" appear regularly in written communications from this period, particularly in newspapers. While some accounts are emotionally charged and may be exaggerated, the sheer volume of reporting makes it evident that the Klan's campaign of terror was effective in keeping freed slaves and their white supporters from exercising their civil rights.

The inclusion of lengthy descriptions of specific acts of mayhem and torture, however, would have had immediate impact on readers of these reports, and would have convinced even the most skeptical to agree that strong countermeasures were required to curb the Klan's activities. Reverend Hoffman's description of the injuries suffered by the "colored man by the name of Jeff," agent Eastman's testimony about the treatment Joshua Ferrell received simply because he supported Governor Brownlow and the Union League, and the manhandling of Minor Fletcher and D. Webb described by agent J. K. Nelson contain little overblown rhetoric. Instead, the graphic language used in a series of declarative sentences filled with strong action verbs conveys without exaggeration the horror of the circumstances in which these men found themselves. The detail with which incidents of brutality are described is clearly intended to provoke both fear and outrage. The elderly Senator Wyatt was pistol-whipped so badly that he suffered a "frightful gash, saturating his shirt with blood, leaving him insensible." Joshua Ferrell, also old and apparently harmless, was similarly beaten, the pistol "cutting a gash half an inch wide, four inches long" into his skull. Little is left to the imagination except the unstated conclusion that incidents like these will continue to occur unless the Klan is neutralized.

Also common among these reports is the tendency to establish clear political and moral differences between perpetrators and victims in the attacks. For example, Senator Wyatt is described as "a Christian gentleman" and "a Union Man." The schoolteacher Dunlap is "a member of the Methodist Church," quiet and inoffensive. Many of the victims are former members of the Union Army. Those who threaten these honest, lawabiding, loyal citizens of the United States are violent, lawless bands intent on sedition. The attack on Senator Case indicates to the writers of the joint committee report that "no loyal man" is safe at present. Additionally, there is a sense running through these reports that these individual groups of "night-prowlers" are part of a larger, sinister organization that was creating a "system of anti-lawry and terrorism" for political motives: to deliver votes in the upcoming presidential election to the Democratic ticket.

The testimony recorded in these reports displays the power of anecdotal evidence in supporting an argument for government support of victims. The specific action sought by both state and federal officials was armed intervention. In his June 1868 report, Carlin makes it clear that Freedmen's Bureau agents were powerless to "remedy" the "evils that cry out for redress," and he predicts exactly what Governor Brownlow feared. The level of Klan activity in the early months of 1868 strongly suggested that "frequent disturbances" would continue to occur during the fall campaigns for president and seats in Congress. The Klan's activities were certain to "bring about a state of affairs that will preclude the possibility for the colored people, and the active, outspoken Union men" to vote in the November election. Carlin is clear in his belief that nothing short of martial law "will preserve the peace and insure safety." No doubt in the summer of 1868 Governor Brownlow was pleased to see this kind of support for his own position against the Klan. For members of Congress receiving this report in 1870, the message was equally clear: some definite action was needed to ameliorate or eliminate Klan violence, or the country as a whole might slip back into anarchy and civil strife.

Essential Themes

The importance of congressional investigations into the activities of the Ku Klux Klan during the first decade following the end of the Civil War can hardly be overstated. Between 1866 and 1870 the Klan had spread to virtually every state in the former Confederacy. Its brutal campaign to intimidate the African American population in those states not only affected the political climate, but also caused many former slaves to fear for their lives and their property. The ability of Klansmen to act with impunity, knowing that sympathetic white officials in law enforcement and government would do little to prosecute them for any crimes they committed, created a virtual state of anarchy that many then and later would equate with terrorism. Although it is impossible to speculate on what might have happened, many scholars agree with those who witnessed Klan violence that the United States may well have slipped back into civil war had the Klan's activities not been checked. Hence, reports that

document the Klan's systematic assault on equal rights were instrumental in bringing about action at the federal level to suppress the organization and restore order and the rule of law in the South.

Various investigations led to decisions that influenced the future of the nation. Undoubtedly the 1868 report prompted Tennessee legislators to reestablish the State Guard. In 1870 the House of Representatives was convinced by its committee's report that the African American population in Tennessee had been denied their civil rights; it voted to allow Tillman to retain the disputed Fourth District seat in Congress. Widespread accounts of Klan violence such as the ones documented in the House committee's report were instrumental in generating further action at the federal level. In 1871, Senator John Scott of Pennsylvania convened a congressional committee to investigate Klan activities in the South. The extensive testimony presented before Smith's committee was published in thirteen volumes in 1872 as *Report of the Joint Select Committee Appointed to Inquire in to the Condition of Affairs in the Late Insurrectionary States*. It became the most important contemporary document outlining the nature and extent of Klan violence during the early years of Reconstruction. The report also prompted passage of a stronger law allowing the federal government to counter Klan activities, which were identified as supporting a specific political agenda, that of the Democratic Party.

As a result of strong enforcement by President Ulysses S. Grant, the Ku Klux Klan's influence was almost completely nullified by 1877, when Reconstruction ended and former Confederate states were once again allowed to participate as full partners in the national government. Unfortunately, once free to act without federal supervision, many Southern states enacted laws that brought about the same result that the Klan had sought through violence: a segregated society in which African Americans remained separate and decidedly unequal.

—*Laurence W. Mazzeno, PhD*

Bibliography and Additional Reading

Alexander, Thomas B. *Political Reconstruction in Tennessee*. Nashville: Vanderbilt UP, 1950. Print.

Bergeron, Paul H., Stephen V. Ash, and Jeanette Keith. *Tennesseans and Their History*. Knoxville: U of Tennessee P, 1999. Print.

Budiansky, Stephen. *The Bloody Shirt: Terror after Appomattox*. New York: Viking, 2008. Print.

Coulter, E. Merton. *William G. Brownlow: Fighting Parson of the Southern Highlands.* Chapel Hill: U of North Carolina P, 1937. Print.

Foner, Eric. *Reconstruction: America's Unfinished Revolution, 1863–1877.* New York: Harper, 1988. Print.

Horn, Stanley F. *Invisible Empire: The Story of the Ku Klux Klan, 1866–1871.* Cos Cob: Edwards, 1969. Print.

Katz, William L. *The Invisible Empire: The Ku Klux Klan Impact on History.* Washington: Open Hand, 1986. Print.

Martinez, J. Michael. *Carpetbaggers, Cavalry, and the Ku Klux Klan: Exposing the Invisible Empire during Reconstruction.* Lanham: Rowman, 2007. Print.

Newton, Michael. *The Ku Klux Klan: History, Organization, Language, Influence, and Activities of America's Most Notorious Secret Society.* Jefferson: McFarland, 2007. Print.

Patton, James Welch. *Unionism and Reconstruction in Tennessee 1860–1869.* Chapel Hill: U of North Carolina P, 1980. Print.

Queener, Verton M. "A Decade of East Tennessee Republicanism, 1867–1876." *East Tennessee Historical Society's Publications* 14 (1942): 59–85. Print.

Rable, George C. *But There Was No Peace: The Role of Violence in the Politics of Reconstruction.* Athens: U of Georgia P, 2007. Print.

Randel, William P. *The Ku Klux Klan: A Century of Infamy.* Philadelphia: Chilton, 1965. Print.

Severance, Ben H. *Tennessee's Radical Army: The State Guard and Its Role in Reconstruction, 1867–1869.* Knoxville: U of Tennessee P, 2005. Print.

Summers, Mark W. *A Dangerous Stir: Fear, Paranoia, and the Making of Reconstruction.* Chapel Hill: U of North Carolina P, 2009. Print.

Trelease, Allen W. *White Terror: The Ku Klux Klan Conspiracy and Southern Reconstruction.* New York: Harper, 1971. Print.

Print shows a campaign banner for the 1872 Republican national ticket. (Baker, Joseph E., ca. 1837-1914 , artist. Library of Congress's Prints and Photographs Division)

■ Documents Relating to the Grant-Greeley Election of 1872

Date: Summer 1872
Authors: Horace Greeley; Congressional Committee of the Republican Party (CCRP)
Genre: Letter (Greeley); political tract (CCRP)

Summary Overview

The election of 1872 was a key contest during the Reconstruction Era, during which the federal government worked to rebuild loyal governments in the former Confederate states. The Reconstruction Era is usually defined as 1865 to 1877, and during this time Republicans occupied the White House and controlled both houses of Congress, in part because many Southern Democratic voters had lost their right to vote due to their role in the rebellion against the national government. Ulysses S. Grant, one of the leading Union heroes of the war, had handily won the 1868 presidential election on the Republican ticket. But by 1872 the political situation was changing, leading a faction of the Republican Party to bolt and form the Liberal Republican Party. In May 1872, the Liberal Republicans nominated Horace Greeley as their candidate. Later, the Democratic Party also nominated Greeley, despite his long identification with the Republican Party. The first document examined here is Greeley's letter accepting the nomination of the Democratic Party, in which he expresses gratitude for their support despite of his long identification with the Republican Party. Greeley did some campaigning similar to what later presidential candidates would do, but Grant stuck to the old tradition that presidential candidates did not actively solicit votes. The second document here is a portion of a report of the Congressional Committee of the Republican Party, which laid out a history of the party and pointed to the successes of Grant's first administration, urging that Grant be elected to a second term.

Defining Moment

The election of 1872 was significant because the emergence of the Liberal Republicans threatened a permanent split in the Republican Party. It also demonstrated that the commitment of the Republican Party to a thorough-going Reconstruction policy, which would guarantee the full civil rights of the freed slaves in the South, was starting to erode. When the Democrats nominated Horace Greeley, the same candidate the Liberal Republicans had chosen, this raised the possibility that the Republicans could lose the White House for the first time since Lincoln's election in 1860.

By the early 1870s, some northern Republicans came to believe that their party, under President Grant, was becoming the party of big business and big money. These "Liberal Republican" insurgents wanted to bring about reform of the federal employment system, ending the "spoils" or patronage system where jobs were handed out to secure or to repay political favors, and replace it with a civil service system by which jobs were awarded on the basis of merit. Ironically, some of the leaders of the Liberal Republicans, who were cooling in their zeal for Reconstruction, had formerly been part of the "Radical Republican" faction that had been the strongest supporters of ending slavery and extending full civil rights to the freedmen (the term used to refer to the former slaves). The Liberal Republicans were also concerned about the rampant corruption in Grant's administration. It is generally thought that Grant was not involved in this corruption, but the fact that many of his appointees were suggested that he was naïve in his judgment of appointees.

The Liberal Republican revolt did not succeed. Greeley failed to attract much support as a candidate, and among faithful Republicans, the attacks on Grant had the result of strengthening support for him. Many northern voters were not ready to trust southern Democrats to treat the freedmen fairly, and the worst of the corruption within Grant's administration was not known until after the election. As a result, Grant won the 1872 election with a popular vote margin of 763,000 votes, and won 286 Electoral College votes to Greeley's 66. The Liberal Republican Party dissolved in the aftermath of Greeley's loss. Greeley died shortly after the election—the only time in U.S. history that a presidential candidate died between the time of the election and the certification of the Electoral College vote by the Senate.

Author Biographies

Horace Greeley was a prominent newspaper publisher and reformer in the mid-nineteenth century. He was born in Amherst, New Hampshire on February 3, 1811. He went into the newspaper business at a young age, and after working for several papers, he founded the *New York Tribune* in 1841. He belonged to the Whig Party and his paper supported their policies. In 1854, as the Whig Party dissolved in the aftermath of the debate over the Kansas-Nebraska bill, Greeley was one of the founders of the Republican Party. In 1872, he became the nominee of both the new Liberal Republican Party and the Democratic Party, running against the Republican President Ulysses S. Grant. Greeley lost that election and died in New York City just a few weeks later, on November 29, 1872.

The second document in this selection is a report of the Congressional Republican Committee. Both the Republican and Democrat parties have usually had such committees, which exist to promote the interests of their party in Congress and to aid the election of members of their party to seats in Congress. Henry Wilson was the chairman of this committee at the time this report was issued. He was born in northern Vermont on February 16, 1812. He was elected to the U. S. Senate in 1855. He had been a founder of the Free Soil Party and then became a Republican when that new party was organized in 1854. He had made an effort to secure the Republican vice presidential nomination in 1868, but lost that bid to Schuyler Colfax. He was nominated to run as Grant's running mate in the 1872 election, and took office in March, 1873. He suffered a debilitating stroke just a few weeks later and died from a second stroke on November 22, 1875.

HISTORICAL DOCUMENTS

Horace Greeley's Letter Accepting the Presidential Nomination of the Democratic Party

Gentlemen,—Upon mature deliberation, it seems fit that I should give to your letter of the 10th inst. some further and fuller response than the hasty, unpremeditated words in which I acknowledged and accepted your nomination at our meeting on the 12th.

That your convention saw fit to accord its highest honor to one who had been prominently and pointedly opposed to your party in the earnest and sometimes angry controversies of the last forty years is essentially noteworthy. That many of you originally preferred that the Liberal Republicans should present another candidate for President, and would more readily have united with us in the support of Adams or Trumball, Davis or Brown, is well known. I owe my adoption at Baltimore wholly to the fact that I had already been nominated at Cincinnati, and that a concentration of forces upon any new ticket had been proved impracticable. Gratified as I am at your concurrence in the nominations, certain as I am that you would not have thus concurred had you not deemed me upright and capable, I find nothing in the circumstance calculated to inflame vanity or nourish self-conceit.

But that your convention saw fit, in adopting the Cincinnati ticket, to reaffirm the Cincinnati platform, is to me a source of profoundest satisfaction. That body was constrained to take this important step by no party necessity, real or supposed. It might have accepted the candidates of the Liberal Republicans upon grounds entirely its own, or it might have presented them (as the first Whig national convention did Harrison and Tyler) without adopting any platform whatever. That it chose to plant itself deliberately, by a vote nearly unanimous, upon the fullest and clearest enunciation of principles which are at once incontestably Republican and emphatically Democratic, gives trustworthy assurance that a new and more auspicious era is dawning upon our long-distracted country.

Some of the best years and best efforts of my life were devoted to a struggle none the less earnest or arduous because respect for constitutional obligations constrained me to act, for the most part, on the defensive, in resistance to the diffusion rather than in direct efforts for the extension of human bondage. Throughout most of those years my vision was uncheered, my exertions were rarely animated by even so much as a hope that I should live to see my country peopled by freemen alone. The affirmance by your convention of the Cincinnati platform is a most conclusive proof that not merely is slavery abolished, but that its spirit is extinct; that, despite the protests of a respectable but isolated few, there remains among us no party and no formidable interests which regret the overthrow or desire the re-establishment of human bondage, whether in letter or in spirit. I am thereby justified in my hope and trust that the first century of American independence will not close before the grand elemental truths on which its rightfulness was based by Jefferson and the Continental Congress of 1776 will no longer be regarded as "glittering generalities," but will have become the universally accepted and honored foundations of our political fabric.

I demand the prompt application of those principles to our existing conditions. Having done what I could for the complete emancipation of blacks, I now insist on the full enfranchisement of all my white countrymen. Let none say that the ban has just been removed from all but a few hundred elderly gentlemen, to whom eligibility to office can be of little consequence. My view contemplates not the hundreds proscribed, but the millions who are denied the right to be ruled and represented by the men of their unfettered choice. Proscription were absurd if these did not wish to elect the very men whom they were forbidden to choose.

I have a profound regard for the people of that New England wherein I was born, in whose common schools I was taught. I rank no other people above them in intelligence, capacity, and moral worth. But, while they do many things well, and some admirably, there is one thing which I am sure they cannot wisely or safely undertake, and that is the selection, for States remote from and unlike their own, of the persons by whom those States shall be represented in Congress. If they do all this to good purpose, then republican institutions were unfit, and aristocracy the only true political system.

Yet what have we recently witnessed? Zebulon B. Vance, the unquestionable choice of a large majority of the present legislature of North Carolina—a majority backed by a majority of the people who voted at its election—refused the seat in the federal Senate to which he was fairly chosen, and the legislature thus constrained to choose another in his stead or leave the State unrepresented for years. The votes of New England thus deprived North Carolina of the Senator of her choice,

and compelled her to send another in his stead—another who, in our late contest, was, like Vance, a Confederate, and a fighting Confederate, but one who had not served in Congress before the war as Vance had, though the latter remained faithful to the Union till after the close of his term. I protest against the disfranchisement of a State—presumptively, of a number of States—on grounds so narrow and technical as this. The fact that the same Senate which refused Vance his seat proceeded to remove his disabilities after that seat had been filled by another only serves to place in stronger light the indignity to North Carolina, and the arbitrary, capricious tyranny which dictated it.

I thank you, gentlemen, that my name is to be conspicuously associated with yours in the determined effort to render amnesty complete and universal in spirit as well as in letter. Even defeat in such a cause would leave no sting, while triumph would rank with those victories which no blood reddens and which invoke no tears but those of gratitude and joy.

Gentlemen, your platform, which is also mine, assures me that Democracy is not henceforth to stand for one thing and Republicanism for another, but that those terms are to mean in politics, as they always have meant in the dictionary, substantially one and the same thing namely, equal rights regardless of creed, or clime, or color. I hail this as a genuine new departure from outworn feuds and meaningless contentions, in the direction of progress and reform. Whether I shall be found worthy to bear the standard of the great liberal movement which the American people have inaugurated is to be determined not by words but by deeds. With me if I steadily advance, over me if I falter, its grand army moves on to achieve for our country her glorious, beneficent destiny.

I remain, gentlemen, yours,

Horace Greeley

Extract from "The Republican Party. Address of the Congressional committee to the party. Review of the History of the party—what it has accomplished—work yet to be done—success of President Grant's administration."

Work To Be Accomplished.

Patriotism principle, the continued existence, reputation and renown of the Republican Party, and a due sense of self-respect and pride of character, demand that Republicans, now, as in the past, should have faith in this capacity to carry forward to completion reforms so auspiciously begun. It came into being as an organization of reform and progress, and should be ever ready to accept the living issues of the hour, and march abreast, with the spirit of the age. Unaided it has fought the battles of reform with constancy and courage. Nor in the work still before it, can it hope for aid from those who still cling to the traditions of the past, pride themselves on their conservatism, and who, during the conflicts of the past 20 years, have resisted reform, and mourned over every effete and hateful abuse as it fell. If there are Republicans who are weary of the ascendancy of a party which has achieved such growing victories, who are tired of the responsibilities of power, and would relinquish it to other hands, they should remember that there are none worthy to accept it. For surely they cannot fail to see that the Democratic party, by its policy during the closing years of its power, and by its blind and unrelenting opposition to reformatory measures while out of power, even now, as if smitten by judicial blindness, refusing to accept the Constitutional Amendments as fixed and final has demonstrated its utter incapacity for such a trust.

President Grant's Administration.

Accustomed to success even against fearful odds, and underrating, perhaps, the intrinsic difficulties of the pending issues, many Republicans looked to Gen. Grant's administration with high raised expectations. Of course they had been impatient, and not always satisfied with results. But while these expectations have not been fully realized in the action of either the President or of Congress, much has been achieved, enough, at any rate, to satisfy them that the difficult problems will be wrought out and the hoped for results accomplished. General Grant came into office pledged to maintain inviolate the public faith, reduce the national debt, diminish taxation, appreciate the currency, reform abuses in the civil and military service, and maintain order in the States lately in rebellion. By the combined action of the President, the Heads of Departments, Congress and the General of the Army, many abuses have been corrected and many reforms inaugurated. President Grant's Indian policy is bringing forth evidences of its justice, its humanity, and

its wisdom. The firm, just and generous policy of the Administration toward the States lately in rebellion has brought much of order and security, and crimes have largely diminished. In the interests of economy the services of thousands of employees, civil and military, have been dispensed with. The currency has been appreciated in value by tens and scores of millions of dollars, and the national credit has been largely strengthened.

The Revenues.

Without any increase in the articles subject to taxation or in the rate of taxation, the revenues of the fiscal year ending 30th of June, 1870, were nearly $409,000,000 against less than $371,000,000 for the year ending 30th June, 1869, showing a gain of nearly $38,000,000. On the other hand, the expenses of the fiscal year, 1870, were less than those of 1869 by more than $27,000,000, thus showing an increased revenue and saving in expenditures of more than sixty-seven millions of dollars in the first fiscal year of Gen. Grant's administration. In the last sixteen months of Mr. Johnson's administration, the receipts from customs and internal revenue were less than three hundred and seventy-two millions of dollars. During the first sixteen months of Gen. Grant's administration they were more than four hundred and sixty-nine millions, showing an increase of nearly ninety-seven millions of dollars. Republicans will remember that during the last two years of Mr. Johnson's administration he removed all Republicans appointed by Mr. Lincoln and others who adhered to the principles of the Republican Party, and appointed Democrats where he could do so. The character of the appointments, and the demoralizing influence which his opinion and conduct had upon them, were seen in the loss of scores of millions of dollars of revenue in those years. The largest gain in the collection is mainly due to the determined and avowed purpose of Gen. Grant to secure an honest administration of the revenue laws, and the appointment of Republicans to office earnestly devoted to his economical policy.

Reduction of Taxation.

During the recent session of Congress taxes have been reduced more than $75,000,000. The taxes have been removed from transportation by canals and railways, from sales by dealers and manufacturers. The income tax has been reduced to two-and-a half per cent, on all incomes above $2,000; and it is to expire at the end of two years. The tax on tea has been reduced from twenty-five to fifteen cents per pound; on coffee from five to three cents, and the tax on sugar and molasses has been reduced in the aggregate twelve millions of dollars per annum. By this reduction of taxation the industries of the people and the necessaries of life have been relieved of burdens amounting to millions. The funding bill is an important financial measure which contemplates the saving of interest upon the public debt by the exchange of outstanding six per cent bonds for those of a lower rate of interest, to the amount of $26,500,000 a year. While a reduction in taxes transfers the burden of the debt from one year to another, from one generation to another, a reduction of the rate interest is an actual saving to the country, not only for the present generation, but for all time. And yet these important and beneficial financial measures, intended to lighten the public burdens, received little countenance and support from the Democratic Party, whose responsibilities for the war, its expenditures, its debts, and its taxation, are fearfully large.

THE GLORIOUS RECORD OF THE PARTY.

Not faultless, but high, noble and glorious is the record of the Republican Party. History will note it, and the world will gratefully remember it. In the light of this brief review of its achievements, for patriotism, liberty, justice and humanity, should not Republicans, one and all, cling to their grand organization, rectify its mistakes, correct its errors, and keep it true to its past traditions and in harmony with the enlightened and progressive spirits of the age? So doing, may they not perpetuate their power until their beneficent principles shall become the accepted policy of the nation?

HENRY WILSON, Chairman of Congressional Republican Committee.

JAMES H. PLATT, Secretary.

Document Analysis

Although these two documents are of significantly different natures, as political documents written in the midst of a presidential campaign, they share certain similarities, in that the authors attempt to rouse support for their party and candidate. Greeley's letter accepting the nomination of the Democratic Party is significant because of the unusual circumstances which led to his nomination, as he notes: "That your convention saw fit to accord its highest honor to one who had been prominently and pointedly opposed to your party in the earnest and sometimes angry controversies of the last forty years is essentially noteworthy." Greeley had broken with Grant and the main body of the Republicans over several issues, and was then nominated by the dissident Liberal Republican faction as their presidential candidate. This presented a dilemma to the Democrats; if they chose a different candidate, then the opposition vote against the Republicans would be divided, probably paving the way for Grant's reelection. While Greeley had long fought for the freeing of the slaves and for the equal rights of the former slaves, he now believed it was time to address what he perceived as the continued injustice facing white Southerners, some of whom are still not allowed to vote because of their role in the Civil War. In terms sure to be received well by the Democrats, especially those in the South, he wrote, "Having done what I could for the complete emancipation of blacks, I now insist on the full enfranchisement of all my white countrymen." "Enfranchisement" means to grant the right to vote, or in this case to restore it to those who had lost it because of the rebellion of the Confederate states.

The Address of the Congressional Committee of the Republican Party also attempts to attract support to their party and to Grant as their nominee. Rather than appeal to some common beliefs in certain ideals, this document is more forthright in its condemnation of the opposing party. The Republican Party, it notes, "has fought the battles of reform with constancy and courage," but points out that it cannot hope "for aid from those who still cling to the traditions of the past, pride themselves on their conservatism, and who, during the conflicts of the past 20 years have resisted reform . . ." The authors of this document knew it was unnecessary to point out that this referred to the Democrats and especially to the Southern wing of that party. The document also lists many of the accomplishments of Grant's first term in office, citing several examples of tax reductions even while the overall revenue of the government had risen. They contrast this to the poor record of Andrew Johnson's time as president. Johnson had been a pro-Union Democrat but was chosen as Lincoln's running mate in 1864 to show broad support for the war effort. But after Lincoln died, Johnson opposed the Radical Republican's Reconstruction agenda so strenuously that they eventually attempted to remove him from office by impeachment. Some of the problems facing the country when Grant was elected were, according to this document, due to the failures of Johnson, who seemed to have reverted to his background as a Democrat. Furthermore, the authors suggest, in all of the Republicans efforts to bring about reform and efficiency in the federal government, they had "received little countenance and support from the Democratic Party, whose responsibilities for the war, its expenditures, its debts, and its taxation, are fearfully large." Thus, these Republican authors allege, the Democrats were not only responsible for the war and its aftermath, but have refused to do anything to help address the problems caused by that war. As a party document, rather than a personal letter like Greeley's document, this report is much more partisan and more direct in attempting to place blame on the opposition party and championing their own party's virtues.

Essential Themes

In Horace Greeley's letter accepting the president nomination of the Democratic Party, a central theme is his acknowledgment that, as one of the founders of the Republican Party, he had long been a fervent opponent of the Democrats. During the sectional crisis before the Civil War, and during the war itself, the Republicans saw southern Democrats as their principle opponents. Greeley had not simply opposed the Democratic Party in the recent years since the Civil War ended, but since the creation of the Republican Party in 1854. Despite his long allegiance to the Republican Party, and his initial support of Grant, Greeley had embraced the Liberal Republicans insurgency against the regular Republicans. He had been nominated as the presidential candidate of the Liberal Republicans at their convention in Cincinnati in May of 1872. The Democratic Party realized that running another candidate would split the vote of those opposing the Republicans, so they also nominated Greeley. Many in the North had become concerned about the fact that some southerners were still denied the right to vote because of their role in the Civil War, and Greeley addresses this concern and stresses the theme of equal-

ity. Whereas the Republicans had earlier been pushing for equality for the freed slaves, Greeley believed it was time to address equality for the white voters in the southern states.

In the report of the Republican Congressional Committee, a central theme is the way in which an incumbent party will usually run on its record. The document begins with a history of the Republican Party, and then highlights the accomplishments of Grant's first administration. Perhaps to suggest a sense of modesty, the authors of this document note that "many Republicans looked to Gen. Grant's administration with high raised expectations. Of course they had been impatient, and not always satisfied with results." Yet, despite the fact that have not achieved everything they wished, the authors go on to argue that the best hope of achieving these goals is to continue their support of Grant and re-elect him to a second term as President. They point to Grant's success in raising the revenues of the government while lowering taxes. In light of these accomplishments, they suggest, "Should not Republicans, one and all, cling to their grand organization, rectify its mistakes, correct its errors, and keep it true to its past traditions and in harmony with the enlightened and progressive spirits of the age?" It is interesting that while the authors admit there have been mistakes, they make no specific mention of the charges of corruption against people in Grant's administration. The results in the election were in line with what this document advocated—Republicans rallied around Grant and re-elected him by a greater margin than he had achieved in his first election.

—*Mark S. Joy, PhD*

Bibliography and Additional Reading

Chernow, Ron. *Grant*. New York: Penguin Press, 2017. Print.

Van Deusen, Glyndon G. *Horace Greeley: Nineteenth-Century Crusader*. New York: Hill and Wang, 1964. Print.

White, Ronald C. *American Ulysses: A Life of U.S. Grant*. New York: Random House, 2016. Print.

Williams, Robert Chadwell. *Horace Greeley: Champion of American Freedom*. New York: New York University Press, 2006. Print.

Campaign print for Horace Greeley. (Library of Congress's Prints and Photographs Division)

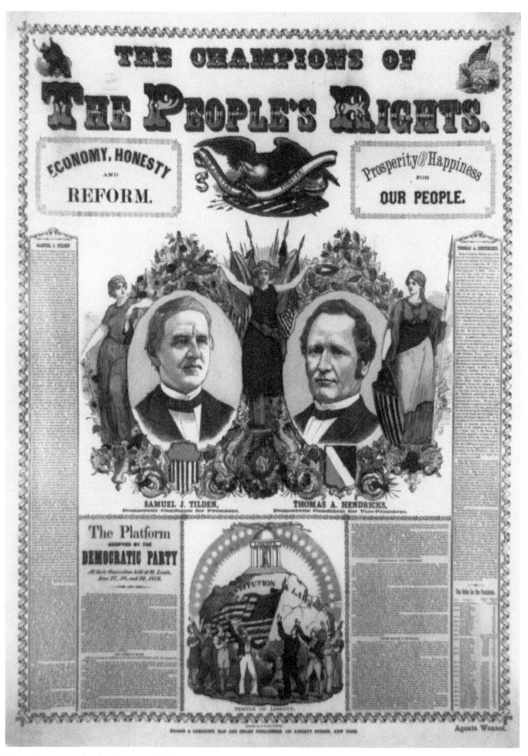

Campaign poster for the election of 1876.

■ Samuel Tilden's Speech Conceding the Election of 1876

Date: June 13, 1877
Author: Samuel Tilden
Genre: Speech

Summary Overview

In the history of American Presidential campaigns, there are numerous examples of electoral results that stretched the boundaries of the Constitutional system and unleashed disharmony and recriminations. Alexander Hamilton's fateful endorsement of Thomas Jefferson over Aaron Burr in 1800 and the accusation of a "corrupt bargain" that placed John Quincy Adams in the White House in the election of 1836 were both watershed moments in American political history. Neither of these, perhaps, was as controversial or carried the significance of the outcome of the election of 1876 between Republican Rutherford B. Hayes and Democrat Samuel J. Tilden. Beyond the basic question of "who won the election?" the contest illustrates the prevalence of backroom political deal making, the changing nature of the Republican party, and the ongoing struggle over civil rights, Reconstruction, and the aftermath of the Civil War.

The document examined here is an informal and (supposedly) impromptu speech, given by Samuel J. Tilden, the Democratic candidate for president in the 1876 election to a group of Democratic Party supporters shortly after the resolution of the election. It was published in the New York *Herald* newspaper on June 13, 1877. In his very brief remarks, Tilden discusses the fact that while he did not receive the presidency (as a result of the "Compromise of 1877") the fight for fair and honest elections was not over. He warns against the growing corruption of the political system in the United States. It is an important snapshot of a moment of profound political change in the United States, as the era of the Civil War and Reconstruction passed away and the so-called "Gilded Age" took hold.

Defining Moment

The context the contested election of 1876 is a complex one, comprising a number of moving parts that require a bit of explanation for readers to fully appreciate the time and place in which Tilden gave this speech. In this sec-

tion, we will break down the major historical trends and event that surrounded the speech in as clear a manner as possible.

Reconstruction, the period of Northern attempts to politically rebuild the Southern states following the Civil War as well as integrate former slaves into the political and economic life of the region had gone through a number of ups and downs in the 11 years between the end of the war and the election of 1876. Southern leaders resented the dominance of the Republican Party and, especially, the fact that former slaves were embracing their newfound political rights by voting and being elected to public offices. In many places, the U.S. Army was in place to keep the peace and supervise the political process. White Southern elites believed that the only way to restore what they perceived to be their rightful place at the top of the social, political, and economic hierarchy was to end the Reconstruction progress. Politically, this pitted Democrats of the South against Republicans—some of whom had migrated from Northern states, some of whom were native Southerners, and many of whom were former slaves. Terrorist organization such as the Ku Klux Klan used violence to dissuade black and white Republicans from exercising their rights. Between 1870 and 1871, Congress approved three "Enforcement Acts" authorizing the use of military force against such organizations. The effort and expense of these Reconstruction efforts, so many years after the end of the war, began to draw criticism from Northern Democrats and even some Republicans.

At the end of the Civil War in 1865, there were a number of prominent Republicans in Congress known as Radical Republicans. The Radicals pushed for a more thorough Reconstruction of the South and fought for laws that guaranteed and protected civil rights for former slaves. While the administration of Republican president Ulysses S. Grant was not radical, Grant did support military action against organizations by the Klan. Regardless, the radicalism of the Republicans decreased during the 1870s. Prominent radical leaders had died or retired and members of the new generation of Republicans were not as heavily committed to civil rights for former African American slaves.

Corruption of the political system—particularly in large cities—was widespread during this time. Cabals and political machines like the Tweed Ring, run by William "Boss" Tweed, provided needed services to poorer neighborhoods, but enriched themselves in the process, accepting bribed, kickbacks, and skimming public money. At the federal level, the Crédit Mobilier scandal and the Whiskey Ring involved high government officials ripping off the American people in a variety of ways for millions of dollars.

The presidential election of 1876 took place in the shadow of a Reconstruction effort that was increasingly unpopular. Books like 1874's *The Prostrate State* depicted the former Confederacy as a region that was corrupt and incompetently led, blaming the political participation of newly freed slaves as the source of the trouble. White, southern Democratic Party elites began winning political office in southern states, as the federal government was increasingly reluctant to use the military to protect African American voting rights. Republicans nominated Ohio's Rutherford B. Hayes, Democrats nominated Samuel J. Tilden of New York. When the votes were counted in November of 1876, there were disputes about the returns from three states: Florida, Louisiana, and South Carolina. In all of these states there were widespread reports of violent intimidation of Republican voters, accusations of bribery and vote fixing on both sides and, astonishingly, a voter turnout rate of 101 percent in South Carolina. While Tilden had won the popular vote by a margin of almost 300,000, the Electoral College returns were close enough that the electoral votes from these disputed states could swing the result either way. In January 1877, after failing to come up with a solution, Congress appointed a special commission consisting of eight Republicans and seven Democrats to determine the fate of the disputed votes.

The commission decided along party lines that Hayes, the Republican, had carried all three states and had won the presidency. However, a number of backroom conversations took place which outlined a deal—often called the "Compromise of 1877" or sometimes the "Bargain of 1877"—in which Democrats agreed to concede the election to Hayes. In response, Hayes would appoint a southerner to the Cabinet, provide federal money for the construction of a new railroad line in the southwest (the Texas and Pacific Railroad), and, most significantly, withdraw the military presence from Southern states, ending Reconstruction.

Author Biography

Samuel Tilden was born February 9, 1814 in Lebanon, New York. Working as a corporate lawyer—chiefly for railroad companies—during the 1840s, he shifted into politics with a seat in the New York state legislature. After the Civil War, he led the Democratic Party in New York, gaining a reputation as a reformer, fighting the corruption of the Tammany Hall political machine. Tilden played a key role in producing evidence of bribery for the trial that eventually took down William "Boss" Tweed.

Tilden returned to the New York legislature and, in 1874 was elected governor of New York. While in office, he continued to fight political corruption in both the Republican Party and his own Democratic party. His reputation as an enemy of corruption made him a strong candidate in the 1876 Presidential election. With the Republican Party still reeling from the Crédit Mobilier scandal that had involved several members of President Ulysses S. Grant's administration, a reformer like Tilden would be an appealing candidate. Following the 1876 election, there was talk in Democratic circles that, given his popular vote victory and the contested nature of the election that Tilden should run again in 1880. Following the election controversy, however, a number of telegrams came to light which suggested that Democratic Party operatives had attempted to bribe election officials in Florida and Oregon. Although the bribery attempts were not successful and Tilden denied all knowledge of the telegrams, the revelations had a negative effect on his popularity and reputation for integrity. Tilden retired to an estate near Yonkers, New York in the early 1880s and lived there for the rest of his life, dying on August 4, 1886.

HISTORICAL DOCUMENT

New York *Herald*, Wednesday, June 13, 1877

Mr. President and Gentlemen of the Manhattan Club:—I accepted your invitation under the idea that this was to be a merely social meeting, the special occasion of which was the presence in this city of Mr. Hendricks and of Governor Robinson and Lieutenant Governor Dorsheimer. One of your guests, Mr. Hendricks, embarks tomorrow on a foreign excursion for rest and recreation. He will carry with him our best wishes for a prosperous voyage, pleasant visit and a safe return, and for the health and happiness of himself and family.

I have been availing myself, for similar purposes, of a brief interval, and find myself now, with some reluctance, drawn away from those private pursuits. But the occasion and the apparent general expectation seem to require that I should say a word in respect to public affairs, and especially that I should allude to the transaction which, in my judgment, is the most portentous in our political history.

Everybody knows that, after the recent election, the men who were elected by the people President and Vice President of the United States were "counted out," and men who were not elected were "counted in" and seated.

NO PERSONAL WRONG.

I disclaim any thought of the personal wrong involved in this transaction. Not by any act or word of mine shall that be dwarfed or degraded into a personal grievance, which is, in truth, the greatest wrong that has stained our national annals. To every man of the four and a quarter millions who were defrauded of the fruits of their elective franchise it is as great a wrong as it is to me. And no less to every man of the minority will the ultimate consequences extend. Evils in government grow by success and by impunity. They do not arrest their own progress. They can never be limited except by external forces.

MUST NOT BE CONDONED.

If the men in possession of the government can, in one instance, maintain themselves in power against an adverse decision at the elections, such an example will be imitated. Temptation exists always. Devices to give the color of law, and false pretenses on which to found fraudulent decisions, will not be wanting. The wrong will grow into a practice, if condoned-if once condoned.

In the world's history changes in the succession of governments have usually been the result of fraud or force. It has been our faith and our pride that we had established a mode of peaceful change to be worked out by the agency of the ballot box. The question now is whether our elective system, in its substance as well as its form, is to be maintained.

THE QUESTION OF QUESTIONS.

This is the question of questions. Until it is finally settled there can be no politics founded on interior questions of administrative policy. It involves the fundamental right of the people. It involves the elective principle. It involves the whole system of popular government. The people must signally condemn the great wrong which has been done to them. They must strip the example of everything that can attract imitators. They must refuse a prosperous immunity to crime. This is not all. The people will not be able to trust the authors or beneficiaries of the wrong to devise remedies. But when those who condemn the wrong shall have the power they must devise the measure which shall render a repetition of the wrong forever impossible.

BE OF GOOD CHEER.

If my voice could reach throughout our country and be heard in its remotest hamlet I would say. "Be of good cheer. The Republic will live. The institutions of our fathers are not to expire in shame. The sovereignty of the people shall be rescued from this peril and be re-established."

THE TWEED RING.

Successful wrong never appears so triumphant as on the very eve of its fall. Seven years ago a corrupt dynasty culminated in its power over the million of people who live in the city of New York. It has conquered or bribed, or flattered and won almost everybody into acquiescence. It appeared to be invincible. A year or two later its members were in the penitentiaries or in exile. History abounds in similiar [sic] examples. We must believe in the right and in the future. A great and noble nation will not sever its political from its moral life. (Applause.)

GLOSSARY

annals: a historical record

disclaim: deny

hamlet: a small village

portentous: important or significant

Document Analysis

Tilden begins his remarks to the Manhattan club by explaining he thought it was an informal gathering and implying that he did not know he would be speaking. However, Tilden seems to have a well-prepared address ready for the occasion. After some pleasantries, particularly about Thomas Hendricks, his vice-presidential running-mate, he launches into his thoughts on the recent "transaction"—the election—an event he considers "the most portentous in our political history." He fires a shot across the Republican bow by expressing that candidates (he and Hendricks) "who were elected by the people" were denied their price and that those who were "not elected" received the victory. From the outset, Tilden is presenting the outcome of the 1877 election as contrary to the will of the American voters.

The third paragraph is where Tilden begins his examination of the election results and their significance. He claims to discount his personal feelings of being wronged and that his disappointment over the returns is not the result of "a personal grievance." Rather, his concern is for the "four and a quarter millions" whose votes were nullified by the backroom deal that decided the election. He warns that "evils in government grow by success and impunity" and that such corruption never stops itself. He continues this line of reasoning into the next two sections ("MUST NOT BE CONDONED" and "THE QUESTION OF QUESTIONS") in which he warns that the easy acceptance of the decisions made by those in power may lead to further abuses in the future. He questions whether the United States' "elective system" can be maintained in the aftermath of the election's outcome. The very fate of popular government and popular sovereignty rests on whether or not the people rise up to "condemn the great wrong which has been done to them" and take measures to ensure that such a thing can never happen again.

The final two sections ("BE OF GOOD CHEER" and "THE TWEED RING") provide some optimism for the audience going forward. Tilden does not expect that American institutions will vanish. Popular sovereignty will survive but, significantly, it needs to be "rescued." He finishes with the example of the Tweed Ring, which he had a hand in bringing down. A corrupt cabal, he explains, always sees strongest before it is finally undone. The Tweed Ring was undone and, Tilden proclaims, right will triumph.

Essential Themes

Tilden's speech, while conceding the election and expressing dismay over the result, never veers from its focus on the implications of the Compromise/Bargain of 1877 for the political life of the nation as a whole. The 1876 contest and its outcome is, in a way, a bellwether, providing a forecast of the increasingly corrupt and decreasing democratic way in which American politics could go. Indeed, political corruption at the local, state, and national levels would certainly not diminish in the coming decades. While it is outside the focus of Tilden's address here, the final end of Reconstruction and the reascendance of the traditional white political power structure in the South which followed certainly ushered in an era of political disenfranchisement for African American voters, bearing out the spirit of Tilden's concerns.

—*Aaron Gulyas, MA*

Bibliography and Additional Reading

Foner, Eric. *Reconstruction: America's Unfinished Revolution, 1863-1877*. New York: Harper, 2014.

Holt, Michael F. *By One Vote: The Disputed Presidential Election of 1876* (American Presidential Elections). Lawrence, Kansas: University Press of Kansas, 2008.

Hoogenboom, Ari. *Rutherford B. Hayes: Warrior and President*. Lawrence, Kansas: University Press of Kansas, 1995

Polakoff, Keith Ian. *The Politics of Inertia: The Election of 1876 and the End of Reconstruction*. Baton Rouge: Louisiana State University Press, 1973.

Presidential Election of 1876: A Resource Guide. https://www.loc.gov/rr/program/bib/elections/election1876.html.

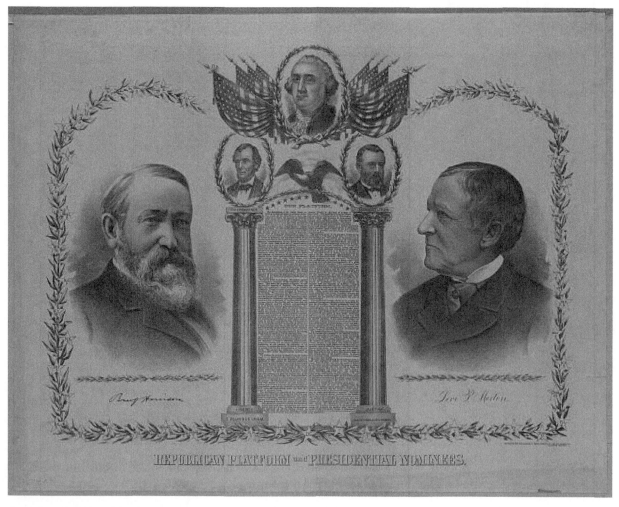

Print of presidential candidate Benjamin Harrison and vice presidential candidate Levi P. Morton with bust portraits of Abraham Lincoln, Ulysses S. Grant, and George Washington.

■ Benjamin Harrison's Speech to the Harrison League of Indianapolis

Date: June 30, 1888
Author: Benjamin Harrison
Genre: Speech; address

Summary Overview

This speech is an example of Republican candidate Benjamin Harrison's so-called front porch campaign, which took place during the presidential election of 1888. Harrison would hold court at his home in Indianapolis, Indiana, and address various groups of supporters on a variety of topics with a brief speech. Taken collectively, these speeches present a broad array of topics that Harrison believed were important for the party and his campaign to address. This particular speech, from June 30, 1888, was delivered to members of the Harrison Club of Indianapolis. The Harrison Club was a group of African American men from Indianapolis who supported the Republican Party in general and Harrison's candidacy in particular. This speech is an important example of the place of African American civil rights in the Republican platform of the 1880s and presents an outline of measures that Harrison would pursue following his victory in the election and four years in office.

In this speech Harrison addresses his childhood in the borderlands between free states and slave states, his service in the Union Army during the Civil War, and the changes he has seen in the legal and social status of African Americans over his lifetime. Perhaps most significantly, in addition to political rights and civil liberties, Harrison's speech emphasizes the need for equal educational opportunities for African Americans. This is a topic and a goal that he had long supported, even before his campaign for the presidency.

Defining Moment

The election of 1888 featured incumbent president Grover Cleveland, a Democrat, seeking re-election, and Republican Benjamin Harrison, seeking to unseat him. The campaign and election took place during a period in American history when presidential elections were typically very close and when the candidates were, often,

merely spokesman for the party platforms they represented rather than significant entities in their own right. Not coincidentally, this was also a period in which the presidents' influence on policy was at a low, as Congress was often deadlocked between parties and there was a general political mood in the nation that regulation and activism at the federal level was unnecessary. The Republican and Democratic political platforms obviously had differences. In the 1880s, perhaps the most critical issue facing national political leaders was the rate to set on tariffs, taxes on imported goods. Republicans often favored higher tariffs, and Democrats lower tariff rates. However, in 1888, there were also references to race and civil rights in each party platform. The Democratic Party platform asserted that under the leadership of Grover Cleveland, "the rights and welfare of all the people have been guarded and defended; every public interest has been protected, and the equality of all our citizens before the law, without regard to race or section, has been steadfastly maintained." The Republican platform, in contrast, is more specific in its goals, with the party pledging itself to "to the supreme and sovereign right of every lawful citizen, rich or poor, native or foreign born, white or black, to cast one free ballot in public elections, and to have that ballot duly counted." The platform then contends that such rights have been lacking during the Cleveland administration, charging that "the present Administration and the Democratic majority in Congress owe their existence to the suppression of the ballot by a criminal nullification of the Constitution and laws of the United States." While this is certainly not a fiery invective in support of a broad defense of African American rights, it establishes the Republicans as the party of civil rights at the time. This is a reference to southern states utilizing loopholes in the 15th Amendment to suppress African American voting rights. While the issue of tariffs was, overwhelmingly, the key issue in the campaign, this speech to African American voters makes clear that Harrison's vision for his candidacy was broader. Further evidence of Harrison's support of civil rights was the endorsement of Civil Rights pioneer and former slave Frederick Douglass.

Harrison would win the election with 233 electoral votes to Cleveland's 168. Cleveland, however, won a plurality of the popular vote, outpolling Harrison 48.6 percent to 47.8 percent.

Author Biography

There have been a handful of presidential "dynasties" in American history, and Benjamin Harrison belonged to, perhaps, the least impressive. He was the grandson of William Henry Harrison, who had served for president for a month before succumbing to pneumonia. Harrison was born August 20, 1833 in North Bend, Ohio. After college, he studied law and in 1854 moved to Indianapolis, Indiana to practice. He joined the Republican Party in 1856, the year it was formed. He served in the Civil War, rising to the rank of brevet Brigadier General, commanding a brigade under William Sherman in his southern campaign.

He returned to the law after the war, and also entered politics, losing the race for Indiana governor in 1876, but winning a Senate seat in 1880. While in the Senate, he supported efforts to improve educational conditions in the southern states, particularly for the children of former slaves. As a senator, he often spoke to groups of African American constituents in Indiana. Losing his Senate seat after 1887 due to a new Democratic majority in the Indiana State legislature (Senators were not directly elected by a states' voters until the early twentieth century), he returned to practicing law.

Harrison received the Republican nomination for president in 1888, after favorite James Blaine refused to run. Despite discussing issue of African American civil rights more often and more fully than some of his campaign advisors desired, he won the election and his presidency would only last one term, but had lasting effects, including the Sherman Anti-Trust Act. Following his defeat, losing a rematch with former president Cleveland in the election of 1892, Harrison returned to Indianapolis, also spending time lecturing in California at Stanford University. He remained active in political and international affairs until his death March 13, 1901 at age 67.

HISTORICAL DOCUMENT

Mr. Bagby and Gentlemen, of the Harrison Club—I assure you that I have a sincere respect for, and a very deep interest in, the colored people of the United States. My memory, as a boy, goes back to the time when slavery existed in the Southern States. I was born upon the Ohio River, which was the boundary between the free State of Ohio and the slave State of Kentucky. Some of my earliest recollections relate to the stirring and dramatic interest which was now and then excited by the pursuit of an escaping slave for the hope of offered rewards.

I remember, as a boy, wandering once through my grandfather's orchard at North Bend, and in pressing through an alder thicket that grew on its margin I saw sitting in its midst a colored man with the frightened look of a fugitive in his eye, and attempting to satisfy his hunger with some walnuts he had gathered. He noticed my approach with a fierce, startled look, to see whether I was likely to betray him; I was frightened myself and left him in some trepidation, but I kept his secret. [Cries

of "Good!" "Good!"] I have seen the progress which has been made in the legislation relating to your race, and the progress that the race itself has made since that day when I came to Indiana to reside the unfriendly black code was in force. My memory goes back to the time when colored witnesses were first allowed to appear in court in this State to testify in cases where white men were parties. Prior to that time, as you know, you had been excluded from the right to tell in court, under oath, your side of the story in any legal controversy with white men. [Cries of "I know that!"] The laws prevented your coming here. In every way you were at a disadvantage, even in the free States. I have lived to see this unfriendly legislation removed from our statute-books and the unfriendly section of our State Constitution repealed. I have lived not only to see that, but to see the race emancipated and slavery extinct. [Cries of "Amen to that !"]

Nothing gives me more pleasure among the results of the war than this. History will give a prominent place in the story of this great war to the fact that it resulted in making all men free and gave to you equal civil rights. The imagination and art of the poet, the tongue of the orator, the skill of the artist will be brought under contribution to tell this story of the emancipation of the souls of men. [Applause and cries of "Amen !"]

Nothing gives me so much gratification as a Republican as to feel that in all the steps that led to this great result the Republican party sympathized with you, pioneered for you in legislation, and was the architect of those great measures of relief which have so much ameliorated your condition. [Applause.]

I know nowhere in this country of a monument that I behold with so much interest, that touches my heart so deeply, as that monument at Washington representing the Proclamation of Emancipation by President Lincoln, the kneeling black man at the feet of the martyred President, with the shackles falling from his limbs.

I remember your faithfulness during the time of the war. I remember your faithful service to the army as we were advancing through an unknown country. We could always depend upon the faithfulness of the black man. [Cries of "Right you are!"] He might be mistaken, but he was never false. Many a time in the darkness of night have those faithful men crept to our lines and given us information of the approach of the enemy. I shall never forget a scene that I saw when Sherman's army marched through a portion of North Carolina, between Raleigh and Richmond, where our troops had never before been. The colored people had not seen our flag since the banner of treason had been set up in its stead. As we were passing through a village the colored people flocked out to see once more the starry banner of freedom, the emblem, promise, and security of their emancipation. I remember an aged woman, over whom nearly a century of slavery must have passed, pressed forward to see the welcome banner that told her that her soul would go over into the presence of her God. I remember her exultation of spirit as she danced in the dusty road before our moving column, and, like Miriam of old, called upon her soul to rejoice in the deliverance which God had wrought by the coming of those who stood for and made secure the Proclamation of Emancipation. [Applause.]

I rejoice in all that you have accomplished since you have been free. I recall no scene more pathetic than that which I have often seen about our camp-fires. An aged man, a fugitive from slavery, had found freedom in our camp. After a day of hard work, when taps had sounded and the lights in the tents were out, I have seen him with the spelling-book that the chaplain had given him, lying prone upon the ground taxing his old eyes, and pointing with his hardened finger to the letters of the alphabet, as he endeavored to open to his clouded brain the avenues of information and light.

I am glad to know that that same desire to increase and enlarge your information possesses the race to-day. It is the open way for the race to that perfect emancipation which will remove remaining prejudices and secure to you in all parts of the land an' equal and just participation in the government of this country. It cannot much longer be withholden from you.

Again I thank you for your presence here to-night and will be glad to take by the hand any of you who desire to see me. [Great applause.]

GLOSSARY

"banner of treason": a reference to the flag of the Confederacy

black code: sets of laws and regulations that restricted the housing, movement, employment and other aspects of life for free African Americans

emancipation: freedom from slavery

Miriam: sister of Moses in the Hebrew Bible; she composed a song of thanksgiving in response to the Hebrew people's release from slavery in Egypt

trepidation: fearful caution

Harrison and the Billion-Dollar Congress are portrayed as wasting the surplus in this cartoon from *Puck*.

Document Analysis

Harrison begins by thanking Mr. Bagby (the head of the Indianapolis Harrison Club) and declaring interest in "the colored people of the United States." He tells a story of his childhood in Ohio, on the river that separated free states from slave states. He recounts how he once came across a runaway slave and made the decision to protect the fugitive. He goes on to offer an overview of the development of civil rights legislation that had been made with regard to civil rights for African Americans over the past few decades, describing how when he arrived in Indiana (in 1854) the state restricted African American freedoms with black codes, as well as how African Americans were not allowed to testify in cases involving whites. He concludes this portion of his speech by admitting that there were significant "disadvantages" for African Americans, even in states that were free from slavery. He expresses happiness that Indiana's laws and state constitution have been amended and that slavery has ended in the United States.

Harrison asserts that history will regard the Civil War primarily as a war not only to liberate African American slaves but also resulted in the guarantee of equal civil rights for the former slaves. He employs some flowery but evocative language ("The imagination and art of the poet, the tongue of the orator, the skill of the artist") to describe the impact that the events of the war will have on future generations of Americans.

Harrison then turns to politics, reinforcing for his audiences that it was the Republican party that had always taken the lead in measures not only that freed the slaves but also the party that established the laws and Constitutional amendments that guaranteed civil rights and equality. Republican creation of agencies such as the Freemen's Bureau during Reconstruction are a good example of what Harrison is talking about when he refers to "great measures of relief." In addition to reminding listeners that Republicans were the "architects" of these measures, it would not escape that audiences' memory that Democrats had actively opposed those laws as well as measures such as the fourteenth and fifteenth amendments. Harrison also references the Emancipation Proclamation monument in Washington DC, which was erected in 1876, which allows for a reference to Lincoln, the "martyred President"—another reminder of Republican commitment to civil rights.

Harrison transitions to a discussion of the Civil War itself, remembering the ways in which slaves had supported the Union Army as it moved through the South, providing information about troop positions, including one moving story of an elderly woman who danced at the sight of the American flag. He then moves toward the conclusion of the speech by praising the audience for the achievements of African Americans since the end of slavery. Consistent with his long-standing support for educational opportunities for former slaves, Harrison recounts the scene of an elderly slave, exhausted from a day's work, studying the alphabet late at night by firelight in an army camp, "endeavor[ing] to open to his clouded brain the avenues of information and light." He concludes by insisting that education is the path to "perfect emancipation"—the removal of prejudice and the key to full political participation. He predicts that it cannot be long before that emancipation comes.

Essential Themes

For a campaign speech, Harrison's address of June 30, 1888 doesn't really extensively discuss the campaign or his candidacy. What it does, however, is position both the Republican Party and Harrison himself as the only logical choice for African American voters. Earlier in the month, at the Republican convention Frederick Douglass had warned the party against assuming they would always have the support of African Americans, even a dozen years after Republican Rutherford B. Hayes had ended Reconstruction. Harrison's speech seems dedicated not only to reinforcing the history of Republican actions on civil rights but also his personal dedication to the cause, as evidenced by his personal history since boyhood.

While the fate of the election of 1888 mostly hinged on the issue of the tariff, Benjamin Harrison's victory ensured that the question of African American civil rights—particularly the voting rights that southern states had successfully circumvented since the end of Reconstruction—would find an audience in the halls of American government. Despite not nominating many African Americans to appointed government positions, he did appoint Frederick Douglass as U.S. Ambassador to Haiti. He also supported the Federal Elections Act, sponsored by Senator Henry Cabot Lodge. This bill would have allowed federal oversight of elections for Congressional seats. Although the measure passed the House of Representatives 155-149, the bill failed in the Senate however. This was the end of Harrison's attempts to push major civil rights reforms and, indeed, the end of federal civil rights legislation for a very long time.

—*Aaron Gulyas, MA*

Bibliography and Additional Reading

1888 Democratic Party Platform, June 5, 1888. The American Presidency Project, http://www.presidency.ucsb.edu/ws/index.php?pid=29584.

1888 Republican Party Platform, June 19, 1888. The American Presidency Project, http://www.presidency.ucsb.edu/ws/index.php?pid=29627.

Calhoun, Charles W. *Minority Victory: Gilded Age Politics and the Front Porch Campaign of 1888*. Lawrence, Kansas: University Press of Kansas, 2008.

Jensen, Richard. *The Winning of the Midwest: Social and Political Conflict, 1888-1896*. Chicago: University of Chicago Press, 1971.

"Presidential Election of 1888: A Resource Guide," Library of Congress. https://www.loc.gov/rr/program/bib/elections/election1888.html.

Summers, Mark Wahlgren. *Party Games: Getting, Keeping, and Using Power in Gilded Age Politics*. Chapel Hill: University of North Carolina Press, 2004.

■ "Cross of Gold" Speech

Date: July 9, 1896
Author: William Jennings Bryan
Genre: Speech

Summary Overview

The Cross of Gold speech was given by the young but ambitious politician William Jennings Bryan at the Democratic Party's 1896 national convention during a period in which the United States was divided on the issue of its monetary system. The nation effectively followed a gold standard for currency, but supporters of adding a silver standard—a policy known as "bimetallism"—were increasingly vocal in their belief that increasing the money supply would more widely distribute prosperity. Bryan's advocacy of silver helped him become the Democrats' presidential candidate for the 1896 election and a long-standing party leader.

Defining Moment

The Cross of Gold speech occurred in an election year that saw intense debate over monetary policy both within the Democratic Party and throughout the nation as a whole. In 1873 the Coinage Act had essentially made gold the only legal tender of the United States following the Civil War. The late nineteenth century was marked by tumultuous economic conditions, including a fall in agricultural prices and the Panic of 1893, and a growing populist movement blamed the gold standard. By the 1890s the so-called Free Silver movement had become a significant political force and had some success reintroducing silver currency, but the issue remained divisive.

Monetary policy particularly split the ranks of the Democratic Party. The "Bourbon" or "Gold Bug" Democrats, such as President Grover Cleveland and other politicians from urban Eastern states, represented the gold standard status quo. The Free Silver movement was associated with rural Western states and argued that the adoption of silver as a monetary standard at a ratio of sixteen-to-one with gold would raise prices, thus benefiting farmers and others of the working class. Gold Bugs argued that the adoption of silver would lead to inflation and make it more difficult for the United States to trade with countries such as Great Britain (then the leading

economic power) that followed a gold standard. The debate over bimetallism was the central element of the party's national convention in 1896 as Democrats sought to establish a platform and select a presidential candidate.

Author Biography

William Jennings Bryan was born on March 19, 1860, in Illinois. After getting a law degree and practicing for a few years he moved to Lincoln, Nebraska, in 1887. There he was elected to the U.S. Congress in 1890 as a Democrat and reelected in 1892, but a Senate run in 1894 ended in failure. He worked as a public lecturer, honing his skills as a gifted and persuasive speaker.

Bryan became active in the Free Silver movement and saw bimetallism as a way to unite the fractured Democratic Party. His Cross of Gold speech at the party's 1896 convention was so stirring that he was nominated as the Democratic presidential candidate despite his youth and inexperience. Yet despite support from the populist movement he lost the general election. He was again nominated and defeated in both 1900 and 1908 as well. Still, he remained an important Democratic leader and was named President Woodrow Wilson's secretary of state in 1912.

Bryan's later career continued to be marked by his strong convictions on controversial subjects. As a pacifist he opposed U.S. involvement in World War I. He was also deeply religious, and in 1925, he joined the prosecution in the highly publicized Scopes trial, in which a teacher in Tennessee was charged for teaching evolution. Bryan died shortly after the trial on July 26, 1925.

HISTORICAL DOCUMENT

I would be presumptuous, indeed, to present myself against the distinguished gentlemen to whom you have listened if this were a mere measuring of abilities; but this is not a contest between persons. The humblest citizen in all the land, when clad in the armor of a righteous cause, is stronger than all the hosts of error. I come to speak to you in defense of a cause as holy as the cause of liberty-the cause of humanity.

When this debate is concluded, a motion will be made to lay upon the table the resolution offered in commendation of the Administration, and also, the resolution offered in condemnation of the Administration. We object to bringing this question down to the level of persons. The individual is but an atom; he is born, he acts, he dies; but principles are eternal; and this has been a contest over a principle.

Never before in the history of this country has there been witnessed such a contest as that through which we have just passed. Never before in the history of American politics has a great issue been fought out as this issue has been, by the voters of a great party. On the fourth of March 1895, a few Democrats, most of them members of Congress, issued an address to the Democrats of the nation, asserting that the money question was the paramount issue of the hour; declaring that a majority of the Democratic party had the right to control the action of the party on this paramount issue; and concluding with the request that the believers in the free coinage of silver in the Democratic party should organize, take charge of, and control the policy of the Democratic party. Three months later, at Memphis, an organization was perfected, and the silver Democrats went forth openly and courageously proclaiming their belief, and declaring that, if successful, they would crystallize into a platform the declaration which they had made. Then began the struggle. With a zeal approaching the zeal which inspired the Crusaders who followed Peter the Hermit, our silver Democrats went forth from victory unto victory until they are now assembled, not to discuss, not to debate, but to enter up the judgment already rendered by the plain people of this country. In this contest brother has been arrayed against brother, father against son. The warmest ties of love, acquaintance, and association have been

disregarded; old leaders have been cast aside when they have refused to give expression to the sentiments of those whom they would lead, and new leaders have sprung up to give direction to this cause of truth. Thus has the contest been waged, and we have assembled here under as binding and solemn instructions as were ever imposed upon representatives of the people.

We do not come as individuals. As individuals we might have been glad to compliment the gentleman from New York [Senator Hill], but we know that the people for whom we speak would never be willing to put him in a position where he could thwart the will of the Democratic Party. I say it was not a question of persons; it was a question of principle, and it is not with gladness, my friends, that we find ourselves brought into conflict with those who are now arrayed on the other side.

When you [turning to the gold delegates] come before us and tell us that we are about to disturb your business interests, we reply that you have disturbed our business interests by your course.

We say to you that you have made the definition of a business man too limited in its application. The man who is employed for wages is as much a business man as his employer; the attorney in a country town is as much a business man as the corporation counsel in a great metropolis; the merchant at the cross-roads store is as much a business man as the merchant of New York; the farmer who goes forth in the morning and toils all day, who begins in the spring and toils all summer, and who by the application of brain and muscle to the natural resources of the country creates wealth, is as much a business man as the man who goes upon the Board of Trade and bets upon the price of grain; the miners who go down a thousand feet into the earth, or climb two thousand feet upon the cliffs, and bring forth from their hiding places the precious metals to be poured into the channels of trade are as much business men as the few financial magnates who, in a back room, corner the money of the world. We come to speak of this broader class of business men.

Ah, my friends, we say not one word against those who live upon the Atlantic Coast, but the hardy pioneers who have braved all the dangers of the wilderness, who have made the desert to blossom as the rose, the pioneers away out there [pointing to the West] who rear their children near to Nature's heart, where they can mingle their voices with the voices of the birds-out there where they have erected schoolhouses for the education of their young, churches where they praise their Creator, and cemeteries where rest the ashes of their dead-these people, we say, are as deserving of the consideration of our party as any people in this country. It is for these that we speak. We do not come as aggressors. Our war is not a war of conquest; we are fighting in the defense of our homes, our families, and posterity. We have petitioned, and our petitions have been scorned; we have entreated, and our entreaties have been disregarded; we have begged, and they have mocked when our calamity came. We beg no longer; we entreat no more; we petition no more. We defy them!

The gentleman from Wisconsin [Vilas] has said that he fears a Robespierre. My friends, in this land of the free you need not fear that a tyrant will spring up from among the people. What we need is an Andrew Jackson to stand, as Jackson stood, against the encroachments of organized wealth.

They tell us that this platform was made to catch votes. We reply to them that changing conditions make new issues; that the principles upon which Democracy rests are as everlasting as the hills, but that they must be applied to new conditions as they arise. Conditions have arisen, and we are here to meet those conditions. They tell us that the income tax ought not to be brought in here; that it is a new idea. They criticize us for our criticism of the Supreme Court of the United States. My friends, we have not criticized; we have simply called attention to what you already know. If you want criticisms read the dissenting opinions of the court. There you will find criticisms. They say that we passed an unconstitutional law; we deny it. The income tax was not unconstitutional when it was passed; it was not unconstitutional when it went before the Supreme Court for the first time; it did not become unconstitutional until one of the judges changed his mind, and we cannot be expected to know when a judge will change his mind. The income tax is just. It simply intends to put the burdens of government justly upon the backs of the people. I am in favor of an income tax. When I find a man who is not willing to bear his share of the burdens of the government which

protects him, I find a man who is unworthy to enjoy the blessings of a government like ours.

They say that we are opposing national bank currency; it is true. If you will read what Thomas Benton said, you will find he said that, in searching history, he could find but one parallel to Andrew Jackson; that was Cicero, who destroyed the conspiracy of Cataline and saved Rome. Benton said that Cicero only did for Rome what Jackson did for us when he destroyed the bank conspiracy and saved America. We say in our platform we believe that the right to coin and issue money is a function of government. We believe it. We believe that it is a part of sovereignty, and can no more with safety be delegated to private individuals than we could afford to delegate to private individuals the power to make penal statutes or levy taxes. Mr. Jefferson, who was once regarded as good Democratic authority, seems to have differed in opinion from the gentleman who has addressed us on the part of the minority. Those who are opposed to this proposition tell us that the issue of paper money is a function of the bank, and that the government ought to go out of the banking business. I stand with Jefferson rather than with them, and tell them, as he did, that the issue of money is a function of government, and that the banks ought to go out of the governing business.

They complain about the plank which declares against life tenure in office. They have tried to strain it to mean that which it does not mean. What we oppose by that plank is the life tenure which is being built up in Washington, and which excludes from participation in official benefits the humbler members of society.

And now, my friends, let me come to the paramount issue. If they ask us why it is that we say more on the money question than we say upon the tariff question, I reply that, if protection has slain its thousands, the gold standard has slain its tens of thousands. If they ask us why we do not embody in our platform all the things that we believe in, we reply that when we have restored the money of the Constitution, all other necessary reform will be possible; but that until this is done, there is no other reform that can be accomplished.

Why is it that within three months such a change has come over the country? Three months ago when it was confidently asserted that those who believed in the gold standard would frame our platform and nominate our candidates, even the advocates of the gold standard did not think that we could elect a President. And they had good reason for their doubt, because there is scarcely a State here today asking for the gold standard which is not in the absolute control of the Republican Party. But note the change. Mr. McKinley was nominated at St. Louis upon a platform which declared for the maintenance of the gold standard until it can be changed into bimetallism by international agreement. Mr. McKinley was the most popular man among the Republicans, and three months ago everybody in the Republican Party prophesied his election. How is it today? Why, the man who was once pleased to think that he looked like Napoleon-that man shudders today when he remembers that he was nominated on the anniversary of the battle of Waterloo.

Not only that, but as he listens, he can hear with ever-increasing distinctness the sound of the waves as they beat upon the lonely shores at St Helena.

Why this change? Ah, my friends, is not the reason for the change evident to any one who will look at the matter? No private character, however pure, no personal popularity, however great, can protect from the avenging wrath of an indignant people a man who will declare that he is in favor of fastening the gold standard upon this country, or who is willing to surrender the right of self-government and place the legislative control of our affairs in the hands of foreign potentates and powers.

We go forth confident that we shall win. Why? Because upon the paramount issue of this campaign there is not a spot of ground upon which the enemy will dare to challenge battle. If they tell us that the gold standard is a good thing, we shall point to their platform and tell them that their platform pledges the party to get rid of the gold standard and substitute bimetallism. If the gold standard is a good thing why try to get rid of it? I call your attention to the fact that some of the very people who are in this Convention today and who tell us that we ought to declare in favor of international bimetallism—thereby declaring that the gold standard is wrong and that the principle of bimetallism is better-these very people four months ago were open and avowed advocates of the gold-standard, and were then telling us that we could not legislate two metals together, even with the aid of all the world. If the gold standard is a good thing, we ought to declare in favor of its retention and not in favor of abandoning it; and if the gold standard is a bad thing why should we wait until other nations are willing to help us to let go? Here is the line of battle, and we care not upon which issue they force the fight; we are prepared to meet them on either issue or on both. If they tell us that the gold standard is the standard of civilization, we reply to them that this, the most enlightened of all the nations of the earth, has never declared for a gold standard and that both the great parties this year are declaring against it. If the gold standard is the standard of civilization, why, my friends, should we not have it? If they come to meet us on that issue we can present the history of our nation. More than that; we can tell them that they will search the pages of history in vain to find a single instance where the common people of any land have ever declared themselves in favor of the gold standard. They can find where the holders of fixed investments have declared for a gold standard, but not where the masses have. Mr. Carlisle said in 1878 that this was a struggle between the "idle holders of idle capital" and "the struggling masses, who produce the wealth and pay the taxes of the country," and, my friends, the question we are to decide is: Upon which side will the Democratic party fight; upon the side of "the idle holders of idle capital" or upon the side of "the struggling masses"? That is the question which the party must answer first, and then it must be answered by each individual hereafter. The sympathies of the Democratic Party, as shown by the platform, are on the side of the struggling masses who have ever been the foundation of the Democratic Party. There are two ideas of government. There are those who believe that if you will only legislate to make the well-to-do prosperous, their prosperity will leak through on those below. The Democratic idea, however, has been that if you legislate to make the masses prosperous, their prosperity will find its way up through every class which rests upon them.

You come to us and tell us that the great cities are in favor of the gold standard; we reply that the great cities rest upon our broad and fertile prairies. Burn down your cities and leave our farms, and your cities will spring up again as if by magic; but destroy our farms and the grass will grow in the streets of every city in the country.

My friends, we declare that this nation is able to legislate for its own people on every question, without waiting for the aid or consent of any other nation on earth;

and upon that issue we expect to carry every state in the Union. I shall not slander the inhabitants of the fair state of Massachusetts nor the inhabitants of the state of New York by saying that, when they are confronted with the proposition, they will declare that this nation is not able to attend to its own business. It is the issue of 1776 over again. Our ancestors, when but three millions in number, had the courage to declare their political independence of every other nation; shall we, their descendants, when we have grown to seventy millions, declare that we are less independent than our forefathers?

No, my friends, that will never be the verdict of our people. Therefore, we care not upon what lines the battle is fought. If they say bimetallism is good, but that we cannot have it until other nations help us, we reply, that instead of having a gold standard because England has, we will restore bimetallism, and then let England have bimetallism because the United States has it. If they dare to come out in the open field and defend the gold standard as a good thing, we will fight them to the uttermost. Having behind us the producing masses of this nation and the world, supported by the commercial interests, the laboring interests and the toilers everywhere, we will answer their demand for a gold standard by saying to them: You shall not press down upon the brow of labor this crown of thorns, you shall not crucify mankind upon a cross of gold.

English: Artist's conception of William Jennings Bryan after the Cross of Gold speech at the 1896 Democratic National Convention (By William Robinson Leigh—*McClure's Magazine*, April 1900, p. 536.)

Judge magazine criticized Bryan for sacrilege in his speech. He is shown with crown and cross, but trampling the Bible. (Cartoon by Grant Hamilton, printed in *Judge* magazine, 1896.)

Document Analysis

Though the central theme of Bryan's speech—that the U.S. should not support the gold standard—is simple, the way he frames and delivers the message is important. He positions himself as a populist champion of the West and the frontier (making no mention of the South, another region that largely supported bimetallism, due to the lingering shadow of the Civil War) in contrast to the established power of the Eastern states and of cities. He describes the movement he leads not only as an insurgency within the Democratic Party but "in defense of a cause as holy as the cause of liberty—the cause of humanity." In this way he builds up the issue as a question of universal morals rather than individual opinions or even simply economic policy.

Bryan uses Christian imagery that is vivid and easily recognizable to his audience. His references to a crown of thorns and a cross of gold put the people—"the producing masses of the nation and the world"—in the position of Jesus Christ at the crucifixion as they allegedly suffer under the gold standard. This powerful symbolism frames gold supporters as harming humankind on a fundamental level. He also evokes the enthusiasm of the crusading warriors of the Middle Ages by comparing the pro-silver Democrats to those who followed the preacher Peter the Hermit on the First Crusade.

In addition to religious imagery Bryan employs the rhetoric of class conflict, railing against the prevailing system that he claims seeks to establish "an office-holding class and excludes . . . the humbler members of our society." Bryan places himself in the tradition of iconic American leaders who represented the interests of the people on monetary issues. He refers to Andrew Jackson and his struggle against the Second Bank of the United States, which ended with a victory "against the encroachments of aggregated wealth" and thereby "saved America." He links himself with Thomas Jefferson, paraphrasing the earlier leader in declaring that the government should control money rather than be controlled by it. He further evokes the spirit of the American Revolution by suggesting that the United States should be able to act independently of England, an upholder of the gold standard. Bryan's rhetoric implies that the United States can and should set its own economic terms and lead by example.

Essential Themes

The Cross of Gold speech had a great immediate impact as audience members at the Democratic National Convention, including many initially hostile to Bryan, expressed their enthusiasm by carrying the speaker around the room as pandemonium broke out. The next day Bryan was nominated as the Democrats' presidential candidate on the fifth ballot, becoming the youngest-ever nominee to that point at thirty-six years old. He also received crossover support as the nominee of both the Populist Party and the Silver Republican Party, a short-lived faction of the Republicans, forming a coalition that would take on the pro–gold standard Republicans in the general election.

In the long run the speech was a failure in that Bryan lost the election to William McKinley and bimetallism was never adopted. Pro-gold Democrats refused to back Bryan and even formed a competing party, the National Democrats. Labor interests also did not provide as much support as expected. The McKinley campaign was able to mobilize America's business community against Bryan, in the process essentially inventing modern campaign financing. The split within the Democratic Party helped lead to a significant shift in U.S. party politics.

Changing economic conditions led to decreasing support for bimetallism in the next few years, and in 1900 the Gold Standard Act officially fixed U.S. monetary policy on gold. Bryan ran for the presidency again that year on a pro-silver platform but was unable to generate the same level of excitement and lost again, as he did once more in 1908. The Democrats would not regain the presidency until Woodrow Wilson's election in 1912. The United States remained on the gold standard until 1933, when the policy was abandoned in the face of the Great Depression.

Perhaps the most lasting effect of Bryan's 1896 speech and candidacy was on the general style and tone of presidential campaigning. He traveled the country giving fiery speeches in contrast to the usual strategy of candidates projecting an aura of being above the fray, and his method soon became standard practice. His highly charged populist rhetoric pitting the working class against the rich continues to be used by politicians from the local to national level and at all points on the political spectrum. The Cross of Gold address is considered one of the strongest political speeches in U.S. history and a key example of the power of rhetoric.

—*William E. Burns*

Bibliography and Additional Reading

Bensel, Richard Franklin. *Passion and Preferences: William Jennings Bryan and the 1896 Democratic National Convention*. New York: Cambridge UP, 2008. Print.

Bryan, Steven. *The Gold Standard at the Turn of the Twentieth Century: Rising Powers, Global Money and the Age of Empire*. New York: Columbia UP, 2010. Print.

Cherny, Robert W. *A Righteous Cause: The Life of William Jennings Bryan*. Norman: U of Oklahoma P, 1994. Print.

Williams, R. Hal. *Realigning America: McKinley, Bryan and the Remarkable Election of 1896*. Lawrence: UP of Kansas, 2010. Print.

THE FOURTH PARTY SYSTEM, 1896-1932

We begin this section on the fourth party system, or fourth phase in U.S. political history, with a speech not by a presidential candidate but by a senatorial candidate, Albert Beveridge of Indiana. Eighteen ninety-eight was a midterm election year, the Republican president William McKinley having been in office for nearly two years by then. The Spanish-American War was recently concluded when Beveridge delivered this campaign speech, "The March of the Flag," in September 1898. We include it here because it marks the start of an age of American imperialism, one that would extend through the twentieth century and into the twenty-first.

As for the fourth party system itself, which lasted from the mid-1890s to the early 1930s, it was again an era of Republican dominance, except for a period between 1912 and 1920 when the Democrats under Woodrow Wilson had the helm. The period began in the midst of a serious economic depression, albeit one tampered by the promise of business growth under McKinley and the rise of the trusts (i.e., monopolies in railroads, oil, and other industries). The Progressive Era unfolded in this period, too, as social reformers, partly in reaction to industrial growth, sought to address such issues as child labor, urban slums, women's suffrage, and political corruption.

World War I unfolded as well, despite initial efforts to keep the United States out of it. The war, whatever else it was, was a boon for business, as corporate interests worked to supply the war effort, to quell the growth of labor unions, to build up the banking system, and to increase trade. After Wilson, who stood for strict regulation of industry, a string of Republican presidents who were staunchly pro-business occupied the White House: Warren Harding, Calvin Coolidge, and Herbert Hoover. The onset of the Great Depression in October 1929, however, damaged the Republican brand—at least as it was represented by Hoover. The fourth party system ends and the fifth begins with the election of Democrat Franklin D. Roosevelt in 1932

■ The March of the Flag

Date: September 16, 1898
Author: Albert J. Beveridge
Genre: Speech

Summary Overview

By the close of the nineteenth century, Americans had done the impossible: they had occupied and settled an entire continent, and they had done it in a single generation. Beginning in the 1840s and completed by the 1890s, settlers and pioneers, mainly coming from the East, had rushed toward the Pacific in a mad orgy of construction, cultivation, and violence. Wherever they went they built towns and cities, laid track, and dispossessed what they considered to be a primitive native population. The force that drove them, beyond the promises of easy riches and the allure of fresh beginnings, was an absolute conviction that they were agents of God himself, tasked by holy writ to bring civilization to savagery. As the frontier finally closed and a new uncertain century loomed ahead, this sense of divine exceptionalism turned outward, toward places like Cuba, Puerto Rico, and the Philippines, culminating in the birth of American imperialism.

Defining Moment

Americans have always been fascinated by the West. The promises of opportunity, prosperity, and reinvention, along with the naturally fertile landscape of the Pacific coast, all coalesce to create an idea often too powerful to resist. Adventure, mystery, and danger, all serve to only sweeten the pot. In the mid-nineteenth century, a generation of Americans and newly-arrived immigrants took it upon themselves to follow the trails, or ride the rails, to a new, undiscovered country. Most of the pioneers who set off from places like Chicago and Independence, Missouri, went in the hopes of claiming a plot of land: a homestead that they could then pass on to future generations. Others followed news of gold and silver strikes, or promises of work in building the vast tracks meant to finally connect the two distant coasts.

All the while, as the government fanned the flames of expansion, as boosters drummed up excitement, a new philosophy was forming in the minds of many Americans, which aimed to explain what was fast becoming one of the largest migrations in human history. It was called Manifest Destiny, the singular belief that the United States generally, and Westward expansion specifically, were consecrated by the divine. Although the view was not universally accepted, most notably by many in the Republican party, the notion that God favored the growth of the United States over other nations, appealed strongly to those struggling to start over on the frontier. America was exceptional. Americans were exceptional, blessed by the Almighty in their deeds, whether that be building homesteads or driving Native peoples off their lands. Such notions of divine authority helped justify the annexation of Oregon Territory and the war with Mexico.

As the frontier finally closed in the 1890s, the notion of Manifest Destiny began to change. In this new version, America had a responsibility to spread its brand of exceptionalism beyond its shores. It was for the United States to civilize and pacify the savage world, to spread democracy, and further national interests. The argument made was that if America was destined to forever change the world, it needed to pursue a policy of perpetual expansion. In April 1898, bolstered by this new imperialist philosophy, the United States went to war against Spain. Officially sanctioned to liberate Cuba, Puerto Rico, and the Philippines from Spanish rule, the move was really made to gain those territories in order expand American interests. Immediately afterward, debate erupted between those for and against annexation. The arguments used would set American foreign policy for the next hundred years.

Author Biography

Albert Jeremiah Beveridge was born in Ohio in 1862. Hailing from an English background, Beveridge was raised with the same frontier attitudes as millions of Americans. To gain success and achieve God's will, one had to work hard and take rather than wait for something to be given. Growing in prominence as a pro-expansionist orator, often speaking on behalf of political candidates for major office, Beveridge was elected to the U.S. Senate under the Republican ticket in 1899. A loyal Roosevelt progressive, Beveridge followed his former commander-in-chief to the Progressive Party in 1912, effectively ending his own political career. Eventually, Beveridge became a historian, writing several highly influential works, including a biography of Justice John Marshall, which earned him a Pulitzer Prize. By the end of his life, the former firebrand imperialist began to regret many of his former expansionist leanings, and before his death in 1927, he gave many speeches warning about the unchecked growth of American power.

HISTORICAL DOCUMENT

It is a noble land that God has given us; a land that can feed and clothe the world; a land whose coastlines would inclose half the countries of Europe; a land set like a sentinel between the two imperial oceans of the globe, a greater England with a nobler destiny.

It is a mighty people that He has planted on this soil; a people sprung from the most masterful blood of history; a people perpetually revitalized by the virile, working-folk of all the earth; a people imperial by virtue of their power, by right of their institutions, by authority of their Heaven-directed purposes-the propagandists and not the misers of liberty.

It is a glorious history our God has bestowed upon His chosen people; a history heroic with faith in our mission and our future; a history of statesmen who flung the boundaries of the Republic out into unexplored lands and savage wilderness; a history of soldiers who carried the flag across blazing deserts and through the ranks of hostile mountains, even to the gates of sunset; a history of a multiplying people who overran a continent in half a century; a history of prophets who saw the consequences of evils inherited from the past and of martyrs who died to save us from them; a history divinely logical, in the process of whose tremendous reasoning we find ourselves today.

Therefore, in this campaign, the question is larger than a party question. It is an American question. It is a world question. Shall the American people continue their march toward the commercial supremacy of the world? Shall free institutions broaden their blessed reign as the children of liberty wax in strength, until the empire of our principles is established over the hearts of all mankind?

Have we no mission to perform no duty to discharge to our fellow man? Has God endowed us with gifts beyond our deserts and marked us as the people of His peculiar favor, merely to rot in our own selfishness, as men and nations must, who take cowardice for their companion and self for their deity—as China has, as India has, as Egypt has?

Shall we be as the man who had one talent and hid it, or as he who had ten talents and used them until they grew to riches? And shall we reap the reward that waits on our discharge of our high duty; shall we occupy new markets for what our farmers raise, our factories make, our merchants sell-aye, and please God, new markets for what our ships shall carry?

* * *

Hawaii is ours; Porto Rico is to be ours; at the prayer of her people Cuba finally will be ours; in the islands of the East, even to the gates of Asia, coaling stations are to be ours at the very least; the flag of a liberal government is to float over the Philippines, and may it be the banner that Taylor unfurled in Texas and Fremont carried to the coast.

The Opposition tells us that we ought not to govern a people without their consent. I answer, The rule of liberty that all just government derives its authority from the consent of the governed, applies only to those who are capable of self-government We govern the Indians without their consent, we govern our territories without their consent, we govern our children without their consent. How do they know what our government would be without their consent? Would not the people of the Philippines prefer the just, humane, civilizing government of this Republic to the savage, bloody rule of pillage and extortion from which we have rescued them? And, regardless of this formula of words made only for enlightened, self-governing people, do we owe no duty to the world? Shall we turn these peoples back to the reeking hands from which we have taken them? Shall we abandon them, with Germany, England, Japan, hungering for them? Shall we save them from those nations, to give them a self-rule of tragedy?

They ask us how we shall govern these new possessions. I answer: Out of local conditions and the necessities of the case methods of government will grow. If England can govern foreign lands, so can America. If Germany can govern foreign lands, so can America. If they can supervise protectorates, so can America. Why is it more difficult to administer Hawaii than New Mexico or California? Both had a savage and an alien population: both were more remote from the seat of government when they came under our dominion than the Philippines are today.

Will you say by your vote that American ability to govern has decayed, that a century s experience in self-rule has failed of a result? Will you affirm by your vote that you are an infidel to American power and practical sense? Or will you say that ours is the blood of government; ours the heart of dominion; ours the brain and genius of administration? Will you remember that we do but what our fathers did-we but pitch the tents of liberty farther westward, farther southward-we only continue the march of the flag?

The march of the flag! In 1789 the flag of the Republic waved over 4,000,000 souls in thirteen states, and their savage territory which stretched to the Mississippi, to Canada, to the Floridas. The timid minds of that day said that no new territory was needed, and, for the hour, they were right. But Jefferson, through whose intellect the centuries marched; Jefferson, who dreamed of Cuba as an American state, Jefferson, the first Imperialist of the Republic- Jefferson acquired that imperial territory which swept from the Mississippi to the mountains, from Texas to the British possessions, and the march of the flag began!

The infidels to the gospel of liberty raved, but the flag swept on! The title to that noble land out of which Oregon, Washington, Idaho and Montana have been carved was uncertain: Jefferson, strict constructionist of constitutional power though he was, obeyed the Anglo-Saxon impulse within him, whose watchword is, "Forward!": another empire was added to the Republic, and the march of the flag went on!

Those who deny the power of free institutions to expand urged every argument, and more, that we hear, today; but the people's judgment approved the command of their blood, and the march of the flag went on! A screen of land from New Orleans to Florida shut us from the Gulf, and over this and the Everglade Peninsula waved the saffron flag of Spain; Andrew Jackson seized both, the American people stood at his back, and, under Monroe, the Floridas came under the dominion of the Republic, and the march of the flag went on! The Cassandras prophesied every prophecy of despair we hear, today, but the march of the flag went on!

Then Texas responded to the bugle calls of liberty, and the march of the flag went on! And, at last, we waged war with Mexico, and the flag swept over the southwest, over peerless California, past the Gate of Gold to Oregon on the north, and from ocean to ocean its folds of glory blazed.

And, now, obeying the same voice that Jefferson heard and obeyed, that Jackson heard and obeyed, that Monroe heard and obeyed, that Seward heard and obeyed, that Grant heard and obeyed, that Harrison heard and obeyed, our President today plants the flag over the islands of the seas, outposts of commerce, citadels of national security, and the march of the flag goes on! Distance and oceans are no arguments. The fact that all the territory our fathers bought and seized is contiguous, is no argument. In 1819 Florida was farther from New York than Porto Rico is from Chicago today; Texas, farther from Washington in 1845 than Hawaii is from Boston in 1898; California, more inaccessible in 1847 than the Philippines are now. Gibraltar is farther from London than Havana is from Washington; Melbourne is farther from Liverpool than Manila is from San Francisco. The ocean does not separate us from lands of our duty and desire—the oceans join us, rivers never to be dredged, canals never to be re paired. Steam joins us; electricity joins us—the very elements are in league with our destiny. Cuba not contiguous? Porto Rico not contiguous! Hawaii and the Philippines not contiguous! The oceans make them contiguous. And our navy will make them contiguous.

But the Opposition is right—there is a difference. We did not need the western Mississippi Valley when we acquired it, nor Florida! nor Texas, nor California, nor the royal provinces of the far northwest We had no emigrants to people this imperial wilderness, no money to develop it, even no highways to cover it. No trade awaited us in its savage fastnesses. Our productions were not greater than our trade There was not one reason for the land-lust of our statesmen from Jefferson to Grant, other than the prophet and the Saxon within them But, to-day, we are raising more than we can consume, making more than we can use. Therefore we must find new markets for our produce.

And so, while we did not need the territory taken during the past century at the time it was acquired, we do need what we have taken in 1898, and we need it now. The resource and the commerce of the immensely rich dominions will be increased as much as American energy is greater than Spanish sloth.

In Cuba, alone, there are 15,000,000 acres of forest unacquainted with the ax, exhaustless mines of iron, priceless deposits of manganese, millions of dollars' worth of which we must buy, to-day, from the Black Sea districts There are millions of acres yet unexplored. The resources of Porto Rico have only been trifled with. The riches of the Philippines have hardly been touched by the finger-tips of modern methods. And they produce what we consume, and consume what we produce—the very predestination of reciprocity—a reciprocity "not made with hands, eternal in the heavens." They sell hemp, sugar, cocoanuts, fruits of the tropics, timber of price like mahogany; they buy flour, clothing, tools, implements, machinery and all that we can raise and make. Their trade will be ours in time. Do you indorse that policy with your vote?

Cuba is as large as Pennsylvania, and is the richest spot on the globe. Hawaii is as large as New Jersey; Porto Rico half as large as Hawaii; the Philippines larger than all New England, New York, New Jersey and Delaware combined. Together they are larger than the British Isles, larger than France, larger than Germany, larger than Japan.

If any man tells you that trade depends on cheapness and not on government influence, ask him why England does not abandon South Africa, Egypt, India. Why does France seize South China, Germany the vast region whose port is Kaou-chou?

Our trade with Porto Rico, Hawaii and the Philip-pines must be as free as between the states of the Union, because they are American territory, while every other nation on earth must pay our tariff before they can compete with us. Until Cuba shall ask for annexation, our trade with her will, at the very least, be like the preferential trade of Canada with England. That, and the excellence of our goods and products; that, and the convenience of traffic; that, and the kinship of interests and destiny, will give the monopoly of these markets to the American people.

The commercial supremacy of the Republic means that this Nation is to be the sovereign factor in the peace of the world. For the conflicts of the future are to be conflicts of trade, struggles for markets, commercial wars for existence. And the golden rule of peace is impregnability of position and invincibility of preparedness. So, we see England, the greatest strategist of history, plant her flag and her cannon on Gibraltar, at Quebec, in the Bermudas, at Vancouver, everywhere.

So Hawaii furnishes us a naval base in the heart of the Pacific; the Ladrones another, a voyage further on; Manila another, at the gates of Asia—Asia, to the trade of whose hundreds of millions American merchants, manufacturers, farmers, have as good right as those of Germany or France or Russia or England; Asia, whose commerce with the United Kingdom alone amounts to hundreds of millions of dollars every year; Asia, to whom Germany looks to take her surplus products; Asia, whose doors must not be shut against American trade. Within five decades the bulk of Oriental commerce will be ours. No wonder that, in the shadows of coming events so great, free-silver is already a memory. The current of history has swept past that episode. Men understand, today, the greatest commerce of the world must be conducted with the steadiest standard of value and most convenient medium of exchange human ingenuity can devise. Time, that unerring reasoner, has settled the silver question. The American people are tired of talking about money—they want to make it. . . . . There are so many real things to be done-canals to be dug, railways to be laid, forests to be felled, cities to be builded, fields to be tilled, markets to be won, ships to be launched, peoples to be saved, civilization to be proclaimed and the Rag of liberty Hung to the eager air of every sea. Is this an hour to waste upon triflers with nature's laws? Is this a season to give our destiny over to word-mongers and prosperity-wreckers? No! It is an hour to remember our duty to our homes. It is a moment to realize the opportunities fate has opened to us. And so is all hour for us to stand by the Government.

Wonderfully has God guided us Yonder at Bunker Hill and Yorktown. His providence was above us At New Orleans and on ensanguined seas His hand sustained us. Abraham Lincoln was His minister and His was the altar of freedom the Nation's soldiers set up on a hundred battle-fields. His power directed Dewey in the East and delivered the Spanish fleet into our hands, as He delivered the elder Armada into the hands of our English sires two centuries ago [Note—actually in 1588]. The American people can not use a dishonest medium of exchange; it is ours to set the world its example of right and honor. We can not fly from our world duties; it is ours to execute the purpose of a fate that has driven us to be greater than our small intentions. We can not retreat from any soil where Providence has unfurled our banner; it is ours to save that soil for liberty and civilization.

GLOSSARY

constructionist: one who adheres to a conservative legal philosophy which limits interpretation to a strict reading of the applicable text contiguous: sharing a common border protectorate: a state that is controlled and protected by another

Document Analysis

In a campaign speech given in late 1898, Albert Beveridge is arguing for annexation of the former Spanish colonies won during the Spanish-American War, but generally, he is also pushing for a policy of unrestrained imperialism. In his opinion, the United States has only to gain by expanding outward beyond its borders—new resources, new markets, and most importantly, a new progression in American authority.

The speech begins with the language of Manifest Destiny. God is invoked several times to describe the special place that America holds in the world. Americans are the chosen people, placed on Earth, on this continent to transform it into a new Eden and, from there, strike out to build God's kingdom across the whole of the world. Over the nineteenth century, Beveridge argues, thanks to the will of great thinking men such as Thomas Jefferson, the United States was transformed from a savage wilderness into a glorious new republic. But if the nation were to stop there, if expansion were to stop with the conquering of the West, Beveridge warns, America will slide backward, becoming something more closely resembling China, or India, or Egypt—a once great empire, now only a shadow of itself.

For Beveridge, the projection of American power is not governance of others without consent, it is the right and responsibility of the American people. How are the populations of places like Cuba and the Philippines to govern themselves when they are incapable of self-rule? Much like the civilized European imperial powers, America must serve as a shepherd, a parent caring for undeveloped children. In the process, the United States stands to gain wealth and resources, which it can then use to better rule over those inferior nations. This imperialist credo, Beveridge continues, is nothing new in American history. It has been a driving force since the nation's founding and must continue to be. Not only out of duty to God, but to the world as a whole. Because America is the driving force for good and freedom throughout the globe. Without the leadership of the United States, Beveridge hints, conflict may be unavoidable in the future.

Beyond Beveridge's arguments for God, for destiny and markets, is the persistent use of the march as a rhetorical device: marching westward, marching forward, marching always toward progress. In this way, Beveridge is able to make an argument for imperialism based not just in a sense of Manifest Destiny, linked to the work of the Founding Fathers, but also as biological inevitability. To resist expansion is to resist the very course of social evolution. It is tantamount to reverting to a more primitive state.

Essential Themes

Drawing on the ideas comprising Manifest Destiny, but also Social Darwinism, evangelism, and patriotism, Albert Beveridge tried to pull together past, present, and future, to make a case for a new, aggressive American imperialism. Built on the foundation of America's breathtaking westward expansion, his speech made a case for a new world order, in which the somewhat isolationist United States would play the role of global leader. The benefits, according to Beveridge were clear: resources; new markets; safety; and, above all, progress. It was a vision of unrelenting, limitless progress, toward a sort of new American utopia. This new imperialism wasn't a choice. It had to happen. It would happen. The very forces of history demanded it.

This speech and others, given by the leading politicians of the time, served to slowly turn American foreign policy increasingly outward. Despite the inherent racism and militarism of such policies, defenders of American expansionism argued that it was a sort of benevolent imperialism. As the United States was a just and democratic nation, it would rule others in a just and democratic fashion. Not strictly for the benefit of the United States, but for that of all nations. Besides, the form of American rule would not be the type practiced by other nations. It would be less direct, more directorial.

After the Spanish-American War, which the expansionists upheld as a bright example of the righteousness of their ideology, America followed a course of increased internationalism, colored by imperialism. Cuba, Puerto Rico, and the Philippines all fell under the sphere of American influence, a state of affairs which served to create long standing resentments and, at times, even open conflict. Although official policy shifted over the course of the twentieth century from one of annexation to intervention, many of the same arguments made by the likes of Albert Beveridge—ideas that America was the sole champion of democracy and freedom, that American exceptionalism demanded that the United States serve as a global leader—remain central to American foreign policy to this day. Recent conflicts in the Middle East, interventions in Central and South America, even the War in Vietnam, are all legacies of America's imperial past, born out of the religious fervor of the settling of the West.

—*KP Dawes, MA*

Bibliography and Additional Reading

Braeman, John. *Albert J. Beveridge: American Nationalist*. Chicago: U of Chicago P, 1971. Print.

Howe, Daniel Walker. *What Hath God Wrought: The Transformation of America, 1815–1848*. New York: Oxford UP, 2007. Print.

Kinzer, Stephen. *Overthrow: America's Century of Regime Change from Hawaii to Iraq*. New York: Time Books, 2006. Print.

Morgan, Robert. *Lions of the West*. Chapel Hill: Algonquin Books, 2012. Print.

■ Platform of the Progressive Party

Date: 1912
Author: Attributed to Theodore Roosevelt
Genre: Charter, political tract

Summary Overview

In August 1912 the newly formed Progressive Party held its nominating convention for president in Chicago and drafted the Progressive Party Platform. The party had emerged as the result of a rift between former president Theodore Roosevelt and his successor, William Howard Taft. Roosevelt had left office in 1909, and Taft, Roosevelt's secretary of war, was his handpicked successor. Taft took office in 1909. During Taft's term as president, Roosevelt became disenchanted with him and his policies, believing that he was too conservative. Accordingly, in 1912 Roosevelt decided to run again for president.

Roosevelt actually outpolled Taft in the Republican primaries, but Taft nevertheless secured the Republican nomination. In response, Progressives hastily organized a new party with Roosevelt as their standard-bearer. The party was later colloquially called the Bull Moose Party after Roosevelt survived an assassination attempt (a fifty-page speech and a metal eyeglass case prevented the bullet from penetrating his lung) and responded to a reporter's question about his health by saying, "I'm fit as a bull moose." Although Roosevelt would garner more than four million votes (more than Taft), Democrat Woodrow Wilson handily won the election. Nevertheless, numerous Progressive Party candidates (and candidates that ran on Progressive ideals) won election that year in Congress and in statewide races.

The Progressive Party Platform, dated August 7, 1912, advocated many positions that were dear to the hearts of early-twentieth-century Progressives, particularly those in the feminist movement, organized labor, and farmers. Although the national party ran out of steam by the end of the decade, many of its proposals have since been enacted, including women's suffrage, direct election of senators, workers' compensation, Social Security measures, a federal income tax, and financial reforms. Thus, while the national political party dissolved, the ideals of progressivism lived on and continue to influence American politics in the twenty-first century. Oregon and Vermont,

for example, have active state-level Progressive Parties.

With the effective collapse of the Republican progressive coalition and the rise in support for progressive-minded issues, such as suffrage, industrial and political reform, and economic justice, the Progressive Party platform served as an appeal to progressives across the political spectrum. By casting themselves as the new party for the modern age, appealing directly to progressive issues and built around a popular former president, the Progressive Party hoped to rise as a new force within the American political system much as the Republican Party had some sixty years earlier. In many ways the platform was an extension of Theodore Roosevelt himself, and his "New Nationalism," born out of his famous Square Deal. The platform, although progressive minded in its domestic agenda, called for a strong military and more powerful executive. So, although the platform was meant to draw in a wide swath of progressives, it also served to repel pacifists and small government reformers. In this sense, the party platform became a mirror of the man at the top of the ticket, making the election, effectively, a referendum on Roosevelt's popularity as president.

Author Biography

Theodore "Teddy" Roosevelt Jr., was born to a wealthy and politically connected New York family on October 27, 1858. Suffering poor health in his youth, Roosevelt, under the influence of his father, took up various sports and physical activities as a means by which to improve his constitution. He became enamored of nature and conservation, often escaping on extended trips into the wild. A voracious reader and brilliant student, Roosevelt excelled at his studies as a student at Harvard, finding solace in intellectual pursuit following the death of his father in 1878. By 1890, Roosevelt had published multiple books and had turned his attention to politics, a vocation he devoted himself to tirelessly after the death of his wife during childbirth (he would later remarry and father five more children). As a New York State Assemblyman, Roosevelt gained a reputation as a progressive, and after unsuccessful bids for President and Mayor of New York, went out West to the frontier where he worked as a cowboy and ranch hand. After serving as New York Police Commissioner and Assistant Secretary of the Navy, Roosevelt fought with distinction and bravado in Cuba during the Spanish-American War, his exploits earning him first the governorship of New York and then the vice presidency under William McKinley. Following McKinley's assassination in 1901, Roosevelt, then the 26th President of the United States, became renowned as a trust-busting progressive, strengthening the rights of

workers while restricting the power of the robber barons. He also gained a reputation as an expansionist, building up the American navy and overseeing the construction of the Panama Canal. In one of his most enduring acts as president, he also established the national parks. After a lackluster second term, and an ill-fated African expedition, Roosevelt ran again for office in 1912 under the Progressive Party, also famously known as the Bull-Moose Party. After defeat to Woodrow Wilson, Roosevelt dove back into conservation and writing. After the loss of his youngest son, Quinten in World War I, Roosevelt's health began to fail. He died on January 6, 1919 at the age of 60.

Electoral program of 1912, 16-page campaign booklet with the platform of the new Progressive Party.

HISTORICAL DOCUMENT

Declaration of Principles of the Progressive Party
The conscience of the people, in a time of grave national problems, has called into being a new party, born of the Nation's awakened sense of justice. We of the Progressive Party here dedicate ourselves to the fulfillment of the duty laid upon us by our fathers to maintain that government of the people, by the people and for the people whose foundation they laid.

We hold with Thomas Jefferson and Abraham Lincoln that the people are the masters of their Constitution, to fulfill its purposes and to safeguard it from those who, by perversion of its intent, would convert it into an instrument of injustice. In accordance with the needs of each generation the people must use their sovereign powers to establish and maintain equal opportunity and industrial justice, to secure which this Government was founded and without which no republic can endure.

This country belongs to the people who inhabit it. Its resources, its business, its institutions and its laws should be utilized, maintained or altered in whatever manner will best promote the general interest.

It is time to set the public welfare in the first place.

The Old Parties
Political parties exist to secure responsible government and to execute the will of the people.

From these great tasks both of the old parties have turned aside. Instead of instruments to promote the general welfare, they have become the tools of corrupt interests which use them impartially to serve their selfish purposes. Behind the ostensible government sits enthroned an invisible government, owing no allegiance and acknowledging no responsibility to the people.

To destroy this invisible government, to dissolve the unholy alliance between corrupt business and corrupt politics is the first task of the statesmanship of the day.

The deliberate betrayal of its trust by the Republican Party, and the fatal incapacity of the Democratic Party to deal with the new issues of the new time, have compelled the people to forge a new instrument of government through which to give effect to their will in laws and institutions.

Unhampered by tradition, uncorrupted by power, undismayed by the magnitude of the task, the new party offers itself as the instrument of the people to sweep away old abuses, to build a new and nobler commonwealth.

A Covenant with the People
This declaration is our covenant with the people, and we hereby bind the party and its candidates in State and Nation to the pledges made herein.

The Rule of the People
The Progressive Party, committed to the principle of government by a self-controlled democracy expressing its will through representatives of the people, pledges itself to secure such alterations in the fundamental law of the several States and of the United States as shall insure the representative character of the Government.

In particular, the party declares for direct primaries for nomination of State and National officers, for Nationwide preferential primaries for candidates for the Presidency, for the direct election of United States Senators by the people; and we urge on the States the policy of the short ballot, with responsibility to the people secured by the initiative, referendum and recall.

Amendment of Constitution
The Progressive Party, believing that a free people should have the power from time to time to amend their fundamental law so as to adapt it progressively to the changing needs of the people, pledges itself to provide a more easy and expeditious method of amending the Federal Constitution.

Nation and State
Up to the limit of the Constitution, and later by amendment of the Constitution, if found necessary, we advocate bringing under effective national jurisdiction those problems which have expanded beyond reach of the individual states.

It is as grotesque as it is intolerable that the several States should by unequal laws in matter of common concern become competing commercial agencies, barter the lives of their children, the health of their women and the safety and well-being of their working people for the profit of their financial interests.

The extreme insistence on States' rights by the Democratic Party in the Baltimore platform demonstrates anew its inability to understand the world into which it has survived or to administer the affairs of a Union States which have in all essential respects become one people.

Social and Industrial Strength
The supreme duty of the Nation is the conservation of human resources through an enlightened measure of social and industrial justice. We pledge ourselves to work unceasingly in State and Nation for:—

Effective legislation looking to the prevention of industrial accidents, occupational diseases, overwork, involuntary unemployment, and other injurious effects incident to modern industry;

The fixing of minimum safety and health standards for the various occupations, and the exercise of the public authority of State and Nation, including the Federal control over inter-State commerce and the taxing power, to maintain such standards;

The prohibition of child labor;

Minimum wage standards for working women, to provide a living scale in all industrial occupations;

The prohibition of night work for women and the establishment of an eight hour day for women and young persons;

One day's rest in seven for all wage-workers;

The abolition of the convict contract labor system; substituting a system of prison production for governmental consumption only; and the application of prisoners' earnings to the support of their dependent families;

Publicity as to wages, hours and conditions and labor; full reports upon industrial accidents and diseases, and the opening to public inspection of all tallies, weights, measures and check systems on labor products;

Standards of compensation for death by industrial accident and injury and trade diseases which will transfer the burden of lost earnings from the families of working people to the industry, and thus to the community;

The protection of home life against the hazards of sickness, irregular employment and old age through the adoption of a system of social insurance adapted to American use;

The development of the creative labor power of America by lifting the last load of illiteracy from American youth and establishing continuation schools for industrial education under public control and encouraging agricultural education and demonstration in rural schools;

The establishment of industrial research laboratories to put the methods and discoveries of science at the service of American producers.

We favor the organization of the workers, men and women as a means of protecting their interests and of promoting their progress.

Business
We believe that true popular government, justice and prosperity go hand in hand, and so believing, it is our purpose to secure that large measure of general prosperity which is the fruit of legitimate and honest business, fostered by equal justice and by sound progressive laws.

We demand that the test of true prosperity shall be the benefits conferred thereby on all the citizens not confined to individuals or classes and that the test of corporate efficiency shall be the ability better to serve the public; that those who profit by control of business affairs shall justify that profit and that control by sharing with the public the fruits thereof.

We therefore demand a strong National regulation of inter-State corporations. The corporation is an essential part of modern business. The concentration of modern business, in some degree, is both inevitable and necessary for National and international business efficiency. but the existing concentration of vast wealth under a corporate system, unguarded and uncontrolled by the Nation, has placed in the hands of a few men enormous, secret, irresponsible power over the daily life of the citizen—a power insufferable in a free government and certain of abuse.

This power has been abused, in monopoly of National resources, in stock watering, in unfair competition and unfair privileges, and finally in sinister influences on the public agencies of State and Nation. We do not fear commercial power, but we insist that it shall be exercised openly, under publicity, supervision and regulation of the most efficient sort, which will preserve its good while eradicating and preventing its evils.

To that end we urge the establishment of a strong Federal administrative commission of high standing, which shall maintain permanent active supervision over industrial corporations engaged in inter-State commerce, or such of them as are of public importance, doing for them what the Government now does for the National banks, and what is now done for the railroads by the Inter-State Commerce Commission.

Such a commission must enforce the complete publicity of those corporation transactions which are of public interest; must attack unfair competition, false capitalization and special privilege, and by continuous trained watchfulness guard and keep open equally to all the highways of American commerce.

Thus the business man will have certain knowledge of the law, and will be able to conduct his business easily in conformity therewith; the investor will find security for his capital; dividends will be rendered more certain, and the savings of the people will be drawn naturally and safely into the channels of trade.

Under such a system of constructive regulation, legitimate business, freed from confusion, uncertainty and fruitless litigation, will develop normally in response to the energy and enterprise of the American business man.

We favor strengthening the Sherman law by prohibiting agreements to divide territory or limit output; refus-ing to sell to customers who buy from business rivals; to sell below cost in certain areas while maintaining higher prices in other places; using the power of transportation to aid or injure special business concerns; and other unfair trade practices.

Commercial Development
The time has come when the Federal Government should co-operate with the manufacturers and producers in extending our foreign commerce. To this end we demand adequate appropriations by Congress and the appointment of diplomatic and consular officers solely with a view to their special fitness and worth, and not in consideration of political expediency.

It is imperative to the welfare of our people that we enlarge and extend our foreign commerce. We are pre-eminently fitted to do this because as a people we have developed high skill in the art of manufacturing; our business men are strong executives, strong organizers. In every way possible our Federal Government should co-operate in this important matter. Anyone who has had the opportunity to study and observe first-hand Germany's course in this respect must realize that their policy of co-operation between Government and business has in comparatively few years made them a leading competitor for the commerce of the world. It should be remembered that they are doing this on a national scale and with large units of business, while the Democrats would have us believe that we should do it with small units of business, which would be controlled not by the National Government but by forty-nine conflicting sovereignties. Such a policy is utterly out of keeping with the progress of the times and gives our great commercial rivals in Europe—hungry for international markets—golden opportunities of which they are rapidly taking advantage.

Tariff
We believe in a protective tariff which shall equalize conditions of competition between the United States and foreign countries, both for the farmer and the manufacturer, and which shall maintain for labor an adequate standard of living.

Primarily the benefit of any tariff should be disclosed in the pay envelope of the laborer. We declare that no industry deserves protection which is unfair to labor or which is operating in violation of Federal law. We believe that the presumptions always in favor of the consuming public.

We demand tariff revision because the present tariff is unjust to the people of the United States. Fair-dealing toward the people requires an immediate downward revision of those schedules wherein duties are shown to be unjust or excessive.

We pledge ourselves to the establishment of a non-partisan scientific tariff commission, reporting both to the President and to either branch of Congress, which shall report, first, as to the costs of production, efficiency of labor, capitalization, industrial organization and efficiency and the general competitive position in this country and abroad of industries seeking protection from Congress; second, as to the revenue-producing power of the tariff and its relation to the resources of government; and third, as to the effect of the tariff on prices, operations of middlemen, and on the purchasing power of the consumer.

We believe that this commission should have plenary power to elicit information, and for this purpose to prescribe a uniform system of accounting for the great protected industries. The work of the commission should not prevent the immediate adoption of acts reducing those schedules generally recognized as excessive.

We condemn the Payne-Aldrich bill as unjust to the people. The Republican organization is in the hands of those who have broken and cannot again be trusted to keep, the promise of necessary downward revision. The Democratic Party is committed to the destruction of the protective system through a tariff for revenue only—a policy which would inevitably produce widespread industrial and commercial disaster.

We demand the immediate repeal of the Canadian Reciprocity Act.

High Cost of Living

The high cost of living is due partly to worldwide and partly to local causes; partly to natural and partly to artificial causes. The measures proposed in this platform on various subject, such as the tariff, the trusts and conservation, will of themselves tend to remove the artificial causes.

There will remain other elements, such as the tendency to leave the country for the city, waste, extravagance, bad system of taxation, poor methods of raising crops and bad business methods in marketing crops.

To remedy these conditions requires the fullest information, and based on this information, effective Government supervision and control to remove all the artificial causes. We pledge ourselves to such full and immediate inquiry and to immediate action to deal with every need such inquiry discloses.

Currency

We believe there exists imperative need for prompt legislation for the improvement of our National currency system. We believe the present method of issuing notes through private agencies is harmful and unscientific.

The issue of currency is fundamentally government function and the system should have as basic principles soundness and elasticity. The control should be lodged with the Government and should be protected from domination manipulation by Wall Street or any special interests.

We are opposed to the so-called Aldrich currency bill, because its provisions would place our currency and credit system in private hands, not subject to effective public control.

Conservation

The natural resources of the Nation must be promptly developed and generously used to supply the people's needs, but we cannot safely allow them to be wasted, exploited, monopolized or controlled against the general good. We heartily favor the policy of conservation, and we pledge our party to protect the National forests without hindering their legitimate use for the benefit of all the people.

Agricultural lands in the National forests are, and should remain, open to the genuine settler. Conservation will not retard legitimate development. The honest settler must receive his patent promptly, without needless restrictions or delays.

We believe that the remaining forests, coal and oil lands, water powers and other natural resources still in State or National control (except agricultural lands) are more likely to be wisely conserved and utilized for the general welfare if held in the public hands.

In order that consumers and producers, managers and workmen, now and hereafter, need not pay toll to private monopolies of power and raw material, we demand that such resources shall be retained by the State of Nation and opened to immediate use under laws which will encourage development and make to the people a moderate return for benefits conferred.

In particular we pledge our party to require reasonable compensation to the public for water-power rights hereafter granted by the public.

We pledge legislation to lease the public grazing lands under equitable provisions now pending which will increase the production of food for the people and thoroughly safeguard the rights of the actual homemaker. Natural resources, whose conservation is necessary for the National welfare, should be owned or controlled by the Nation.

Waterways

The rivers of the United States are the natural arteries of this continent. We demand that they shall be opened to traffic as indispensable parts of a great Nation-wide system of transportation in which the Panama Canal will be the central link, thus enabling the whole interior of the United States to share with the Atlantic and Pacific seaboards in the benefit derived from canal.

It is a National obligation to develop our rivers, and especially the Mississippi and its tributaries, without delay, under a comprehensive general plan covering each river system from its source to its mouth, designed to secure its highest usefulness for navigation, irrigation, domestic supply, water power and the prevention of floods.

We pledge our party to the immediate preparation of such a plan, which should be made and carried out in close and friendly co-operation between the Nation, the States and the cities affected.

Under such a plan, the destructive floods of the Mississippi and other streams, which represent vast and needless loss to the Nation, would be controlled by forest conservation and water storage at the headwaters, and by levees below; land sufficient to support millions of people would be reclaimed from the deserts and the swamps, water power enough to transform the industrial standing of whole States would be developed, adequate water terminals would be provided, transportation by

river would revive, and the railroads would be compelled to co-operate as freely with the boat lines as with each other.

The equipment, organization and experience acquires in constructing the Panama Canal soon will be available for the Lakes-to-the-Gulf deep waterway and other portions of this great work, and should be utilized by the Nation in co-operation with the various States, at the lowest net cost to the people.

Panama Canal

The Panama Canal, built and paid for by the American people, must be used primarily for their benefit.

We demand that the canal shall be so operated as to break the transportation monopoly mow held and misused by the transcontinental railroads by maintaining sea competition with them; that ships directly or indirectly owned or controlled by American railroad corporations shall not be permitted to use the canal, and that American ships engaged in coastwise trade shall pay no tolls.

The Progressive Party will favor legislation having for its aim the development of friendship and commerce between the United States and Latin-American nations.

Alaska

The coal and other natural resources of Alaska should be opened to development at once. They are owned by the people of the United States, and are safe from monopoly, waste or destruction only while so owned.

We demand that they shall neither be sold nor given away, except under the homestead law, but while held in Government ownership shall be opened to use promptly upon liberal terms requiring immediate development.

Thus the benefit of cheap fuel will accrue to the government of the United Stated and to the people of Alaska and the Pacific Coast; the settlement of extensive agricultural lands will be hastened; the extermination of the salmon will be prevented, and the just and wise development of Alaskan resources will take the place of private extortion or monopoly.

We demand also that extortion or monopoly in transportation shall be prevented by the prompt acquisition, construction or improvement by the Government of such railroads, harbor and other facilities for transportation as the welfare of the people may demand.

We promise the people of the Territory of Alaska the same measure of local self-government that was given to other American territories, and that officials appointed there shall be qualified by previous bona-fide residence in the Territory.

Equal Suffrage

The Progressive Party, believing that no people can justly claim to be a true democracy which denies political rights on account of sex, pledges itself to the task of securing equal suffrage to men and women alike.

Corrupt Practices

We pledge our party to legislation that will compel strict limitation on all campaign contributions and expenditures, and detailed publicity of both before as well as after primaries and elections.

Publicity and Public Service

We pledge our party to legislation compelling the registration of lobbyists; publicity of committee hearings except on foreign affairs, and recording of all votes in committee; and forbidding Federal appointees from holding office in State of National political organizations, or taking part as officers or delegates in political conventions for the nomination of elective State or National officials.

The Courts

The Progressive Party demands such restriction of the power of the courts as shall leave to the people the ultimate authority to determine fundamental questions of social welfare and public policy. To secure this end it pledges itself to provide:

1. That when an act, passed under the police power of the State, is held unconstitutional under the State Constitution, by the courts, the people, after an ample interval for deliberation, shall have opportunity to vote on the question whether they desire the act to become a law, notwithstanding such decision.

2. That every decision of the highest appellate court of a State declaring an act of the Legislature unconstitutional on the ground of its violation of the Federal Constitution shall be subject to the same review by the Supreme Court of the United States as is now accorded to decisions sustaining such legislation.

Administration of Justice

The Progressive Party, in order to secure to the people a better administration of justice and by that means to bring about a more general respect for the law and the courts, pledges itself to work unceasingly for the reform of legal procedure and judicial and methods.

We believe that the issuance of injunctions in cases arising out of labor disputes should be prohibited when such injunctions would not apply when no labor disputes existed.

We also believe that a person cited for contempt in the disputes, except when such contempt was committed in the actual presence of the court or so near thereto as to interfere with the proper administration of justice, should have a right to trial by jury.

Department of Labor

We pledge our party to establish a Department of Labor with a seat in the cabinet, and with wide jurisdiction over matters affecting the conditions of labor and living.

Country Life

The development and prosperity of country life as important to the people who live in the cities as they are to the farmers. Increase of prosperity on the farm will favorably affect the cost of living and promote the interests of all who dwell in the country, and all who depend upon its products for clothing, shelter and food.

We pledge out party to foster the development of agricultural credit and co-operation, the teaching of agriculture in schools, agricultural college extension, the use of mechanical power on the farm, and to re-establish the Country Life Commission, thus directly promoting the welfare of the farmers, and bringing the benefits of better farming, better business and better living within their reach.

Health

We favor the union of all the existing agencies of the Federal Government dealing with the public health into a single National health service without discrimination against or for any one set of therapeutic methods, school of medicine, or school of healing with such additional powers as may be necessary to enable it to perform efficiently such duties in the protection of the public from preventable diseases as may be properly undertaken by the Federal authorities; including the executing of existing laws regarding pure food; quarantine and cognate subjects; the promotion of appropriate action for the improvement of vital statistics and the extension of the registration area of such statistics and co-operation with the health activities of the various States and cities of the Nation.

Patents
We pledge ourselves to the enactment of a patent law which will make it impossible for patents to be suppressed or used against the public welfare in the interests of injurious monopolies.

Inter-State Commerce Commission
We pledge our party to secure to the Inter-State Commerce Commission the power to value the physical property of railroads. In order that the power of the commission to protect the people may not be impaired or destroyed, we demand the abolition of the Commerce Court.

Good Roads
We recognize the vital importance of good roads and we pledge out party to foster their extension in every proper way, and we favor the early construction of National highways. We also favor the extension of the rural free delivery service.

Inheritance and Income Tax
We believe in a graduated inheritance tax as a National means of equalizing the obligations of holder of property to government, and we hereby pledge our party to enact such a Federal law as will tax large inheritances returning to the States an equitable percentage of all amounts collected.

We favor the ratification of the pending amendment to the Constitution giving the Government power to levy an income tax.

Peace and National Defense
Progressive Party deplores the survival in our civilization of the barbaric system of warfare among nations with its enormous waste of resources even in time of peace, and the consequent impoverishment of the life of the toiling masses. We pledge the party to use its best endeavors to substitute judicial and other peaceful means of settling international differences.

We favor an international agreement for the limitation of naval forces. Pending such an agreement, and as the best means of preserving peace, we pledge ourselves to maintain for the present the policy of building two battleships a year.

Treaty Rights
We pledge our party to protect the rights of American citizenship at home and abroad. No treaty should receive the sanction of our government which discriminates between American citizens because of birthplace, race or religion, or that does not recognize the absolute right of expatriation.

The Immigrant
Through the establishment of industrial standards we propose to secure to the able-bodied immigrant and to his native fellow workers a larger share of American opportunity.

We denounce the fatal policy of indifference and neglect which has left our enormous immigrant population to become the prey of chance and cupidity.

We favor governmental action to encourage the distribution of immigrants away from the congested cities, to rigidly supervise all private agencies dealing with them and to promote their assimilation, education and advancement.

Pensions
We pledge ourselves to a wise and just policy of pensioning American soldiers and sailors and their widows and children they Federal Government. And we approve the policy of the Southern States in granting pensions to the ex-Confederate soldiers and sailors and their widows and children.

Parcels Post
We pledge our party to the immediate creation of a parcels post, with rates proportionate to distance and service.

Civil Service
We condemn the violations of the civil service law under the present administration, including the coercion and assessment of subordinate employees, and the President's refusal to punish such violation after a finding of guilty by his own commission; his distribution of patronage among subservient Congressmen, while withholding it from those who refuse support of administration measures; his withdrawal of nominations from the Senate until political support for himself was secured, and his open use of the offices to reward those who voted for his re-nomination.

To eradicate these abuses, we demand not only the enforcement of the civil service act in letter and spirit, but also legislation which will bring under the competitive system postmasters, collectors, marshals and all other non-political officers, as well as the enactment of an equitable retirement law, and we also insist upon continuous service during good behavior and efficiency.

Government Business Organization
We pledge our party to readjustment of the business methods of the National Government and a proper co-ordination of the Federal bureaus, which will increase the economy and efficiency of the Government service, prevent duplications and secret better results to the taxpayers for every dollar expended.

Government Supervision over Investment
The people of the United States are swindled out of many millions of dollars every year, through worthless investments. The plain people, the wage-earner and the men and women with small savings, have no way of knowing the merit of concerns sending out highly colored prospectuses offering stock for sale, prospectuses that make big returns seem certain and fortunes easily within grasp.

We hold it to be the duty of the Government to protect its people form this kind of piracy. We, therefore, demand wise carefully-thought-out legislation that will give us such Governmental supervision over this matter as will furnish to the people of the United States this much-needed protection, and we pledge ourselves thereto.

Conclusion
On these principles and on the recognized desirability of uniting the Progressive forces of the Nation into an organization which shall unequivocally represent the Progressive spirit and policy we appeal for the support of all American citizens without regard to previous political affiliations.

Document Analysis

The Progressive Party Platform begins by outlining the party's ideals. Claiming to be the party of "public welfare," the Progressive Party is sharply critical of the existing Democratic and Republican Parties, arguing that "they have become the tools of corrupt interests which use them impartially to serve their selfish purposes." The platform promises "to dissolve the unholy alliance between corrupt business and corrupt politics."

The planks of the platform can be sorted into four broad groups. The first group addresses social welfare and proposes an inheritance tax, a federal income tax (achieved by means of the Sixteenth Amendment to the U.S. Constitution in 1913), workers' compensation (achieved incrementally at the state level from 1906 to 1949), farm relief, limitations on injunctions against labor strikes, social insurance for the elderly (realized in the Social Security Act of 1935), and a national health service. Additionally, the platform calls for many labor reforms that are taken for granted today: prohibition of child labor, the eight-hour workday, the minimum wage, abolition of convict labor, and establishment of schools for industrial education. The platform also addressed issues involving conservation, the use of the nation's waterways, and the opening of the territory of Alaska (not yet a state) for resource exploitation.

The second group consists of political reforms and includes women's suffrage (attained in 1920 with ratification of the Nineteenth Amendment), direct election of U.S. senators (accomplished with the ratification of the Seventeenth Amendment in 1913), and the adoption of primary elections for state and federal nominations. The third group emphasizes direct participatory democracy in proposals for recall elections, referenda and citizen initiatives, and judicial recall (allowing the citizenry to overturn a court decision by popular vote).

The final group has to do with the broad theme of the platform: "To destroy this invisible government, to dissolve the unholy alliance between corrupt business and corrupt politics is the first task of the statesmanship of the day." Thus, the platform recommends limits on campaign contributions (finally enacted in part in 1972 with passage of the Federal Election Campaign Act), registration of lobbyists, and publication of the proceedings of congressional committees.

Interestingly, the platform has little to say about international affairs. It calls for an end to warfare and the establishment of "friendship and commerce" between the United States and the Latin American nations, but its most specific proposals are to maintain use of the Panama Canal for the benefit of the American people to break the railroad monopoly and continuation of the construction of battleships at the rate of two per year.

With deep roots in the populist and suffrage movements of the mid nineteenth century, and a progressive-minded, reform spirit at the turn of the twentieth century, a new progressive element had begun to emerge in American politics in the early years of the new century. Built on a deep mistrust of modernity and the crusading efforts of social reformers and muckrakers, progressives began to demand massive social-political-economic change. In addition to women's right to vote and prohibition, progressives called on government to strengthen worker pay and safety, establish standards for food and drugs, abolish practices like child labor, and reform the political system to allow for direct elections and mechanisms by which the citizen body could enact direct change. For a brief time progressives found a champion in Theodore Roosevelt, but when TR stepped down in 1909, selecting Howard Taft, his Secretary of War, to succeed him, the progress made since 1901 began to collapse. Unlike Roosevelt, Taft was a staunch conservative, and although he did push through some reforms, his close ties to business and insistence on reaching compromise angered many progressives including Roosevelt himself. Disagreement turned to open hostility, and in 1912, Roosevelt openly challenged Taft for the Republican nomination. Despite a strong challenge from TR, Taft prevailed, leading Roosevelt and his progressive supporters to walk out of the convention. The next day, Roosevelt supporters founded the Progressive Party. Despite strong support from many progressives and financial backing from wealthy donors, the Progressive Party lacked the organizational structure of the Democrats and Republicans. Furthermore, it antagonized many potential allies by effectively challenging progressives from other parties up and down the ticket. Regardless of shortcomings, the Progressive Party met late that summer at a nominating convention, in which it nominated Roosevelt by popular acclamation and quickly passed a party platform it hoped would unify progressives across the nation.

Despite the fact that the Progressive Party's platform was effectively a laundry list of progressive policy positions, and even went beyond that of the Democratic Party in making universal suffrage a key spoke, it was by no means without controversy. Industrial reformers, who had lobbied for strong trust-busting language, were angered when George W. Perkins, Chairman of International Harvester Company and Roosevelt's hand-picked party secretary, watered down the language only to call for strong regulation. Some, especially radical suffragists, opposed notions of Roosevelt's New Nationalism, a philosophy deeply entrenched in patriarchy. Finally, pacifists and isolationists, such as Jane Addams, were unhappy with the platform's foreign policy positions, especially those calling for a strengthening of America's military and increased internationalism. These issues weakened the overall platform and created deep fissures within the progressive coalition. However, despite these problems, the election of 1912 became one of the most spirited and reform-centric in American history. With Roosevelt and Wilson battling it out on the left, Taft was increasingly marginalized. In the end Wilson won the presidency with only 42% of the vote, with Roosevelt second (27%), Taft third (23%), and Eugene V. Debs, the Socialist candidate, coming in at a distant third. Although the loss would mark the end of Roosevelt's political career and the end of the Progressive Party, it remains the strongest showing by a third party in the history of American politics. Furthermore, despite its many flaws, the Progressive Party Platform became an important founding document for the American Left. Some twenty years later, Theodore Roosevelt's cousin, Franklin, would champion ideas grounded in progressive issues and causes when he was elected president as, ironically, a Democrat. Today we can still see echoes of the platform in its positions on economic justice, reform, and equality in modern-day liberalism.

—KP Dawes, MA
—Michael J. O'Neal, PhD

Bibliography and Additional Reading

Brands, H.W. *T.R.: The Last Romantic*. Basic Books, 1998.

———. *Traitor to His Class: The Privileged Life and Radical Presidency of Franklin Delano Roosevelt*. Anchor, 2009.

Goodwin, Doris Kearns. *The Bully Pulpit: Theodore Roosevelt, William Howard Taft, and the Golden Age of Journalism*. Simon and Schuster, 2014.

Mikis, Sydney M. *Theodore Roosevelt, the Progressive Party, and the Transformation of American Democracy (American Political Thought)*. University Press of Kansas, 2009.

Morris, Edmund. *Colonel Roosevelt (Theodore Roosevelt Series Book 3)*. Random House, 2010.

Wolraich, Michael. *Unreasonable Men: Theodore Roosevelt and the Republican Rebels Who Created Progressive Politics*. St. Martin's Press, 2014.

■ The "New Freedom"

Date: 1912 (various dates during campaign)
Author: Woodrow Wilson
Genre: Speech

Summary Overview

Over the course of the 1912 presidential campaign, New Jersey Governor Woodrow Wilson gradually elucidated his philosophy of government. While the journalist William Allen White famously claimed that the difference between Wilson's "New Freedom" and his chief rival Theodore Roosevelt's "New Nationalism" were about the same as between the famously similar *Alice in Wonderland* characters "Tweedledee" and "Tweedledum," Wilson came to believe that the differences between their two positions were vast, and that they represented the difference between a future of economic freedom versus economic slavery for average Americans. The first chapter of his collected speeches, "The Old Order Changeth," is illustrative both of Wilson's fears of monopoly and of his general belief in the importance of government interventionism on behalf of under-represented individuals during a time of laissez-faire capitalism.

Wilson had been in politics for only two years when he made this speech. While he was known as a political scientist and a reform governor, his exact policy prescriptions were little known. They would remain so after the campaign. Wilson campaigned on a philosophical position rather than on a specific set of policy proscriptions. He made general statements about economic justice and social reform. As a result, many Progressives gradually came to his side—even when presented with a newly radicalized Theodore Roosevelt, who had broken with the Republican Party, as an alternative.

In this speech, Wilson makes American corporations the enemy, in much the same way that slave masters had been made the enemy of Northerners in the antebellum period. Fear of corporations, however, showed no regional distinctions, thus explaining how economic populism could be used as a successful strategy for becoming the first Democratic president since Grover Cleveland (served 1885-89; 1893-97) and Wilson could present himself as the first reform-minded Democratic president since Andrew Jackson (served 1829-37).

Defining Moment

This speech is the clearest statement Wilson ever made about what his concept "the New Freedom" actually meant. The speech is simultaneously a summary of radical changes in society and a call for further radical changes in American social and political organizations in response to previous developments. Many of the changes that Wilson alludes to here came as a result of industrialization. His general call to make government more active in protecting individuals marks a sea change from the late-nineteenth century, when government became an engine for protecting corporate profits at almost any cost. Instead of protecting the freedom of corporations, Wilson wanted the federal government to protect the freedom of individuals from corporations. In that respect, the speech demonstrates the links between Wilsonian Progressivism and the later New Deal ideology of Franklin D. Roosevelt. It also highlights, in retrospect, the difference between Wilson's "New Freedom" and Theodore Roosevelt's "New Nationalism."

Wilson's campaign strategy was to forge a coalition of Progressives in both the Democratic and Republican parties. The lack of specific policy proposals in his speeches was important to achieving that goal. What Wilson could do safely is diagnosis the problems in America, one of which was the domination of the "trusts," or large, monopolistic enterprises. While Theodore Roosevelt had been a proven trust-buster while in office (served 1901-09), he believed that some trusts were good for national development and should not be broken up. Wilson was much more hostile to any kind of unfair accumulation of economic power. Understanding how trusts developed was key to understanding what should be done about them, and this is where Wilson offers that explanation, in contradistinction to Roosevelt's position. This speech, in other words, gets precisely to the most important difference between two otherwise very similar candidates.

Author Biography

Before Woodrow Wilson became Governor of New Jersey, he had been a prominent political scientist and political historian. Even while serving as President of Princeton University, he continued to write and speak about political issues. Wilson's primary mission as an academic was to champion aspects of the British political system that he felt could be imported to the American system. For example, Wilson would be the first president to directly address Congress with an annual State of the Union Speech, because he found the British prime minister's practice of visiting Parliament frequently to be very worthwhile. As a political scientist, as with his career in politics, Wilson was a "small d" democrat, supporting efforts to make the government more accountable to the will of the people. (Whether he succeeded in that respect is debatable.)

Such tendencies are apparent in his first campaign speeches. Wilson's democratic leanings became apparent in the Progressive policies he supported as president (many of which did not, however, originate with him, such as the direct election of U.S. Senators). As president, Wilson would help move the Democratic Party toward a more democratic stance on many issues – racial politics being the one major exception. The "New Freedom" is sometimes used to refer to the Progressive reforms passed during the early years of Wilson's presidency, such as the Clayton Antitrust Act of 1914 and the federal income tax (1913). However, Wilson did not have as big a role in the passage of many of these laws as did Franklin Roosevelt in the legislation related to the New Deal or Lyndon Johnson with the legislation making up his Great Society.

HISTORICAL DOCUMENT

THE OLD ORDER CHANGETH

There is one great basic fact which underlies all the questions that are discussed on the political platform at the present moment. That singular fact is that nothing is done in this country as it was done twenty years ago.

We are in the presence of a new organization of society. Our life has broken away from the past. The life of America is not the life that it was twenty years ago; it is not the life that it was ten years ago. We have changed our economic conditions, absolutely, from top to bottom; and, with our economic society, the organization of our life. The old political formulas do not fit the present problems; they read now like documents taken out of a forgotten age. The older cries sound as if they belonged to a past age which men have almost forgotten. Things which used to be put into the party platforms of ten years ago would sound antiquated if put into a platform now. We are facing the necessity of fitting a new social organization, as we did once fit the old organization, to the happiness and prosperity of the great body of citizens; for we are conscious that the new order of society has not been made to fit and provide the convenience or prosperity of the average man. The life of the nation has grown infinitely varied. It does not centre now upon questions of governmental structure or of the distribution of governmental powers. It centres upon questions of the very structure and operation of society itself, of which government is only the instrument. Our development has run so fast and so far along the lines sketched in the earlier day of constitutional definition, has so crossed and interlaced those lines, has piled upon them such novel structures of trust and combination, has elaborated within them a life so manifold, so full of forces which transcend the boundaries of the country itself and fill the eyes of the world, that a new nation seems to have been created which the old formulas do not fit or afford a vital interpretation of.

We have come upon a very different age from any that preceded us. We have come upon an age when we do not do business in the way in which we used to do business,—when we do not carry on any of the operations of manufacture, sale, transportation, or communication as men used to carry them on. There is a sense in which in our day the individual has been submerged. In most parts of our country men work, not for themselves, not as partners in the old way in which they used to work, but generally as employees,—in a higher or lower grade,—of great corporations. There was a time when corporations played a very minor part in our business affairs, but now they play the chief part, and most men are the servants of corporations. You know what happens when you are the servant of a corporation. You have in no instance access to the men who are really determining the policy of the corporation. If the corporation is doing the things that it ought not to do, you really have no voice in the matter and must obey the orders, and you have oftentimes with deep mortification to co-operate in the doing of things which you know are against the public interest. Your individuality is swallowed up in the individuality and purpose of a great organization.

It is true that, while most men are thus submerged in the corporation, a few, a very few, are exalted to a power which as individuals they could never have wielded. Through the great organizations of which they are the heads, a few are enabled to play a part unprecedented by anything in history in the control of the business operations of the country and in the determination of the happiness of great numbers of people, in the determination of the happiness of great numbers of people. Yesterday, and ever since history began, men were related to one another as individuals. To be sure there were the family, the Church, and the State, institutions which associated men in certain wide circles of relationship. But in the ordinary concerns of life, in the ordinary work, in the daily round, men dealt freely and directly with one another. To-day, the everyday relationships of men are largely with great impersonal concerns, with organizations, not with other individual men.

Now this is nothing short of a new social age, a new era of human relationships, a new stage-setting for the drama of life.

In this new age we find, for instance, that our laws with regard to the relations of employer and employee are in many respects wholly antiquated and impossible. They were framed for another age, which nobody now living remembers, which is, indeed, so remote from our life that it would be difficult for many of us to understand it if it were described to us. The employer is now generally a corporation or a huge company of some kind; the employee is one of hundreds or of thousands brought together, not by individual masters whom they know and with whom they have personal relations, but by agents of one sort or another. Workingmen are marshaled in great numbers for the performance of a multitude of particu-

lar tasks under a common discipline. They generally use dangerous and powerful machinery, over whose repair and renewal they have no control. New rules must be devised with regard to their obligations and their rights, their obligations to their employers and their responsibilities to one another. Rules must be devised for their protection, for their compensation when injured, for their support when disabled.

There is something very new and very big and very complex about these new relations of capital and labor. A new economic society has sprung up, and we must effect a new set of adjustments. We must not pit power against weakness. The employer is generally, in our day, as I have said, not an individual, but a powerful group; and yet the workingman when dealing with his employer is still, under our existing law, an individual.

Why is it that we have a labor question at all? It is for the simple and very sufficient reason that the laboring man and the employer are not intimate associates now as they used to be in time past. Most of our laws were formed in the age when employer and employees knew each other, knew each other's characters, were associates with each other, dealt with each other as man with man. That is no longer the case. You not only do not come into personal contact with the men who have the supreme command in those corporations, but it would be out of the question for you to do it. Our modern corporations employ thousands, and in some instances hundreds of thousands, of men. The only persons whom you see or deal with are local superintendents or local representatives of a vast organization, which is not like anything that the workingmen of the time in which our laws were framed knew anything about. A little group of workingmen, seeing their employer every day, dealing with him in a personal way, is one thing, and the modern body of labor engaged as employees of the huge enterprises that spread all over the country, dealing with men of whom they can form no personal conception, is another thing. A very different thing. You never saw a corporation, any more than you ever saw a government. Many a workingman to-day never saw the body of men who are conducting the industry in which he is employed. And they never saw him. What they know about him is written in ledgers and books and letters, in the correspondence of the office, in the reports of the superintendents. He is a long way off from them.

So what we have to discuss is, not wrongs which individuals intentionally do,—I do not believe there are a great many of those,—but the wrongs of a system. I want to record my protest against any discussion of this matter which would seem to indicate that there are bodies of our fellow-citizens who are trying to grind us down and do us injustice. There are some men of that sort. I don't know how they sleep o' nights, but there are men of that kind. Thank God, they are not numerous. The truth is, we are all caught in a great economic system which is heartless. The modern corporation is not engaged in business as an individual. When we deal with it, we deal with an impersonal element, an immaterial piece of society. A modern corporation is a means of co-operation in the conduct of an enterprise which is so big that no one man can conduct it, and which the resources of no one man are sufficient to finance. A company is formed; that company puts out a prospectus; the promoters expect to raise a certain fund as capital stock. Well, how are they going to raise it? They are going to raise it from the public in general, some of whom will buy their stock. The moment that begins, there is formed—what? A joint stock corporation. Men begin to pool their earnings, little piles, big piles. A certain number of men are elected by the stockholders to be directors, and these directors elect a president. This president is the head of the undertaking, and the directors are its managers.

Now, do the workingmen employed by that stock corporation deal with that president and those directors? Not at all. Does the public deal with that president and that board of directors? It does not. Can anybody bring them to account? It is next to impossible to do so. If you undertake it you will find it a game of hide and seek, with the objects of your search taking refuge now behind the tree of their individual personality, now behind that of their corporate irresponsibility.

And do our laws take note of this curious state of things? Do they even attempt to distinguish between a man's act as a corporation director and as an individual? They do not. Our laws still deal with us on the basis of the old system. The law is still living in the dead past which we have left behind. This is evident, for instance, with regard to the matter of employers' liability for workingmen's injuries. Suppose that a superintendent wants a workman to use a certain piece of machinery which it is not safe for him to use, and that the workman is injured by that piece of machinery. Some of our courts have held that the superintendent is a fellow-servant, or, as the law states it, a fellow-employee, and that, therefore, the man cannot recover damages for his injury. The superintendent who probably engaged the man is not his employer. Who is his employer? And whose negligence could conceivably come in there? The board of directors did not tell the employee to use that piece of machinery; and the president of the corporation did not tell him to use that piece of machinery. And so forth. Don't you see by that theory that a man never can get redress for negligence on the part of the employer? When I hear judges reason upon the analogy of the relationships that used to exist between workmen and their employers a generation ago, I wonder if they have not opened their eyes to the modern world. You know, we have a right to expect that judges will have their eyes open, even though the law which they administer hasn't awakened. Yet that is but a single small detail illustrative of the difficulties we are in because we have not adjusted the law to the facts of the new order.

Since I entered politics, I have chiefly had men's views confided to me privately. Some of the biggest men in the United States, in the field of commerce and manufacture, are afraid of somebody, are afraid of something. They know that there is a power somewhere so organized, so subtle, so watchful, so interlocked, so complete, so pervasive, that they had better not speak above their breath when they speak in condemnation of it.

They know that America is not a place of which it can be said, as it used to be, that a man may choose his own calling and pursue it just as far as his abilities enable him to pursue it; because to-day, if he enters certain fields, there are organizations which will use means against him that will prevent his building up a business which they do not want to have built up; organizations that will see to it that the ground is cut from under him and the markets shut against him. For if he begins to sell to certain retail dealers, to any retail dealers, the monopoly will refuse to sell to those dealers, and those dealers, afraid, will not buy the new man's wares.

And this is the country which has lifted to the admiration of the world its ideals of absolutely free opportunity, where no man is supposed to be under any limitation except the limitations of his character and of his mind; where there is supposed to be no distinction of class, no distinction of blood, no distinction of social status, but where men win or lose on their merits.

I lay it very close to my own conscience as a public man whether we can any longer stand at our doors and welcome all newcomers upon those terms. American industry is not free, as once it was free; American enterprise is not free; the man with only a little capital is finding it harder to get into the field, more and more impossible to compete with the big fellow. Why? Because the laws of this country do not prevent the strong from crushing the weak. That is the reason, and because the strong have crushed the weak the strong dominate the industry and the economic life of this country. No man can deny that the lines of endeavor have more and more narrowed and stiffened; no man who knows anything about the development of industry in this country can have failed to observe that the larger kinds of credit are more and more difficult to obtain, unless you obtain them upon the terms of uniting your efforts with those who already control the

industries of the country; and nobody can fail to observe that any man who tries to set himself up in competition with any process of manufacture which has been taken under the control of large combinations of capital will presently find himself either squeezed out or obliged to sell and allow himself to be absorbed.

There is a great deal that needs reconstruction in the United States. I should like to take a census of the business men,—I mean the rank and file of the business men,—as to whether they think that business conditions in this country, or rather whether the organization of business in this country, is satisfactory or not. I know what they would say if they dared. If they could vote secretly they would vote overwhelmingly that the present organization of business was meant for the big fellows and was not meant for the little fellows; that it was meant for those who are at the top and was meant to exclude those who are at the bottom; that it was meant to shut out beginners, to prevent new entries in the race, to prevent the building up of competitive enterprises that would interfere with the monopolies which the great trusts have built up.

What this country needs above everything else is a body of laws which will look after the men who are on the make rather than the men who are already made. Because the men who are already made are not going to live indefinitely, and they are not always kind enough to leave sons as able and as honest as they are.

The originative part of America, the part of America that makes new enterprises, the part into which the ambitious and gifted workingman makes his way up, the class that saves, that plans, that organizes, that presently spreads its enterprises until they have a national scope and character,—that middle class is being more and more squeezed out by the processes which we have been taught to call processes of prosperity. Its members are sharing prosperity, no doubt; but what alarms me is that they are not originating prosperity. No country can afford to have its prosperity originated by a small controlling class. The treasury of America does not lie in the brains of the small body of men now in control of the great enterprises that have been concentrated under the direction of a very small number of persons. The treasury of America lies in those ambitions, those energies, that cannot be restricted to a special favored class. It depends upon the inventions of unknown men, upon the originations of unknown men, upon the ambitions of unknown men. Every country is renewed out of the ranks of the unknown, not out of the ranks of those already famous and powerful and in control.

There has come over the land that un-American set of conditions which enables a small number of men who control the government to get favors from the government; by those favors to exclude their fellows from equal business opportunity; by those favors to extend a network of control that will presently dominate every industry in the country, and so make men forget the ancient time when America lay in every hamlet, when America was to be seen in every fair valley, when America displayed her great forces on the broad prairies, ran her fine fires of enterprise up over the mountainsides and down into the bowels of the earth, and eager men were everywhere captains of industry, not employees; not looking to a distant city to find out what they might do, but looking about among their neighbors, finding credit according to their character, not according to their connections, finding credit in proportion to what was known to be in them and behind them, not in proportion to the securities they held that were approved where they were not known. In order to start an enterprise now, you have to be authenticated, in a perfectly impersonal way, not according to yourself, but according to what you own that somebody else approves of your owning. You cannot begin such an enterprise as those that have made America until you are so authenticated, until you have succeeded in obtaining the good-will of large allied capitalists. Is that freedom? That is dependence, not freedom.

We used to think in the old-fashioned days when life was very simple that all that government had to do was to put on a policeman's uniform, and say, "Now don't anybody hurt anybody else." We used to say that the ideal of government was for every man to be left alone and not interfered with, except when he interfered with somebody else; and that the best government was the government that did as little governing as possible. That was the idea that obtained in Jefferson's time. But we are coming now to realize that life is so complicated that we are not dealing with the old conditions, and that the law has to step in and create new conditions under which we may live, the conditions which will make it tolerable for us to live.

Let me illustrate what I mean: It used to be true in our cities that every family occupied a separate house of its own, that every family had its own little premises, that every family was separated in its life from every other family. That is no longer the case in our great cities. Families live in tenements, they live in flats, they live on floors; they are piled layer upon layer in the great tenement houses of our crowded districts, and not only are they piled layer upon layer, but they are associated room by room, so that there is in every room, sometimes, in our congested districts, a separate family. In some foreign countries they have made much more progress than we in handling these things. In the city of Glasgow, for example (Glasgow is one of the model cities of the world), they have made up their minds that the entries and the hallways of great tenements are public streets. Therefore, the policeman goes up the stairway, and patrols the corridors; the lighting department of the city sees to it that the halls are abundantly lighted. The city does not deceive itself into supposing that that great building is a unit from which the police are to keep out and the civic authority to be excluded, but it says: "These are public highways, and light is needed in them, and control by the authority of the city."

I liken that to our great modern industrial enterprises. A corporation is very like a large tenement house; it isn't the premises of a single commercial family; it is just as much a public affair as a tenement house is a network of public highways.

When you offer the securities of a great corporation to anybody who wishes to purchase them, you must open that corporation to the inspection of everybody who wants to purchase. There must, to follow out the figure of the tenement house, be lights along the corridors, there must be police patrolling the openings, there must be inspection wherever it is known that men may be deceived with regard to the contents of the premises. If we believe that fraud lies in wait for us, we must have the means of determining whether our suspicions are well founded or not. Similarly, the treatment of labor by the great corporations is not what it was in Jefferson's time. Whenever bodies of men employ bodies of men, it ceases to be a private relationship. So that when courts hold that workingmen cannot peaceably dissuade other workingmen from taking employment, as was held in a notable case in New Jersey, they simply show that their minds and understandings are lingering in an age which has passed away. This dealing of great bodies of men with other bodies of men is a matter of public scrutiny, and should be a matter of public regulation.

Similarly, it was no business of the law in the time of Jefferson to come into my house and see how I kept house. But when my house, when my so-called private property, became a great mine, and men went along dark corridors amidst every kind of danger in order to dig out of the bowels of the earth things necessary for the industries of a whole nation, and when it came about that no individual owned these mines, that they were owned by great stock companies, then all the old analogies absolutely collapsed and it became the right of the government to go down into these mines to see whether human beings were properly treated in them or not; to see whether accidents were properly safeguarded against; to see whether modern economical methods of using these inestimable riches of the earth were followed or were not followed. If somebody puts a derrick improperly secured on top of a building or overtopping the street, then the government of the city has the right to see that that derrick is so secured that you and I can walk under it and not be afraid that the heavens are going to fall on us. Likewise, in these great beehives where in every corridor swarm men of flesh and blood, it is the privilege of the government, whether of the State or of the United States, as the case may be, to see that human life is protected, that human lungs have something to breathe.

These, again, are merely illustrations of conditions. We are in a new world, struggling under old laws. As we go inspecting our lives to-day, surveying this new scene of centralized and complex society, we shall find many more things out of joint.

One of the most alarming phenomena of the time,—or rather it would be alarming if the nation had not awakened to it and shown its determination to control it,—one of the most significant signs of the new social era is the degree to which government has become associated with business. I speak, for the moment, of the control over the government exercised by Big Business. Behind the whole subject, of course, is the truth that, in the new order, government and business must be associated closely. But that association is at present of a nature absolutely intolerable; the precedence is wrong, the association is upside down. Our government has been for the past few years under the control of heads of great allied corporations with special interests. It has not controlled these interests and assigned them a proper place in the whole system of business; it has submitted itself to their control. As a result, there have grown up vicious systems and schemes of governmental favoritism (the most obvious being the extravagant tariff), far-reaching in effect upon the whole fabric of life, touching to his injury every inhabitant of the land, laying unfair and impossible handicaps upon competitors, imposing taxes in every direction, stifling everywhere the free spirit of American enterprise.

Now this has come about naturally; as we go on we shall see how very naturally. It is no use denouncing anybody, or anything, except human nature. Nevertheless, it is an intolerable thing that the government of the republic should have got so far out of the hands of the people; should have been captured by interests which are special and not general. In the train of this capture follow the troops of scandals, wrongs, indecencies, with which our politics swarm.

There are cities in America of whose government we are ashamed. There are cities everywhere, in every part of the land, in which we feel that, not the interests of the public, but the interests of special privileges, of selfish men, are served; where contracts take precedence over public interest. Not only in big cities is this the case. Have you not noticed the growth of socialistic sentiment in the smaller towns? Not many months ago I stopped at a little town in Nebraska, and while my train lingered I met on the platform a very engaging young fellow dressed in overalls who introduced himself to me as the mayor of the town, and added that he was a Socialist. I said, "What does that mean? Does that mean that this town is socialistic?" "No, sir," he said; "I have not deceived myself; the vote by which I was elected was about 20 per cent. socialistic and 80 per cent. protest." It was protest against the treachery to the people of those who led both the other parties of that town.

All over the Union people are coming to feel that they have no control over the course of affairs. I live in one of the greatest States in the union, which was at one time in slavery. Until two years ago we had witnessed with increasing concern the growth in New Jersey of a spirit of almost cynical despair. Men said; "We vote; we are offered the platform we want; we elect the men who stand on that platform, and we get absolutely nothing." So they began to ask: "What is the use of voting? We know that the machines of both parties are subsidized by the same persons, and therefore it is useless to turn in either direction."

This is not confined to some of the state governments and those of some of the towns and cities. We know that something intervenes between the people of the United States and the control of their own affairs at Washington. It is not the people who have been ruling there of late.

Why are we in the presence, why are we at the threshold, of a revolution? Because we are profoundly disturbed by the influences which we see reigning in the determination of our public life and our public policy. There was a time when America was blithe with self confidence. She boasted that she, and she alone, knew the processes of popular government; but now she sees her sky overcast; she sees that there are at work forces which she did not dream of in her hopeful youth.

Don't you know that some man with eloquent tongue, without conscience, who did not care for the nation, could put this whole country into a flame? Don't you know that this country from one end to the other believes that something is wrong? What an opportunity it would be for some man without conscience to spring up and say: "This is the way. Follow me!"—and lead in paths of destruction!

The old order changeth—changeth under our very eyes, not quietly and equably, but swiftly and with the noise and heat and tumult of reconstruction.

I suppose that all struggle for law has been conscious, that very little of it has been blind or merely instinctive. It is the fashion to say, as if with superior knowledge of affairs and of human weakness, that every age has been an age of transition, and that no age is more full of change than another; yet in very few ages of the world can the struggle for change have been so widespread, so deliberate, or upon so great a scale as in this in which we are taking part.

The transition we are witnessing is no equable transition of growth and normal alteration; no silent, unconscious unfolding of one age into another, its natural heir and successor. Society is looking itself over, in our day, from top to bottom; is making fresh and critical analysis of its very elements; is questioning its oldest practices as freely as its newest, scrutinizing every arrangement and motive of its life; and it stands ready to attempt nothing less than a radical reconstruction, which only frank and honest counsels and the forces of generous co-operation can hold back from becoming a revolution. We are in a temper to reconstruct economic society, as we were once in a temper to reconstruct political society, and political society may itself undergo a radical modification in the process. I doubt if any age was ever more conscious of its task or more unanimously desirous of radical and extended changes in its economic and political practice. We stand in the presence of a revolution,—not a bloody revolution; America is not given to the spilling of blood,—but a silent revolution, whereby America will insist upon recovering in practice those ideals which she has always professed, upon securing a government devoted to the general interest and not to special interests.

We are upon the eve of a great reconstruction. It calls for creative statesmanship as no age has done since that great age in which we set up the government under which we live, that government which was the admiration of the world until it suffered wrongs to grow up under it which have made many of our own compatriots question the freedom of our institutions and preach revolution against them. I do not fear revolution. I have unshaken faith in the power of America to keep its self-possession. Revolution will come in peaceful guise, as it came when we put aside the crude government of the Confederation and created the great Federal Union which governs individuals, not States, and which has been these hundred and thirty years our vehicle of progress. Some radical changes we must make in our law and practice. Some reconstructions we must push forward, which a new age and new circumstances impose upon us. But we can do it all in calm and sober fashion, like statesmen and patriots.

I do not speak of these things in apprehension, because all is open and above-board. This is not a day in which great forces rally in secret. The whole stupendous program must be publicly planned and canvassed. Good temper, the wisdom that comes of sober counsel, the energy of thoughtful and unselfish men, the habit of co-operation and of compromise which has been bred in us by long years of free government, in which reason rather than passion has been made to prevail by the sheer virtue of candid and universal debate, will enable us to win through to still another great age without violence.

GLOSSARY

Labor Question: a late-nineteenth century intellectual debate over how to get workingmen to accept the problems associated with industrialization

Document Analysis

In this speech, Wilson is arguing that American life has (at the time) become increasingly unfair over the previous twenty years because of the problems associated with industrialization, and that if America does not change so as to become more fair again there will be a violent revolution aimed at restoring the prospect for ordinary Americans to improve their economic standing. The language is quite vague. For instance, Wilson makes a direct appeal to working people, without explicitly mentioning trade unions. He mentions socialists—a direct nod to the constituency of the Socialist candidate, Eugene V. Debs—but appeals to their spirit of protest instead of denouncing their specific policies. His goal is to co-opt the spirit of unhappiness related to the Republican status quo, without, however, giving opponents like Theodore Roosevelt any concrete policy points on which to attack him.

The problems that Wilson describes all stem from industrialization. "The life of the nation has grown infinitely varied," he writes, by which he means that change has come so fast that it has blown past the old structures and constraints that once kept all operating smoothly. Evidence of such changes includes the new relations between capital and labor, under which employers no longer know their employees as individuals. Even more important, the changes in the system have made it impossible for good men to rise within the system as they once could. In other words, corporations have threatened the American Dream. To Wilson, such capitalist aggregations threaten the viability of society itself.

Wilson does not specifically blame Republicans for the changes he wants to temper. Instead, his enemies are corporations. "Our government has for the past few years been under the control of heads of great allied corporations with special interests," he explains. These corporations, under Wilson's formulation, are powerful enough to destroy people's freedom—not just the freedom of employees, but the freedom of all Americans because corporate interests have too much influence over how government is conducted. Wilson is afraid that strong corporations will crush weaker ones, thereby giving them too much power. He is particularly disturbed that the laws of the United States—specifically, the antimonopoly laws as currently enforced—do not make that behavior illegal. In this way, Wilson is trying to protect not just working people but small business, as well. The spirit of innovation embodied by smaller businesses can make life better for everyone. Antitrust enforcement,

then, is central to Wilson's political philosophy and his campaign rhetoric.

While Wilson's positions, so described, may sound left wing-ish to modern ears, the candidate justified them as a way to conserve the core structures that he wished to reform and revive. If the economics became too unequal, he argues, there could be a violent revolution. The popularity of Eugene Debs, then a four-time third-party presidential candidate (1900, 1904, 1908, and 1912; he also ran in 1920), was one indicator of that potential revolutionary development; but in some ways so too was the continuing popularity of Roosevelt, who was often accused of being a political demagogue. "Don't you know that some man with eloquent tongue, without conscience, who did not care for the nation, could put this whole country into a flame?," Wilson asks. The question applied to both Roosevelt and Debs at a time of uncertainty regarding national governance and the direction of the nation as a whole. More important, the statement implies that the very system that Wilson revered as a political scientist might check his powers as president, because of ongoing debates.

Wilson used this speech to successfully stake out the political center. Moderate reform was enough, he argued, and, ultimately, voters in 1912 largely agreed with him, making him the only reform-minded Democratic president during a long period of Republican ascendancy.

Essential Themes

Wilson's rhetoric about the changes brought about industrialization became increasingly less important over time, as those changes became largely accepted, if not entirely welcomed. Efforts to change the distribution of economic power in the United gradually rested more on people's right to live as individuals than on the hardships they experienced. The theme of Wilson's speech that would be expanded on by the Democratic presidents that succeeded him was the need for moderate, rather than radical, reform. In other words, Wilson's framing devices concerning the voice of what would become known as "the common man" versus corporate influence proved far more important than any specific policies that he proposed.

Franklin Delano Roosevelt (FDR) took up much the same political position during the New Deal. While there was less than is commonly thought that united the disparate policies of the New Deal, FDR told his cabinet in private that his efforts were all designed to promote security for average Americans. During FDR's 1935 speech in signing the Social Security Act, he specifically cited the "startling industrial changes" that "tended more and more to make life insecure" as the reason for creating a new, elaborate social insurance system. This harkened back to Wilson and the New Freedoms. Other Democratic presidential candidates, including Harry Truman and Bill Clinton, would likewise echo themes first enunciated by Woodrow Wilson in 1912.

—Jonathan Rees, PhD

Bibliography and Additional Reading

Chambers II, John Whiteclay. *The Tyranny of Change: America in the Progressive Era, 1900-1917.* New York: St. Martins, 1980.

Cooper, John Milton, Jr. *Woodrow Wilson: A Biography.* New York: Alfred A. Knopf, 2009.

Link, Arthur S. *Woodrow Wilson and the Progressive Era 1910-1917.* New York: Harper & Row, 1954.

Roosevelt, Franklin D. "Statement on Signing the Social Security Act." August 14, 1935. The American Presidency Project, University of California Santa Barbara, http://www.presidency.ucsb.edu/ws/?pid=14916.

Wilson, Woodrow. *The New Freedom: A Call for the Emancipation of the Generous Energies of a People.* New York: Doubleday, Page & Company, 1918.

■ Woodrow Wilson's Second Inaugural Address

Date: March 5, 1917
Author: Woodrow Wilson
Genre: Speech

Summary Overview

Each inaugural address is crafted to focus the nation upon the issues which the president believes are paramount for the nation to confront. In his Second Inaugural Address, Woodrow Wilson focuses on foreign affairs, specifically the ongoing international conflict that the United States would soon join. As reflected in his speech, throughout his first term in office Wilson had diligently attempted to keep the United States from becoming actively involved in the war in Europe. However, by March 5, 1917, it had become clear to Wilson, and many others, that these attempts would soon be coming to an end. Just as nation after nation had been drawn into the war in Europe, Wilson knew that before too many months, the United States would join the war against Germany. And so, in his Second Inaugural Address, Wilson does not examine on legislation or partisan issues, but raises issues created by the Great War in Europe and the role he anticipated the United States would play. In confronting these challenges, he sought the support of the American people.

Defining Moment

Although when first elected, in 1912, Wilson had wanted to focus upon domestic issues, the course of events did not allow him to do that exclusively. Slowly, but surely, the global conflict, centered in Europe, had come to dominate everything else. Even though one of his campaign slogans was "He Kept Us Out of War," it seemed that each week made this more and more difficult. The steps which Germany was willing to take to hurt the British and French forces caused more and more problems for the United States and other neutral nations. And so, with the beginning of his second term, Wilson decided that it was the proper time to begin a major new campaign. This was not a campaign to win an election, but rather it was to help the public realistically understand the situation. By doing this, Wilson hoped to slowly change public sentiment so that when the time for action came, the nation

would stand behind the call to arms.

Woodrow Wilson was a gifted orator whose public addresses embodied the main stylistic elements of his day. He was one of a new generation of orators who emphasized plain language and avoided the classical allusions used by older, noted speakers such as William Jennings Bryan. Nonetheless, he was able to relate contemporary issues to larger philosophical themes. As a lawyer and academic, Wilson had spent most of his life speaking in front of audiences, and he was very comfortable before crowds. He usually spoke extemporaneously, which allowed him to develop eye contact with his audience. Wilson revived the practice of appearing before Congress to deliver the annual message, beginning with his 1913 address. A scholar of history and politics, Wilson appreciated the success that Theodore Roosevelt had garnered by taking his message directly to the American people and sought to replicate that success. And so, in this Second Inaugural Address, Wilson hoped to use these skills to help the nation understand the task, which Wilson believed, it would be called to undertake.

Author Biography

Woodrow Wilson was born in Staunton, Virginia, in 1856 and grew up in Augusta, Georgia, and Columbia, South Carolina. He overcame a learning disability to become a lawyer in 1882 and earned a doctorate from Johns Hopkins in history and political science four years later. He had a distinguished academic career, becoming president of Princeton University in 1902. While leading the university, Wilson developed a reputation as a reformer. He won New Jersey's gubernatorial election in 1910 and oversaw enactment of a number of Progressive measures. Wilson secured the Democratic presidential nomination in 1912. With the Republican Party split between the incumbent William H. Taft and former President Theodore Roosevelt, Wilson won the election and became the first Democratic president elected since 1892 and the first southerner elected since Zachery Taylor was in 1848. In one of his earliest addresses as president, on the fiftieth anniversary of the Battle of Gettysburg, Wilson sought to soften regional tensions and unite the country.

During the 1912 campaign Wilson had titled his ambitious program of domestic policies "New Freedom." The president supported various reforms during his first term. He worked with Congress to undertake tariff reductions through the 1913 Underwood-Simmons Act. Wilson was the first president to benefit from the ratification of the Sixteenth Amendment, which authorized a federal income tax; the new, progressive tax allowed him to offset any revenue losses from lower tariffs. He also endorsed the 1913 Federal Reserve Act, which created the modern system to oversee monetary policy, including credit and currency supplies and regulation of banks. The president likewise benefited from the adoption of the Seventeenth Amendment in 1913, which mandated the direct election of U.S. senators. The result was an increasing number of Progressive senators who endorsed Wilson's reforms. The Department of Labor was created under Wilson, as was the Federal Trade Commission. The president was instrumental in the passage of the 1914 Clayton Antitrust Act, which further regulated business practices to prevent monopolies.

Wilson adopted an idealistic foreign policy that emphasized free trade, self-determination, and democracy. He was credited with ending the brief age of American imperialism that had begun in the 1890s. For instance, he persuaded Congress to grant the Philippines greater political control over their affairs. Puerto Rico became a territory, with its people being granted U.S. citizenship. Under Wilson, the United States was the first country to offer diplomatic recognition to the Chinese Republic. Wilson was willing to use force to promote democracy. The result was a series of military interventions in Latin America and the Caribbean, including Nicaragua (1914), Haiti (1915), and the Dominican Republic (1916). He also intervened in the Mexican Revolution, sending troops to occupy Vera Cruz in 1914 and dispatching five thousand soldiers to northern Mexico in 1916. That year, Wilson bought the Danish Virgin Islands for $25 million.

The president tried to keep the United States neutral in World War I, but by his second term the county began to be drawn into the global conflict, which he acknowledged in his Second Inaugural Address. In January of 1917, he spoke to Congress about the terms of a possible negotiated peace. He personally supported the Allied forces and endorsed U.S. sales of weapons, foodstuffs,

and industrial products to France and Great Britain. Unrestricted German submarine warfare and the publication of the famous Zimmermann telegram, in which Germany promised to aid Mexico in recapturing territories lost during the Mexican-American War, led the United States to enter the war in 1917. During the war Wilson supported curtailments to civil liberties through the Espionage Act of 1917 and the Sedition Act of 1918. He managed the largest military and industrial mobilization that the country has witnessed to date, with industrial output increasing 20 percent between 1917 and 1919.

The entry of the United States into the war led to the defeat of Germany and the Central powers. At war's end Wilson was one of the architects of the Treaty of Versailles, but isolationist sentiment within the United States constrained his postwar foreign policy. He hoped that the nations of the world would adopt new measures, outlined in what became known as his "fourteen points proposal," which prevented another global conflict by encouraging self-determination and creating a League of Nations to resolve disputes. His program was weakened, however, by the victorious Allied forces, who sought to punish Germany. Meanwhile, Republicans took control of Congress in 1918 and blocked several of Wilson's initiatives, including U.S. membership in the League of Nations. Wilson supported the Eighteenth Amendment (1919), which banned alcohol, and, after initially opposing women's suffrage, endorsed the Nineteenth Amendment (1920), which granted women the vote. In 1920 the president received the Nobel Peace Prize. He suffered a stroke that left him incapacitated during the final months of his presidency. After he left office, Wilson retired from public life and died on February 3, 1924.

Although he left office unpopular and humiliated by the failure of the United States to ratify the Treaty of Versailles, Woodrow Wilson has come to be regarded as one of the more effective presidents in U.S. history. His early domestic programs, including the creation of the Federal Reserve System and the Federal Trade Commission, remain important components of the contemporary U.S. government. Wilson's greatest legacy was in the realm of foreign policy. He sought to create a global international system marked by democracy and self-determination, international law, and collective security. He correctly foresaw that the spread of democracy would ameliorate conflict and lead to economic and political stability in Europe. His proposal for the League of Nations would be refined and developed more fully in the aftermath of World War II with the establishment of the United Nations. His main diplomatic principles would lay the foundation for U.S. foreign policy throughout the twentieth century.

HISTORICAL DOCUMENT

Although we have centered counsel and action with such unusual concentration and success upon the great problems of domestic legislation to which we addressed ourselves four years ago, other matters have more and more forced themselves upon our attention—matters lying outside our own life as a nation and over which we had no control, but which, despite our wish to keep free of them, have drawn us more and more irresistibly into their own current and influence.

It has been impossible to avoid them. They have affected the life of the whole world. They have shaken men everywhere with a passion and an apprehension they never knew before. It has been hard to preserve calm counsel while the thought of our own people swayed this way and that under their influence. We are a composite and cosmopolitan people. We are of the blood of all the nations that are at war. The currents of our thoughts as well as the currents of our trade run quick at all seasons back and forth between us and them. The war inevitably set its mark from the first alike upon our minds, our industries, our commerce, our politics and our social action. To be indifferent to it, or independent of it, was out of the question.

And yet all the while we have been conscious that we were not part of it. In that consciousness, despite many divisions, we have drawn closer together. We have been deeply wronged upon the seas, but we have not wished to wrong or injure in return; have retained throughout the consciousness of standing in some sort apart, intent upon an interest that transcended the immediate issues of the war itself.

As some of the injuries done us have become intolerable we have still been clear that we wished nothing for ourselves that we were not ready to demand for all mankind—fair dealing, justice, the freedom to live and to be at ease against organized wrong.

It is in this spirit and with this thought that we have grown more and more aware, more and more certain that the part we wished to play was the part of those who mean to vindicate and fortify peace. We have been obliged to arm ourselves to make good our claim to a certain minimum of right and of freedom of action. We stand firm in armed neutrality since it seems that in no other way we can demonstrate what it is we insist upon and cannot forget. We may even be drawn on, by circumstances, not by our own purpose or desire, to a more active assertion of our rights as we see them and a more immediate association with the great struggle itself. But nothing will alter our thought or our purpose. They are too clear to be obscured. They are too deeply rooted in the principles of our national life to be altered. We desire neither conquest nor advantage. We wish nothing that can be had only at the cost of another people. We always professed unselfish purpose and we covet the opportunity to prove our professions are sincere.

There are many things still to be done at home, to clarify our own politics and add new vitality to the industrial processes of our own life, and we shall do them as time and opportunity serve, but we realize that the greatest things that remain to be done must be done with the whole world for stage and in cooperation with the wide and universal forces of mankind, and we are making our spirits ready for those things.

We are provincials no longer. The tragic events of the thirty months of vital turmoil through which we have just passed have made us citizens of the world. There can be no turning back. Our own fortunes as a nation are involved whether we would have it so or not....

These, therefore, are the things we shall stand for, whether in war or in peace:

That all nations are equally interested in the peace of the world and in the political stability of free peoples, and equally responsible for their maintenance; that the essential principle of peace is the actual equality of nations in all matters of right or privilege; that peace cannot securely or justly rest upon an armed balance of power; that governments derive all their just powers from the consent of the governed and that no other powers should be supported by the common thought, purpose or power of the family of nations; that the seas should be equally free and safe for the use of all peoples, under rules set up by common agreement and consent, and that, so far as practicable, they should be accessible to all upon equal terms; that national armaments shall be limited to the necessities of national order and domestic safety; that the community of interest and of power upon which peace must henceforth depend imposes upon each nation the duty of seeing to it that all influences proceeding from its own citizens meant to encourage or assist revolution in other states should be sternly and effectually suppressed and prevented....

Upon this as a platform of purpose and of action we can stand together. And it is imperative that we should stand together. We are being forged into a new unity amidst the fires that now blaze throughout the world. In their ardent heat we shall, in God's Providence, let us hope, be purged of faction and division, purified of the errant humors of party and of private interest, and shall stand forth in the days to come with a new dignity of national pride and spirit. Let each man see to it that the dedication is in his own heart, the high purpose of the nation in his own mind, ruler of his own will and desire....

The shadows that now lie dark upon our path will soon be dispelled, and we shall walk with the light all about us if we be but true to ourselves—to ourselves as we have wished to be known in the counsels of the world and in the thought of all those who love liberty and justice and the right exalted.

GLOSSARY

"governments derive their just powers from the consent of the governed": an allusion to the American Declaration of Independence

provincials: backward, rural people

Document Analysis

Wilson's Second Inaugural Address, delivered on March 5, 1917, is relatively short compared with the inaugural addresses of other presidents. Yet it was extremely significant, in that it was part of a broader effort by the administration to prepare the country for war. In response to Germany's resumption of unrestricted submarine warfare, the president broke diplomatic relations with Germany in February. Wilson hoped the action would prompt the Germans to respect the rights of neutral vessels, but the government in Berlin refused to change its policy. In addition, on February 23, the British government turned over to Wilson a telegram that had been sent by Germany's foreign minister, Arthur Zimmermann, in which Germany proposed an alliance with Mexico in the event that the United States entered the war. In exchange for Mexican military action against the United States, Germany promised military and financial support and pledged to help Mexico regain Texas, New Mexico, and Arizona, lost during the Mexican-American War. When the telegram became public, it created an uproar in the United States and increased pressure on Wilson to take stronger action against Germany.

In the address, Wilson briefly acknowledges the domestic accomplishments of his first term but notes that the ongoing international conflict had forced the nation to reevaluate its priorities and focus on foreign affairs. Wilson states that it had "been impossible to avoid" the ramifications of World War I and that the results of the conflict had "shaken men everywhere with a passion and an apprehension they never knew before." The president recognized the cleavages within the United States which the global conflict had engendered. He exclaims that "we are of the blood of all the nations that are at war." At the time, one in eight Americans had been born overseas, and many had ties to the countries involved in the war. There was a large German American community in the United States and an even larger community of immigrants and descendants of immigrants from the British Isles. Aware that U.S. involvement in the conflict was increasingly likely, Wilson sought to unify the nation. He expresses his belief that the war had not pushed Americans apart but rather had brought them together, stating that "despite many divisions, we have drawn closer

THE AMERICAN WAR–DOG

(The American-German crisis, January–March, 1916)

The American War-Dog. The American-German Crisis, January-March 1916. Depicts U.S. President Woodrow Wilson looking out his door at howling dog labeled "Jingo"; representing those in the U.S. eager to join the Great War against Germany contrary to the administration's policy of neutrality.

together."

Wilson declares that although the United States had suffered "intolerable" actions by the Central powers, the nation still sought peace over war. He affirms that the country stood "firm in armed neutrality" and that it was willing to use force to protect its interests. Wilson acknowledges that the nation's efforts to remain neutral might not be successful and that the United States could be drawn into the war. He asserts that if the United States did become involved in the war, the nation's wartime goals would remain consistent with its principles. He states that the United States desired "neither conquest nor advantage." Instead, he reiterates the main principles of his address in support of a world league for peace and argues that the United States sought only a resolution to the war that would prevent future conflicts and grant people around the globe the right to choose their own government.

With an eye to the future, Wilson also contends that nations had "the duty of seeing to it that all influences proceeding from its own citizens meant to encourage or assist revolution in other states should be sternly and effectually suppressed and prevented." This was a reference to German efforts to encourage revolution in Russia. (Wilson conveniently forgot the United States incursion into Mexico in 1914.) Exhausted and bankrupt from the war, Russia saw a series of revolutions sweep the country by March 1917. The czar was overthrown, and eventually a Communist government was established under Vladimir Lenin.

The president exclaims that Americans were "provincials no longer" and that the nation increasingly understood the nature of the war, even if they were horrified by its brutality. He sees it as "imperative that we should stand together" and that the nation was "being forged into a new unity amidst the fires that now blaze throughout the world." He finishes the address by reminding Americans of the need to be "true to ourselves"; by doing so, the nation could serve as a beacon for those who sought justice and democracy around the world.

Although the speech was part of a public effort to prepare the nation for war, the administration had already begun preparations. The 1916 National Defense Act increased the size of the peacetime Army to 175,000 regular troops and quadrupled the National Guard to 450,000. It also authorized further increases in the size of the military in the event of war. The National Defense Act also gave the president the authority to compel industries to produce arms and wartime supplies, and it created the Council of National Defense, comprising industrialists, labor leaders, and politicians to oversee wartime production. The administration undertook other actions as well to begin the transition to a wartime economy.

While reminding the nation of the trials which the country is facing due to German attacks upon American merchant vessels, Wilson does not want the American response to be based only upon anger over these attacks. Wilson wants the nation to move forward unified by the ideals which had been a part of the national heritage since its inception. Thus, as he concludes the speech, Wilson depicts the unity which has transformed the immigrants into Americans, the unity based upon the ideals of the nation. In listing the "things we stand for, whether in war or in peace," Wilson reminded not only those gathered in Washington to hear the speech, but all who would later read it in their newspapers, of who it is that Americans strive to be. This is a nation in which all share in freedom, equality, democratic rights, with domestic security, according to Wilson. Similarly, Wilson states his belief that among the nations of the world there should be mutual respect, peaceful intentions, safe transit on the seas, and only minimal armaments. In Wilson's view, the "family of nations" should democratically work toward a common goal of justice and freedom for all.

The hopes and ideals which Wilson expressed in this speech do represent his hopes and dreams. However, the warnings and fears of which he speaks are just as real. Less than a month after giving this speech, Wilson called together a joint session of Congress and requested a declaration of war against Germany. If he had had any hope that this speech would be heard by German leaders, that did not happen. However, most people in the United States did seem to understand the ongoing events, and supported the entry of the United States into the Great War, as it was then known.

Essential Themes

As Woodrow Wilson outlined his vision for his second term, he understood that it was time for a change in focus. His first term priority had been domestic policy. However, the international situation had changed dramatically since early 1913. The United States would probably be forced to join in the conflict which already touched much of the world. Wilson had hopes that he would be able to return to domestic concerns, but in the immediate future the Americans must play their part as "citizens of the world."

Although in this passage Wilson did not identify Germany by name, it would have been clear to all when he spoke of the United States as having been "deeply wronged upon the seas." The U-boats (submarines), which were operating against vessels carrying goods to the Allies, directly interfered with American interests. He believed that whether he, or the nation, liked it or not, the United States was being pulled into the war. As a result, Wilson made it clear that preparations would be undertaken to assure that America would be able to achieve its goals, whether in peace or war.

Wilson closed with an appeal to American idealism. Perhaps over-idealistically, he ascribed to all nations the same desires as had been those of the Founding Fathers. These included freedom for all people, a peaceful world, security from militaristic threats, and domestic security. He lifted up the United States as the example for all nations, in that he proclaimed it as being composed of those "who love liberty and justice." This being the case, Wilson proclaimed to the nation and the world that the United States would do whatever it took to make the ideals outlines in this speech an actuality around the globe.

—*Tom Lansford, PhD*
—*Donald A. Watt, PhD*

Bibliography and Additional Reading

Berg, A. Scott. *Wilson.* New York: G. Putnam's Sons, 2013.

Brands, H. W. *Woodrow Wilson.* New York: Times Books, 2003.

Clements, Kendrick A. *The Presidency of Woodrow Wilson.* Lawrence: University Press of Kansas, 1992.

Cooper, John Milton. *Breaking the Heart of the World: Woodrow Wilson and the Fight for the League of Nations.* New York: Cambridge University Press, 2001.

Ferrell, Robert H. "Woodrow Wilson: Man and Statesman." *Review of Politics* 18, no. 2 (April 1956): 131–145.

Heckscher, August. *Woodrow Wilson.* New York: Scribners, 1991.

Knock, Thomas. *To End All Wars: Woodrow Wilson and the Quest for a New World Order.* New York: Oxford University Press, 1992.

Link, Arthur S., ed. *Woodrow Wilson and a Revolutionary World.* Chapel Hill: University of North Carolina Press, 1982.

Martin, Daniel W. "The Fading Legacy of Woodrow Wilson." *Public Administration Review* 48, no. 2 (March–April 1988): 631–636.

Stid, Daniel D. "Woodrow Wilson and the Problem of Party Government." *Polity* 26, no. 4 (Summer 1994): 553–578.

Walker, Larry. "Woodrow Wilson, Progressive Reform, and Public Administration." *Political Science Quarterly* 104, no. 3 (Autumn 1989): 509–525.

"How Does He Do It?" In this Clifford Berryman cartoon, Harding and Cox ponder another big story of 1920: Babe Ruth's record-setting home run pace. (By Clifford Berryman (1869-1949) Library of Congress)

■ Warren G. Harding's "Not Nostrums, but Normalcy" Speech

Date: May 14, 1920
Author: Warren G. Harding
Genre: Speech

Summary Overview

Warren G. Harding delivered this speech before the Home Market Club in Boston, Massachusetts, in the spring of 1920, before he was selected as the Republican nominee for president. His speech presented a critique of the political reforms and Progressivism of Democratic President Woodrow Wilson. This was the first speech in which Harding called for a return to "normalcy," a major theme of his campaign. Throughout the speech, Harding drew a number of contrasts between what he saw as the needless experimentation of Wilson's Progressive agenda and his desire to see the United States return to traditional, more conservative ideals and practices that he believed the Republican Party embodied. He called for less dependence on government, more reliance on the character and accomplishments of the people, and an abandonment of the internationalism associated with U.S. participation in World War I and Wilson's attempt to draw the country into the League of Nations.

Defining Moment

In the 1920 presidential election, American voters chose the Republican candidate, Warren G. Harding, by a large margin, thus largely repudiating the Progressivism and internationalism represented by the Democratic platform. The first term of President Woodrow Wilson's administration (1913–17) is often cited as the high point of Progressive reform. During Wilson's second term (1917–21), the United States' entry into World War I and Wilson's attempt to establish the League of Nations largely diverted attention away from domestic reform. Progressivism was a reform movement that embraced government as a major agent of change in American society and sought to rein in the power of big business through strict government regulation. Progressives wanted the government to have a more direct role in managing and regulating the U.S. economy and undertook a major overhaul of the U.S. banking and monetary system with the passage of the Federal Reserve Act in 1913. Progressives also

sought to give more political power to the people through measures such as the direct election of U.S. senators by popular vote, which was achieved with the ratification of the Seventeenth Amendment in 1913, and the enfranchisement of women, which was achieved with the ratification of the Nineteenth Amendment in 1920.

Progressivism was not strictly aligned with only the Democratic Party; for example, Theodore Roosevelt was a Progressive Republican. But Warren G. Harding identified more with the conservative wing of the Republican Party. The best way to understand Harding's call for a "return to normalcy" is to see it as a rejection of what he considered to be the reckless innovation and experimentation of Wilson's Progressivism. The fact that Harding was elected in a decisive fashion in 1920, along with Republican majorities in both houses of Congress, demonstrates that Harding correctly perceived that there was a popular reaction against Progressivism and Wilson's policies. Wilson had suffered a stroke in September 1919 and was largely incapacitated for the remainder of his term, and, therefore, he was not a candidate in 1920. But Wilson hoped voters would back the platform of the Democratic nominee, James M. Cox, and support his ultimately unsuccessful efforts to persuade the Senate to ratify the Treaty of Versailles and to bring the United States into the League of Nations.

Harding delivered this speech in May 1920, before he had been selected as the Republican nominee for president. Although Harding was not considered a front-runner for the nomination that year, he emerged as a compromise candidate after the convention deadlocked.

One of the earliest supporters of Harding's presidential bid, E. Mont Reily, coined the phrase "Harding and Back to Normal," and marketing executive Albert D. Lasker, who directed much of the campaign's advertising, popularized the slogan "Back to Normalcy." On November 2, 1920, Harding won a decisive victory over Cox, pulling 60.3 percent of the popular vote.

Author Biography

Warren Gamaliel Harding was born near Marion, Ohio, on November 2, 1865. After graduating from Ohio Central College in 1882, he attempted various business endeavors before he bought the Marion Daily Star and began serving as the newspaper's editor. He was elected to the Ohio Senate in 1899, and in 1903, he was named the lieutenant governor of Ohio. In 1914, he was elected to the U.S. Senate. When the Republican National Convention deadlocked in 1920, Harding emerged as a compromise candidate and was selected as the presidential nominee. He decisively defeated the Democratic candidate, James M. Cox. As president, Harding tried to live up to his campaign promises of returning to normalcy by reining in the growth of government, adopting a pro-business strategy, and pursuing an isolationist foreign policy. However, his administration was tarnished by the corruption of some of his cabinet officials. The worst of these scandals, known as the Teapot Dome scandal, was not yet widely known when Harding died of a heart attack in San Francisco, California, on August 2, 1923. Harding was succeeded by his vice president, Calvin Coolidge.

HISTORICAL DOCUMENT

There isn't anything the matter with world civilization, except that humanity is viewing it through a vision impaired in a cataclysmal war. Poise has been disturbed, and nerves have been racked, and fever has rendered men irrational; sometimes there have been draughts upon the dangerous cup of barbarity, and men have wandered far from safe paths, but the human procession still marches in the right direction.

America's present need is not heroics, but healing; not nostrums, but normalcy; not revolution, but restoration; not agitation, but adjustment; not surgery, but serenity; not the dramatic, but the dispassionate; not experiment, but equipoise; not submergence in internationality, but sustainment in triumphant nationality.

It is one thing to battle successfully against world domination by military autocracy, because the infinite God never intended such a program, but it is quite another thing to revise human nature and suspend the fundamental laws of life and all of life's acquirements.... This republic has its ample tasks. If we put an end to false economics which lure humanity to utter chaos, ours will be the commanding example of world leadership today. If we can prove a representative popular government under which a citizenship seeks what it may do for the government rather than what the government may do for individuals, we shall do more to make democracy safe for the world than all armed conflict ever recorded. The world needs to be reminded that all human ills are not curable by legislation, and that quantity of statutory enactment and excess of government offer no substitute for quality of citizenship.

The problems of maintained civilization are not to be solved by a transfer of responsibility from citizenship to government, and no eminent page in history was ever drafted by the standards of mediocrity. More, no government is worthy of the name which is directed by influence on the one hand, or moved by intimidation on the other....

My best judgment of America's needs is to steady down, to get squarely on our feet, to make sure of the right path. Let's get out of the fevered delirium of war, with the hallucination that all the money in the world is to be made in the madness of war and the wildness of its aftermath. Let us stop to consider that tranquillity at home is more precious than peace abroad, and that both our good fortune and our eminence are dependent on the normal forward stride of all the American people....

Document Analysis

"Normalcy" has become a key word associated with Harding's 1920 presidential campaign. Perhaps the best way to understand what Harding meant by normalcy is to look at how he intended it to contrast with certain trends and policies that were established during his predecessor President Woodrow Wilson's eight-year administration, which pushed Progressive reform legislation and also saw the United States drawn into active participation in World War I. Harding believed that the reform-minded experimentation and innovation of Wilson's Progressive agenda was a departure from the norms of American politics and society.

Harding's reference to "normalcy" appears in one long sentence in which he draws a number contrasts. The United States, Harding claims, needed normalcy rather than "nostrums." The term "nostrum" refers to untried, "quack" medical cures—and thus untried political measures. Each of the phrases in Harding's paragraph-long sentence was intended to contrast something undesirable about Wilson's Progressivism with a more normal, less dramatic return to traditional concepts and practices.

Harding concedes that the United States' entry into World War I might have been necessary, but he suggests it is not necessary or desirable to try to "revise human nature"—thus implying that such revisions had been attempted in Wilson's reform agenda with the expansion of government. Harding suggests that the United States needs to "put an end to false economics" and return to a mindset where people seek what they can do for their country rather than what their government can do for them (a theme echoed in John F. Kennedy's famous line, "Ask not…"). In doing this, Harding asserts, "we shall do more to make democracy safe for the world than all armed conflict ever recorded." Harding intended for this phrase to recall Wilson's characterization of the United States' entry into World War I as an effort to "make the world safe for democracy."

Another way to understand Harding's concept of normalcy can be seen in the last paragraph of this excerpt. Harding says the United States needs to "steady down, to get squarely on our feet, to make sure of the right path." Again, all of these phrases suggest that the nation had just recently passed through a period of rapid, perhaps haphazard change and now needs to simply back away from the "fevered delirium of war" and to return to what is normal. The country's greatness and good fortune, Harding asserts, are ultimately dependent simply upon "the normal forward stride of all the American people."

Nowhere in this speech did Harding try to provide specific evidence for his assertions. Speaking before a largely Republican crowd in Boston, Massachusetts, he likely assumed that many in the audience would agree with him. Given his decisive victory in the 1920 election, it is evident that many voters throughout the nation did embrace Harding's call for a return to "normalcy."

Essential Themes

In this speech, Harding introduced the notion of returning to "normalcy," which became a hallmark of his 1920 presidential campaign. Harding believed the postwar era represented a decisive time of crisis for the United States and that a continuation of President Woodrow Wilson's policies would be a grave mistake for the country and democracy worldwide. Harding's basic argument that the Progressive reforms embodied in the domestic policies of Wilson's administration and the internationalism represented by the attempts to secure U.S. membership in the League of Nations represented a departure from what he saw as the "normal" trends in U.S. politics and society. As he believed these departures were doomed to failure in the long run, Harding wanted the United States to return to traditional ideals and practices. While Harding never mentioned Wilson or any particular piece of Progressive legislation in this speech, it is clear that he intended to draw a contrast between Progressivism's reform agenda and Wilson's internationalism on the one hand and, on the other, what he believed was the normal American emphasis on a quiet, responsible society, in which individuals of strong character sought to direct their own affairs without government interference or assistance.

Harding believed that the Progressives had tried to "revise human nature" and to institute a "false economics" by increasing government influence and regulation, and he argued that such attempts were doomed to failure. Progressive ideals and policies were what Harding termed "nostrums"—untried but popular remedies that he saw as a quick fix for complex problems. Success would instead be found in a return to emphasis upon "quality citizenship" in which the people took responsibility for their own welfare and sought to do good for the nation rather than to think of what the government might do for the individual. What the United States needed, in Harding's eyes, was to back away from this time of rapid change, to take stock, and to move ahead steadily along traditional lines.

—*Mark S. Joy, PhD*

Bibliography and Additional Reading

Murray, Robert K. *The Harding Era: Warren G. Harding and His Administration*. Minneapolis: U of Minnesota P, 1969. Print.

———. *The Politics of Normalcy: Governmental Theory and Practice in the Harding- Coolidge Era*. New York: Norton, 1973. Print.

Trani, Eugene P., and David L. Wilson. *The Presidency of Warren G. Harding*. Lawrence: Regents P of Kansas, 1977. Print.

■ "The Destiny of America"

Date: May 30, 1923
Author: Calvin Coolidge
Genre: Speech

Summary Overview

During the 1923 Memorial Day commemoration ceremony in Northampton, Massachusetts, Vice President Calvin Coolidge paid tribute to both the U.S. form of government and the prevailing sense of patriotism among Americans. The vice president cited a wide range of examples from American history, each of which demonstrated the distinctiveness of Americans, particularly during times of tumult and conflict. Coolidge also celebrated the wealth of resources and opportunities available in the country, suggesting that such an abundance of assets would be maintained if the government avoided unnecessary regulation and taxation. Furthermore, Coolidge looked to distinguish the economic, political, and social environment in the United States from that of war-torn Europe and elsewhere.

Defining Moment

The decade of the 1920s was dubbed the "Roaring Twenties," referring to the sense of cultural exuberance and renewed optimism in the years following World War I. Since the beginning of the twentieth century, the United States had experienced a major economic boom. Virtually every sector of the economy grew, aided by the growing prevalence of electricity and other energy sources and the expansion of transportation, from the vast railway system to the appearance of automobiles.

Labor productivity was at 3.8 percent per year, a much higher rate than in the previous decades. World War I, which ended in 1918, had completely devastated Europe, but left the United States largely unaffected. With prosperity the common theme during the 1920s, Americans began to spend and invest more money than before. Consumers started investing heavily (and often at great risk) in the stock markets. Capital flowed freely between financial institutions and businesses.

The "bull market" during this period appeared unsustainable and headed for an eventual slowdown, but Americans were unconcerned with such warnings. Politically, the 1920s were worthy of another nickname: the Republican Era. The activist Progressive Era, exemplified by Democrat Woodrow Wilson's efforts to use government to foster social reform, bolster organized labor, and create an international network of nations, was on the wane. Americans wanted less government involvement by the 1920s, and the platform of President Warren G. Harding and his vice president, Calvin Coolidge, reflected this notion.

The Republicans were aided by a general fear of left-wing ideals associated with the Red Scare, during which Americans were increasingly worried about the rise of Bolshevism and Communism in eastern Europe. Indeed, one of the most prominent issues in the minds of Harding and Coolidge was the reconstruction of Europe. Harding's administration remained focused on the European stage, in terms of not only rebuilding that continent's infrastructure but also avoiding the apparent left-wing radicalism that was starting to surge in the region.

The fear of radicalism and the desire for continued economic growth also contributed to the decline of labor unions. Organized labor was finding itself under attack from government, business, and the general public. Flush with profits from the strong economy, businesses were increasingly able to negotiate higher wages with their employees, without involving the unions. With fear of Bolshevism and distrust of Progressivism prevalent in the United States, citizens grew disillusioned with the role of their federal government.

Known to resist confrontation and controversy, Harding used the phrase "return to normalcy" as his campaign slogan. Despite the eventual ineffectiveness of Harding's presidency, the Republican Era continued with his successor, Coolidge, who became president in August 1923 after Harding's death. Coolidge continued to focus on ensuring the moral and social stability of the nation by drawing from his own thoughtful, Christian upbringing.

Author Biography

John Calvin Coolidge was born on July 4, 1872, in Plymouth Notch, Vermont. His mother and sister died early in his life; his father was a prominent public official. Coolidge graduated from Amherst College and pursued a career in law and government. While still living in Northampton, he won a seat on the city council in 1900, chairmanship of the Northampton Republican Committee in 1904, a position on the Massachusetts General Court in 1907, and, eventually, the office of governor in 1919. He left office to serve as vice president to Harding. In August 1923, Harding died, leaving Coolidge as president. In 1924, Coolidge won reelection, holding office until 1929. He retired to Northampton and died on January 5, 1933.

HISTORICAL DOCUMENT

Patriotism is easy to understand in America. It means looking out for yourself by looking out for your country. In no other nation on earth does this principle have such complete application. It comes most naturally from the fundamental doctrine of our land that the people are supreme. Lincoln stated the substance of the whole matter in his famous phrase, "government of the people; by the people, and for the people."

The authority of law here is not something which is imposed upon the people; it is the will of the people themselves. The decision of the court here is not something which is apart from the people; it is the judgment of the people themselves. The right of the ownership of property here is not something withheld from the people; it is the privilege of the people themselves. Their sovereignty is absolute and complete. A definition of the relationship between the institutions of our government and the American people entirely justifies the assertion that: "All things were made by them; and without them was not anything made that was made." It is because the American government is the sole creation and possession of the people that they have always cherished it and defended it, and always will.

There are two fundamental motives which inspire human action. The first and most important, to which all else is subordinate, is that of righteousness. There is that in mankind, stronger than all else, which requires them to do right. When that requirement is satisfied, the next motive is that of gain. These are the moral motive and the material motive. While in some particular instance they might seem to be antagonistic, yet always, when broadly considered or applied to society as a whole, they are in harmony. American institutions meet the test of these two standards. They are founded on righteousness, they are productive of material prosperity. They compel the loyalty and support of the people because such action is right and because it is profitable.

These are the main reasons for the formation of patriotic societies. Desiring to promote the highest welfare of civilization, their chief purpose is to preserve and extend American ideals. No matter what others may do, they are determined to serve themselves and their fellowmen by thinking America, believing America, and living America. That faith they are proud to proclaim to all the world. It is no wonder that the people are attached to America when we consider what it has done and what it represents. It has been called the last great hope of the world. Its simple story is a romance of surpassing interest. Its accomplishments rise above the realm of fable. To live under the privileges of its citizenship is the highest position of opportunity and achievement ever reached by a people.

If there be a destiny, it is of no avail for us unless we work with it. The ways of Providence will be of no advantage to us unless we proceed in the same direction. If we perceive a destiny in America, if we believe that Providence has been the guide, our own success, our own salvation require that we should act and serve in harmony and obedience.

Throughout all the centuries this land remained unknown to civilization. Just at a time when Christianity was at last firmly established, when there was a general advance in learning, when there was a great spiritual awakening, America began to be revealed to the European world. When this new age began, with its new aspirations and its new needs, its new hopes, and its new desires, the shores of our country rose through the mist, disclosing a new hemisphere in which, untrammeled by Old World conventions, new ideals might establish for mankind a new experience and a new life.

Settlers came here from mixed motives, some for pillage and adventure, some for trade and refuge, but those who have set their imperishable mark upon our institutions came from far higher motives. Generally defined, they were seeking a broader freedom. They were intent upon establishing a Christian commonwealth in accordance with the principle of self-government.

They were an inspired body of men. It has been said that God sifted the nations that He might send choice grain into the wilderness. They had a genius for organized society on the foundation of piety, righteousness, liberty, and obedience to law. They brought with them the accumulated wisdom and experience of the ages wherever it contributed to the civilizing power of these great agencies. But the class and caste, the immaterial formalism of the Old World, they left behind. They let slip their grasp upon conventionalities that they might lay a firmer hold upon realities. . . .

The main characteristics of those principles [of government] from which all others are deduced is a government of limited and defined powers, leaving the people supreme. The executive has sole command of the military forces, but he cannot raise a dollar of revenue. The legislature has the sole authority to levy taxes, but it cannot issue a command to a single private soldier. The judiciary interprets and declares the law and the Constitution, but it can neither create nor destroy the right of a single individual. Freedom of action is complete, within moral bounds, under the law which the people themselves have prescribed. The individual is supported in his right to follow his own choice, live his own life, and reap the rewards of his own effort. Justice is administered by impartial courts. It is a maxim of our law that there is no wrong without a remedy. All the power and authority of the whole national government cannot convict the most humble individual of a crime, save on the verdict of an impartial jury composed of twelve of his peers. Opportunity is denied to none, every place is open, and every position yields to the humblest in accordance with ability and application.

The chief repository of power is in the legislature, chosen directly by the people at frequent elections. It is this body, which is particularly responsive to the public will, and yet, as in the Congress, is representative of the whole nation. It does not perform an executive function. It is not, therefore, charged with the necessity of expedition. It is a legislative body and is, therefore, charged with the necessity for deliberation. Sometimes this privilege may be abused, for this great power has been given as the main safeguard of liberty, and wherever power is bestowed it may be used unwisely. But whenever a legislative body ceases to deliberate, then it ceases to act with due consideration.

That fact in itself is conclusive that it has ceased to be independent, has become subservient to a single directing influence or a small group, either without or within itself, and is no longer representative of the people. Such a condition would not be a rule of the people, but a rule of some unconstitutional power. It is my own observation and belief than the American Congress is the most efficient and effective deliberative body, more untrammeled, more independent, more advised, more representative of the will of the people than any body which legislates for any of the great powers. An independent legislature never deprived the people of their liberty. Such is America, such is the government and civilization which have grown up around the church, the town meeting, and the schoolhouse. It is not perfect, but it surpasses the accomplishments of any other people. Such is the state of society which has been created in this country, which has brought it from the untrodden wilderness of 300 years ago to its present state of development. Who can fail to see in it the hand of destiny? Who can doubt that it has been guided by a Divine Providence? What has it not given to its people in material advantages, educational opportunity, and religious consolation? Our country has not failed, our country has been a success. You are here because you believe in it, because you believe that it is right, and because you know that it has paid. You are determined to defend it, to support it, and, if need be, to fight for it. You know that America is worth fighting for.

But if our republic is to be maintained and improved it will be through the efforts and character of the individual. It will be, first of all, because of the influences which exist in the home, for it is the ideals which prevail in the homelife which make up the strength of the nation. The homely virtues must continue to be cultivated. The real dignity, the real nobility of work must be cherished. It is only through industry that there is any hope for individual development. The viciousness of waste and the value of thrift must continue to be learned and understood. Civilization rests on conservation. To these there must be added religion, education, and obedience to law. These are the foundation of all character in the individual and all hope in the nation. . . .

A growing tendency has been observed of late years to think too little of what is really the public interest and too much of what is supposed to be class interest. The two great political parties of the nation have existed for the purpose, each in accordance with its own principles, of undertaking to serve the interests of the whole nation. Their members of the Congress are chosen with that great end in view. Patriotism does not mean a regard for some special section or an attachment for some special interest, and a narrow prejudice against other sections and other interests; it means a love of the whole country. This does not mean that any section or any interest is to be disproportionately preferred or disproportionately disregarded, but that the welfare of all is equally to be sought. Agriculture, transportation, manufacturing, and all the other desirable activities should serve in accordance with their strength and should be served in accordance with the benefits they confer.

A division of the people or their representatives in accordance with any other principle or theory is contrary to the public welfare. An organization for the purpose of serving some special interest is perfectly proper and may be exceedingly helpful, but whenever it undertakes to serve that interest by disregarding the welfare of other interests, it becomes harmful alike to the interest which it proposes to serve and to the public welfare in general. Under the modern organization of society there is such a necessary community of interests that all necessarily experience depression or prosperity together.

They cannot be separated. Our country has resources sufficient to provide in abundance for everybody. But it cannot confer a disproportionate share upon anybody. There is work here to keep amply employed every dollar of capital and every hand of honest toil, but there is no place for profiteering, either in high prices or in low, by the organized greed of money or of men. The most pressing requirement of the present day is that we should learn this lesson and be content with a fair share, whether it be the returns from invested capital or the rewards of toil. On that foundation there is a guarantee of continued prosperity, of stable economic conditions, of harmonious social relationships, and of sound and enduring government. On any other theory or action the only prospect is that of wasteful conflict and suffering in our economic life and factional discord and trifling in our political life. No private enterprise can succeed unless the public welfare be held supreme.

Another necessity of the utmost urgency in this day, a necessity which is worldwide, is economy in government expenditures. This may seem the antithesis of military preparation, but, as a matter of fact, our present great debt is due, in a considerable extent, to creating our last military establishment under the condition of war haste and war prices, which added enormously to its cost. There is no end of the things which the government could do, seemingly, in the way of public welfare, if it had the money. Everything we want cannot be had at once. It must be earned by toilsome labor. There is a very decided limit to the amount which can be raised by taxation without ruinously affecting the people of the country by virtual confiscation of a part of their past savings.

The business of the country, as a whole, is transacted on a small margin of profit. The economic structure is one of great delicacy and sensitiveness. When taxes become too burdensome, either the price of commodities has to be raised to a point at which consumption is so diminished as greatly to curtail production, or so much of the returns from industry is required by the government that production becomes unprofitable and ceases for that reason. In either case there is depression, lack of employment, idleness of investment and of wage earner, with the long line of attendant want and suffering on the part of the people. After order and liberty, economy is one of the highest essentials of a free government. It was in no small degree the unendurable burden of taxation which drove Europe into the Great War. Economy is always a guarantee of peace.

It is the great economic question of government finances which is burdening the people of Europe at the present time. How to meet obligations is the chief problem on continental Europe and in the British Isles. It cannot be doubted that high taxes are the chief cause for the extended condition of unemployment which has required millions to subsist on the public treasury in

Great Britain for a long period of time, though the number of these unfortunate people has been declining. A government which requires of the people the contribution of the bulk of their substance and rewards cannot be classed as a free government, or long remain as such. It is gratifying to observe, in our own national government, that there has been an enormous decrease in expenditures, a large reduction of the debt, and a revision of taxation affording great relief.

But it is in peace that there lies the greatest opportunity for relief from burdensome taxation. Our country is at peace, not only legal but actual, with all other peoples. We cherish peace and goodwill toward all the earth, with a sentiment of friendship and a desire for universal well-being. If we want peace it is our business to cultivate goodwill. It was for the promotion of peace that the Washington Conference on the Limitation of Armaments and Pacific Questions was called. For the first time in history the great powers of the earth have agreed to a limitation of naval armaments. This was brought about by American initiative in accordance with an American plan, and executed by American statesmanship. Out of regard for a similar principle is the proposal to participate in the establishment of a World Court. These are in accordance with a desire to adjust differences between nations, not by an overpowering display or use of force but by mutual conference and understanding in harmony with the requirement of justice and of honor.

Our country does not want war, it wants peace. It has not decreed this memorial season as an honor to war, with its terrible waste and attendant train of suffering and hardship which reaches onward into the years of peace. Yet war is not the worst of evils, and these days have been set apart to do honor to all those, now gone, who made the cause of America their supreme choice. Some fell with the word of Patrick Henry, "Give me lib-erty, or give me death," almost ringing in their ears. Some heard that word across the intervening generations and were still obedient to its call. It is to the spirit of those men, exhibited in all our wars, to the spirit that places the devotion to freedom and truth above the devotion to life, that the nation pays its ever enduring mark of reverence and respect.

It is not that principle that leads to conflict but to tranquillity. It is not that principle which is the cause of war but the only foundation for an enduring peace. There can be no peace with the forces of evil. Peace comes only through the establishment of the supremacy of the forces of good. That way lies only through sacrifice. It was that the people of our country might live in a knowledge of the truth that these, our countrymen, are dead. "Greater love hath no man than this, that a man lay down his life for his friends."

This spirit is not dead, it is the most vital thing in America. It did not flow from any act of government. It is the spirit of the people themselves. It justifies faith in them and faith in their institutions. Remembering all that it has accomplished from the day of the Puritan and Cavalier to the day of the last, least immigrant, who lives by it no less than they, who shall dare to doubt it, who shall dare to challenge it, who shall venture to rouse it into action? Those who have scoffed at it from the day of the Stuarts and the Bourbons to the day of the Hapsburgs and the Hohenzollerns have seen it rise and prevail over them. Calm, peaceful, puissant, it remains, conscious of its authority, "slow to anger, plenteous in mercy," seeking not to injure but to serve, the safeguard of the republic, still the guarantee of a broader freedom, the supreme moral power of the world. It is in that spirit that we place our trust. It is to that spirit again, with this returning year, we solemnly pledge the devotion of all that we have and are.

Document Analysis

Coolidge's speech celebrates the values and principles that gave rise to American patriotism. He views patriotism as a positive force in the United States, fostering the protection of individual rights and liberties. Patriotism also serves as the foundation for the American democratic system of government, which he extols as worth defending at all costs. The United States' political, economic, natural, and social resources, he says, are the reasons the United States remains intact while European countries struggle to rebuild after World War I.

American patriotism, Coolidge argues, represents the foundation of the American way of life. In particular, he says, patriotism involves both a desire to ensure the freedoms and rights of every individual and loyalty to the overall society. Patriotism is at the core of the American political system, which was designed to protect the people rather than to impose a political will over them.

The country's destiny, he adds, relies on continually re-committing to the nation's fundamental values. Coolidge echoes the view that the United States is "the last great hope of the world" that, if left unaltered, would survive any effort to destabilize it.

American government, Coolidge argues, is an organic product of the nation's historically imbued morals and values. The myriad types of people who settled the country, he adds, had to collaborate to create a strong, but not domineering, legal and political system. Although it is not perfect, Coolidge acknowledges, the American system of checks and balances serves the country well, particularly in light of the limitations it put on all branches of government.

The key to continuing the American success story, Coolidge argues, is the indivisibility of and equality among the nation's people. He says that there are enough resources in the country for every American and that no disproportionate shares of those resources should be given to any one level of society. Furthermore, government should ensure that the poorest citizens have an opportunity to gain education and employment. "There is no end of the things which the government can do" with regard to the public welfare, he says. Coolidge adds that Americans should take notice of the issues facing postwar Europe. Europeans are being stifled under excessive taxation to pay down debts, he says. The U.S. government, he advises, should avoid excessive taxation and regulation or else risk similar economic issues.

Coolidge concludes his speech by marking the occasion's significance, paying homage to the American spirit and to the peace that U.S. soldiers have fought to maintain. The peace the United States enjoys, he says, flows not only from these soldiers but also from every American. After all, he comments, peace is central to the values espoused by the settlers, colonists, and the earliest Americans, and it is a tenet that endures in the modern country as well.

Essential Themes

Coolidge used the Northampton Memorial Day celebration not only to honor the men (particularly those from Northampton) who gave their lives to protect the values and virtues of the United States, but also to pay homage to those principles themselves. Coolidge states that the American way of life stems from patriotism, liberty, and independence, and that such concepts distinguished the United States from the war-torn nations of Europe.

Coolidge espouses the Republican notion of a minimally intrusive government. To be sure, every American should have the opportunity to pursue his or her own goals. Where there are social and economic inequities, he says, government should help correct that imbalance. Then again, as the European example showed, American government should avoid unnecessary taxation or regulation. Such burdens, he says, slow the growth of national economies.

American social, political, and economic principles, Coolidge suggests, emerged naturally from the values and ideals of the men and women who helped build the country. The country's destiny, as he describes it, remains as long as Americans continue to hold on to their values—especially patriotism, which is a concept that focuses on preserving democratic ideals, the country's political system, and the highest concern for the public good. Therefore, Americans should embrace their heritage, he says, and continue the traditions of self-governance and liberty.

—*Michael P. Auerbach, MA*

Bibliography and Additional Reading

Allen, Frederick Lewis. *Only Yesterday: An Informal History of the 1920s.* Marblehead: Wiley, 1931. Print.

Ferrell, Robert H. *The Presidency of Calvin Coolidge.* Lawrence: UP of Kansas, 1998. Print.

Goldberg, David J. *Discontented America: The United States of the 1920s.* Baltimore: Johns Hopkins UP, 1999. Print.

Himmelberg, Robert F., ed. *Antitrust and Regulation during World War I and the Republican Era, 1917– 1932.* New York: Routledge, 1994. Print.

Lowi, Theodore J. *The End of the Republican Era.* Norman: U of Oklahoma P, 1996. Print.

Herbert Hoover on "The Constructive Side of Government"

Date: November 2, 1928
Authors: Herbert Hoover
Genre: Speech

Summary Overview

During a campaign speech in St. Louis, Missouri, Herbert Hoover underscored what he believed to be the most significant attributes of a constructive American government. Citing the uniquely American political, social, and economic structures, Hoover said government is most constructive when it is invested in the country's infrastructure, fostering the nation's education, trade, and natural resource management programs, and providing services that help the country's neediest citizens.

Defining Moment

In the eyes of many historians, the 1920s were aptly dubbed "The Roaring 20s." Since the turn of the century, the country had been experiencing a major economic boom. Virtually every sector of the economy saw growth, aided by the prevalence of electricity and other energy sources as well as a vast railway system and even the widespread use of automobiles. Labor productivity grew at a rate of 3.8 percent per year between 1917 and 1927—a much higher rate than in the previous decades. World War I, which ended in 1918, had completely devastated Europe, but left the United States largely unaffected.

With prosperity the common theme during the 1920s, Americans began to spend and invest more. Consumers started investing heavily (and often at great risk) in the stock markets. Capital flowed between financial institutions and businesses. The "bull market" during this period appeared unsustainable and headed for an eventual slowdown, but Americans were, at the time, unconcerned with such possibilities.

Politically, it was the Republican Party's country. The Progressive Era—exemplified by Democrat Woodrow Wilson's efforts to bolster organized labor and create an international network of nations—had fallen into history. By the 1920s, Americans wanted less government involvement, and the platforms of Warren G. Harding and Calvin Coolidge reflected this desire. Presidents Harding and Coolidge were aided by a general fear of liberal ideals stoked by the first "Red Scare," in which Americans were being increasingly mindful of the rise of Bolshevism and Communism in Eastern Europe.

The fear of radicalism and the desire for continued economic growth also contributed to the demise of the labor unions. Organized labor was finding itself under attack from government, business, and the general public. Flush with profits from the strong economy, businesses were increasingly able to negotiate higher wages with their employees without involving the unions.

With fear of Bolshevism and distrust of progressivism prevalent in America, citizens grew disillusioned with the role of the federal government. Warren Harding, who was known to resist confrontation and controversy, was elected on the notion of a "return to normalcy." Despite his eventual ineffectiveness as president, the "Republican Era" would continue with his successor. Calvin Coolidge, who moved into the White House after Harding's death, continued to focus on ensuring the moral and social stability of the nation by drawing from his own Christian upbringing.

In 1928, when Coolidge declined to run for a second term, the Secretary of Commerce for both Coolidge and Harding, Herbert Hoover, opted to take up the mantle. Hoover was something of an anomaly among Republicans, showing a moderate, "progressive" temperament that distinguished him from other members of his party. However, his reputation as a humanitarian and a political outsider (he had never held elected office) endeared him to voters. As he continued his 1928 campaign against New York Governor Alfred E. Smith, he offered to a St. Louis crowd his views of how the federal government should operate in the new era.

Author Biography

Herbert Clark Hoover was born in West Branch, Iowa, on August 10, 1874. Orphaned at age nine, Hoover attended the newly opened Stanford University, graduating with a degree in mining engineering. During World War I, Hoover established the Commission for Relief in Belgium to provide food for civilians trapped in war zones. For his work, President Woodrow Wilson tapped him to be his U.S. Food Administrator. Hoover later became Warren Harding's Secretary of Commerce, a post he would continue to hold during Calvin Coolidge's administration.

In 1928, he successfully won the Republican nomination for President of the United States and easily won the election. Victimized politically by the onset of the Great Depression, Hoover lost the 1932 election to Franklin Delano Roosevelt. He remained active in public service after his presidency, including helping President Harry Truman with the post-World War II reconstruction effort. He died on October 20, 1964.

HISTORICAL DOCUMENT

I propose tonight to discuss the constructive side of government. I propose to outline something of the principles which must underlie the relation of government to the constructive tasks which confront us. A few nights ago in New York I had occasion to discuss these principles in application to matters which the government should not undertake. Tonight I discuss them in connection with matters which the government should and must undertake. Government is only in part a negative function. Its purpose is not merely to stand as a watchman over what is forbidden; government must be a constructive force.

The Unique American System

Our country has a political, social and economic system that is peculiarly our own. It is the American system. It grew out of our revolt from European systems and has ripened with our experience and our ideals. We have seldom tried to express it or define it. It has been the moving force of our progress. It has brought us into the leadership of the world.

The founders of our republic under Divine inspiration set up not alone a great political system of self-government, but they set up also a revolutionary social system in the relation of men toward men.

Our political system is unique in the world. It is unique because of its decentralization of self-government and its checks and balances which safeguard ordered liberty and freedom to each individual. Our social system is unique in the world. It is unique because it is founded not only upon the ideal that all men are created equal and are equal before the law, but also upon the ideal that there shall be equal opportunity among men. We have no frozen classes or stratification of caste in our country.

We allow nothing to prevent the ride of every boy and girl to the position to which their initiative and talents will carry them. We have no titles except the descriptions of our jobs.

From our unique political and social ideals we are evolving a unique economic system. We have discarded the original European theory that there is a class struggle between the capital of the few and the labor of the many. Under that theory it was held that labor was a commodity and the laborer in general could never rise far above bare existence, for if he did so the supply of labor would increase and thus constantly pull him back into the cesspool of inevitable poverty.

We Americans have proved this conception wrong. By what amounts to a revolution in ideas and methods, we have developed a new economic system. The dominating idea of that system is that labor on the one hand and capital, which in America means the savings of the people, on the other hand, by joint effort can steadily increase the efficiency of production and distribution. In other words, we find that by join effort we can steadily increase the production of goods by each individual and we can at the same time decrease the cost of goods. As we increase the volume of goods, we have more to divide, and we thereby steadily lift the standard of living of the whole people. We have proved this to be true, and by this proof we have laid away the old theory of inevitable poverty alongside the theory of human slavery.

These three revolutionary American ideas, political, social, and economic, are interlocked and intermeshed. They are dominated and cemented by the ideal and practice of equal opportunity. They constitute one great system protecting our individualism and stimulating initiative and enterprise in our people. This is the American system. One part of it cannot be destroyed without undermining the whole. For us to adopt other social conceptions, such as federal or state government entry into commercial business in competition with its citizens, would undermine initiative and enterprise and destroy the very foundations of freedom and progress upon which the American system is built....

Constructive Government

There are three potential fields in which the principles and impulses of our American system require that government take constructive action. They comprise those activities which no local community can itself assume and which the individual initiative and enterprise of our people cannot wholly compass. They comprise leadership of the government to solve many difficult problems.

The first of these fields includes the great under-takings in public works such as inland waterways, flood control, reclamation, highways, and public buildings.

The second of these is necessary interest and activity of the Federal Government in fostering education, public health, scientific research, public parks, conservation of national resources, agriculture, industry, and foreign commerce.

The third great field lies in broadening the assistance of the government to the growing efforts of our people to co-operation among themselves to useful social and economic ends.

Federal Highways

This administration has recognized the public necessity of Federal Government contribution to the creation of a definitive system of modern interstate highways. This program is far from completion, and I stand for its continuance. Congress has lately authorized a large program of much-needed public buildings. And there are other important public works of less immediate interest to the Midwest to which I have referred upon other occasions. The whole comprises the largest engineering construction ever undertaken by any government. It means an expenditure of nearly a billion of dollars in the next four years, or nearly four times the outlay on the Panama Canal. As I have said before, these undertakings are justified by the growth, the need, and the wealth of our country. The organization and administration of this construction is a responsibility of the first order. For it we must secure the utmost economy, honesty, and skill. These works, which will provide jobs for an army of men, should, so far as practical, be adjusted to take up the slack of unemployment if it should occur.

A Federal Farm Board

In addition to the tariff and cheaper waterway transportation in assistance to agriculture, the Republican Party proposes to go farther. It proposes to set up an institution which will be one of the most important institutions in our government, designed to meet not only the varied problems which confront us today but those which may arise in the future. We propose to create a Federal Farm Board composed of men of understanding and sympathy for the problems of agriculture; we propose that this board should have power to determine the facts, the causes, the remedies which should be applied to each and every one of the multitude of problems which we mass under the general term "the agricultural problem."

This program further provides that the board shall have a broad authority to act and be authorized to assist in the further development of co-operative marketing; that it shall assist in the development of clearing-houses for agricultural products, in the development of adequate warehousing facilities, in the elimination of wastes in distribution, and in the solution of other problems as they arise. But in particular the board is to build up, with initial advances of capital from the government, farmer-owned and farmer-controlled stabilization corporations which will protect the farmer from depressions and demoralization of summer and periodic surpluses. It is proposed that this board should have placed at its disposal such resources as are necessary to make its action effective.

Thus we give to the Federal Farm Board every arm with which to deal with the multitude of problems. This is an entirely different method of approach to solution from that of a general formula; it is flexible and adaptable. No such far-reaching and specific proposal has ever been made by a political party on behalf of any industry in our history. It is a direct business proposition. It marks our desire for establishment of the farmer's stability and at the same time maintains his independence and individuality.

This plan is consonant with our American ideals to avoid the government operation of commercial business, for it places the operation upon the farmer himself, not upon a bureaucracy. It puts the government in its real relation to the citizen—that of co-operation. Its object is to give equality of opportunity to the farmer. I would consider it the greatest honor I could have if it should become my privilege to aid in finally solving this, the most difficult of economic problems presented to our people, and the one in which by inheritance and through long contact I have my deepest interest....

The Principle of Co-operation

...We have in the past quarter of a century evolved a higher sense of organized co-operation than has ever been known before. We have ten thousand examples of this conscious co-operative development in the enormous growth of associational activities. Civic associations, chambers of commerce, trade associations, professional associations, labor unions, trade councils, farm organizations, farm co-operatives, welfare associations—these are so all-embracing that there is scarcely an individual in our country who does not now belong to one or more of them. They represent every phase of our national life both on the economic and on the welfare side. They constitute a vast ferment toward conscious co-operation. They have become a part of the very fabric of American life. While some of them engage in highly objectionable attempts to wrongly influence public opinion and the action of government, the majority of them recognize a responsibility to the public as well as to themselves; and a large part of them are founded solely on public interest.

Wherever these associations undertake high public purposes I wish to see active co-operation by the government with them. Without intrusion the government can serve to bring together discordant elements and to secure co-operation between different industries and groups. It gives great hope of a new basis of solution for many of our problems and progressive action in our people. It should be the response of government to our new economic conceptions.

It is consonant with the American system. It is a method that reinforces our individualism by reducing, and not increasing, government interference in business

and the life of our citizens. Such co-operation strengthens the whole foundations of self-government and serves to maintain equality of opportunity and constructive leadership. This co-operation can take two distinct directions. It can assist in the promotion of constructive projects of public interest on one hand, and it can assist in the cure of abuses by the voluntary establishment of a higher code of ethics and a stricter standard in the conduct of business.

Illustrative Examples

First, I may review a case of assistance to labor and business. In 1923, under my chairmanship, there was organized a series of committees representing the manufacturers, contractors, engineers, real estate men, and labor in the building trades. Its purpose was to reduce the loss of time due to the seasonal character of these industries. As a result of the organization set up, the average winter unemployment in these trades has been reduced from about one hundred days to about half that number. There has been no decrease in daily wages. The annual income of the workers in these trades has been substantially increased by the decrease in idle days, and the business given greater stability.

Another instance of action of fundamental importance to the farmer, the businessman, and the worker consists of the measures taken in co-operation between the government and business agencies to mitigate the violence of the so-called business cycle. Booms and slumps have occurred periodically for one hundred years. No one suffers more from these periodic hard times, with their hideous unemployment, decrease in wages, and bankruptcy in business, than both labor and the farmers. Time forbids a discussion of the intricate problems involved and the remedies which have been inaugurated. The proof of the effectiveness lies in the fact that we have had a far longer period of stability in industry and commerce, far greater security in employment, and larger buying power for farm products than ever before in our history. The solution of this question was just as intricate as those which we face in agriculture....

Avoidance of Unnecessary Regulation

An illustration of another direction of these activities has been in eliminating abuses in a particular industry without resort to legislation and regulation. For a great many years legislation had been debated in Congress providing for the regulation of the lumber industry somewhat on the lines of the pure food laws, in order to protect the honest manufacturers and dealers and the public. In 1923, however, we created a series of committees amongst associations in the lumber industry at their request. In the course of a gradual extension over five years we finally perfected a system for the grading of lumber and for the guaranteeing of those grades to the public, which is now carried out wholly within and by the lumber industry itself. Consequently during these last few years there has been no suggestion of such legislation from Congress. The savings to the public in the elimination of waste and fraud have been estimated by the industry as upwards of two hundred and fifty million dollars a year. This is a clear case where by co-operative methods we have avoided the necessity of regulation with the bureaucracy and interference that flow from it.

It is also a clear case of building up of self-government…. In this broad field of co-operation by government lie potentialities which have been barely touched. The government can give leadership and co-operation. It can furnish scientific research. It can give prestige and influence. All of these call for but trivial expenditures. They require no increased bureaucracy. They are of first importance to every branch of American life. It is by these means of co-operation by the government that we contribute mightily toward business stability and greater productivity in industry. And it is stability that every business man needs that he may thus work out for himself his own destiny without those ill tides over which he has no control.

It is by means of the sort of co-operation from the government that we may contribute greatly to the very foundations of economic progress, that is, to provide continuous and full employment. General employment comes not only with sound policies of government but equally from vigorous co-operation by the government to promote economic welfare. It is by these means that we build such organization of our economic system as to provide a job for all who have the will to work.

Equality of Opportunity

Government has the definite and manifest obligation of giving constructive leadership to the people. In doing so it must not lessen their initiative and enterprise, upon which we must rely for the progress of the race and of the nation. Our system has been built upon the ideal of equality of opportunity. For perhaps a hundred years after the foundation of the Republic, the opportunities of a moving frontier preserved that equality of opportunity. Now with the settlement of the country and with the astonishing speed and intricate complexity of industrial life, the preservation of equality of opportunity becomes yearly and yearly more difficult, and for that very reason is of higher and higher importance. If we would maintain America as the land of opportunity, where every boy and girl may have the chance to climb to that position to which his ability and character entitle him, we shall need to be on increasing guard. If I could drive the full meaning and importance of maintained equality of opportunity into the very consciousness of the American people, I would feel I had made some contribution to American life. It is the most precious of our possessions that the windows of every home shall look out upon unlimited hope. Equality of opportunity is the right of every American, rich or poor, foreign or native born, without respect to race or religion. By its maintenance alone can we hold open the door of full achievement to every new generation and to every boy and girl? Only from confidence that this right will be upheld can flow that unbounded courage and hope which stimulates each individual man and woman to endeavor and to accomplishment. By this principle we should test every act of government, every proposal, whether it be economic or political. I insist upon the most strict regulation of public utilities, because otherwise they would destroy equality of opportunity. I object to the government going into business in competition with its citizens because that would destroy equality of opportunity. And equality of opportunity is the flux with which alone we can melt out full and able leadership to the nation.

The first step to maintained equality of opportunity amongst our people is, as I have said before, that there should be no child in America who has not been born, and who does not live, under sound conditions of health; who does not have full opportunity for education from the kindergarten to the university; who is not free from injurious labor; who does not have stimulation to ambition to the fullest of his or her capacities. It is a matter of concern to our government that we should strengthen the safeguards to health. These activities of helpfulness and of co-operation stretch before us in every direction. A single generation of Americans of such a production would prevent more of spirit and of progress than all of the repressive laws and police we can ever invent—and it would cost less.

The American Home

I have said often before in this campaign that we need always to interpret our discussions of economic and material proposals by how they affect the peace, the happiness, and the security and prosperity of every American home. I have tried to interpret to my fellow-countrymen what government means to that home. I stand for a prosperous country because I want good homes. You cannot

divide those things that are seen from those that are unseen. The things that we call material are the foundation stones upon which we build the temple of those things that we call spiritual.

Prosperity, security, happiness, and peace rest on sound economic life. Many of the subjects with which we have had to deal are intricate and complex. We must support the maintenance of peace amongst nations, economy in government, the protective tariff, the restriction of immigration, the encouragement of foreign trade, the relief of agriculture, the building of waterways, and a score of other great governmental policies which affect every home in our land. Solution of these questions is not always easy. Only the inexperienced can be positive in offering solutions of great problems. The first necessity in handling of such problems is the assembling of the facts in their proper perspective. The truth must be forged from the metal of facts.

Document Analysis

In a November presidential campaign speech delivered in St. Louis, candidate Herbert Hoover carefully identifies a number of areas in which the American government could be most constructive. Hoover says that the American government is less effective when it engages in heavy regulation and otherwise injects itself into private matters. Instead, he says, government is best suited to acting as steward over the country's infrastructure, agency operations, and programs that help the nation's neediest citizens.

Hoover argues that the country's political, economic, and social systems reflect the unique interests of the American mission. The government, therefore, should also be reflective of this particularity. Government, he says, was designed to be decentralized, protecting and not infringing upon the individual rights and liberties of the people and their business and personal pursuits. Furthermore, the federal government would only be relevant in areas in which state and local governments were limited by their resources and/or geographic jurisdictions.

Hoover next cites three major areas in which the federal government would play a useful—if not vital—role. The first of these areas is infrastructure. The country's waterways, highways, public buildings, and natural resources would fall under this category. Hoover says that

his predecessor, Calvin Coolidge, had advocated for the construction of modern highways and public buildings. As a part of that administration, Hoover advocates for the continuation of this effort, as its successful completion would address the needs of a modern America.

Hoover also stresses usefulness of centralized government in managing national programs, such as education, trade, and agriculture. In this vein, he advocates for the creation of a Federal Farm Bureau, which would work to address the issues facing the country's entire agricultural sector. The Bureau's role would be to establish an environment in which farms could thrive absent a level of regulatory oversight that would remove control from the farmers.

In the third arena, Hoover says that, over the previous twenty-five years, citizens had established thousands of trade associations, civic organizations, labor unions, and other interest groups. These groups played an integral role in fostering cooperation among private citizens and industries. Hoover says that it is his hope that his administration would build strong relationships with these groups, particularly in matters of public interest, without intruding upon their private activities. Government, Hoover argues, should play a role in promoting and protecting American interests. Instead of applying heavy regulations, it should create opportunities for commerce, he says. Hoover adds that government should avoid intervening in private matters, but foster environments for interparty issues to be addressed. Such opportunities, he states, must be equally attainable by all interested parties. Every American, he says, should enjoy the same ability to take advantage of every opportunity the country has to offer.

Essential Themes

The 1920s was a time in which Americans sought less of a presence from their federal government. The social reform movements (including the passage and repeal of Prohibition) were matters of the past, as were the progressive leanings of Woodrow Wilson. The country was now entering a "Republican Era"—one that was marked by unprecedented economic growth and prosperity. Americans, bolstered by this growth and success, looked for less government oversight, intervention, and regulation than was prevalent during the Progressive Era. Herbert Hoover, the third Republican presidential candidate to succeed the Progressive Era, offered a view that satisfied this desire.

Hoover states that government's role was to be constructive rather than overly involved. It should serve as a steward of the country's infrastructure, assisting only where state and local governments lacked sufficient resources. Additionally, Hoover says, government should only offer intercession in matters in which an impasse would threaten the common good. His example of the Farm Bureau supports this idea—the government, as a partner to the farmers, landowners, and other interested parties, would serve as an intermediary in addressing pivotal issues facing one of the country's most vital industries.

Additionally, he says, government should be focused on ensuring that every American has equal access to opportunity. Prosperity, security, happiness, and peace, he says, are all concepts to which every American has a right. According to Hoover, these concepts are reliant on the even hand of government. Government should be willing to assist its poorest citizens (especially in terms of education), but it should also be willing to stand aside so that citizens can pursue these goals without unnecessary hindrance.

Hoover says that the United States is unlike any other nation or society. Because of this uniqueness, American political and social institutions were designed in a fashion particular to the American way of life. Americans desired a government whose presence was minimal and positive, Hoover says. Government, he says, should be cognizant of this fact, willing to assist in matters in which its involvement will avail opportunities, and willing to stand back when its involvement would only present hindrances.

—*Michael P. Auerbach, MA*

Bibliography and Additional Reading

Allen, Frederick Lewis. Only *Yesterday: An Informal History of the 1920's*. Marblehead: Wiley, 1931. Print.

Goldberg, David J. *Discontented America: The United States of the 1920s*. Baltimore: Johns Hopkins UP, 1999. Print.

Hansen, Bradley A. *The National Economy*. Westport: Greenwood, 2006. Print

"Herbert Clark Hoover." Herbert Hoover Presidential Library and Museum. National Archives and Records Administration, 2014. Web. 20 May 2014.

"Herbert Clark Hoover." Miller Center. University of Virginia, 2013. Web. 20 May 2014.

Himmelberg, Robert F., ed. *Antitrust and Regulation During World War I and the Republican Era, 1917–1932*. New York: Routledge, 1994. Print.

Lowi, Theodore J. *The End of the Republican Era*. Norman: U of Oklahoma P, 1996. Print.

Whisenhunt, *Donald W. President Herbert Hoover*. Hauppauge: Nova, 2007. Print.

The earliest surviving sheet music of "The Star-Spangled Banner," from 1814.

■ The National Anthem Established: The Star-Spangled Banner

Date: March 3, 1931
Authors: Francis Scott Key; John Stafford Smith; U.S. Congress
Genre: Song; legislation

Summary Overview

The U.S. national anthem is made up of two parts, lyrics based on the Francis Scott Key poem "Defence of Fort M'Henry" and music written by John Stafford Smith. The poem was written in 1812, after Key witnessed the Battle of Fort McHenry during the War of 1812, but it was not set to music and adopted for official use by the U.S. Navy until 1889. Then, in 1916, President Woodrow Wilson, through an executive order, authorized its use in official state functions. Only in 1931 did Congress pass a resolution affirming Wilson's order and adopting the song as the nation's official anthem. President Herbert Hoover signed the measure into law the same year, making it part of the U.S. Code (the statutes that control government actions). The law, reproduced below, describes the approved procedure for a proper "rendition of the national anthem." Also reproduced here are the four stanzas of the Francis Scott Key poem making up the anthem's lyrics. However, only the first stanza is commonly recited during public renditions of the anthem.

Defining Moment

Before this legislation was passed in 1931, the United States of America had been without a national anthem. While a simple song might not seem very important, it is an integral part of the national identity of many countries' inhabitants. Much like a university's fight song or creed, a national anthem is a rallying point around which a country's citizens can gather and feel a part of something larger than themselves. By the 1930s, the United States had been a county for over 150 years, and throughout much of the nineteenth century and early twentieth century, "The Star-Spangled Banner" had been popular and was played at military events, particularly during the raising of the American flag. Indeed, President Woodrow Wilson required its use at certain types of events in 1916; and in 1918, it played for the first time at a baseball game,

during the World Series. Based on its wide use, its broad popularity, and its patriotic imagery, "The Star-Spangled Banner" was an obvious choice for the U.S. national anthem.

The year 1931, then, was the first time that a set of rules had been written down and made part of the public record as to how and when to perform the official national anthem. The performing of the national anthem, especially in conjunction with the presentation of the American flag, was and is a symbol of the nation as a whole and all that that entails. Uniformed military personnel and civilian individuals were given separate actions to perform during the playing of the anthem, highlighting the differences between those two categories of citizens. Given that the song is based on a poem about a battle fought by soldiers, any military personnel present at the anthem's performance are, in effect, honoring their fellow soldiers before them and those who will come after. The War of 1812 was a chance for a young United States of America to prove its strength and enduring nature and a song from that period immortalized that nature and projected it forward for each successive generation.

Author Biographies

Francis Scott Key was born in 1779 in Georgetown, Maryland, on his family's plantation. He studied law at St. John's College and eventually became a lawyer. He took on many high-profile cases, such as prosecuting President Andrew Jackson's would-be assassin, Richard Lawrence, and was appointed a U.S. District Attorney in 1833. He was also a slave-owner and very active in defending slavery, even prosecuting those who spoke out against the institution. (This is not an unusual position in light of his upbringing.) Key participated in the American Bible Society, the American Colonization Society. He married Mary Tayloe Lloyd in 1802 and the couple had two children. Key is best known for his amateur poetry. Most of his poems reflect his faith and have heavy religious overtones. While "The Star- Spangled Banner" calls upon God, its main theme is the enduring strength of the nation. Key died in 1843, almost ninety years before his poem was made into the national anthem.

John Stafford Smith (1750–1836) was a British composer and organist who is best known for writing the score that later was married with the Francis Scott Key poem to form "The Star-Spangled Banner." The original music is thought to have been written by Smith in the 1760s and was first published in 1778 as "The Anacreontic Song," the official song of a gentlemen's society made up of amateur musicians and students of music.

HISTORICAL DOCUMENT

36 U.S. Code § 301—National Anthem

(a) Designation.—The composition consisting of the words and music known as the Star-Spangled Banner is the national anthem.

(b) Conduct During Playing.— During a rendition of the national anthem—

(1) when the flag is displayed—

(A) individuals in uniform should give the military salute at the first note of the anthem and maintain that position until the last note;

(B) members of the Armed Forces and veterans who are present but not in uniform may render the military salute in the manner provided for individuals in uniform; and

(C) all other persons present should face the flag and stand at attention with their right hand over the heart, and men not in uniform, if applicable, should remove their headdress with their right hand and hold it at the left shoulder, the hand being over the heart; and

(2) when the flag is not displayed, all present should face toward the music and act in the same manner they would if the flag were displayed.

* * *

The Star-Spangled Banner

O say can you see by the dawn's early light,
What so proudly we hailed at the twilight's last gleaming,
Whose broad stripes and bright stars through the perilous fight,
O'er the ramparts we watched, were so gallantly streaming?
And the rockets red glare, the bombs bursting in air
Gave proof through the night that our flag was still there;
O say does that star-spangled banner yet wave,
O'er the land of the free and the home of the brave?
On the shore dimly seen through the mists of the deep,

Where the foe's haughty host in dread silence reposes,
What is that which the breeze, o'er the towering steep,
As it fitfully blows, half conceals, half discloses?
Now it catches the gleam of the morning's first beam,
In full glory reflected now shines in the stream:
'Tis the star-spangled banner, O! long may it wave
O'er the land of the free and the home of the brave.

And where is that band who so vauntingly swore
That the havoc of war and the battle's confusion,
A home and a country, should leave us no more?
Their blood has washed out their foul foot steps' pollution.
No refuge could save the hireling and slave
From the terror of flight, or the gloom of the grave:
And the star-spangled banner in triumph doth wave,
O'er the land of the free and the home of the brave.

O thus be it ever, when freemen shall stand
Between their loved home and the war's desolation.
Blest with vict'ry and peace, may the Heav'n rescued land

Praise the Power that hath made and preserved us a nation!

Then conquer we must, when our cause it is just,

And this be our motto: "In God is our trust."

And the star-spangled banner in triumph shall wave

O'er the land of the free and the home of the brave!

GLOSSARY

ramparts: a broad mound (of earth) created as a fortification around a place; usually topped with a parapet; anything used as a defensive blockade

vauntingly: in a boastful manner; vaingloriously

Document Analysis

The relevant portion of the U.S. Code (36, section 301) addresses the military and civilian requirements when the national anthem is played, especially when the American flag is also present. While there is no specific penalty stated for breaking these rules (except, perhaps, for military personnel under the Uniform Code of Military Justice), the strictures noted here have become the norm for all public performances, creating a situation in which one is expected to conform to the guidelines under penalty of public disapproval. Also noted, again, are the different forms of conduct expected of military personnel, in and out of uniform, and civilians.

As for the lyrics, Key's poem touches on several ideals that remain relevant today and perhaps are timeless. While the language of the poem may be somewhat archaic for today's reader, the themes are still clear even 200 years after they were laid down. The spark of inspiration for the creation of the poem was the fact that Fort McHenry, in Baltimore, Maryland, managed to stay standing after being attacked by British forces. The poem opens the morning after the battle, with the speaker daring to hope that he might see the American flag waving over the fort. It is not until near the end of the second stanza, after describing the enemy who lurks outside the fort, that the speaker is able to state with certainty that, "Tis the star-spangled banner, O! Long may it wave… ."The third stanza begins more triumphantly, showing that even though the British, who were the dominant world-power at the time, may have boasted that they would destroy the young American country, they were unable to do so. Yet, the last four lines of stanza three show that terror and death were not absent; rather, they were the price paid for the continued liberty of "the free."

The final stanza is more typical of Key's other poems. He shows the power of men who seek to protect their homeland, an act that gives them a strength and a purpose that cannot be overestimated. He also thanks God for his intervention in helping to preserve the lives of Key's countrymen. Key was devoutly religious, as were many others of his era, and he believed that the country should embrace the ideals of religion and freedom, in order to create the strongest nation possible.

Essential Themes

The central ideas of the national anthem are the strength and freedom of the United States of America, especially while it is under attack from outside forces. This is particularly relevant to the modern world, where threats seem to come from many sources, even if they are not as obvious or overt as the British sending their ships to engage U.S. forces inside military forts. According to Key's poem, fighting for one's country, protecting it from outside threats, is one of the most important things a person can do. At the same time, he emphasizes the importance of being free. There is a delicate balance, in other words, that can too easily be upset during a crisis.

Key also forswears those who boast of their power, because it is that type of person who often comes before a fall. "The [British] band who so vauntingly swore" that they would destroy the Americans were defeated in battle (although for the war as a whole it is more difficult to identify a clear winner). In alluding to the defense of one's home and the reliance on a god, Key shows his belief that many obstacles can be overcome, even at great odds. Such faith in the power of religion and belief was a large part of the founding era of the country, even though the Constitution created an official separation of church and state.

Finally, the adoption of a national anthem created a formal rallying point for American citizens. Although, before "The Star-Spangled Banner," there was some debate about whether to choose and anthem and which one it should be, the Francis Scott Key poem seems to have touched on many of the ideals that were then and still are held dear by the widest possible swath of U.S. citizenry. Not always the easiest piece to read or sing (with its somewhat antiquated language and its great musical range, from deep low notes to soaring high notes), still, "The Star-Spangled Banner" has, for two hundred years, given people solace and inspiration. Played at concerts, ball games, military events, Fourth of July ceremonies, flag raisings ("colors"), and many other events, the national anthem is a unifying symbol of the enduring quality of the American people and the nation they created.

—*Anna Accettola, MA*

Bibliography and Additional Reading

Cerulo, Karen. "Symbols and the World System: National Anthems and Flags." *Sociological Forum* 8.2 (1993): 243–71. *Print.*

Delaplaine, Edward Schley. *Francis Scott Key: Life and Times.* Biography Press, 1937. Print.

Silkett, John T. *Francis Scott Key and the History of the Star Spangled Banner.* Washington: Vintage America Pub., 1978. Print.

Muller, Joseph. *The Star Spangled Banner; Words and Music Issued between 1814–1864; an Annotated Bibliographical List with Notices of the Different Versions, Texts, Variants, Musical Arrangements, and Notes on Music Publishers in the United States.* New York: Da Capo, 1973. Print.